ESSAYS ON NATURE

An Anthology of
Selected Writings from

The Living Museum

by

Virginia S. Eifert

The Living Museum, a monthly publication of the Illinois State Museum,
was edited from May 1939 through July 1966 by Virginia S. Eifert

[Printed by authority of the State of Illinois.]
1967

*Dedicated to the
Memory of
Virgina S. Eifert*

AN ILLINOIS SESQUICENTENNIAL BOOK

*T*HIS YEAR, 1968, the State of Illinois is observing its 150th anniversary. Three years ago Governor Otto Kerner appointed a commission, authorized by the General Assembly, to decide upon the most effective and suitable means of commemorating this milestone in the state's history. The commission decided that a series of publications was called for, and an advisory committee selected the subjects to be covered. High on the list was a natural history of Illinois, which we hoped Virginia S. Eifert would write. Her untimely death put an end to this hope. However this collection of Mrs. Eifert's writings goes far toward filling the gap, and the commission gladly extends its sponsorship.

For their support of the sesquicentennial historical program I wish to thank Governor Otto Kerner, the Illinois General Assembly, and the members of the Illinois Sesquicentennial Commission: Hon. Hudson R. Sours, 1st Vice Chairman; Hon. J. W. "Bill" Scott, 2nd Vice Chairman; Gene H. Graves, Secretary; William K. Alderfer; James W. Cook; Hon. Lawrence DiPrima; Patrick H. Hoy; Goffrey Hughes; Hon. Henry J. Hyde; Hon. J. David Jones; Hon. Richard R. Larson; Hon. Edward Lehman; Daniel MacMaster; Virginia L. Marmaduke; Hon. Edward McBroom; Hon. Robert W. McCarthy; Hon. Tom Merritt; Hon. Richard H. Newhouse; Hon. James Philip; Hon. Paul Powell; Hon. Paul. J. Randolph; Walter Schwimmer; John H. Sengstacke; Glenn H. Seymour; Hon. Paul Simon; Hon. Harold D. Stedelin; Milton D. Thompson; Clyde C. Walton.

RALPH G. NEWMAN, *Chairman*
Illinois Sesquicentennial Commission
October 1967

PREFACE

The Living Museum, the monthly publication of the Illinois State Museum, was edited and, in the main, written by Virginia Eifert from May 1939 through July 1966. "Essays on Nature" is an anthology of selected writings from these issues.

Virginia had a unique way of describing the obvious and simple everyday happenings which make up our natural environment, a style of writing which could capture the unusual in the usual. She had a creative flare for expressing the technical detail in understandable, accurate, and poetic language; she had a "turn of phase" that could capture the imagination. Her descriptions of nature were vivid to the point of creating vicarious experiences for those who read *The Living Museum.* Her writings had the quality of personalizing an experience—of bringing you into her world of authority and inspiration.

It is with these thoughts that we have chosen the essays in this memorial anthology—sketches "devoted to a better understanding of living things and the surroundings in which we live."

MILTON D. THOMPSON
Museum Director

October 1967

When city noise and city stress
Conspire to wreck my happiness;
When television, cars and noise
Usurp the place of forest joys,
Then to my heart come memories
Of lakes and bogs and quiet trees.
I listen, and again I hear
The cries of wild geese drawing near.
I listen, and my heart's deep core
Knows lake waves lapping on a shore,
The gentle sounds of leaves at night,
The wakening of flowers to light.
Once more the fox is on the ridge;
A bluebird nests beside a bridge.
The hummingbird, a whirring gem,
Adorns the lily's diadem,
While every bird song heard again
Helps to alleviate my pain.
The misty silver of the bay,
Where gull-wings pattern early day,
The hermit thrush's wistful chime
Beside a bog at sunset time,
The message of a meteorite
Pencilling fire across the night,
The fragrance of the pines in rain,
Cloud shadows drifting over grain—
All these are surcease, balm and joy
When work is hard and tasks annoy.
And so I mortgage city stress,
Anticipating wilderness.

V. S. E.

Virginia S. Eifert

The LIVING MUSEUM

| Vol. XXVIII | AUGUST, 1966 | No. 4 |

DEVOTED TO THE RECOGNITION AND TO THE MEMORY OF VIRGINIA S. EIFERT

This issue of *The Living Museum* marks the end of an era which began in May 1939 when Dr. Thorne Deuel, Museum Director, with Virginia Eifert as Editor, published through the Illinois State Museum Volume I, Number 1, of this popular publication.

Virginia continued to serve as editor and principal author for twenty-seven years until her sudden death on Thursday, June 16, 1966. Her growth in skill and as an interpreter of the natural world is wonderfully documented in *The Living Museum's* three hundred twenty-six issues.

Although *The Living Museum* will be continued, we know it will not be the same for Virginia lent it a personal touch that can not be replaced.

A very modest and reserved person, she was remarkably articulate in expressing her feelings for the world about her. Through her writings and her personal leadership, thousands have come to know and understand the natural world. We who knew her personally and the thousands of you who enjoyed her writings have lost a friendly, quiet but potent force in our lives.

Considerable thought has been given to the creation of a suitable memorial to Virginia, something appropriate which would express appreciation in a permanent way and at the same time exemplify her philosophy. The selection is a 36-foot mural to be in the Museum Lobby opposite the entrance to depict pictorially the natural world and the convictions she developed as presented in her writings, art, and photography during these past twenty-seven years. We hope, through the skills of the artist, Virginia's contribution to "the better understanding of living things and the surroundings in which we live" may be portrayed. By this means, we may show some appreciation for one who has so deeply enriched our lives.

—MILTON D. THOMPSON,
Museum Director

From early years Virginia Eifert was attracted to the natural world, much of her appreciation instilled originally by her parents who spent many hours with their three children in the out-of-doors.

Being knowledgeable in nature study, she was asked to be counselor at the Springfield YWCA Camp and to lead nature walks for local groups. Short sketches of the trips taken led to a four-page mimeographed nature paper which she composed and distributed to interested people for a charge of five cents. An acquaintance over the backyard fence with Mr. J. Emil Smith, Editor of the *Illinois State Journal*, opened the way to a series of nature articles in the newspaper.

In 1939, Dr. Thorne Deuel, Museum Director, conceived the idea of a monthly publication to tell the story of the Museum's exhibits and activities in terms of living things out-of-doors. Impressed with the little nature paper and the newspaper column, Dr. Deuel secured Virginia to be Editor. And so in May, 1939, *The Living Museum* began. Now in its twenty-eighth year, *The Living Museum* is a tangible record of her development in writing skill, her deeper insight and profound belief in the great inner need for nature.

In addition to *The Living Museum*, she wrote other publications for the Museum. The first five booklets in the Story of Illinois Series are hers—on Illinois history, mammals, mushrooms, flowers, and birds, the latter three illustrated with her drawings. *Birds in Your Backyard* contains accounts and drawings of 121 Illinois birds. In *Illinois Wild Flowers*, she wrote the text to accompany photographs taken by Dr. John Voss. These descriptions were described just recently in a letter from an admirer in Pennsylvania as "ecological vignettes."

Always she was writing. In an upstairs storeroom were pages and pages of material in manuscript form, some which had been submitted to publishers, some which had not. The one she favored most was a field guide in botany, but it never seemed to suit a publisher; it was put aside. In the early 1950's she decided to try a whole new approach; she wrote about Abraham Lincoln. The result was a historical novel about Lincoln's flatboat trip down the three rivers —the Sangamon, Illinois, and Mississippi. This manuscript, written on an adult level, was sent to several publishers; each time it was returned. She chose one more, Dodd, Mead and Co. A letter came saying the manuscript could be accepted if it were on a teen-age level. She rewrote the whole thing in three days, and *Three Rivers South* became her first independently published book. This was in 1953. Since then there have been 14 more, and another, *Of Men and Rivers*, is in press now.

The Lincoln book was so well received that the publisher requested two more. These she supplied: *Buffalo Trace, the Story of Lincoln's Ancestors;* and *Out of the Wilderness, Young Lincoln Grows Up*—both preceding the first one in sequence. Much unused material remained from her research; so she wrote two more to complete Lincoln's life—*With a Task Before Me, Abraham Lincoln Leaves Springfield;* and *New Birth of Freedom, Abraham Lincoln in the White House.*

Rivers held a great fascination for Virginia Eifert. Through the interests of friends, she had the unusual opportunity to take several river trips by towboat. From this vantage point she gained much of the inspiration and information for *Mississippi Calling, River World,* and *Wonders of the Rivers.* During one of these trips, she saw the *Delta Queen,* the last overnight, stern-wheel passenger boat still operating on any river in the U. S. She immediately set out to learn more about this steamboat. There were interviews with the owners and with officials of the Greene Line Steamers, Inc. in Cincinnati and first-hand information from the captain and the crew as she traveled the rivers aboard the boat. In 1960, *Delta Queen, Story of a Steamboat,* was published.

One of her favorite vacation areas was Northern Wisconsin where she, her husband and son often spent summers. *Land of the Snowshoe Hare* relates experiences there. Another place dear to her was Door County, Wisconsin, which she came to know as leader of nature classes at The Clearing, an adult school-in-the-woods founded by Jens Jensen near Ellison Bay. The Door Peninsula and the Ridges Sanctuary, unique habitats of many unusual and rare plants, are explored in *Journeys in Green Places.*

Her intense interest in birds and plants prompted her to write *Men, Birds, and Adventure, the Thrilling Story of the Discovery of American Birds;* and *Tall Trees and Far Horizons, Adventures and Discoveries of Early Botantists in America.*

Two more historical novels were interspersed: *George Shannon, Boy Explorer with Lewis and Clark;* and *Louis Jolliet, Explorer of Rivers.*

In her thinking she was always at least three books ahead of the one on which she was working. She composed quickly and with a minimum of revision. There was never a lack of ideas for subjects, either for books or *The Living Museum.* A lifetime, no matter what its span, could never be long enough to exhaust the resources of a receptive mind such as hers.

—ORVETTA M. ROBINSON,
Museum Librarian

Virginia Eifert, like Gene Stratton Porter, Thoreau and Darwin, accepted school and the lighthearted social life that accompanied it with some impatience. Among the many who more or less readily followed the road of formal learning, Virginia was one of those rare spirits who was continually lured away from her books by the chirp of a cricket, the flight of a bird or the web-spinning of a spider. These activities beckoned this inquisitive observer as irresistibly as a magnet attracts a nail. It was not that she disliked the restriction and stilted silence of the classroom; she longed for the first-hand discoveries she knew awaited her in the forest, beside a wilderness river and in a quaking bog.

Possibly during these years she dreamed of scientific expeditions to strange lands and ruined temples. I doubt it. She was far too busy investigating the living creatures in her own backyard, in the Springfield city parks, along the banks of the Sangamon River, and in the Illinois woods and streams. Not that Virginia was a recluse; far from it. She thoroughly enjoyed her friends and particularly exchanging experiences with bird- and star-watchers and other searchers of the little known.

In her early years she enjoyed telling others of her experiences through occasional newspaper articles. Later she wrote a mimeographed leaflet that appeared at irregular intervals for groups of local nature seekers. About this time she was called upon to undertake the editorship of a small paper, the purpose of which was to familiarize people with the Museum exhibits, to make the displays live for them, and to lead them to search for counterparts in the wild. The Museum was scant of funds; it was without a printing appropriation and had neither position nor salary for an editor. The prospect of continued support for such a paper was dim; but to Virginia this was a challenge, and she accepted the responsibility and the uncertainties with quiet enthusiasm. Her first "subscribers" were a thousand names selected from the local telephone directory. The following month (May 1939) *The Living Museum,* a four-page leaflet on Illinois birds, beasts and blossoms, appeared in mimeographed form, the contents and illustrations from the editor's pen. It was an immediate success.

Six months later, *The Living Museum* was expanded to eight pages; and by the end of the first year, Governor Horner had approved funds to produce it in printed form with halftone illustrations. Its size has remained the same ever since. Readers have increased from the original one thousand to 25,000 —scientists, professors, poets, writers and just people who were fascinated by the creatures of the wild and their open secrets. Since 1949 a Braille edition has been printed; it is available without charge to any blind person.

Letters have come in by the hundreds from housewives, farmers, teachers, persons in the public eye and of the workaday world, praising an article, asking for a copy for a friend, or telling of a new "toadstool" or trap-door spider, a summer tanager, or strange tracks in the mud—things they have seen and now find pleasure in observing and recognizing.

Virginia continued her learning wherever she was—in the Wisconsin woods, the Indiana dunes, the Rocky Mountains—and extended her adventures to the.

rivers, particularly the Ohio and the Mississippi. She explored the Tennessee and Cumberland rivers from their mouths to the limits of navigation where the *Delta Queen* carefully nosed its way to avoid being caught on a sandbar. She enjoyed several river trips by towboat, one to New Orleans from where she returned reluctantly by train because she could not spare the time from home and work for the slower upstream trip.

These were not just trips for her personal amusement though I know she enjoyed them thoroughly. Her experience became "word pictures and prose poems," as Edgar Lee Masters once described her writing, in which she shared with the readers of *The Living Museum* and of nearly a score of published books her intense pleasure in the wildlife of the river regions. Many readers were led to take the steamer trips and make her adventures theirs.

Through *The Living Museum* she brought the Illinois State Museum, its displays and activities, before the people of the State. She thus did much to secure the modern new building in which the Museum is now located.

So the education of Virginia Eifert, and incidentally of her many friends and admirers, continued throughout a brief, busy, and satisfying lifetime. It never occurred to her that she had a mission, but many thousands of lives were enriched and inspired to higher levels of thought and ambition because Virginia Eifert lived and loved living creatures and plants in their native haunts and taught others to look for them there and see them with their own eyes and minds.

—THORNE DEUEL,
Museum Director Emeritus

There are those who look; and there are those who see. The difference is determined by depth of perception.

Virginia Eifert was one who saw, who was cognizant of that at which she looked. Oftentimes she stood motionless by the window, on the lakeshore, among tall trees, on the foot-bridge, and gazed intently, listening perhaps, but seemingly oblivious to all else. In the mind of the observer were the questions: What is she really seeing? Does she think descriptively? Are these thoughts some which will appear in print later? As she stooped to examine a flower, she seemed to ponder on its delicate beauty. Did she, at the same time, think "bloodroot blossoming like small white waterlilies on pinkish stems" which she later wrote? (*The Living Museum*, April 64).

Her writing was informational, sometimes philosophical, sometimes fanciful. Its charm lay in the apt descriptions, the similes and metaphors, expressed easily and esthetically. A snowflake was "a celestial marvel" and trees in winter were "decorated with ice-glaze" (Jan. 65). Haw trees in autumn were "a blur of soft scarlet" (Nov. 64). A lake in moonlight became "an oval pewter platter" (May 64); a zebra swallowtail butterfly, "a pen-and-ink sketch" (May 65). A fox with "lovely orange-russet fur" was described as "leaping on steel-spring, long black legs" (Oct. 64). The Pleiades were an "ornament of the glittering winter night" (Dec. 64) and dragonflies, "pure speed and light embodied in wings" (July 64). A snake appeared as "a long, lithe, animated ribbon of brown, black and yellow stripes" (July 53). She saw wild blue phlox as "a drift of lavender" (Apr. 41).

Her subtle sense of humor often came through: ". . . the ducklings, which had been pretty well fortified with the packed lunch each had had in its egg, began to feel hunger" (Sept. 58); ". . . frogs were sitting haunch-deep in the shallows" (May 64); oriole's nest in winter "suspended like an old sock high above the street" (Feb. 66); dogwood flowers after a rain "hung like wet laundry" (Apr. 66).

She liked alliteration: ". . . tiny frogs clinging with tight toes to grass tufts" (Mar. 59); pine needles "swish and rush against each other in a far sound like surf on a sandy shore" (May 59); "A large yellow moon ballooned up beyond the black trees and put light on pools but lately dyed with sunset" (Mar. 59).

Through her printed pages and personal contacts, she has led hundreds, perhaps thousands, to see, to appreciate, to be perceptive. Last February she wrote: "To walk with an awareness of one's surroundings is to discover new delights on every . . . expedition" (Feb. 66). She felt that an opportunity missed was an opportunity lost: "Old as it is, spring is eternally new to every man who watches it—and there are all too few springtimes in his life to ignore a single one of them" (Feb. 42).

Perhaps we can find some consolation now in these words written in April 1942: "Morale is a curious thing: simple habits like watching birds and clouds and stars and hearing frogs in spring can strengthen it for our own deep good."

—ORVETTA M. ROBINSON,
Museum Librarian

CONTENTS

CONTENTS

CONTENTS

SNOW AND WINTER

"FROM THE FALLING SNOWFLAKES . . ."

In the beginning, say the old Icelandic legends, there were two worlds, Nifelheim, the Frozen, and Muspelheim, the Burning. From the falling snowflakes in Nifelheim was born the giant Ymir, from whose body later on was formed the earth. "There was in times of old," says the Edda, "where Ymir dwelt, nor sand nor sea nor gelid waves; earth existed not, nor heaven above; 'twas a chaotic chasm, and grass nowhere."

Thus, vividly, the ancient people of the North spoke of their wintery world which was created from the giant who was born of the snowflakes.

Yet in itself a snowflake is a gentle thing. It is nothing. It is a fleeting fragment of frozen moisture congealed in a perfect six-sided star that falls out of a grey sky and either lies for a while on ground or tree or roof, or vanishes swiftly as human breath bends upon it. Yet in force, the millions of snowflakes battering out of the north can be as evil and as powerful as the old Icelanders knew in the times of their gods and giantesses.

The snow that comes in December has a certain charm which no other snow at other times of the year may have. Now in December snow is new; it is a novelty in its purity and whiteness and infinite delicacy. We rush to see the first flake that comes sifting in silence from a low sky, marvel at a flake caught in a spider's web or set like a jewel on coat sleeve or muffler. With Thoreau we exclaim: "How full of creative genius is the air in which these stars are generated! I should hardly admire them more if real stars fell and lodged on my coat. Nature is full of genius, full of divinity. Nothing is cheap and coarse, neither dewdrops nor snowflakes. And as surely as the petals of a flower are fixed, each of these countless snowstars comes whirling to earth, pronouncing thus, with emphasis, the number six." And so, through the timeless words of Icelander and of naturalist, we find a deeper kinship with the snow. (*Dec. 1948*)

1

ICE STORM

The temperature one January day hovered just above freezing, hovered at that indecisive point which is so menacing. It was not quite cold enough to snow, too chilly to send down proper rain . . . but rain began to fall, chill and somber, with bits of ice in it. The fine drops pattered with a heavy, sodden sound and froze where they landed. Now in that leaden day in which there was no spark of sunshine, "no sun, no moon, no morn, no noon, no dawn, no dusk, no proper time of day," the trees slowly became crystallized with a thin coating of ice. It continued as the grey day deepened into night. The roads were becoming glassy. And now at dusk there was an ominous, heavy sound from dripping, icy branches which, as they swayed in the wind, uttered dismal groanings and creakings befitting a horror movie.

The people in the forest cabin were uneasy. They could not settle down for an evening with books and warm fire and popcorn. Every hour or so one of them got up to see what was happening to the woods. A splintering crash—that was the top of a pine up the road. A dull crack and a long swish as a birch went down. Pine needles were slivers of solid ice, each tipped with a congealing drop of water. The balsams were weighted with ice, sleeked miserably like wet cats. The young pines already were bending to the ground and so were the pliable birches. Another birch down the road couldn't stand the load of ice or the increasing arc of the bend; it snapped off. The watchers shuddered and went inside again. And still the freezing rain came down.

Night moved on with dripping ice-rain and groaning trees. There was a deepening sense of impotence of man against the power of natural forces. The cold rain falls and freezes; trees break. Man can do nothing about it.

The usual silence of a winter night was broken all this night by the sounds of the trees. Brittle birches and maples uttered little splintering noises; the ground beneath them was littered with wreckage. A crash in the distance; another big tree had gone down. Pine branches swished heavily back and forth; branch against branch made rubbing noises. Night, growing colder, moved on toward dawn.

And when morning came, the temperature had dropped enough to stop the ice-rain. The sky cleared and the sun illuminated a glittering, unbelievable world of glass. The exquisite lace-work of the trees was gleaming, unreal, and cold. In all their terribleness, they were magnificent. The sun struck a thousand sparks and made colors like those seen through a prism. And everywhere was the wreckage of trees in the grip of ice.

Yet, even as a forest recovers from hurricane, blizzard, drouth, or fire, the ice-damaged trees in another year will have healed many of their wounds, new growth will take the place of broken branches and needle clusters. Only the trees which went down in the icy night, and those bent in strange arches, will mark where the ice formed on a night in January and changed the aspect of the woods. (*Jan. 1951*)

STORIES IN THE SNOW

When snow hides bare earth and blankets fallen leaves, it puts upon the woods and fields a fresh covering which is almost immediately imprinted with tracks and stories of the local inhabitants. The creatures themselves usually are difficult to see. They travel about at night, preferably, move inconspicuously under bushes, or hide among leaves so that human beings are seldom aware of the extent of the wild populations dwelling so close to houses and roads. Except for the tell-tale marks left on dusty paths and muddy shores in summer and on snowy fields in winter, we would know little of what has been going on around us.

But when snow comes, the creatures cannot move about without leaving their autographs. After a newly fallen snow has been arranged with crystalline nicety over log and meadow, upon slope and woodland, we may go out and, as with a newly sharpened vision, find fresh chapters in the story of the wild.

Now it is plain to be seen that clumps of prairie grass jutting from the snow really are fortresses of the meadow mice. The stalks provide a citadel with old, tough leaves matted around the bases of the plants where the mice retreat for shelter. Heaped over with snowflakes, the shelter is warm and is concealed from the hungry eye of hawk or fox. The mice, however, cannot stay inside forever. They must go out to forage; and although for a time they may tunnel beneath the snow, they also emerge and leave small quartets of tracks, the tail marks nicely imprinted to show which way their makers have gone. Mouse tracks lead to the stalk of a wild aster still holding seeds; to the corn stubble to find forgotten nubbins; to the ebony-dark stalks of partridge pea whose splitting pods still hold seeds.

By dawn, also, the rabbits have marked the new snow. The young ones which have never before seen snow are gay and reckless in their dancing about, imprinting numberless tracks in a most dangerous sort of prodigality while the old rabbits are more cautious. They follow well-traveled paths, putting their tracks together so that they eventually pat down the snow in rabbit-roadways which blur the identity of individual scents. Only the very young or the very reckless strike off for themselves in independent directions which are marked with dreadful clarity for any fox or weasel to follow.

In pursuit, the hunters leave their own tracks. The fox sets down its small, dog-like feet in an almost straight line, tracks made with purpose, following along the top of a log, disappearing when the fox changes course and walks in the still-open shallows of the creek, emerging again . . . and pouncing. The pounce marks are plain, and so are the small splatters of blood and scattering of brown feathers where a bobwhite was not quite fast enough to escape the hunter. The rest of the covey—the snow is plain in its narration here—had slept in a circle, tails together, heads out, in a hollow in the snow. They had been lightly covered with it as it fell last night, had all burst out in a concerted rush and a roar of wings as the fox leaped—all but the slow one. The slow and the inept and the weak are quickly taken to give energy to other creatures which are fast and efficient and strong. The story is all told there in the snow.

And the star-shaped tracks of an opossum show where it walked cautiously and with some distaste over the cold snow to look for fallen persimmons under leaves and snow or to dig out the remains of a dead robin, or an apple core thrown away by yesterday's hiker. The opossum searches, and its ambling tracks, as photographed in a city park last winter, tell stories in the snow, meeting and mingling with others on different errands and with different tales to tell, and going on again as part of the small drama of a winter's day. *(Dec. 1964)*

JANUARY

January . . . low point of life out of doors . . . . but a southward sun is beginning its journey back to the north and days are noticeably longer . . . . sunsets are clear, cold, lemon color behind black trees. . . . . There is the squeal of snow under hiking heels that tramp the paths the rabbits made when they skipped on light-hearted toes in the icy moonlight . . . footprints turned pink by the morning sun. January . . . . chickadees and cardinals managing a bare existence which is not too bare or too hard . . . a cardinal on a thawing day begins to sing again . . . . a chickadee, in brittle woods on a day of below-zero cold, turns flip-flops on a sycamore ball and pipes a cheerful note. January . . . . tight buds on all the trees, buds containing the leaves and flowers of spring, the whole leaf-crop, flower-crop, fruit-crop of summer. Snow again . . . a miracle of six-sided stars . . . the lonely hooting of an owl in the dusk across purple woods . . . and in the sky, beyond the cold flame of Sirius and Betelgueze and Aldebaran, the warmer light of Arcturus, star of spring, just before midnight, rises in the east. *(Jan. 1949)*

EDGE OF SNOW

This is January, the lowest point of life in the year. It is cold and the hand of snow is everywhere. Yet even on the carved drifts, life makes its presence known. The footprints of rabbits are everywhere; birds leave their marks; there are the rapid-fire running tracks of a shrew on a desperate hunt for bird or mouse; there are the staccato leapings of a white-footed mouse that skipped about in last night's icy moonlight.

These are the outward signs of life in January. There are others not so obvious. In the leftover heads of old grass are the carefully put-away eggs of insects, waiting for spring. Strung on sturdy silks between grass stems is the pear-shaped egg sac of a spider. There are living seeds in the grass heads, seeds in old vines on the fence.

Away from the grass-clump leaps a rabbit; he leaves behind him a warm hollow which is just the shape of his body. He had rested here to escape the eyes of the hawk in the bright cold sky. If the rabbit does not return to this hummock, perhaps the bobwhites, piping in the cold blue dusk, will gather here for the night, sit in a circle with their tails to the middle and their heads out, ever watchful of danger and ready to burst away in all directions when danger appears. Their keen ears hear the fox that comes over the wind-carved crust and noses the grass for food.

Beneath the snow itself there is other life. Some of it slumbers, but it is very much alive. Here the grasshoppers deposited their eggs just beneath the surface of the ground last summer when life was prolific and sunshine assured. There are a dozen sleeping lady beetles under a leaf and chinch bugs among the old grass leaves beneath the snow. In the earth itself is the burrow of a ground squirrel. In a snug room at the end of a long passageway deep beneath the frost line, the ground squirrels lie curled asleep in the almost death-like slumber of hibernation.

Here is life in the midst of intense cold and snow. Here is the promise of the coming season's growth, its song and its skipping, hopping, flying inhabitants. Here is life reduced to its most compact state, a concentration of heat and the life-element in such an efficient way that in spite of hardship, living things persist.

Now as the January days pass by, the edge of snow which catches the fullest strength of the sun's rays melts at noonday. Slowly the snow draws back; slowly little by little the live things and the growing things increase their life tempo until, one day, the snow has gone and a foretaste of spring is in the air. *(Jan. 1945)*

WINTER MAGIC

The freezing of water bears a multitude of forms. A snowflake is a celestial marvel. A snowstorm is worthy of the best efforts of Wotan or Kaleva. Hoar frost on weed stalks is an ornament of delicacy and delight. An ice-covered lake seals a mysterious world beneath an impervious shield. Great storm waves on Lake Michigan, with majestic and awe-inspiring might, cast freezing spray on pilings and rocks. As the rivers freeze, their ice is different in some degree from that on lake or pond; for the river is still flowing beneath its cover, and its efforts create strains and stresses which form patterns of fissures and ridges. The magic of winter creates snowdrifts carved by winds, trees decorated with ice-glaze, holly berries encased as if in glass, "hard water" to puzzle the birds which have never seen this wonder before. Winter, besides, is a creator of icicles.

An icicle is a product of both warmth and cold. It is ice in action, forming before our eyes. It grows in melting, until the melting overtakes growth and the whole structure vanishes. It is one of the splendors of the northern winter which, with the coming of longer days in January, often reaches the greatest development.

When there has been snow, the warmth of the noonday sun on the south slopes of roofs causes the melt-water to trickle into gutters and spill over eaves. When the gutters are still filled with snow and ice (and with some of last autumn's leaves, too, without a doubt) they brim over, a drop at a time, and freeze on the colder edge of the roof. The ideal, and usually the only, possible temperature for this forming of icicles is between thirty and thirty-two degrees. Lower temperatures discourage melting; higher degrees prevent freezing.

At first there is only a row of small, bright bumps of ice, but as the afternoon moves on and the drops continue to run, they slide over the ice-bumps and freeze around them. Layer after layer of ice is formed around the embryo icicles, with always a fresh, unfrozen drop hanging on the tip of what is now a stalactite of ice. When night comes and, in the growing cold, the dripping stops, the icicles remain in a hard, sparkling fringe along the eaves. Next day, if the dripping resumes, they increase in length. There are times, especially in January, when the supply of snow on the roof is large, when a fringe of icicles may elongate to three feet or more. Each is marked with circular ridges which indicate changes in the freezing and thawing or where each drop paused and froze before the next one came along. Some show definite concentric growth rings inside, like annual rings in wood or the layers of a hand-dipped candle. At times, if two drops hang side by side from one tip, the result may be a forked icicle. Wind may produce changes in direction. Tree branches getting in the way may be decorated with a shawl of ice.

The ice itself is not wholly transparent, for it contains within its structure myriads of tiny air bubbles which pick up and refract the light to give sparkle and whiteness. The living drop of water on the tip shoots off sparks of pure prismatic color in all the hues of the spectrum. Now and again a kinglet or a chickadee may dart out from the nearby tree to hover beside an icicle and sip the cold, sparkling drop of water.

Ice is a mineral. It belongs in the same hexagonal system of crystals as quartz itself, and, like quartz, it separates and refracts those rainbow colors hidden in sunlight. Although the crystals of ice are often invisible, the true six-sided forms are best seen when they manifest themselves as snowflakes.

Be an icicle-watcher. Time their growth. Keep notes on weather which is most favorable to icicle formation, and learn how the longer days of late winter bring the longest icicles. Bring one of these fascinating, tapered productions indoors and, before it melts, use a hand lens on its structure. Lay the icicle in a container of water. Unlike most solids, which are heavier than water, ice floats with only about one-ninth of itself above the surface. The floating icicle and the floating iceberg displace the same percentage of themselves.

And the icicle melts and it is gone. In the puddle of melt-water there is no hint of the magical formation which lately grew on roof or twig or dripping rock. (Jan. 1965)

ORNAMENT OF SNOW

Frosts came, leaves fell, birds cleared out, animals changed their habits, and the landscape became open and brown. Only where there were coniferous trees did the countryside hold its green, and in winter it was bright against the muted brown and gray framework of the deciduous trees. Quiet, almost voiceless, the landscape lay waiting for winter.

And then it snowed. The day had been gray, lowering, with a penetratingly damp cold which seemed more uncomfortable than downright winter weather. Snow began in the early gray dusk. The thin flakes flittered down like mosquitoes, tickling the cheek and dancing across the forehead, vanishing in a breath, yet coming and coming until the hosts in their billions began to whiten the ground.

By eight o'clock everything was covered. By midnight the snow had fallen so heavily that in the windless quiet it had heaped itself inches deep on every twig and bough, had created a Christmas card decoration of every pine and spruce and hemlock. As the flakes became fewer, the air held that mystic, crystalline purity of cold in the presence of innumerable snow crystals.

The midnight world was transformed. Although it was night, it was light, for the woods were illuminated by the snow itself. As the clouds tore apart, the stars came out in a glitter, so that the winter night had no need for light other than that provided by its own glory.

Loaded spruce boughs, bent nearly to the ground, sprang erect as the snow slid off. Handfuls of snow tumbled from the lightly-held tuftings of the pine needle clusters, and the maples were a splendid filagree-work of twigs, each piled perfectly with the nice balancing of flakes. A small, dark bubble of a thing leaped in a disembodied lightness from beneath an earth-touching bough and made off in airy bounds up the path, leaving only the delicate impress of feet and tail to show where the wood mouse had gone. A rabbit in a sudden flurry skipped off, kicking snow, and all about lay the silence of winter and snow and the muffled feeling of insulation from the flakes.

The first snow marked the change to a new series of experiences in the wild. To the young creatures of the year, it is a totally new and unexplainable thing. When morning breaks and the world is a glitter beneath the chill, southerly sun, the squirrels and rabbits come out in wonderment, touch their noses to the snow, and frisk about in a half-intoxicated delight. The older squirrels will dive purposefully into the light snow to dig down for nuts cached there in autumn; and the bluejay, searching for his own cache of sunflower seeds, comes up with snow all over his astonished face. The search for food is the thing, the immediate and vital goal of every day of the long winter.

As the boughs drip and the snow cascades off the pines and spruces in park and garden and woods, the whole immensity and drama of winter is begun. The first snow, ornament and delight, is the signal. *(Dec. 1963)*

THE JANUARY WOODS

Real winter had come at last, now that January was here; and the low ebb of heat from the sun, aided by the loss of summer-stored heat of the earth, brought long cold nights and days that sometimes were bitter-bright. Sometimes the days were mild and sunny, fresh with the smell of a false spring. For the Illinois winter may be like that, too. We never know. January may be like March, and dandelions may hasten into bloom; or it may be real winter like the one known as Eighteen-Hundred-and-Froze-to-Death, or a winter like the Winter of the Deep Snow.

If there is going to be any real winter weather, then, it had better begin in January or there won't be much chance for it. Though there can be snows and cold in February and in March, the opportunity of long duration is spoiled by the disconcerting appearance of a bluebird on February 1st, or the sight of crocuses and aconites pushing up through the leaves in a garden, or ruddy, curled-over heads of spring beauty buds on a sunny bank in the woods. There may be a robin or two even in January. Some stay over and spend the winter here. When February comes, the likelihood of robins grows even brighter, and by March it's all up with winter. It can make a comeback with some effort and effect, and often it does so with some of the deepest snows of an almost snowless winter, but it won't last. Everyone knows it, even the robins who, fluffed up and a trifle indignant at all that cold stuff on the ground, contrive to find a thawed place on a southern exposure and haul forth the worms lurking there. If there's to be any winter in most of Illinois, it usually comes in January.

And when it does, and the mercury slides in chilly silence down into the nether regions of the thermometer, and open waters finally freeze to an expanse of shining glass, and there may be snow sweeping viciously out of the north, the wild things are ready for it. Ready now, or not at all. By this time, most of the summer birds long since have gone to South America and Mexico where even now they may begin to feel an inexplicable pull toward the north again. Weaklings, months ago, were eliminated from the ranks of remaining winter birds, and the survivors are equipped to handle blizzards and below-zero cold if they come. The chickadees maintain a temperature of around 114 degrees by the simple expedient of wearing an extra-thick under-layer of downy feathers to keep heat in, and they man-ufacture that heat by turning every bit of protein food they can find into the fuel which keeps a small body alive. You can see the chickadees hunting meat on a bitter day—spider-egg sacs, tiny cocoons, the chain of eggs laid by a katydid along a twig, sleeping insects tucked into crevices of bark. Cardinals and juncos and sparrows are endlessly busy eating rich seeds in the weed patches.

Many birds fare well. On a winter's walk in the woods of Illinois, you will find a surprising population of birds comfortably living through the cold. With feathers fluffed to maintain dead-air spaces which conserve warmth, the birds live through the day and sleep through the January night. Like the junco most wild things will ride out the storms of any January severity which comes to Illinois *(Jan. 1954)*

WINTER INSECTS

In the northern hemisphere when winter comes, insects seem to disappear without a trace. When the first hard freeze sears the last greenery, seals waters with ice, and tightens the ground with frost, billions of insects which have hummed or whirred or flitted or bitten since spring, have vanished, but not so completely that they have not provided for renewed life next year.

On a cold day when there is no wind and the sunny side of the hill is deceptively warm, a short walk may turn up the clues to what has happened to our insects. Nature provides for coming generations of some of her most transient children; in the amazing survival of insects, we discover some of the deep truths of continuity in the natural world.

To focus on insects in winter requires a special sort of perception. Cultivating it is like putting a strong magnifying glass to one's eyes, a mental magnifier which makes minute things important and gives meaning and reason to the smallest insect egg or pupa. This mental lens suddenly gives meaning to the host of neat gray pendants hanging from the twigs of evergreens, from bare branches, from fence ledges. Bagworms are one of the easiest seen examples of winter survival among insects.

The provident bagworm moth has laid her eggs in these neatly tapered, very strong silk cases which no wind will easily dislodge. Insulated from cold, the eggs are safe until warm weather when they hatch into larvae which will emerge, eat, and grow, then busily spin new bags which will harbor the eggs for next year's young.

Another obvious sign of advance preparation—the large brown silk cocoon of a cecropia moth lashed tightly along a twig. The polyphemus cocoon dangles from another twig, but the cocoons of luna and promethea moths have fallen with the leaves on which they were built and now lie beneath dead leaves and snow until spring. The sphinx moth's big green caterpillar, the tomato worm, has long since crawled into loose earth and spun a cocoon or become encased in a cell. The earth itself is well occupied by many a slumbering insect—by millions of grasshopper eggs, the eggs of Carolina locusts, and the larvae of cicadas, which stop sucking sap from tree roots to become inactive in the cold earth during the winter.

If we had the eyes of a chickadee, we could find myriads of insect eggs in crevices of tree bark and on twigs. We would spot the neatly overlapping chains of eggs laid by the katydid along a twig, the masses of mantis eggs. As a woodpecker, we would uncover, deep in dead wood, the little sawdust-insulated bedrooms of the hibernating carpenter ants, would find engraver beetles in their snug tunnels, and termites, cold and motionless, in their labyrinthine halls.

A dead log would tell other stories of survival. Inside the pulpy decayed wood the fertilized queens of hornets, wasps, and yellow jackets, sole survivors of their colonies, hibernate. In other places are sleeping bumblebees, mourning cloak butterflies, red admiral butterflies, and woolly bear caterpillars. But the honeybees, in their hives or dead trees, stay awake in winter. They gather in a great close cluster, in the center of which certain bees set up an energetic dance which generates heat that warms the whole enclosure. According to Edwin Way Teale, the winter temperature inside the hive may be sixty-five degrees higher than outside.

But the majority of insects do not make heat; they simply adapt to cold. Some emerge on mild days to soak up the weak sunshine of January or early February—the mourning cloaks and red admirals, the lady beetles, the box-elder bugs, the mud dauber wasps, mosquitoes, water striders, midges, gnats, tiger beetles, and springtails. These are the obvious ones, the adult survivors. In midwinter, we can only guess at some of the numbers which survive in the form of eggs or larvae, and which are waiting all about us for the coming of the spring. *(Jan. 1960)*

ROBINS ARE A STATE OF MIND

It is a grim day in late winter with a bite in the air and a cold wind blowing out of the north again. Nowhere is there the slightest sign of spring, for January in Illinois is stern midwinter which seems to stretch interminably ahead. And yet—and yet—perhaps spring cannot be so far away; for there is a robin, a plump, russet-breasted bird with white-rimmed bright eyes, who shouts impatiently into the weak January sunshine, claps his wings, and runs importantly on the lawn. Now winter never again will be too despairing. One robin makes all the difference.

That robin on a January lawn may be one of those which annually spend the winter in a northern neighborhood where food is plentiful. Perhaps he is one of a flock wintering in the river bottomlands. Properly these have no right to be called "first robins."

But in southern Illinois and in the Mississippi bottomlands there are others wintering, marking time until early spring. It is usually some of these which impatiently head northward on the first passably spring-like days of late winter—or even in cold weather—to surprise us. They are hardy creatures; when the inevitable return of winter freezes the worms in the ground, the robins fluff themselves round as balls; they are cheerful, chubby, and bright-fronted, and they chirp indignantly as they gobble raisins and chopped apples put out for them. Somehow even in the worst snowstorm or zero weather, these robins convey the impression of waiting until this, too, shall pass.

If they time themselves properly, certain first robins may bear that title for at least two months and in consequence receive the acclaim of all who see them. They travel in leisurely fashion from Tennessee to northern Wisconsin and Canada, and all along the way, in town and village and farm, each one is heralded as the "first robin." As they go on, others follow, and as they, too, go on, those which may have wintered in the long-leafed pines of Florida and the Gulf country finally come almost unnoticed to nest in Illinois. For by that time, as Emily Dickinson said, "The robins stand as thick today as did the snows of yesterday."

But now January still is on the land; it is still winter. Nevertheless, that first robin is a good omen. He becomes the possession of a person who discovers him, for robins have the quality of earthiness which belongs to man. Some folk may be a little late in catching up with what has been seen by sharper eyes before, and yet it does not matter. The first robin is a personal thing—it is a state of mind. The person who sights what to him is the first robin of the year definitely has put winter behind, and spring at last is in his heart. (*Jan. 1944*)

GREEN IN JANUARY

Illinois, which is not primarily a coniferous country nor blessed with many broad-leaved evergreens, has little all-winter greenery to carry over the color of life from one year to the next. Green leaves are here for months; they go; we must wait many more months before they return to fill the landscape with the look of summer.

We in the Middle West accept what winter is; we rather like the transition and the challenge of the seasons. We do not have the shocked horror of two Hawaiian Air Force cadets who came to see the Lincoln shrines one bleak February day: "We didn't realize that all your trees died in winter!"

We know they haven't died; only greenery has left the landscape, and not all of that has vanished. To track down these remnant greens of January may become a game on a pleasant winter day, for although the majority of plants may have vanished, the hardy, winterized leaves of certain deciduous plants withstand cold that has destroyed the others. The over-all picture of the landscape is, however, largely gray and brown, with lavender shadows and overtones; with the orange-copper hue of turkeyfoot grass on loess slopes; of— why, that field is *green!* Winter wheat, a great green lawn nourished by snows and released by thaws, is green as summer. In January it is a magnificent sight.

Along the country road near the wheat field are the gray-green rosettes of mullein; the basal rosettes of dandelion and yarrow and daisy and aster. There are dark green junipers on a hill; Norway spruces and pines in a farm yard; Japanese honeysuckle, gone wild over embankments and draped on trees, sparks color in the winter woods.

In those woods there may be the bright viridian bark of the greenbrier vines and their berries which the cardinals eat all winter. There are beds of low, tender, green, wild chervil leaves, delicate as springtime yet astonishingly sturdy all winter long. There are the violet-like basal leaves of *Ranunculus;* the dark leaves of hepatica which, by spring, will have turned purple-brown.

On slopes above the woods are Christmas ferns as green as summer. They lie low now because the weight of the snow earlier in winter bent them down.

They spread across the emerald beds of moss which seem to be changeless in their hue around the year, yet have their own seasonal transitions, too. And the dark green of liverworts is there; the green paint of algae on tree-trunks; the gray-green of lichens.

In summer, many of these small plants would be inconspicuous among the burgeoning wealth of greenery. In winter they are precious, must be sought and the sight of them cherished. Theirs is a small green fire burning through the grimmest January day, green under snow, green under ice . . . green, at last, with a springtime sun upon it. And none are more colorful, perhaps, than the polished twigs of the sassafras along the road, with green buds and the flavor of sassafras tea when chewed contemplatively as we walk the woodland paths in search of life's immortality as it is expressed in the presence of January green. (*Jan. 1962*)

BLACK WATER IN FEBRUARY

Black against the curving shoulders of the snow, the rushing waters of the open creek dashed through the sunshine. Now sparkling with a dazzle of sun on myriad whirls and curvets, now black as obsidian as it slid under a mass of ice and snow, the water went on its way. And slowly, silently, as the sun shone a little longer each day, the black water was conquering the snow and ice.

This is the eternal hope of winter, the courage of February. It is a time in which any kind of weather may happen, and usually does, and most of it is still sternly winter and not at all like spring. Yet the story of the progress of the season lies in the creek. The ice still covers the quieter waters, but even during most of the winter there was some open water, ebony-dark and silently rushing. Zero weather sealed more of the creek under ice; milder weather permitted the water to eat away some of the ice and dissolve it, churning and tumbling, among the rapids.

And the fish, the sunfish, the crappie, and the perch, lay along the bottom, their noses pointing against the endless push of the current. They fed when it was mild, existed when it was cold, but now always above them the February sunshine filters through the kaleidoscope of the rushing dark water and brings some measure of the improving season to those that wait below.

Today an otter came along the hard, crusted, curving shoulder of snow and down to the edge of the black water. The otters have a slide on a steep bank along the open creek where the snow is packed into a miniature ski-slide; here the gay otters coast on their slim bellies into the cold water. But today the otter was fishing and had not time for play. With a graceful curve of its long dark body it slid into the black water and swam through its iciness down to where the fish lay motionless against the current. And in another moment the water parted with a froth of silver bubbles as the otter, gripping a perch, emerged and came out on the bank, then loped off with the fish in its mouth.

Chickadees piped hopeful little spring songs in the willows. A downy wood-pecker doggedly hammered and probed on willow bark which had been explored too many times lately to find much else that was good to eat. Food supplies are reaching that low point of the winter which comes in February, yet most of the creatures find a way to survive. The portent which comes with the opening of the creek, with the breaking away of a little more ice and a little more ice, with the reddening of maple twigs and a gloss of gold on the willows, with the scattering of birch seeds on the snow and the release of seeds from the conifers, all mean that the worst of the winter is past. For although February may mean deep winter in the north and high spring in the south, and may mean either or both in Illinois, where the seasons sometimes become badly mixed, the live black waters of the open creek surely have much of meaning in their sparkle. (*Feb. 1952*)

SO MUCH TO SEE IN FEBRUARY

To the Indians, February was the lean month, the starving month, the month when even the wolves went hungry and howled like lost spirits on the prairie. To one who knows the calendar of events out of doors, February is still a lean and hungry month, yet, as in every month, there always is so much to see. Here, in the last stand of winter and the first tentative touch of spring, are the living things whose very scarcity gives them an aura of excitement.

Compared with the grandeur and abundance of June, February truly may appear bald and empty. Yet February's wealth is not in vastness nor in numbers. The song of one cardinal on a February morning takes the place of the chorus of a hundred birds in May, and is the sweeter for having been heard alone in its perfection. The flowers of February may be limited to one half-frozen crocus and a handful of maple flowers flung upon the sky, but after a long winter that is not yet past, this blossoming interlude in February is all the more wonderful. So it is with all the things which one may see in this wintery month—within the woods, along the roads, beside the streams, upon the wind. There is so much to see in February.

There are the first weak-winged stoneflies crawling upon the wet rocks of a thawed stream, and the first phoebe efficiently snapping them up as they venture into the sunshine. There are the dancing clouds of winter mosquitoes, and the same mild day that brings them forth may see the flitting, ragged, black and golden wings of that butterfly, the mourning cloak, which winters behind a tatter of hickory bark.

There may be those glowing bits of mushroom flesh, the scarlet cups, brilliant as a tanager's feather lost among the winter's leaves. There may be orange-capped, sticky, velvet-stem mushrooms jutting determinedly from the trunk of a willow or an elm. Upon a sunny hillside there may be a basking garter snake, up from its winter burrow in the deceptive warmth of the day, thawing its chilly blood in the weak sunshine. There may be a rabbit leaping from its cupped bed of dry grass, squirrels gathering mouthfuls of dry shingle-oak leaves to mend the big leaf-nests that have worn a trifle thin under the winter storms.

There is always a robin or two chirruping importantly in town, robins that are dignified and a trifle smug with the honor of being the First Robin and making all the front pages of the local press. There very likely are bluebirds, too, infinitely bluer than any bird possibly could be, in the orchard or along the road. The prairie horned larks come flying in a scattered migration over the February sky and return to the wet, plowed fields where northern horned larks have fed all winter. Mourning doves may appear before the end of the month, and so may the caroling redwinged blackbirds in the marsh. Short-eared owls cruise low over the dead grass of the prairie fields, hunting for the mice that have grown scarcer than they were in autumn. Juncos and tree sparrows in the weed patches begin to sing sweet tinkling songs that presage the flight to Canada. And in the woods, on wet banks where ice still lingers, the beds of moss are brilliant emerald. They are the greenest things in the whole February landscape just now—greener than the winter wheat, brighter by far than the algae and water cress in the slow stream, or the leaves of Christmas fern that wintered under the snow.

There is indeed so much to see in February—small things, exciting things, that are part of February and the doorstep to the spring. *(Feb. 1947)*

❁

❁ # SPRING

❁

❁

SPRING IS A JIGSAW PUZZLE

Take the dull face of late winter and add a bit of green that looks like new grass, and add a plump robin running importantly across it, and you have the beginning of the jigsaw puzzle called Spring. Take winter and put the pieces of spring together upon it, and in a few weeks you have the great composite picture which is, surprisingly enough, not spring, but summer.

But whatever begins it, the rest of the picture is still scattered broadly from Illinois to Argentina, scattered from the tops of the trees and the open sky to the lowest grasp of root in the earth. Still, one thing is intended to fit into another. Somehow, piece by piece, from far places, they come back or they spring from the ground, or they grow, and, magically, they all fit together. Each bird that returns from the south adds one more bit to the picture, and it would forever seem incomplete if the orioles forgot to come back, or if the myrtle warblers skipped over our woods and kept going nonstop to Canada. If the spring beauties forgot to bloom, or if a blight hit all the dogtooth violets, how empty would be the April woods, how imperfect the picture of spring.

In two weeks from bare ground, wild flowers bloom. Terns over the lake casually but mightily came up from southern Argentina and may go on to the Arctic. Trees are covered with new leaves that develop from tiny buds which were there almost unnoticed all winter—you get a hatful of flowers from one horse-chestnut bud, bouquets on every redbud, the promise of lavish crops on every apple tree.

That is the sly wonder of this jigsaw puzzle of spring. It may give us the feeling that it is being done for the first time and for our special joy. It may come as freshly as if this were the first springtime ever known, come with an enthusiasm and a newness which is innocent and gay, but it is really old stuff, very old indeed. It is as old as the seasons. The ancient picture puzzle

15

has been put together every springtime for millions of years, yet in spite of that and in spite of the obvious skill in which the pieces put themselves in place, we who look at it today find it forever new. *(April 1948)*

INEVITABLY, SPRING

A world upset by war, lives stirred and tightened, luxuries denied, motor cars in abeyance—this is today. A return to simplicity, therefore, is at hand, a return to entertainment which costs no money, needs no conveyance, and is so varied and delightful that no end to it has ever yet been reached. Out-of-doors lies the perfect recreation. Spring is coming, and now in spite of himself mankind in America takes his eyes from the newspapers and his ears from the radio. There's a spring smell in the air, swelling buds on the street-side trees, and an insistent, far-too-early robin that claps its wings and shouts from the roof-top. Now America watches the return of spring, breathes air that puts new color in the face, new light in the eyes, new buoyance in the step, and offers a source of new courage for the future.

The man-made world may seem all wrong, but the natural world is still, reassuringly, comfortingly, the same as it always has been. In spite of head-lines, there soon will be meadowlarks and robins, bluebirds and doves. In spite of priorities, the raccoon soon will be dabbling for crawfish in the creek, snakes will be basking in the warming sun, young rabbits will be born, and among birds there will be nesting as usual. In spite of death and destruction abroad, a million billion buds will be getting ready to cover the trees with the 1942 crop of leaves.

With superb preparedness, those fat buds were formed last summer when the leaves were still on the trees. At the base of each leaf a new bud formed, and when autumn came, and the leaves fell, the buds hardened, grew brown, and proof against the cold. There they stayed all winter, and now when the first warmth comes, some of them, often in late January or February, burst open with early flowers.

Now when larger, more elaborate, and more distant entertainment for leisure time is denied, the joy of watching spring rise from its earliest beginnings becomes one of the fullest satisfactions of the year. Old as it is, spring is eternally new to every man who watches it—and there are all too few springtimes in his life to ignore a single one of them.

Step by step, inch by inch, spring comes. Left behind is the unhappy winter; behind must be fear and worry and dread. Springtime is the fine solution to man's wartime moods, to his motorized restrictions, and to his feet which are now largely on their own. Out-of-doors, as well as within the walls of that illustrated nature book, the Museum, lies the answer to what to do with leisure time on foot without expense. That bouquet of twigs is only one of the countless small yet infinitely satisfying things to do that are suddenly rediscovered and made available out of doors. *(Feb. 1942)*

THE BANNERS OF SPRING

To us of the north who have been so long starved of greenery and blossoms and birdsong, it could seem at least a thousand years since we last had spring-time. Autumn seems half an eon away, and last spring so distant that every bird and flower and leaf comes now as if for the first time in the history of the world. Perhaps it is this feeling of separation which we have for all past springs which makes this one undoubtedly the most beautiful, the most splendid, the most satisfying of any we have ever known.

Spring in the north is never that whole-hearted surge of azaleas and dogwood and greenery which never really went away, as the south knows it. We suffer through the delays of a northern spring, we urge it along, we scan every small shoot and every incipient snowdrop as if by our earnest efforts and encouragement we can make them bloom. We in Illinois have to work so hard for our springtime—perhaps never more than in 1962— it is no wonder we love it.

Thoreau, after his first long winter at Walden, watched spring as we do, watched it come inch by inch, robin by robin, and could know it intimately because he was so close to it. The melting of the pond was a triumph. Green grass called for celebration. He wrote: "The grass flames up on the hillsides like a spring fire, as if the earth sent forth an inward heat to greet the returning sun; not yellow but green is the color of its flame;—the symbol of perpetual youth, the grassblade, like a long green ribbon, streams from the sod into the summer. . . ."

And so our grass pushed up almost visibly; daffodil shoots extended themselves an inch in a night; dandelions put forth flowers; and there was on every tree a visible expansion of the buds which had remained on the twigs all winter. The expansion was visible as early as late February, if we looked. Compared with their dimensions last fall, there was a minute fraction of a difference in size by late winter. The cells of the miniature leaves and flowers inside those buds had all taken on a meager portion of sap, but not until exactly the right time when the temperature and the light-hours and the moisture were proper for each kind, would they expand, put out leaves, and open their flowers. Then it all happened rapidly. By mid-March the maples were all but out of bloom, the elms by April; but not until mid-May in northern Illinois would the large-toothed aspens put out their white leaves.

In April most of the wild fruit trees blossom—even in late March, some-times, the buds of wild plum expand suddenly on a mild, rainy night and burst into a tangle of fragrant white flowers that fairly drip perfume in the rain. They are the first really flavorful blossoms, and they come in such masses before the leaves, in the thickets along country roads, that the air even at a distance is scented with them. Canada plum, goose plum, Indian plum —close your eyes, smell wet plum blossoms, and know that spring is here at last! (*April 1962*)

THE PROMISE OF MARCH

The morning was mild, the sunshine warmer than it had been for months, and a robin in a tree-top had saluted the chilly dawn. While the robin sang, the night's frosts still lay on the brown grasses and capped the maple buds, but by ten there was such promise in the air that spring itself seemed to have come in the night.

Yet, the March landscape was very much as it had been all winter. The trees outwardly showed no signs of change, no leaves, no flowers, no opening buds. The earth revealed no evidence of blossom or leaf, nothing but the evergreen rosettes of mullein, primrose, or dock. The river flowed quietly between its muddy banks, and as yet there were no swallows to dart back and forth above it, nor any mosquitoes to swarm along its reaches, nor any frogs to sing along the shores. It was March and, in most of Illinois, it was certainly not yet spring. March was only offering its tempting promises.

For March, perhaps more than other months in the year, is exciting because of the promises it offers and the assurance it presents for what is about to happen. Without March, we might leap too quickly from winter to summer. March is the merger. Although it may bear only the outward look of endless winter and may, in fact, produce some of the deepest snows of the year, there are now so many subtle spring beginnings, both visible and invisible, that, when March arrives, we cannot have anything else but hope for an early spring.

The sycamores along the river now take on a brighter shine, a whiter whiteness against the pale March sky. The maples on the river banks seem dark and lifeless; yet, far in advance of sycamore buds, they are usually in bloom by mid-March. The soft maples hold small, tight, carmine bouquets so high against the sky that they are all but unseen. Often, not until the large seed-keys shower down in April and May do we realize that this early blossoming has taken place. The elms also bloom in March—very high, seldom seen; yet the tiny clusters of little bells with orange and maroon stamens are extraordinary things when seen under a hand lens.

The only mammal in sight is a cheeky fox squirrel nibbling elm buds. Several blue jays in procession fly with bugling calls over the woods. A titmouse whistles; another challenges him from across the river. A Carolina wren flirts and flits along the wooded bank, poking under the exposed tree roots where the river has chewed out the earth, quite vanishing into small crannies, and popping out again to sing once more. Among the trees or dallying out over the water there is a black and pale yellow butterfly, the mourning cloak, wakened from hibernation by the warming sunshine.

On the sand bar there are fresh tracks imprinted by a raccoon that foraged there the night before for clams and crayfish. Last night it had been too cold for frogs to stir, but today, as the sun grows warmer toward noon, there comes the first rasping, hesitant piping and jingling of the small cricket frogs and spring peepers. With maple flowers and singing frogs, with butterflies and caroling birds—with music and motion and sunshine—March offers promise for the coming of spring. (*March 1964*)

DAY IN MARCH

This now is spring, this day of mildness and freshness and life after many days of cold. Now at last the grip of frost has relaxed. Thawed and wet, the earth is ready for growth to begin.

The lake still has much ice, but on the blue open water the late winter and early spring ducks are gathering. American mergansers, long and rakish with their scarlet saw-beaks brilliant in the sunshine, sit like penguins along the edge of ice and preen and gesture and stretch their black and white wings. The goldeneyes on open water are courting. Several males perform for a female goldeneye who obviously isn't watching nor is much concerned. The male goldeneye suddenly snaps back his glossy black head with the white spot near the eye, until the puffy crown feathers almost touch his back. Then forward with a zip he bows, to touch beak to water, then is back to normal position. All over the open water, wherever the goldeneyes gather, these strenuous antics go forward.

Crowds of streamlined pintails get up in restless flights around the sky, and more sedate gatherings of hundreds of mallards and black ducks sit and doze on the water. A great flock of Canada geese, pausing on the long flight north, sits in close formation on the water; there is much honking, talking, flapping, or they get up in sudden mass flights which are as exciting and as full of excitement as the buglings of spring itself. And a bluebird carols plaintively in wind that shakes the willows of the marsh.

The marsh is full of newly arrived redwinged blackbirds, all males, all singing and gurgling in a tangle of sound which is as if the marsh with its bleached old cattail stalks had come alive in the sunshine. The buds of the soft maples along the edge of the marsh are ruddy and swollen; by tomorrow they will be in bloom.

Everywhere there is mud—mud, the prelude to spring. The trails through the woods are muddy, the country roads are muddy, the hills and pastures are muddy, the whole world seems muddy, yet it is all an indication of the progress of the season. In a little while it will have drained, the last ice below the surface will be gone, and then indeed will things grow and summer will come. There is as yet no evidence of renewed green . . . except in the woods where the thin, ruddy little stems of spring beauties are up and there are tiny, down-curved clusters of buds. No green . . . except the dark green of Christmas ferns left from last year. No green . . . . except for the bright pale green of lichens damp in the moisture of a March day.

Now at sundown flocks of redwings and grackles stream over in the glow. A robin in the top of a maple sings a brief song. And in the long twilight, while an orange sky lingers behind black trees, the wet black fields with pools of melt-water reflect the dregs of light. Over an orange pool flies a stubby, long-billed bird which whirls upward with a whickering of wings, up, up, against the glow—the woodcock, calling nasally, spirals in its spring evening flight. Horned larks in small groups fly low over the muddy fields to grass clumps for the night, and in the transcendent light of dusk the great glowing body of Venus, the evening planet, is huge and low and bright. (*Mar. 1951*)

AWAKENING OF THE MARSH

Until that day, the marsh had lain cold and unstirring. There had been no evidence of any life until that first blackbird came back and set up an impatient calling which was not half what he would utter when the rest of the flock returned. This redwing was the outpost, one lone bird ranging ahead of the coming hordes which at that March moment perhaps were filling a cattail marsh along the river bottoms of western Kentucky or southern Illinois, and filling it with song and wings and bright spots of red.

The blackbird came that morning into a land which might have been discouraging to any bird less sturdy. He was shining-satin black with shoulders of scarlet and gold and handsome in his spring plumage, but his soon-to-be-mellow voice sounded rusty in the cold wind. There was no sunshine; the wind was coming out of the north again—he had moved to this empty marsh on a kindly south wind which, during the night, had most unkindly changed back to this bitter breeze with the sting of winter still upon it. He was hungry. It seemed that in all that broad expanse of marsh with a fringe of ice in its edges of water and the brown acres of old bent-over cattail stalks, there was not one morsel of food for a bird. The blackbird creaked his song again and went down among the old cattails, foraging.

There wasn't much. It was too cold that morning for insects to be out, or snails either. He did find a few early spiders, a meager meal, but enough for the moment. It was warmer down there out of the wind which almost had a hint of snow in it. The thin ice around the stalks and in the pools tinkled and crackled, seemed to extend a little farther to reclaim the open water.

The blackbird stayed in the marsh. It is not customary for a bird that has migrated northward to retreat in the face of stern weather. He was not unaccustomed to cold. He and his flock had been in the marshes along the Mississippi River this past winter when the temperature had dropped far below zero. Many of the birds had ranged farther down the river into Louisiana where they could eat again, but had quickly started north as soon as the weather was moderating—and their own instinct told them it was time, weather or not, to come to Illinois and the Middle West.

This blackbird spent the night down among the cattails. It was dangerous there, open to any weasel or mink prowling for food, but the scout was alive when morning came. He hopped stiffly up the stalks to the bending stem still topped with an old fluffed-out seed head. He spread his wings and got out a rusty carol into the chill sunrise. It was going to be a clear day, and there was a new feeling in the air. Although the thin ice had extended and covered whole pools in the night, it seemed to be dissolving. The wind was back in the south again, air had a softness; and the sun, as it climbed higher, had a lovely warmth.

By noon the ice was gone. The blackbird was singing most of the time. He had caught some early stoneflies and was feeling good again. And now there were new sounds in the marsh. A flock of mallards had come down to feed and dabble and quack. A song sparrow was singing as if it were summertime.

And in the shallows a tiny brown frog an inch long climbed slowly out onto a clump of old grass. His throat-sac pulsated, and he let out a tentative, shrill, bird-like whistle. The sun felt warm on his back. He whistled again, and was answered by another little frog.

By the time the sun was setting in the fragrant March afternoon, the marsh was full of the high-pitched whistles of the spring peepers in a grand chorus which almost drowned out the voice of the blackbird. He gave a last guttural call, shook his feathers, signed off, and went to sleep. He had found enough to eat that day. And perhaps in the morning, brought on that gentle south wind, would be the black-satin, scarlet-epauletted flocks of his kind. They would be all males at first, singing in a mad jumble of competitive song, impatient for the later arrival of the streaked brown females which would not come for perhaps another two weeks. He, the scout, the advance guard, had led the way for them all. (*March 1963*)

NIGHT IN MARCH

When the cool March sunset paled behind the bare maples beyond the marsh, the water lying between black grass hummocks caught up the last lemon and apricot colors bathing the sky. Wet fields across the road lay purple-black, patterned with pools of color. Now the sky arching over field and marsh was an apple green, darkening to purple in the east, and night drew on in a long, fragrant twilight.

It was March, and from the wet clods in the unplowed field the horned larks were twittering, then leaping on rapidly beating wings into the damp twilight air, higher, higher, until the singing bird was lost against the sky. But from up there somewhere fell down a gush of small notes of music, a quick tinkling of song before a small bird plummeted to the dark oblivion of the field. The female larks were down there, and in a few days there would be nests built in the sodden old grass along the fence rows, where eggs would be laid and exposed to late snows. Young larks would emerge to a cold, windy March world.

With deepening twilight, the peepers tuned up in the marsh. Their high, insistent voices, shrill, bird-like musical whistles, grew in numbers and in volume with the coming of night. The marsh grasses were full of tiny frogs clinging with tight toes to grass tufts; the peepers were invisible but astonishingly vocal. They were so loud and continuous in their chorus that the steady, sudden whickering of another sound was all but lost.

But it came again, a loud whirring, like a pliable willow switch rapidly whipped back and forth. There came a strange sort of twittering, not like larks nor like peepers, then a loud "peent!" like a nighthawk, but with a difference.

There was another farther off in the marsh; several more were among the maples standing at the marsh edge. Unseen in the darkness, the woodcocks were at their nuptial flights. Stout, long-billed waders and probers in mud, the woodcocks in spring leap on whirring wings into the twilight, whickering their way upward like a small projectile, with ardent twitterings, then dropping back and uttering that nasal "peent!," only to leap up and do it all over again.

And the peepers shrilled and the woodcocks spun upward, the moist smell of wet spring earth, renewed waters and the stirring of innumerable forms of life were all about in the March night. A large yellow moon ballooned up beyond the black trees and put light on pools but lately dyed with sunset, and the peepers piped with more vigor, the woodcocks whickered again and again, and in the dark reaches of the night there came the far sounds of geese. High, momentarily blotting out the pale stars of spring, calling resonantly, in a close communion among themselves far above the earth, the geese were moving north. Briefly they patterned the face of the moon and were gone, calling.

A bat, newly out of hibernation, cut parabolas in the moonlight. A barred owl called across the swampy woods and was answered by another; the owls talked back and forth, volubly, drawing closer, shortening the distance between each other, until soft wings shadowed across the open water and swerved up into a blur of darkness in the trees.

And the night and the stars and the springtime moved on a few more hours toward the coming of a new dawn and of a day which would have two more minutes of sunlight, and a steadily growing vigor in the renewed life of spring. (*March 1959*)

ALL ON AN APRIL MORNING

It was spring. There was no doubt about it. A fragrance on the wind told of willow catkins blossoming, of young leaves coming out on the maples, of wild plums in bloom, and of earth and old leaves which had been well dampened by last night's April rain and warmed by the morning's sun. There was no question about it; spring had really come. You didn't need the rollicking, just-back-from-the-south carols of the first rose-breasted grosbeak, nor the wave of robin song which had rolled like a tide over the woods and town at half past four in the morning, nor even the purple martins cutting great sweeps across the sky and chortling in downright mirth and good feeling. It was really spring—the dandelions were in bloom, the wild plums were full of bees and pollen, and the woods were perfectly carpeted this morning with one of the most exciting visions of the year.

There they all were, the manifestations of April. Spring beauties, tenuous and frail, their thin petals veined with pink; bloodroot blossoming like small white waterlilies on pinkish stems above the floor of the woods; white and yellow trout lilies, like miniature Easter lilies; and blue violets, yellow violets, white violets; Dutchman's breeches, crisp as popcorn; lavender phlox; and the somber stalks of red trilliums—they were all there.

Flowers were not confined solely to the earth. Some were in the tops of the sugar maples where pale, green-gold tassels were dangling slender threads tipped with tiny bells. The redbud was in bloom; each tree held thousands of miniature pink, "sweetpea" blossoms on thin carmine stems which jutted in clusters from the wood itself. The thickets of wild plums presented a lower strata of bloom in which the bees seemed to be half intoxicated with that concentrated fragrance.

And, very inconspicuous, very quiet, hardly to be seen until looked for, on bare brown twigs the papaw flowers were opening. Theirs was part of the picture and perfume of April. Even though the papaw is by ancestry a tropical tree, member of the Custard Apple family, the Annonaceae, this northern species dwells with us in river bottoms and lowland woods. A thousand species grow in the tropics; only two live in North America. Now, long before the thin, oval leaves cover the tree to hide it in the over-all camouflage of greenery, the papaw's flowers are one of the most interesting facets of the Illinois springtime.

The flower emerges from a round, pea-sized, brown-furred bud on the side of a twig. There is a small, three-parted brown calyx. Hanging beneath it are three maroon petals an inch long, while three smaller petals inside the cup shelter the globular pistil and the stamens. The blossom has a vague resemblance to the red trillium, but the rich, fruity fragrance is almost tropical in its implication. When sunshine strikes through the petals, they gleam with a silken sheen. Papaw flowers are one of the unique and delightful specialties of certain springtime woods. Although they are not easily found in the wild, they may be seen in the new habitat exhibit of the Eastern Illinois Hardwood Forest in the Museum. (*April 1964*)

APRIL IN THE HILLS

Tall white limestone cliffs shone in the sunshine and on their ancient surfaces there shimmered a reflected light cast up by the sun on the river. The Mississippi, immensely broad and brown, surged southward. On it a paddle-wheeler, kicking foam and pulling a great train of loaded barges, came upstream.

It was late April, and between the white cliffs the village of Elsah was full of the glory of dogwood and the singing of birds. Everywhere spring was at its height; after a period of coldness and rain, everything surged and sang and bloomed in the warm sunshine. On two levels which opened out to the river, the old village with its native-stone houses and neat gardens lay between the hills. Everywhere that day was the white snow of dogwood, the rosiness of redbud, opening coral buds of wild crab apple, new leaves on all the trees, bleeding-hearts and violets beside an old house. Oaks had hung out their yellow tassel-flowers; the new leaves were as if cut from velvet, perfect leaves in miniature—russet, pink, white, pale green, buff, lilac. The woods had taken on a shadowing of leaves that was different and vastly refreshing from the openness of winter that so long had held the land. Trees covered the hills and grew in the village; now from the hill-top the village almost was hidden.

All about were birds. A dozen scarlet tanagers in a dogwood ravine; hosts of warblers singing; an oriole, newly back from South American jungles, flashing and singing and dashing about in a frenzy of song and color. A brilliant wood duck with head tucked in its shoulder-feathers dozed in mid-morning on a snag by the river; an osprey with wings bowed sailed up-stream high above the river and the paddle-wheeler; a flock of bobwhites followed their private trail through the prairie grass on the cliff-top; two brown thrashers in opposite trees wildly and loudly tried to out-sing each other.

All day long the birds sang and sun shone warmly for the first time that spring, until even the crispness of the dogwood blossoms all through the woods seemed a trifle wilted by mid-afternoon. Along the stream that wound down through the ravine there were colonies of unrolling croziers of Christmas ferns, white-woolly, and crisp; whole hill-sides were decked with the curled fronds of young brittle-ferns; wild columbine nodded from the sheer cliffs. Lavender sweet william flowers were everywhere. Scents, sights, sounds: Spring!

It is not often that there comes a truly perfect day in spring. Most days are too warm, too cold, too windy, too rainy. This seemed perfection. All about in the countryside the fruit trees were in bloom. Upstream in the apple country the hills were white, and the last of the peach blossoms thrust against the blueness of sky and the brownness of plowed earth. Winter wheat was emerald; cocks crowed madly; there were butterflies in the woods.

The day passed goldenly. As the sun slipped behind the great white bluffs, the hollow with the village in it was in shadow that suddenly grew cool and scented with April. There was an opalescent glow in the little stream where a waterthrush, teetering from stone to stone across the satiny water, sang to itself. As dusk came, a whip-poor-will flew up from the stream-side to the ridgepole of a barn to utter its evening call over and over again.

Frogs near the river jingled and chirruped, and in the soft dusk there came the long, throaty trilling of the toads. Out beyond the white cliffs the river ran strongly toward New Orleans, and, in the stone houses of the village, lights shone out in patches along the dusky streets. And still the dogwood, lighted as if with a glow of its own, gleamed in the dark woods where the whip-poor-wills were loud. (*April 1944*)

THE SINGING POND

Now in the warmth of the summer evening fireflies flick and glimmer in the wet grass by the pond; hour by hour the stars move over the dark sky; and the voices of frogs and toads rise in a chanting chorus that becomes a part of the night.

At sunset the cricket frogs start their dry clickings, a sound as of pebbles shaken briskly together in the hand. There is a hearty, calf-like bawling from the swelled-out throat of a Fowler's toad, and bird-like whistlings from a pair of tree frogs in elms at opposite sides of the pond. Then the bullfrog awakens and thunders forth to shake the pond, to make the cattails wiggle and the young redwings stir in their nests.

Frogs and toads are comedians of the wild, broad in their grins, unexpected in their antics, laughable whether they croak, or leap, or just sit on a bank and stare with gold-rimmed eyes. Since ancient times folk have had notions about them. In the old medieval days of witchcraft, a toad was considered a poisonous creature, one which gave warts and was good only as an ingredient in a witch's brew, or as part of a spell to cast evil. Pleasanter legends surround the clean-skinned frog—Aristophanes wrote a lyric play called "The Frogs" to take men's minds off a war, and Aesop used frogs as an example of pompousness in a fable. Prehistoric Indians carved frogs on pipes and totems; and many a fine Chinese jade depicts a grinning Oriental frog. Frogs have been used as food for a long time, and in parts of the south there are bullfrog farms where the big creatures are reared just for their plump and meaty legs. But this evening in the pond they are just ordinary toads and frogs that sing amiably in the warm, damp air, and add their voices to the myriad sounds which make up the summer night. *(Aug. 1942)*

ONE HOUR OF APRIL

The wild things are unaware of it, but to clock-controlled human beings, there comes a night in spring when we lose one hour of April. Two o'clock in the morning becomes three o'clock; an hour of springtime is lost to us. Robins that began to sing promptly at half-past four in the morning, now, by the clocks, begin at half-past five, and conversely the robins sing an hour later in the evening—but only by the clock, not the sun.

We who have lost an hour of April think back on that hour. At two o'clock in the morning, if we go to the window and listen, we can hear small, high sounds of birds flying over in the dark. They have been flying all night, guided by their inner sense of direction, from some point a hundred or more miles to the south, and may continue yet another hundred before they drop down when dawn is touching the tree-tops, to rest and feed. They need that early light of dawn to survive the night.

At two o'clock in the morning, the barred owl may be out in the river-bottom forest, shouting a mellow eight-hoot call which is answered by one from across the river, for the barred owls are courting in April. This is long after the great horned owls mated, laid their eggs and hatched their young. Some of the little birds which are flying in during the night may serve as food for the young horned owls, but the barred as yet has only himself to feed, and in the starlit darkness of an April night he is looking for mice.

At two o'clock in the morning, the deer mouse feels secure in the cloak of night and in the absence of a moon, and may come on lightly flitting feet across an open space in the woods. And the owl may see, and float down, and the mouse will lose its life during that hour of April which man-made time obliterates.

In that hour, the water-filled cells of new leaves expand a little more, each like a little balloon inflated with liquid, until the leaf's pleated appearance spreads and enlarges. On a mild spring night there is much growth, and in one hour there can be much which speeds springtime on its way. In an hour, the crisp, curved pink buds of the wild crab apple expand, and the petals separate and open a little way. No one will hear that small sound when the buds part and the petals open; but in one magic hour of the night, it happens.

Spring has not lost that hour which we have lost when we wake to a Sunday morning which begins daylight saving time. Our day will have only twenty-three hours for our use. In the wild, the full span of the twenty-four is needed and used. No matter to the creatures of April that an extra hour will be returned to us in October. In autumn their lives are reaching a state of completion which has no need for any extra time. It is in the fullness of spring that they must use it all. *(April 1960)*

QUEEN OF THE MAY

It is May—it is high spring. It is next door to summer, as sometimes summer itself makes its appearance in Illinois before the month of May is half done. It hurries the migrating birds into the north, speeds the leaf-growth on the trees so that the new leaves reach a great size, yet are thin and fragile under a hot sun. It brings into bloom the first of the summer flowers, and sends into a wilting oblivion the last of the violets and leggy buttercups and bleaching wild geraniums.

Yet the Illinois May perhaps is slow and cool. It may be a period of soft rains in which the blur of wild crab apple bloom is like wet pink silk, full of the flitting of migrant warblers and the piping of the white-throats. It may be a time when the delicate new velvet leaves on the oaks remain a soft pastel hue—leaves in miniature which, in muted colors, paint the distant landscape.

May is all these things. It is the first irises in the garden and the first morel mushrooms in the woods. It is mayapples in bloom and jack-in-the-pulpits crisp as wax; it is bob-tailed young robins already out of their nests, and the coming of the laggard cuckoos to complete the resident bird population. It is that settled feeling which comes when migration is over and we know that the birds which remain belong to us for the summer.

All through the centuries, for thousands upon thousands of years, May has been all this and far more to the people of the world. This month of transition between winter and summer for ages has been celebrated by mankind more than any other month has been celebrated. Now is the time, said the people, now we must celebrate the end of cruel winter that has taken all our food and fuel; now it is past and summer is at hand. Rejoice!

So the ancient Romans, who dearly loved a festival and made one at any excuse, held annual festivities called the Floralia in honor of Flora, Goddess of Flowers and Springtime. From April 28 to May 3, there were dancing and feasting and a gathering of flowers to decorate the houses of rich and poor.

The Druids, who worshipped trees, had a May festival of their own and perhaps were the first to originate the Maypole. They decorated a beautiful birch tree with flowers and garlands and held religious rites and feasting and carousing around it. Much later, the Britons, who inherited both the Roman Floralia ceremonies from the Roman occupation, and the old Druidic May rites, made a great to-do over the coming of this month. They set up a Maypole and danced around it. They went to the woods before sunrise and gathered branches of may, or hawthorn, and other flowers to decorate both the Maypole and to ornament houses, and held games and sports and feasting all day long. Folk dressed in carnival costumes, and everyone from chimney sweeps in their holly pyramids to the King himself dressed as a harlequin, made the most of the glorious informality of May Day.

It was a most important day. It was the day to make a wish in a wishing well, a day to exorcise witches from crops and cattle, a day to improve one's complexion if it was inclined to be blotchy. For even the dew on that breathless morning was precious. If a maiden wished to remove freckles for a year, she had only to go to a secret place before dawn on May Day, and bathe her face in the sparkling dew upon the new grass. Every woman, from milkmaid to Queen, made May Day pilgrimages to grassy places to have her share of May dew.

In America, May Day festivities never were as popular nor as widespread as they were in England, for the reason that the Puritans frowned upon such obviously pagan sports. When someone in 1660, in the exuberance of spring, had the temerity to set up a Maypole on Merrymount in Massachusetts, Governor Endicott himself went with a party of righteous folk to cut down this symbol of Baal.

So for want of encouragement in the New World, May Day languished, and when it revived a bit in schools and colleges, it had lost its old lusty meaning. Maypole dances were insipid things. May Day became a time when little girls made variously successful baskets of paper and ribbons, filled them with the flowers they could find, and hung them on doorknobs of friends, teachers, and kinfolk.

Although the present day sees little of the outward celebration of May Day, the background is still there. When the haw trees bloom, they tell again of long gone English maids and men trooping before sunrise to the woods to gather hawthorn blossoms; or, when a birch tree, shimmering in its new leaves, stands like a woods-goddess among the duller trees, it tells of the Druids and that first Maypole in an ancient British wood. *(May 1947)*

BACK OF THE AMERICAN GARDEN

Now in May the seeds that were planted hopefully in March and April have become strong plants. Already there have been early radishes and lettuce and onions for the table as the first tangible results of this year's gardens.

For almost unknown thousands of years, gardens have been planted and the products eaten. Four hundred years before the Christian era the Greeks and Romans were growing their gardens, in which beets and lettuce were favorites. Many a philosopher in classic Greece, digressing for a moment from more sober matters, argued eloquently about the proper dressing for a "sallet." Lettuce in the Victory garden makes today akin with the past.

So do radishes—they were popular in China and ancient Europe a long time ago. So were turnips, especially in northern Europe and Siberia. Sturdy cabbage, taken from the wild in Denmark, England, Ireland, and the Channel Islands, gradually through the years developed a lusty heading and became a favorite food of rich and poor.

Spinach came from Spain and carrots from Holland, where the finest carrot seeds were grown until today's war plowed the fields with tanks and armaments. Onions, a grateful flavor for oftentimes unpalatable foods, were cultivated so long ago that no one seems to know their origin, while garlic, as part of the poor man's diet, was listed as one of the foods eaten by the builders of the pyramids. When Cortez came to Mexico he found great papery piles of onions, leeks, and garlic sold in the market places of ancient Tenochtitlan. During this present war, onions have been among the most highly prized of garden comestibles produced by the English. There is so much, they say, that you can do with an onion, so much that is quite lacking without one.

From all corners of the earth have come the ancestors of our garden seeds. New Zealand spinach actually came from New Zealand, was brought to England by Captain Cook's expedition in the 18th century; watermelons were eaten by the Israelites; garden peas were planted in the early gardens of the Swiss Lake Dwellers many thousands of years ago in the Age of Bronze.

But from the New World itself have come certain vegetables that give the garden a truly American flavor, a fresh, sunshine-filled taste that is unequalled by Old World crops. Primarily there is corn, luscious, milky sweet corn—golden bantam just off the stalk and popped into boiling water, country gentleman, pearly and tender, and the fun of popcorn at Christmas. Corn was known to the Indians who passed on their treasure to the European invaders, who became as American as the corn they cultivated. Tomatoes came from Peru and so did white potatoes, which travelled by means of Spanish explorers to Europe. Here they were looked on with suspicion until in time of famine, potatoes became a life saver for the hungry. Potatoes came back to the Americas, perhaps on board the Mayflower itself.

Green beans and limas came from Peru and the valley of the Amazon. Sweet potatoes came out of South and Central American jungles into primitive gardens, were taken as a special gift by Columbus to his queen, and at last were grown throughout Europe and America. "Batatas," they were called, and they became a favorite vegetable of the south.

And pumpkins and squash are truly American, were known long ago by the Southwestern Indians. Here on the fertile tops of the mesas the Indians planted their gardens and grew sun-warmed beans and corn and squash. All these, together with the other succulent vegetables which are the product of past centuries of patient gardening and cultivating by many peoples of the world, are America's heritage in the soil of Victory gardens. (May 1943)

A LITTLE NIGHT MUSIC

Although the night had begun in darkness, the dark was seeping away in a dim white glow which heralded the half-moon's rising behind the tamaracks. The lake, glimmering in reflected light, lay as an oval pewter platter of faint illumination which grew all the brighter, moment by moment, in contrast to the black shores and the mystery of the surrounding night. That mystery and darkness came alive in voices singing the special music of a May night.

There was a veritable anvil chorus of frogs. Their songs were deafening—spring peepers whistling like shrill birds, cricket frogs in a clicking chorus, tree frogs chirping, leopard frogs cackling their wry laughter, green frogs grunting. They all ceased abruptly when a deer splashed in the shallows. But the warmth of the evening and the exuberance of spring were too much for the singers to endure; they could not remain quiet for very long. Shortly, the first peeper, unable to be still, thrust out one questioning whistle with a rising inflection—*wheet?*—and was immediately answered, was surrounded again with the mounting urgency of the whole great chorus. In the distance there came the low, sweet, bubbling trilling of the toads.

There were small splashes, moonlit rings moving out from small things in the inch-deep water—the frogs were sitting haunch-deep in the shallows, their throats distended and quivering in tight balloons full of May music. Along the line of the curving shore, the moonlight picked out the glint of the swelling throats while small red points, in pairs, were frogs' eyes. Two aquamarine lights were extinguished in a sudden splash and long ripples pushing outward marked where a muskrat swam into the glory of moonlight lying upon the lake.

The frog voices picked up volume, decreased, stopped, commenced again. The mellow hooting of a barred owl in the oaks up the slope, a song sparrow casting a loud melody into the night, an ovenbird, like the song sparrow, wakening to sing, uttering a song unlike what it knows by day—they filled the May night. The customary quiet of the north was submerged in music. Now a whip-poor-will chanted a hundred and forty staccato calls before pausing for breath. In the distance another challenged that figure and made it two hundred. The owl barked again, and in a dark and silent shadow it floated across the moonlit lake, dipped to the shore, picked up a leopard frog, and was gone. Abruptly, on half a note, the singing stopped, the singers frozen. As a raccoon, foraging quietly along the shore, pounced on a green frog, all the rest erupted in a sudden flurry of leaps and splashes into the water.

When the fox from a den on the hill, out hunting for food, headed for the lake shore to look for frogs, not one was in sight, and she trotted back into her secret trail among the ferns where wood mice might be found. The ovenbird sang again, the owl called from the distance, and the frogs, short of memory but with a strong sense of tradition, one by one climbed out of the water and arranged themselves, haunch-deep in the shallows, to sing again.

As the moonlight grew with the mounting of the moon, turning the pewter of the lake to shining silver with a band of glitter laid upon it, a dark creature swam down the silver avenue and lifted a sleek head to yodel an unearthly, wild, and wonderful call. For this was a northern lake, and to be complete it must have a loon upon it. To make the May concert complete it must have loons' voices awakening the full wildness of the landscape, adding that one needed instrument to the orchestra of night *(May 1964)*

THE MARSH IN MAY

There had been no real or prolonged silence all that short May night. The frogs had clamored endlessly, the first night insects of the year had jingled and the calls of birds had sounded all through the night. There were the eerie barks of black-crowned night herons passing in the darkness, the yapping and purring of two barred owls talking in the distant woods, the half-awake night songs of yellowthroat, goldfinch, and cardinal. At midnight the chat awoke in his dew-drenched willow, cackled a while, and slept fitfully but with furtive chucklings until dawn. And there were other mysterious sounds from creatures which live secretively in a marsh and at night are vocal.

For a marsh contains an element of fascination and mystery not found elsewhere in the wild. Marsh birds are elusive and shy. Often they are only voices—guttural, resonant, primitive sounds that belong peculiarly and forever to the wet acres of waving grasses and sedge, to the wide sky, and to the immense, watery peace which covers the marsh.

In the expanse of cattails and sedges and grass, with open pools of still water between that reflect the dawn, the pulsating sensation of life stirring and awakening is all about. Now there are dry wingbeats of redwings rising out of the cattails, the thin trill of a swamp sparrow among the sedges, the wakened chirrups of robins, and the thoroughly-awakened chat gabbling in the top of its willow.

The dawn light catches a small, cautious motion of a chicken-like sora rail that steps carefully along the pool's edge, and as if this slight movement were a signal, there comes a scattering of ghostly "ha-ha-ha's" from the wet sedges out in the marsh. It is a mirthless cackling from nowhere and everywhere, whose makers are unseen—the rails salute the sunrise with their laughing.

The marsh awakens. The sky is full of martins; a flight of tree swallows, dawn-color on their burnished white breasts and blue wings, swirls past. Goldfinches burst bubbling and singing from the weeds, bound in black and gold flight everywhere into the air, down into the willows, to the pools for a drink, up again, tweeting. The redwings sing and gabble in a torrent of confused song that dominates the cattail zone. There must be hundreds of redwings, some of them skreeking dissonantly, others singing, but in their excitement hardly ever finishing a song before beginning another. Males sit on twig-tips, spread blood-and-gold shoulder patches, bend forward, seem to expand as the song bursts forth. They almost fill the marsh with their clamor. Yet calmly above it, from the acres of marsh still comes the laughter of the soras, comes the strange grunting of the big brown king rail, with the rapid-fire conversation and clickety-clack of the marsh wrens weaving through it all.

Across the sky come the ponderous wingbeats of a great blue heron; four black-crowned night herons, barking, rise from a pool where they silently fished since before dawn; a brown bittern flies low and drops into the wet oblivion of the sedges.

These are the apparent things, the visible things, yet hidden in the marsh are the unseen creatures—the retiring birds, the snakes and turtles and frogs, the muskrats and mink and the raccoon that fishes on the shore of an open pool. It is the Unseen and their voices which constantly accent the pleasant mystery of the marsh. *(May 1946)*

ILLINOIS JUNE

This is June in Illinois: Sunshine, clover blossoms, song. It is the time when the new strength that comes to the sun begins to bake the soil between rows of growing corn, when soft dust powders up in the road, and the river level nightly falls. It is the time when pale pink wild roses blossom fleetingly along the railroad tracks and highways of Illinois; when the morning knows a stream of blue spiderwort in bloom beside the road. June is the renewed sound of insects in the grass, in the air, in the sunshine, in the night— a humming, churring, buzzing, zinging, clicking that swells to a crescendo as the warmth increases.

Now the scent of ripe wild prairie strawberries fills the warm air of the sunny roadside; here are strawberries, clover, wheat. The berries are small, sweet, ruby fruits in clusters on long stems; you pick a stem-full and fill your hand with berries. Nearby is the rosy color of the red clover fields whose perfume blows on the wind or hangs almost visibly in the sunshine.

And the wheat in June—the winter wheat that lay bright green under a snow blanket all winter, and with the thaw grew and expanded and waved in the wind— ripples like deep fur on a sleeping animal under the prairie sun. The wheat grows tall in June and begins to head. Now the promise of the harvest is well at hand.

It is June, and a meadowlark sings in the wheat. On bowed wings he flits with a harsh sputtering and a flashing of white tailfeathers to a fencepost across the field. Into the sun he thrusts his golden bosom with its great black V, so that he glints in his pride as he opens a long beak widely to sing over and over again. Beneath him along the fence-row are the flat rosettes of snowy Queen Anne's lace, emblem of June, with delicate clusters of tiny off-center blossoms with a single maroon floweret uniquely in the center of the cluster. Meadowlarks and Queen Anne's lace—these, too, are June.

June is all these, and it is delphinium standing blue in the garden, and rambler roses, and nasturtiums blossoming. It is the fussing of young wrens being fed on the trellis, and the chortling of martins around their houses. It is new fresh peas just off the vines—June peas picked and hulled and cooked and eaten all in less than an hour. And crisp young onions, fresh green lettuce, new carrots, earthy beets. June is the reward, the high point, the climax of the spring.

Never again will the summer be so fresh, never again until another June will the days be so long and full, the year be so complete. Now is the fullness of June on the prairie: look, it is everywhere. *(June 1945)*

THE GROWING FIELDS

It is June, and the face of the fields wears a new greenery which has crept over it, softly and quickly after spring rains fell and spring suns warmed the earth. The corn is up, inches high, and now the earth around the growing stalks has grown dry and caked. Weeds have sprung up, as weeds do, hastily and urgently, and if the fields are not cultivated, and quickly, the corn may vanish under the faster-growing clotburs and horseweeds.

And so in the weedy fields the cultivators are working beneath the skies of June. There are the mechanized, efficient cultivators whose wheels and those of the tractors supplying the power are cunningly placed to neatly miss all the tender little corn plants. There are still the horse-drawn cultivators, too; as carefully as the tractors move, the horses step between the rows of precious green.

Life moves over and around and within the growing fields. Down to the cultivated soil come the grackles to pick up grubworms to feed the young clamoring in a nest nearby. The brown-headed cowbirds come, following the horses or the tractors. A robin with a nest in the elm across the field runs importantly in the open soil and fills her beak with earthworms to carry back to the gaping yellow mouths.

The cornfield is a space of earth in which man has chosen to plow and cultivate and harvest crops. It is land which he may have obtained for himself by cutting the forest and pulling the stumps, or by plowing the prairie, or by draining the bottomland.

Out of that harnessed earth comes life in June. Plants grow; insects emerge; birds and mammals feed. The sphinx pupa case buried in the earth splits and the grey-and-rose hawk moth which emerges will visit the farmer's petunias at dusk. Grubs become beetles and beetles climb forth. Ants dig their burrows, ant lions set their traps, worms tunnel, and the sphinx caterpillars burrow into the earth and become pupa cases. Birds eat some of the insects in the field, but not all. Some insects remain and attack growing things, but not all. The corn grows and the tassels shake pollen over the silks, and there is corn "in the milk." Raccoons from the bottomland forest tear down the ears and feast in the moonlight; but they take only a few. As the ears ripen, blackbirds tear open some of the husks and eat the kernels; but they, too, take only a few. In the nice balance of the year, creatures eat and are eaten, the fields grow and produce, so that both man and the wild things are fed. *(June 1952)*

JUNE IS A CLOVER FIELD

Over the landscape, meeting the sky, the clover fields are in bloom. The acres of red clover are covered with a rich, dusty-rose color that is set off by the emerald of the nearby wheat and the fluff of wild carrot along the road; and the perfume from the fields is a rich and heady odor from a thousand-thousand blossoms on a thousand-thousand stems.

The fields of alfalfa are purple and silver; their scent is sweet and the butterflies know it. They hover all day over the slender sprays of purple flowers, and the bees are there with a murmuring that is so much a part of a clover field that one no longer is conscious that the sound is there, but would feel the lack if it stopped. And if the bees stopped and went away, the clover would not set its seed.

The white clover on the lawns of city and village are full of round, sweet-scented heads beloved of honeybees and children. The children, as they have done for years, perhaps as long as children and clover have lived as neighbors, pick the wiry stems and braid them into wreaths and bracelets, make chains and baskets and ornaments which quickly wilt but retain their sweetness.

June is the froth of white and yellow melilot, the tall and bushy sweet clover along the roadsides and the fields. Melilot is fragrant from the moment the leaves grow in spring, to the time, well past its bloom, when the old stalks stand dry in the sun. And the clover hay in the barn is sweet with the memories of June.

June is a clover field—June is all the creatures which live or find their living in and under and over a clover field. It is the dickcissel clacking all day from a flower head, and swooping to the nest of pale blue eggs hidden on the ground among the clover. It is the meadowlark nesting at the edge of the field; it is the bobwhite finding insects there, and the grey spermophile which comes streaking in a streamlined journey between cars—across the highway and into the shelter of anonymity of the clover. There where every plant is like its neighbor and the sameness of clover flowers is multiplied a million times, bird and animal and insect find haven.

June is a clover field, and it is the perfume and character of clover, and the long roots the plants send into the soil. It is the silent, unseen activity of the microscopic bacteria on clover roots, at work in the soil to make nitrogen to enrich the land.

For the June clover field is not all beauty. It is a vast chemical laboratory. It is a crop that does not tear down the soil nor deplete it of its nutrients. Instead, the clover, together with other legumes, continually adds the beneficial nitrogen that will feed the crops which follow clover in a wisely rotated program. Nitrogen is a part of all living tissue, and it is the legumes that, of all known plants or animals, are able to produce it by means of the partnership of the nitrogen-fixing bacteria on the roots.

The clover is an old, old plant, as reckoned by its terms of cultivation under the hand of man. It is believed to grow wild in all countries of the world, and for several thousand years certain clovers have been grown by man. Alfalfa is one of the oldest of cultivated plants. It was grown in Greece, where it was called "medica" because it had been obtained from the people of Media. The Arabs called it "al-fac-facah," "the best sort of fodder," but it has only been grown successfully in America since the early twentieth century. Red clover, grown for a shorter time historically but known longer than alfalfa in the New World, came from Flanders to England in 1676 and later came to America—some 2000 years after the ancient alfalfa in the Old World was an established crop plant.

June is a clover field. Perhaps the world over, June is a clover field, just as it is representative of Illinois at that bright season of the year. Now under a shining sky and a warm sun, the pink and purple fields send a rich and incomparable perfume into the air. *(June 1947)*

SUMAC IN THE WORLD OF JUNE

The country lane which winds its unhurried route between fragrant fields of summer alfalfa and the shady oak woods is the entryway to summer. A trifle dusty, but still cool in the morning shadows cast by the overhanging trees, the road is the footpath to the discovery of small, quiet, stirring little things.

These are the components of June: the spider leaving a curiously patterned track across the dust; a field sparrow with a mouthful of inchworms slipping into the nest hidden in a hummock of unmowed grass; the sounds of bees in the alfalfa—alfalfa heavy with perfume, regal with purple blossoms, warm in the sun. Adventure lies around every bend of the road, past every tree—who knows what lives in or on or beneath that tree?—and in the downright enjoyment of living in June.

The little road is bordered with growing things. It may be rich green panic grass, or the fountains of turkeyfoot. Grass . . . but within its concealment the meadow mice may hide their young; or a tiger beetle may be dragging the luckless corpse of a fly or caterpillar; a large yellow and black spider may hang on its web strung skillfully between grass stalks. And the grass may be in bloom. The tassels of the turkeyfoot are three-parted and long, and the joints of the stems are azure-blue, dyed rose-color and pale green above and below. Even the anonymity of grass itself is lost in the discovery that grasses are different in a thousand ways, that they have strange forms and colors and characters, all of them an integral part of the world of June and summer and Illinois.

And where the woods-edge still remains, though the woods itself has given way to the cornfield, there may be thickets of low sumac bushes full of summer blossoms.

The sumacs are an island of discovery. Perhaps commonest to be found in this area, so often a part of country roads, is the smooth sumac (*Rhus glabra*) with its long, shining, bronze-green, compound leaves spreading from finely powdered, pale green stems. In May and June, the centers of the leaf whorls hold tight clusters of greenish-yellow or cream-colored flowers, fragrant enough for the bees to hunt them out, attended all day long by varied insects. With the going of the blossoms, sumac fruits replace most of the individual flowers in the tight cluster. Autumn sees the sumacs, clothed by then in scarlet and yellow and orange, decorated with clubs of dark maroon fruits. The seeds are very hard, covered with a thin, juicy, red skin which is pleasantly acid-tasting to the tongue. "Sumac lemonade," made by soaking the seeds in water, is an old standby of the play-house and backyard-shack set.

Scarcely big enough to be called a tree, yet classified as such, the smooth sumac has few branches or twigs. They and the thin trunk are smooth and pith-filled. Spiles made of hollowed sumac tubes were used by pioneers and their descendants to conduct maple sap from tree to bucket in the spring of the year.

With the smooth sumacs along the country road may be the low bushes of fragrant sumac which is among the earliest flowers to bloom in spring. And there may be that other member of the family, that ever-present woods-menace, that well-known, often contacted sumac, poison ivy. In Illinois it takes the place of the poison sumac which grows in northern bogs and very effectually ruins the good name of sumac. Poison ivy, like the smooth sumac, in June puts forth its greenish-white flowers which add their own essence to the special quality of June along the country road. *(June 1956)*

❀

❀ # SUMMER

❀

❀

THE RARE DAY

It is June, and an Illinois June means summer. It is that fleeting moment in Time when life is at its height and the year knows the completeness of all the slowly fitted-together jig-saw puzzle of spring. Since the days of long ago when men first became aware of the changing seasons, June has delighted humankind. It was an assurance that the hardships of winter and the set-backs and disappointments of a cantankerous springtime were over and the certainty of summer was at hand.

The climax to all that preparation which has been going on since last July and August is the substance of the present June. In it are the thin, broad, new, green leaves which were formed in inconspicuous buds on the trees last summer. In it are the frogs that were tadpoles all winter; in it are the young cardinals and robins for whom special nests were carefully built; in it are the baby orioles whose parents traveled a hazardous route from Mexico to Illinois to make a nest for eggs and young. There are the dragonflies that zip in the sun above the pond, and which were sluggish nymphs in the pond all winter long. There are the butterflies that hatched from last year's hidden eggs, the hosts of infant mantids hatching from an egg-mass under a board, the big-eyed grass-hoppers in the blossoming redtop, the determined stirrings inside cocoons, and the emergence of velvet moths to flutter in the June dusk.

For "Every clod feels a stir of might,
    An instinct within it that reaches and towers,
    And, groping blindly above it for light,
    Climbs to a soul in grass and flowers."

June may be the high point but it is not the stopping point of the year. It is the end of many cycles and the beginning of many more. Now in June the seeds of spring-flowering wildlings are ripe; now the grass is in bloom for next year's seeding; now there are maturing young robins already able to care for themselves, and in whom there is implanted that mysterious instinct

36

of flight to the south and back again. Next year they very likely will be back in the neighborhood in which they were born, from a journey into a land they had never known. June is the time when the new growth on the trees perhaps is at its greatest, and even now the tiny buds for next year's leaves are beginning to form on the twigs.

June is that rare day when the world is shining and fresh and new; perhaps never again will it be so fresh and clean and unmarred. Never again, perhaps, in this cycle of a year, can the one who is conscious of the miracle of June and of midsummer, see and feel and hear and smell so much that is exciting.

"No price is set on the lavish summer.
June may be had by the poorest comer." *(June 1947)*

THE POND TERRAPIN

The quiet waters of Illinois—the mud-bottomed, often shallow, warm ponds and sluggish rivers—are the haunts of many turtles.

Turtles belong in the wild. They are an inescapable part of the atmosphere of our summer waters, especially of backwater sloughs where there are plenty of old logs and pieces of driftwood lying close to shore. These are places on which turtles may climb out and sun themselves with greater safety and watchfulness than the baked mud of the bank itself. How they do seem to enjoy the sun! The turtles face into the searing sunshine of a summer's day and seldom blink in its fury. Their shells—upper, or carapace; lower, or plastron— grow dry and dull and dusty-looking. A log may be so crowded that, although there may be half a dozen unoccupied ones nearby, turtles may be piled up two or three deep, all basking in the sunshine. Yet, the slightest alarm sends them in a series of well-timed splashes into the water, and not a turtle is in sight where, three minutes before, there may have been a dozen.

The pond terrapin, slider, or cooter, one of the common turtles in the area, is often eight to ten inches long and rather flat. The carapace of adults is dark, the plastron yellow, polished, often marked with black. The head and legs are greenish brown, striped with bright yellow, with a red-orange band on the side of the head and neck.

The great protection which a turtle has when it pulls its head inside its shell is vividly shown as a pond terrapin peers warily from inside an armored, well-padded shelter. *(June 1963)*

FISHING WEATHER

Early morning in July has that pleasant coolness which comes to mid-summer shortly after dawn, when the fragrance of a new day is on the world and the heat of the day as yet is still ahead. It is July—the pond is cool and mirrored—it is fishing weather.

A kingfisher, bright in the sunshine, hovers cackling over the shining water, plunges, comes up, shaking drops, with a slim perch in his beak. He is first fisherman of the wild, and all who come later must take his leavings. But the kingfisher, together with the other fish-eaters of the wild, takes only what he needs for food. It is only to feed himself and his young— the bristly kingfisher babies in the shadowy burrow dug by the parent birds in the side of a clay hill—that he fishes the pond.

In the growing heat of the morning sunshine, dragonflies skim the water, zip and whiz around about and back again, whirl and skirl on powerful gauze wings. Shiny black whirligig beetles, their one-eyed vision sending them in endless circles, race like magic over the surface, dart in carnivorous frenzy when a fly, losing its balance, falls into the water and wets its wings beyond recovery. Like wild beasts the whirligigs tear the fly to pieces and race off with minute mouthfuls. Finally, the body devoured, they allow the fly's thin wings to float off unpursued. The beetles resume their aimless whirling. Life in the pond goes on. A leopard frog, comfortable in the cool mud of the shore, takes a headlong leap into the pond as a fisherman comes along.

There is a peculiar quality to fishing that comes to scarcely another outdoor sport, unless it is to the bird watcher or the star gazer. The fisherman must be able to sit still and let life go on around him. He has no need to pursue his quarry; he lets it come to him. And to the true fisherman, the point is not alone in coming home with a fish—many times a fishing trip is only an excuse to get outdoors—for he always comes back with some reward of the day. Perhaps it is a memory of a dragonfly glinting a moment on his bobber. Perhaps it is the memory of half-heard thrush songs in the woods behind him, or the distant whistling of bobwhites in the buckbrush pasture.

Fishing is all these things and many more. It is just as much these as it is the hot-weather flies endlessly biting, or mosquitoes gathering for blood. It is the blue glint of a sunfish's "ear-spot," the black and yellow swirl of a fighting catfish, the silver flash of a bass breaking water. Fishing is that sunburned contentment which comes of just sitting by the water on a summer day, with a rod and line and a can of bait for excuse, perhaps a pan of newly caught, freshly fried fish for supper as reward, and the benediction of high summer everywhere. *(July 1946)*

THE MOTH

The oval, whitish thing rocked a bit among the moist, fallen leaves on the floor of the woods. It was shaped something like an egg, a little less than two inches long, but it was not an egg. It was a firm, silken cocoon, and it moved because life inside it was stirring and making its determined efforts to get out. A luna moth was about to leave the residence in which it had spent the winter and to which it would never return.

Last summer a luna moth had laid eggs on a birch leaf. One of the surviving caterpillars ate birch leaves, grew, shed its skin several times, and ate more leaves. When at last its leaf-green color changed to a ripened yellow and the caterpillar moved more sluggishly, it crept out on a leaf and began a strange, rhythmic movement of the head and body. From the mouth issued a fine, liquid, white silk which hardened as soon as it met the air. The caterpillar spun the silk around itself, wrapping leaf and body until at last, in a miracle of self-containment, it was hidden inside an ovoid cocoon.

When autumn came and yellow leaves fell to the ground, the cocoon fell with them and lay hidden among fallen leaves. Snows came. The long winter, with temperatures far below zero, enfolded the woods as the caterpillar had been wrapped in silk.

On a warm, soft night in June, there began a quivering inside the cocoon. Shortly after daylight, a damp spot began to form at one end. As the action increased inside, the cocoon rolled over several times, and about ten o'clock in the morning the silk at the end gave way. A pair of large, satiny brown eyes and straw-colored, ferny antennae thrust out. Two sharp-clawed feet clung to the small opening; the emerging creature struggled, and the silk gave way farther. With more working and straining, the moth finally made a convulsive lunge and fell forward as if exhausted . . . but it was free at last of the cocoon in which it had lain as a pupa all winter.

The wet, white and lavender body still seemed almost caterpillar-like; it was loose, wriggling, twitching. What passed for wings was a pitiful set of crumpled green things not more than an inch long. The moth climbed up a twig and hung there, resting, while the downy body and wings dried. The body contracted, lost its caterpillar-like look. It pulsed as if the creature were drawing long, gasping breaths which pumped life and power into body and wings . . . and the wings grew, expanded, became smooth and taut. An hour after emerging from the now outgrown cocoon, a splendid creation in green, white, and lilac velvet clung quietly to the twig. Lettuce-green wings with a five-inch spread were accented with purple. An eye-spot on each upper wing was margined with lilac, covered with a thin material like cellophane. The lower wings ended in two twisted green tails. The legs were purple, the body lavender and white velvet.

The luna moth would stay there all day and, as dusk came into the woods, would flit through the trees. After a courtship dance which would send two lunas up and up among the trees, dropping lightly down like green feathers, then spiraling upward again, there would be more white eggs laid on birch leaves. The cycle of life, the assurance of more green moths dancing in another twilight, in another year, would thus continue. *(June 1963)*

A TIME FOR SPIDER WEBS

When August comes and that feeling of late summer and impending autumn is in the air, the world seems to become peopled with spiders and their webs. Where they seemed not too noticeable before, now they are abundant; the webs are built over night and those which are wrecked during the day appear remade by the next morning.

A spider's web is essentially a trap to obtain food. From the spider's spinnerets issues a thin stream of liquid silk which is securely fastened to a point on leaf, stem, or other firm support, and then the spider proceeds according to its own methods to create a masterpiece of delicate webbing. Some, like those built by the large black and yellow garden spider, *Argiope,* are strong and symmetrical with guy lines, spokes, and circular parts all nicely spaced. The spokes are rather stiff and inelastic and are not sticky, but the spirals are very sticky. It is on these that insects become hopelessly entangled, and upon the spokes the spider runs quickly to wrap more silk about its prey and devour it at leisure.

But there are other webs than these. There is the handkerchief of silk which is the funnel web of a grass spider, laid over grasses or among low plants or in a corner of a fence. The spider lurks down at the end of the funnel, out of sight, till an insect lands in the web. Cobwebs in houses are built by tiny black house spiders, and there are many webs of irregular shape. One of these is the filmy dome web spun by a small spider which hangs beneath the fragile silken bubble. The spider is extremely neat—no dead insect or bit of foreign matter is permitted to remain in the web, but is cut out immediately and the spot mended. Now that August is on the land, there are filmy domes waiting patiently for prey, in garden, wood, and thicket. *(Aug. 1949)*

THE SUBTLE SIGNS OF AUTUMN

In most of Illinois, September is too early for the more obvious signs of autumn to have become very apparent. As color moves like a conflagration down the continent, by September it has only come into its best in northern Wisconsin and Michigan. Slowly, through October, color burns its way southward. Nevertheless, even in August the subtle signs of autumn were evident in secret places and in quiet ways. The color was there, too, though largely hidden under chlorophyll. But not entirely. The sassafras leaves early were showing an underpinning of yellow and orange; the dogwood had a bronzy wash over the dark green; the wild cherries dangled a few yellow feathers among summer-like greenery.

But more subtle autumn signs are there. A greater readiness of leaves to be detached from their twigs is one sign. The corky layer of separation, indication of ripeness and of autumn, is not ready to effect the total loss of leaves, but it is there, invisible, the key to the falling of all the leaves of autumn.

The hidden signs grow day by day. Migration began as early as August when the warblers and sandpipers were moving south from the Arctic or far northern nesting grounds; swallows have been gathering in great swarms on wires and fences near marshes and river bottoms. And now the woolly bear caterpillars are walking.

The restlessness of the woolly bears is as certain a sign of autumn as any ripened apple or southbound warbler. The inch-and-a-half caterpillar may be all brown, the color of a mink coat, or may be brown and black in broad bands, or a creamy blond. Certain superstitions claim to discover from the color pattern of the caterpillars just what the winter portends. But, brown or black or beige, no matter the hue, when the woolly bears are on the move, we know autumn is exerting its inner influences. The furry caterpillars crawl rapidly along on their secret routes and are seldom deflected from the courses they have previously decided upon. A passing car whirling a caterpillar into a curled-up ball, or the reversing of its original direction in any way, seems to have no effect upon the direction-finder of the insect, which unrolls itself, rights itself, and continues on in the way it intended to go. It will eventually crawl into a place of hibernation, to wait out the winter in a thick fur coat, and, after a brief period in a cocoon, to emerge as the Isabella moth.

The subtle signs of autumn—mosquitoes whirling in a dance of death in a damp, chill, willow bottomland; the lonesome night-sounds of high-flying birds; the rising of the autumn constellations of Pegasus and Andromeda; the coming of the blue lobelias along wet ditches; the avid storing of food by chipmunks and squirrels; the greater lethargy of the over-stuffed woodchuck; blue jay, robin and grackle feathers scattered in the woods and parks, indication of the late summer moult—they are all about. Bright, newly-feathered robins with white eye-rings and white tail spots eat ripening red haws; there is a crunching of acorns underfoot; a fluffing of cattail stalks in the marsh, which is deserted of the redwing hordes which lived there all summer.

Yet, with all the subtle hints, autumn in September seems to have gained little hold on the world of the long summer which is part of the character of Illinois. The secret signs, however, the coming promise, speak up here and there, loud and clear with a clarion of portent to those who hear. *(Sept. 1960)*

THE TURN AWAY FROM SUMMER

In September the landscape turns visibly away from summer. The change has been gradual; it is change which takes place so slowly that one is scarcely aware of what is going on. It is a deliberate ripening, a darkening of greens, a sudden flaming bough upon a tree, a patch of goldenrod beside a road, the first of the wild asters, a blue lobelia beside a stream, milkweed silks upon the air, robins and grackles and redwings flocking. The beginning of the changes comes in July, comes when the days are noticeably shorter, and becomes more apparent all through August while the egrets wade in the withered lotus beds and wood ducks eat lotus seeds. The change becomes a reality in mid-September, when the buckeyes are bright with scarlet leaves, the sandpipers swarm on the mudflats, and migrant warblers are in our city trees.

It is, suddenly, autumn, but it is not sudden at all. No one may point to a particular thing, a particular moment, a particular sensation, and say, "This is when autumn began." Yet as surely as the locust trees turn gold and the juncos come back from the north, *this* is autumn. *(Sept. 1949)*

AUTUMN

THE VISION OF AUTUMN

The vision of autumn is a gradual building up of color, sound, smell, taste, and change. It may begin in July with a scattered yellowing of leaves on a wild cherry tree, with a burst of early goldenrod along an August road, with scarlet leaves on early-turning buckeye trees glowing in woods which still bear the look of summer. Autumn may actually have begun last spring when new buds formed at the bases of the young leaves, and, in the roots of spring flowers, food was stored to set them growing next year. By autumn the buds are hardened, the roots well stocked.

Yet all these things are only a premonition, a part of the overlapping of the seasons. To really see the autumn, however, is thus to be aware of the first inklings of change, to realize that no season is unaffected by the one before and by the one to follow, and that each carries a portion of the others within its complex structure. That first hint of color-to-come is a signal to be alert for what lies ahead.

Early September may bring some of the hottest weather of the year, while the corn ripens and the leaves grow dry. After autumn storms which bring moisture and a sudden drop in temperature, there is a cool, fresh atmosphere which is obviously no longer that of summer. The breath of autumn is now felt in the misty dawns, and the haze of leaf smoke blurs the golden afternoons. Here is the distillation of all the smells of summer mingled with the ripening of leaves and fruits across the countryside.

The autumn smells, sounds, flavors, and sensations are all part of the growing festival of color. Autumn, perhaps more than any other season, is one to be enjoyed and savored by all the senses. One need not have sight in order to delight in autumn, for the rich, ripe smells in themselves are as good as a picture. They are as varied as those of burning leaves and the scent of pineapple weed, the stout aroma of Jimson-weed and sycamore leaves, of

42

apple orchards and the yellow-green wild crab apples mellowing under fallen leaves.

The sense of touch is gratified by such diverse textures as thistledown and acorn contours, by leathery oak leaves and velvety mushroom skin, by tree bark and the little canoe paddles of ash seeds, by the furry bonnets of hazel nuts and the rhythmic patterns of pine cones. Taste is also gratified in autumn. Here are the ripened fruits—the cool pear picked up from the ground, wild grapes, tart and juicy, hanging on a fence, the fire of a prickly ash fruit, the nutlike seeds of the lotus, the pungence of a sassafras leaf, the flavor of a papaw, the tang of mint.

The sounds of autumn are indicative of what is happening when the almanac beckons toward winter. Squirrels rustle about in the fallen leaves, while other sounds transcend time and space as the small voices of warblers and finches, downbound from Canada, are heard in the trees. Cries of migrating cuckoos, sandpipers, or thrushes come down through the night darkness. The thrilling trumpets of the geese are heard over the marsh, with the clamor of ducks just in from Saskatchewan. There are the slowing sounds of grasshoppers in the brief heat of the day, and the final, feeble scrapings of crickets approaching the finality of frost.

Sight is inordinately gratified by autumn. Color burns in glory across the countryside, illuminates once dark maple woods with a brilliant daffodil light, turns into extravagantly painted plumes the leaves of sumac, and ornaments the Virginia creeper vines with stars of scarlet decorated with blue fruits.

It is a season of so many facets that no autumn is long enough to see it all. There can only be the annual attempt, the promise to see more next year, to absorb, to remember: most of all, to be aware. An old Pima Indian prayer stated: "The Creator made the world—come and see it." The invitation is always there. (*Oct. 1965*)

AROMA OF AUTUMN

Away from the smells of civilization which fill the air with scents which are often far from agreeable—automobile exhausts, smoke from burning trash, oil fumes, factory smells, smog—the pure purfumes of the wild are half intoxicating in their sweetness. The warm smell of the sun on fallen pine needles makes us wish to capture it for use later on. Thoreau himself, more than a hundred years ago and long before the American air over cities was as yet heavily polluted, also felt this and said: "Morning air! If men will not drink of this at the fountainhead of the day, why, then, we must even bottle up some and sell it in the shops, for the benefit of those who have lost their subscription ticket to the morning time of the world."

The aroma of autumn leaves in particular is one of the rich and splendid experiences of the year. The scents are distinguishably different in each kind of tree—in oak and elm (different, too, between white elm and slippery elm), in willow and in sycamore, in maple and in walnut. Each kind of leaf and flower has its odor, although some are not easily discerned by our often untrained and blunted sense of smell, while others are distinctive and part of our indelible impressions of the wild. The memory of one of these smells, or its recurrence, is enough to bring a surge of nostalgia for a past which may have held the perfumes of arbutus or arbor vitae, balsam needles or ripe oak leaves.

The air itself is full of scents which are distilled from the organic vapors given off by every leaf and flower during the growing season. These vapors contain enough scent to give us that fresh smell in the morning, the perfume of a cornfield on a warm night, or the autumn smell itself with its attendant blue haze in the air.

The blue haze is believed to be caused by those same vapors which are given off by the leaves of grasslands, fields, marshes, and forests. These volatile oils are called terpenes; those from pine and balsam forests, called pinenes, give the air in such an area its characteristic delicious smell. The fragrances of autumn leaves themselves are caused by terpenoid compounds which are believed to have come from decomposing carotinoids—the red and yellow pigments which produce colors in autumn leaves. It has been estimated that a million tons of these volatile substances are given off in a year by the land plants of the world—by meadow grass, clover fields, sage brush, pine forests, corn fields, autumn leaves, orchards, weedy bottomlands, orange groves, deciduous woods, and by every fragrant flower of the year.

The blue haze is especially predominant in the Middle West which is a land of greenery; blue haze is always in the air during growing periods and is concentrated by autumn. We used to think it was caused by burning leaves; the old legend was that the blue haze was made by the ghosts of Indian campfires. But the haze, it is now believed in a theory offered as a logical solution by Dr. Fritz Went, St. Louis Botanical Garden, is caused by the partial oxidation of those aromatic oils of the terpenes given off by vegetation. These are condensed into large molecules which refract blue light—to make the azure haze and the blue distances of the American autumn.

Blue haze and autumn perfume—these are a pleasurable part of one of our most glorious seasons of the year, this distillation of the long golden weeks of summer and the coming brilliance of October's trees. (*Sept. 1962*)

THE STIR OF SEPTEMBER

The pulse of summer slowed its beat in August. Birds were moulting and were not easily seen; songs were few, and the flocking blackbirds showed ragged wings and sparsely feathered tails. Cardinals were dull; scarlet tanagers were a patchwork of green and scarlet; indigo buntings seldom looked as brilliantly blue as they did in June. As long as the heat held high, insects were noisy and abundant; their crescendo of sound soared to heights of insect ecstasy. Young mammals had reached a state of independence if not of wisdom —young rabbits, young squirrels, young muskrats, young mice. But August was a quiet time, a period of physical recharging for many wild things. It was the prelude to autumn.

Suddenly it is September and suddenly there is a stir in the woods and roadsides and across the fields and sky. "What stir of winged creatures, hark!" The burst of activity is marked on a sunny September day which is not so far removed from August on the calendar, but which is eons away in point of activity and state of mind. Now is the time to get ready for winter. There may be only the yellowing of locust trees and elms, a scattering of orange and scarlet leaves among the sassafras, a surge of goldenrod along the roads and in the woods, a few little white frost asters foaming among roadside weeds. But the hand of autumn is visible and the wild creatures sense it.

Heading south, migrating monarch butterflies float on the breeze. On any breeze, in any direction, milkweed and thistle seeds, catching the light, float silkily, set free by goldfinches busily eating seeds in the weed patches.

Chipmunks and ground squirrels have been working for weeks to store seeds in their burrows, but now the work reaches almost fever pitch. Dry leaves in the woods rustle under the busy feet of the chipmunks. The wood mice gather hackberry seeds and hide them in a hollow log. Meadow mice gather grass seeds and carry them into their burrows. Up in the pasture the woodchucks solemnly stuff themselves and grow steadily fatter to meet the winter in their own stolid way.

And the birds—suddenly after the quiet August, the birds seem to be everywhere. September days see a constant coming and going of wings and voices. Wrens are migrating early in the month; briefly there appear to be wrens everywhere, and then there are none. Another day or two sees the migrating cuckoos and brown thrashers; at the end of the month, flickers go through, heading south. And every day there come more of the migrant warblers, vireos, thrushes, sparrows, some in fall plumage, all of them quick in movement and difficult to see, yet giving notice of their presence in the movement of wings among leaves and in flight across the sky.

There is a little song again—the broken, youthful attempts of young towhees, and catbirds, even robins chirruping as they gather in growing flocks. And at sundown in the swamp the newly feathered blackbirds gather. In flocks whose like has not been seen since they came back in spring, the blackbirds congregate, creaking and clacking in a surge of wild, autumnal excitement, in preparation for the great exodus which is to come. It is all part of the stir of September, the surge of life and motion which comes just before autumn itself is an actuality. (*Sept. 1951*)

THE SEPTEMBER MARSH

The autumn sun rose cool and lit the marsh with a light that shot sparks across the pools and glinted on the spears of cattail leaves that covered an acre of marsh with an army of close-set plants. A strange quiet lay everywhere. The chorus of bird voices that had begun the dawn ever since springtime was oddly lacking now as autumn lay upon the land. September and autumn had come over the marsh and things had subtly changed since spring and summer had come and gone.

But the temperature even now was almost summery. By noon the heat shimmered over the cattails, made the crisp brown bulrushes even more crisp and brown, curled the willow leaves and opened the last of the turtle-head flowers. The lotus leaves stood dried and sere, as if a frost had parched them, and the tall stems that once had held the huge fragrant flowers of the moon-blossom lotuses now held great pods full of seeds. Among the lotus stems, in the shadow of the drying leaves, the wood ducks paddled about or dozed, or squeaked shrilly and petulantly among themselves. Out on the mud flats that baked in the hot sun stood the egrets whose numbers now were increasing daily and would continue to increase until the whole flight went south. Around their cautious feet scampered the sandpipers that were here for a while on their way to far places, and the killdeers bobbed and spread their russet tails and fumed in endless arguments.

Along the drier places of the willow-grown shores were great beds of milk-weed and thistles into whose white silk seed-tufts the sun flashed with an almost prismatic light. As the sun went westward all that long golden autumn afternoon, the light gleamed on the silks and on the bright gold and black goldfinches that were there picking the meaty parts away from the silks.

On the September air the silks floated away from the marsh, floated away from the finches, off across the marsh and across the fields, into the town where they lazily drifted between houses and into and out of the windows of tall buildings. And went on and on in an aimless autumn cruise.

Back in the marsh the sun was hot. If it had been midsummer, and hot, there would have been songs that dared the heat—songs of indigo bunting, yellowthroat, chat, field sparrow, dickcissel, marsh wren, for these all are birds of the sun. But now most of these are gone from the marsh, and to those that remain, September is not a time for song.

Now as the sun slants toward the western willows and a coolness comes upon the marsh, a coolness that is of still pools and silent cattail stalks and ripening willow leaves, the birds of the marsh suddenly make themselves known. For the marsh is a place of protection and food for the flocks. Now come the thousands of redwings and cowbirds, the grackles and rusty black-birds, with a sweep and swish of dry wingbeats, a rush of voices, down to the cattails, to the willows, the smartweeds, the lotuses. From all directions across the sunset they come, converge in the marsh to feed and talk far into the evening. Song sparrows cheep lonesomely. A bobwhite calls. And the mellow quaver of a screech owl somewhere in the silent willows is one with the autumn dusk. *(Sept. 1947)*

AUTUMN OVER THE LAND

There is no doubt that October is elaborate. From whole mountain-sides yellow as goldfinch feathers in Idaho, to a thousand whistling swans winging down the Atlantic coast to Currituck, or the paint-box colors of sumac, sassa-fras, and goldenrod along an Illinois lane, the season does things in a large and lavish way. It is a time for broad masses of color and great gatherings of wild creatures. Yet the small things—a chipmunk cramming his cheeks with panic-grass seeds to store in his burrow; the late flowering of violets; and the sparkling silk of ballooning spiders caught among the ironweeds—these, too, are October.

Over all the land, October makes its presence known. In Maine it may bring the first snows down from Katahdin and the St. Lawrence. It means a path of red leaves along the bloody Mohawk Trail from the Hudson to the sea. It means a clearing-out of migrant birds, and hawks drifting down Kittatinny Ridge. Autumn is a ruffed grouse drumming in the Alleghenies, and chinquapins ripe along the Susquehanna. It is the oyster tongers busy in Chesapeake Bay, and canvasbacks feeding among the eel-grass beds. It is a warm blue haze over the red fields of Virginia, fogs rolling up from the Cumberlands, and the tobacco crop drying in Kentucky barns. It is the beginning of The Season in Florida, a tawny look to the Everglades, a thousand egrets gathering in the cypresses.

The coming of autumn means that the days of the ore freighters on Lake Superior are numbered; it means white birches scattering yellow leaves in Michigan and Wisconsin and Minnesota; a glory of color in the Indiana dunes; scarlet partridge berries in the North Woods; a growing wariness among the deer; red and yellow apples ripe on the midwest hills. It is robins gathering to eat haws and poke berries, blackbirds by millions assembling at sundown, the first juncos down from the North. It is the blazing oaks of Illinois, the sugar maples of Ohio, winter wheat showing green in Kansas, and jackrabbits on the run before the hunters. It is frosts and early snows up in Montana and Dakota where the northern lights now flash every night, and the stars twinkle with that wintery look. October brings the mountain goats down from the high crags, flashes yellow over the aspens and then drops their gold-doubloon leaves at the feet of the firs. October means an ageless, timeless, added blueness to the depths of Grand Canyon and the pink castles of Bryce. It is the time when the creatures of the high country feel the approach of winter. The cony finishes his hay pile; the marmot sniffs the sharpening air and retires underground; the bears fatten on berries and roots and small creatures, and roll contentedly into their hibernation dens.

October, and along the Pacific the tides come in with tattered seaweeds that have broken loose far at sea under the surging currents of distant storms. October, and the thousands upon thousands of monarch butterflies, in an undulating, scintillating crowd over Monterey Bay, have come to spend the winter in the pines and gardens of Pacific Grove.

It is October—High Autumn—a time of ripening, of traveling, of change, of coloring, of the falling of leaves, of preparation for winter. It is a good season which is painted in many hues upon the continent by the lavishness of October. (Oct. 1947)

THE COUNTRY ROAD

It is a crisp autumn day with a sky too blue for reality, the kind of sky that lives above the Colorado peaks and the Painted Desert, the kind of blue that is part of October and the turning of the year. Now on a Saturday afternoon this sky becomes a backdrop for orange sassafras, brown weeds, and the colors of the maples. Against the sky the milkweed silks are flying, and monarch butterflies on delicate wings migrate toward the south.

The road is brown and soft. It was oiled last summer, but this year the oil supply was cut, and the old road lapsed into a pleasant mellowness that works into a fine powdering of dust. And beneath the dust there is solid, packed earth over which, since the road was developed from an old footpath or an Indian trail, there have passed many feet and many wheels and hoofs.

This is a road of little purpose now. A straight, efficient highway runs parallel only a few miles away, and one travels quicker by taking it in preference to the old, ambling, narrow country road that rambles around crooked curves and over gentle hills and rattling bridges. But on a Saturday afternoon with the sun bright in the west and frost asters white in a tangle beside the road, the country lane is a place to walk just for the fun of walking. There are things to see all along the way: precise tracks of a beetle in the dust; an arrogant chipmunk, out of his own territory, cheeks stuffed with hazel nuts, challenging the rights of the road; crab apples glistening merrily in the slant sunlight. The silks of travelling spiders are flung headlong on the wind. There are yellow elms and a splash of scarlet sumac at the edge of the woods; white-throated sparrows pipe brokenly in the horseweed tangle by the creek, and in the woodlot, heavy walnuts drop with satisfying thuds.

Perhaps autumn is the best time of all the year to find the joy of walking on a country road. There is not only the exercise of walking, which in itself is a renovator of mind and body, but there are all those unimportant, interesting scents, sounds, and sights along the way which year after year recur and are a link with the past; they are changeless in a world of change.

It is a cool autumn day with a bright October sky; it is a day for a walk, a striding out with vigor in one's step and a sandwich in one's pocket, or a leisurely rambling with a stop here and there to look at things or to bask in the sunshine.

And then there is the setting sun, a small fire with sweet wood smoke curling upward, crows flying over to their night roosts, the scents of an autumn evening, and stars gleaming out on the walk back to town. Now in October the little country road offers much to the seeker after simplicity, to those to whom walking now is a selected form of recreation. (*Oct. 1942*)

OCTOBER COMES TO ILLINOIS

It began in August when the first buckeye leaves turned red and orange. It developed in September with the yellowing of the elms and hickories and the shrivelling of the lotus leaves. Then when October finally arrived in the Illinois Country, the stage was set, the non-essentials banished by frosts, and October, the great drama of autumn, was ready to take place.

Illinois may have its less pleasant aspects; its too-hot and humid summers, its interminably slippery and sleeted winters, its too-wet or too-cold spring-times, but its autumns are superb.

There are the large-scale splendors of October, and there are the small but important nonentities, the little things which, taken as part of the whole, contribute vitally to its charm. They are the bright purple violets which blossom now as they did in April, the witch hazel flowers in bare woods at the end of the month. The caramel fragrance of pearly everlastings. The aftermath asters and goldenrods. The glitter of sunlight on a stray milkweed silk drifting in vast unconcern into town. The brown and orange wings of a monarch butterfly going south. The piping of white-throated sparrows in the weed patches—sparrows newly returned from nesting in Wisconsin and Canada. Small things—a clump of cool brick-top mushrooms beside an old stump. Stick-tights on every dog that goes wandering about the countryside. A blue lobelia in a ditch. A yellow leaf floating on a brown pool. These are all things which are part of the Illinois October.

There are the large things, too, the miles upon miles of woods flaming with colors of autumn. Now the mixed oak forests are brilliant with the intense colors of oaks, hickories, hard maples, wild cherries, honey locusts, sassafras and dogwood. Now the green chlorophyll in the leaves ripens, dies, and reveals the other pigments which have been hidden until the ripening of the individual leaf. Frost has nothing to do with it; frost often ruins the leaf colors. It is simply that now in October the work of making food and of storing it in the tree, which is the duty of leaves, is finished for the season. A corky plate has formed where the leaf joins the twig. This cuts off the outgo of food to be stored, but permits water to enter the leaf and keep it alive as its colors grow. Then at last in the peak of autumn the leaf drops off the tree and the colors fade to brown.

All over Illinois the forests, the woodlots, the parks, the city trees, blaze with color. It flows in a wonderful tide up from the yellowing cypresses in the bottomlands along the Ohio and the Mississippi at the tip of the State, moves into the heights of the Illinois Ozarks where the oak colors are tre-mendous, is splendid in the limestone country of Pere Marquette Park, Giant City, the village of Elsah, and Calhoun County flames along the rivers, burns on the hills. It is gay in the sugar maple country around New Salem and Funk's Grove and Rockford. It colors the countryside from Cairo to Galena, from Nauvoo to Chicago.

And between the color areas there are the fields of autumn corn shocks in careful rows, the newly plowed and planted wheat fields, the emerald of cut-over alfalfa, the brown bean stubble, the pastures green after the rains. And off across the hills where color lies blurred, there is that haze which blends the colors and the fields and the sky into one great stirring picture which is October in Illinois. *(Oct. 1949)*

ONE DAY IN OCTOBER

We followed a narrow lane through autumn woods where fallen leaves and remnants of last summer's smells made a nostalgic perfume, like memories of delicious foods in an old kitchen. We had entered the quiet world of autumn. It was suddenly remote from the outer world of highways and motor fumes and noise, far more remote in spirit, perhaps, than in actual physical distance. Stillness dwelt here along this wooded path where nothing larger than a fox or a deer had passed in a week.

These woods had been dusky all summer. Sugar maple shade is one of the darkest shades there is, and because of that the woodland floor produces little but a few ferns in summer. The flowers came in spring when sunlight poured through bare trees and bathed the ground with life-giving light. As leaves grew, shade deepened, and, even in the warmest days of midsummer, the deer could rest in the perpetual cool twilight of maple shade. But on this day, although the leaves still remained pretty much in place, they had lost their green; they were illuminated. Instead of absorbing sunlight or bouncing it back as they had done all summer, now they let it pass through a golden fabric. Maples and birches thus produce a lovely daffodil light which is one of the brief and fleeting glories of the year.

The woods were indeed floodlighted. Every tree stood out darker against that yellow glow, while minute details on ground and tree seemed pinpointed and accented. In the deep stillness of autumn, this flooding of light is extraordinary. The silence itself accents any small sounds; the golden light points out details.

We stood and looked at the woods and at first saw just that—trees in autumn sunlight, and a scattering of fallen leaves, dampened by rains, on the woods floor. But so much else was there besides. We could guess that a deer might be standing just beyond those maples. A squirrel would come along at any moment. Chickadees, talking softly and paying no attention to anything but the business at hand, were swinging among the twigs and picking up insect eggs or pupae or little spiders—whatever it is that can keep chickadees alive throughout a long winter. We knew that vireos had been nesting in these woods in the summer and that the well-built nest must still be there. It might be hanging in the crotch of a maple twig. Ornamented with thin shreds of birchbark, the nest was there, part of the picture, if we could only discover it.

A chipmunk scuttled across the path and disappeared. Its cheeks bulged with something, perhaps basswood seeds, to be added to its underground store of winter food. If we could turn back the fallen leaves we might find many holes as well as those of chipmunks, for the underworld of the woods has many doorways through which beetles, larvae, earthworms, snakes, mice, salamanders, and other creatures come and go. In late autumn, however, most of the inhabitants were already asleep; others would wait until dusk to emerge.

There is always so much in the picture which is tantalizingly invisible. For any woodland, no matter how small, no matter at what time of the year, is full of secrets. It is, after all, not so much what is plainly discovered, but what is not; it is those sounds which are not quite heard, and those things still left undiscovered which must bring us back here again and again. (*Oct. 1963*)

THE SHAD FISHERS

In the spring the hickory shad laid their eggs in the shallows of the lake, and now in October the half-grown young are swarming. Six inches long, silvery white, with a purple spot just back of the gills, the slender little shad are massed in the water. The water moves with the concerted swimming and dashing about of millions of fish; it is as if there were a semi-solid mass of living creatures surging just below the surface.

It is on such a day when the shad are swarming—a day in October when the sun is warm but the air is cool, when there are gulls once again in the sky and migrant thrushes in the trees—that the shallow swampy portions of the lake are alive with birds. They are the shad fishers, the birds that, by diving or wading, gorge on the succulent little bony fish.

The shad fishers clamor in the shallows where at sunset the surface is flicked with silver by the constant nibbling of the fish. Out in the bay the birds still dine noisily. There is the eerie squalling and keening of the grey-winged gulls as they dip and dive and fight each other over their catch. Crows come down on the lotus leaves or walk upon a snag, and from there they cautiously reach out to snatch unwary fish. The restlessness of the shad transmits itself to the birds, to all but the cormorants which already have fed to satiety and now sit about dourly, like creatures from another geologic age, on posts and snags. The cormorants are heavy with fish and scarcely can manage flight. Further out in the bay, however, a dozen cormorants that arrived later than these others swim madly about, come up a moment for air, dive again, green eyes agleam and waterproof feathers flashing in the sunlight.

Nearby are pied-billed grebes. Forty of them are scattered over the smooth opal waters of the bay. Grebes usually are quiet creatures, but now in the frenzy of feeding which has attacked the other birds, even the grebes dash about, spatter across the surface, beat their inadequate wings in pursuit of each other when one has caught a fish. Others soberly dive and dive again, and feed steadily.

Many great blue herons stand knee-deep in the shallows where the lotus pods are ripe. The herons are gaunt and solemn and very still, and every muscle is poised as the long necks unfold and the beaks strike the water. It has been a long time since food was so easily come by. Here and there among the ragged lotus leaves are white egrets, also fishing, and some stand, dozing, on muskrat houses far out in the swamp.

Then the sun is gone. The glow fades. The crows get up from their awkward position and fly off to their roosts. The herons majestically beat their enormous wings across the swamp to the great dead roost tree on the far shore. Half a dozen egrets, tinged with pink in the last of the glow, head toward the west swamp. The gulls and grebes camp out on the open bay for the night, to be near the source of food when morning comes. And the little shad, restless and milling about, undisturbed by the inroads the birds have made on the multitudes, continue their urgent movements through the darkening waters. *(Oct. 1946)*

TIME OF FLOCKING

Thousands of flocking blackbirds pattern the skies of October. The curious urgency of autumn is upon them as they surge in tremendous crowds, traveling with a unison of wings and a singleness of purpose which characterizes the season of migration. The flocking of the blackbirds, in particular, is one of the miracles of the world of nature, a thing so commonplace that it happens almost everywhere across the land, yet is little understood. What signals are transmitted to those swiftly moving birds, that they all swerve at once, in a magnificent swirl of darkness? What makes them rise all together, in an aerial whirlpool of wings, leveling off above a field, climbing above trees, circling, sweeping, in mass flight at its most profound?

Man may never discover what makes ten thousand grackles, redwings and other blackbirds move in complete accord, ten thousand obeying the direction of one, yet no single bird apparently standing out as a leader. In the flocking of geese, there is an obvious commander, usually the father of the family, or the recognized leader of the group of a hundred or more powerfully flapping birds. They follow in the wake of the leader, lining up in a long V, or an echelon, or a long, wavering line, only to merge in a group or in another V, yet continuing to follow the strong course of the leader. But in the blackbirds' autumn flight, no leader is apparent. The great swirling mass of birds, like a single entity, performs a definite pattern of aerial evolutions, then sweeps, still as one bird, across the autumn cornfield.

The corn is noisy with the dry swish of wings and the clattering of the birds. Big grackles with their long tails and snapping white eyes sit about in the corn. The redwings cling to other cornstalks or surge out to the cattail marsh.

The cornfield and the marsh have been empty of blackbirds, silent of song, since late summer. Now, swept southward on a north wind, the hordes crowding the drying acres, as if overwhelmed with the sparkle of autumn, the promise of sun and the gaiety of flight, have all burst into song. Under a peaceful October sky, an ecstatic chorus greets the morning. On ten thousand wings, the songs of the past have returned, reborn in the autumn air, performed dreamily once more as play-backs of old concertos. *(Oct. 1958)*

ILLINOIS NOVEMBER

In spite of war and human difficulties, the whole orderly procession of a year has moved onward as it always does, and once again it is November. This is a point which has not been attained without innumerable advance moves which have combined in a vast jigsaw puzzle of the year. In Illinois there cannot be November without there having been April and June and October, without the return of migratory birds and the passage of many of them to far nothern points to nest. There cannot be November without there having been a June in which wild strawberries were fragrant on the prairie and meadowlarks sang among the Queen Anne's lace, nor November without the long hot days of July and the short starry nights of midsummer. There cannot be November without September's newly yellowing hickories and October's dropping walnuts, and the orderly retreat of migratory birds along the airways to the south.

In all the intricate maze of the year which culminates in November, there are the spring flowers which came up early and bloomed and made seeds and disappeared in only a few weeks above ground. Their food-filled roots or bulbs lie now in the cool, dark, damp soil of November, embryo flowers and leaves already formed and ready to grow next spring. Into the ground push the sturdy red taproots of the sprouting acorns which weeks ago began the lengthy business of growing into trees. It is a time to plant bulbs in the garden and prepare for spring. For now in November one does not prepare for winter, but for the spring which is inevitably ahead.

November—a last aftermath violet in bloom near the marsh, and thousands of wild ducks coming down on the waters and into the acres of rusty smartweed stalks. November—the witch hazel is still blossoming in pale yellow tendrils in a canyon at Starved Rock, and a few late robins still run about or fly with the sunset on their ruddy fronts.

November—and the chill, damp silence of dusk closes down on the silent woods where a single cardinal calls once and then is still. And as the November night moves over the sky, the stars of November again take their places in the endless, orderly sequence of the year. Now rise Taurus the Bull and the twinkling cluster of the Pleiades; the summer stars sink into the west, and the first stars of Orion, constellation of winter, rise late on a November evening. And early in the morning, just before the dawn, there are stars of springtime in the sky. *(Nov. 1950)*

NOVEMBER MOON

Frost sparkles on the grass blades, on the fluffed-out seedheads of goldenrod, on the cattails along the water. There is no wind, no sound, no motion. It is November and the moon puts a dead-white brilliance upon hill and lake, makes the frost more tangible, makes the approach of winter more assured. Behind the black branches of bare trees the stars glitter, and the dry pods on a locust tree, for no reason at all, beat a sudden sharp tattoo that is loud in the silence.

There can be great silence—seldom more deep than in November when the crickety noises of summer are gone and the world settles down for sleep — that is heightened by sound. Small voices in the vastness of the night-silence in November are part of that stillness and increase it, emphasize it.

Now against the stars there is the sound of flying ducks. It is a thin whistling of wings, a momentary blotting out of stars, a brief procession across the moon. Flock after flock, invisible, voiceless, their wings alone announce their passing. South, south. A flock of geese, high in the upper darkness that is so bright under the moon, for a brief moment sends down wild calls that are part of the night and of November. The cold moon sees many things.

It sees the small wings of birds passing south in its brilliance. There are only faint cheeps, small trills, indistinguishable calls that sound like nothing heard in daylight, but which are the migrant calls of familiar birds that are departing for the winter. They are lonely voices. They are scattered here and there, alone in cold moonlight, alone in the terrible hugeness and emptiness of the November night, with winter pacing close upon their retreating wings.

Frost grows on the grass blades. The motionless surface of the lake is marked by a sudden splash as a small fish leaps out to escape a large fish, and the moving rings of ripples catch the gleams of moonlight until they break and are lost upon the shore.

There is a snarling, a squawling, a thin, angry turmoil of yapping that ends as quickly as it began, as two raccoons on the dark shore argue over a fish. It is a sound that, like the sounds of night wings, is infinitely fitting to the wildness of the November moon.

Still in the sky the ducks go over. Still there are the sounds of wings and the calls of passing birds. A cold, white, creeping fog, like smoke, pours soundlessly from the valleys, from the lake, envelops the upland, and the frost, under this gentle urging, glitters whiter and more wintry than before. It is November, and the cold moonlight is everywhere. *(Nov. 1946)*

THANKSGIVING WALK

The grey sky is full of withheld snow; white frost crystals lie thinly on the stiffening earth; hoarfrost clings to dead weeds by the road. It is the morning of Thanksgiving Day. This is the end of autumn, the day before winter, the brown time, the period when pastel shadings of brown and russet and beige are everywhere. The landscape has grown restful; it lays a calmness over everything, including man, a waiting sense of quietness . . . . waiting.

Ragweeds by the roadside have grown dusky, and every twig, every seed stalk, every shrivelled old leaf is silhouetted against the discerning greyness of the sky. Among them is the musical cheeping of tree sparrows from the northern woods, the scratch-scramble sounds of small feet among fallen leaves where the weed seeds lie.

Thanksgiving Day, and in town there is cooking food and the traditional scents that always have meant the Day in America; roasting fowl, the spice of hot pumpkin pies just out of the oven, cranberry sauce like a ruby in a glass bowl. But out in the cold, frosty air of that morning, the

values of today's Thanksgiving may be seen more clearly. The stern landscape of November is like a Puritan in its soul-searching demands and its
inspiration to courage.

Down the road stand the quiet winter woods. Low shingle oaks full of
russet leaves gather at the edges, and further in the woods are the taller
oaks and elms that hold their bare lacy twigs against the sky. Three blue
jays, clarioning, fly on rhythmic wings across the oak-edge, not rapidly but
with a purposeful beat measured to the meter of their clanging voices.
Crows in a treetop shout nasally into the exhilarating, cold morning air;
a squirrel with a rattling of claws on bark races up an elm, out on a
branch, and lands in the next tree—scurrying as if to hasten the slowing
pulse of the year.

These are the woods on Thanksgiving Day in the morning. And then
suddenly there comes a hint of acid fragrance in the still air, a cold, lemony
scent somewhere, anywhere. And there in the woods a bare bush is full of
delicate pale yellow flowers. Here is the final flower of the year, defier of
cold and frost, a wild flower for Thanksgiving Day, the witch hazel. Not
until late autumn and early winter do the small yellow calyces open, from
which emerge four thin, narrow, twisted petals an inch long; the gnarly
twigs are fringed with them. There also are hard brown seed pods which
burst open suddenly after frost, and the little stony black seeds, a pair in
each pod, are catapulted many feet away into the woods. But long after the
seeds have gone, the yellow flowers of the witch hazel make a glow in the
dark November days. Faithful to tradition, they represent a strength to
meet the winter. At sight of them, that brooding sense of waiting is
changed to a brave certainty of Spring. *(Nov. 1943)*

ALL-AMERICAN THANKSGIVING

Thanksgiving Dinner is a meal dedicated to the foods whose story is
interwoven with the history of the nation. For three hundred twenty years
many of these same foods have been a part of the American feast.

The turkey itself is a native American bird which was found by the
Colonists in the forests of Massachusetts and Virginia. It was a meaty bird
that graced the family platter at Thanksgiving and became an American
tradition which has not lost meaning with the years.

Long ago also cranberry sauce became a traditional accompaniment of
turkey, and even today cranberries come largely from the original sand bogs
of Cape Cod which furnished the early settlers with a tart wild fruit.

Out of Chesapeake Bay came oysters for early Thanksgiving dinners,
as oysters have been coming since the Indians of Maryland knew them.
Potatoes, though probably not a part of the earliest feasts, later became an
integral part of the American meal. White potatoes came from the Andes,
were cultivated in Europe, and were brought back vastly improved to

America. Sweet potatoes were also of American origin and were roasted and eaten by the Indians long before white men knew them. If the Pilgrims had potatoes for their Thanksgivings dinners, they had yams, not white potatoes.

Maize or Indian corn was there that first Thanksgiving Day, and the whole story of America thereafter became associated with the yellow and white kernels. The Pilgrims were introduced to maize by the friendly Indians of Plymouth, who taught them how to plant, tend, and reap the new grain. They had green corn in summer, and dried corn in winter, and succotash, corn bread, samp, and the famous, delightful Indian pudding with maple sugar shaved over the top.

Indian pudding was a probable dessert for the first Thanksgiving, but later it was joined by a dish that became a tradition—pumpkin pie, made from a fruit which was also of Indian origin. Still later in the history of America, the spices which went into the making of these pies wrote not a few pages of American history. Out of Salem and Boston and Barnstable went fast Yankee ships bound for the Indies to bring home silks and porcelains and teas, and the spices without which pumpkin was nothing more than a vegetable.

It is all these things—from the Yankee spice trade to the vegetables, nuts, fruits, and fowls which the American Indians introduced to the white colonists—which make up the secrets of all those aromas steaming up from our Thanksgiving dinner today. *(Nov. 1941)*

⚙
⚙

CHRISTMASTIME

⚙

⚙

THE WISE MEN AND THE STAR

"What do the stars mean?" "What do they portend?" The stars hung there, menacing, so that whenever a man looked at them he looked only for a sign, an omen, an indication of what they might mean in his life. Always the stars puzzled generations who watched and feared. And because it was so much easier to frighten a man than to make him happy, the star-interpreters of two thousand years ago preferred to put a sinister meaning on almost every sky-event. These men, the astrologers and seers, undoubtedly were far wiser than anyone knew at that time. They worked out the equivalent of modern horoscopes, charted rich men's destinies, and made themselves indispensable in the daily lives of Greeks, Sumerians, and Egyptians. And in many instances the wise men discovered things which they kept to themselves simply because the people of those days were not educated to understanding the great truths that even so early were being ferreted honestly out of the skies.

In those days, also, the stars, to mariners and travellers, were compass and pointer and map. Without the Pole Star in sight they often were lost. Greek sailors as early as 330 B.C. were taught to steer by the North Star, and 3000 years before that the Egyptians were steering their slender boats by Thuban, which at that time was the North Star. The stars might be oracles and avengers, but the night was even more awful when clouds shut them out.

It was with all these things in mind that the wise men, travellers, and common people watched the skies in the year 747 after the building of Rome, and saw two planets move ever closer until at last they were almost as one star. Nightly the people gathered in the darkness and looked up fearfully at the two and wondered what they portended. When, a year later, a third planet joined them, the world each night stared heavenward, bound as with a common awe and fear. The astrologers and wise men worked late trying to figure out the phenomenon, but nobody knew what it meant. But something, everyone felt, was going to happen.

In China a brilliant star that came and went was recorded, and there was a comet that filled the night with light and terror. This was the situation at the time set by the Christian religion as the probable birth date of Christ. For once, perhaps, the wise men predicted nothing but good which was to come upon the earth. But in those far-off days even they could not know what had happened.

These celestial happenings are the basis for the story of the Christmas star. From old records kept in China, Mesopotamia, and Egypt, and by tracing backward the orbits of comets, planets and novae, or new stars, many astronomers believe that instead of one Christmas star, there were at least three at about the time set for the first Christmas. It is no wonder that there arose the story of the Star in the East. *(Dec. 1943)*

THE FIRE ON THE HEARTH

Christmas Eve, and on the hearth the flames are red. The house is full of friendliness, is scented with spruce needles and the odors of Christmas. The shimmering tongues curl around the logs; the ashes glow red—red as the embers a certain cave-man found in a charred log when the forest fire had burned itself out. . . .

He knew nothing of the uses of fire. He only knew that when he touched it, it hurt him, that fire was stronger than he. Like the wind and the sea and the sun, it was a power and he dared not defy it.

But in the log there were only little harmless red coals. He put a dried leaf on them, laughed when it smoked and burst into small flame. He took coals home with him and put them in the door of his cave, and found that fire kept out unwelcome visitors from the forest, made the cave warmer than before. Now fire was servant and he was master. Yet for ages he could only feed the fire; he could not make it.

The flames flicker on the hearth, as an arrowhead maker by chance strikes flint against mineral rock and makes sparks. Faster, faster, the sparks fall on dry leaves and tinder, and a tiny flame leaps up. Man has found a new power. He can command fire at his will.

The scene shifts rapidly now as fire changes man's simple life. All the arts of cookery grow out of the first act of singeing meat. A clay pot hardens in the fire . . . dishes and utensils one by one are invented and perfected. Near a hot fire, a rock melts out its copper and tin, the cooling metal becomes bronze and a whole new age opens for man.

Tribal flame is guarded by autocratic fire priests and virgin priestesses. Terrible fire gods come into being. Now the picture in the flames grows twisted and awful, as Baal and Gibil and Xiuhtecutli demand human sacrifice in the temple fires. The Children of Israel are cast into the fiery furnace, and the voice of Yahveh comes to Moses from a burning bush on the slopes of Mount Horeb.

The flames lick into the logs, burn through, as the story of man's age-old hunt for fuel to feed the ever-hungry fire engages him in life-time searchings for stuff to burn for light and warmth. Year by year and century by century, he climbs to today. Chimneys come into being, and fires burn great cities. For fire is servant only as long as it is restrained; unleashed, it destroys the wealth which, often by means of fire, man laboriously has built.

Again the fire flickers as the story moves on to industry and manufacture, all made possible by fire.

Yet through all its work and adaptation by man, fire has remained the same raw, primitive element that molded the world. Today it is still raw and pagan, yet, as if it were a hold upon our remote past which we cannot quite let go, we like to see a little fire in our daily lives. We enjoy fireworks, the contentment of a campfire, candlelight at dinner and in church; even the birthday cake and the Christmas tree are small fire-festivals in themselves. The benediction of fire is not out of place, somehow, in a modern home with today's way of life. Yet it is still the primitive blaze whose charm is as mysterious as it was long ago when men first were drawn to worship it.

And now the logs roll over and send a stream of yellow sparks up the black mouth of the chimney. It is Christmas Eve, and the fire burns low. *(Dec. 1942)*

CHRISTMAS OVER THE LAND

This now is Christmas—this, the scent in the air, the sound of the bells, the sparkle of candles, the fragrance of spruce. This is Christmas in America as it always has been, and as it may never have been before.

It has as many meanings as there are people in the land. Christmas may mean cold waves pounding the red rocks of Scituate and the barnacled pilings of fish houses from Maine to Buzzard's Bay; it may mean white houses in New England buttoned up tight and warm against the near-Arctic cold. Christmas means children coasting on Boston Common, and snow on the Great Stone Face. It is extra pancakes in honor of the Day at a logging camp above the Saco or the Androscoggin; it is a great, lighted tree on the White House lawn; it is traditional lebkuchen, pfeffernuss, and spring-erle cookies exchanged in the homes of Pennsylvania Dutch down Lancaster way.

And Christmas may mean scarlet hibiscus blowing in the breeze off Florida's Indian River—Christmas in the south means the golden globes of ripened oranges, a warm surf rolling in from Tybee City to Key West, pelicans diving after fish in the Gulf, frogs singing like springtime in a bayou swamp. It is Spanish moss and colored lights on a long-leaf pine in

New Orleans; it is the bells of St. Louis cathedral calling the faithful to Christmas mass, and azaleas blooming in Audubon Park. Christmas is the shrimp fleet coming in to celebrate on shore; it is the rich scent of pralines bubbling in a copper pot; it is turkey with cornbread stuffing, and Texas mistletoe over the door.

This is all Christmas and it is all American. There is nothing really like it any place else in the world. It is decorated streets and crowded shops in every village, town, and city from New York to San Francisco—it is Santa Claus in a department store, and a lake wind whipping the garlands along Michigan Avenue. It is the largest cedar anyone could find for miles around, cut by men of the congregation and set up for lights and ornaments in an Illinois country church. It is the solemnity of the sunrise service on a quiet December morning, and the hushed wonder of a child looking at a lighted Christmas tree.

Christmas is as fragile as crystals of snow on a coatsleeve. It is as breathless as December 24th, when the atmosphere is keyed to its highest pitch and Christmas Day itself can be only an anti-climax. Christmas is as exciting as the sound of sleigh bells, as the blueness of winter dusk, as the glow of a star on Christmas Eve. It is as fragrant as logs burning on the hearth, as tantalizing as the odors of oyster stew, fruit cake, or an orange in the toe of a stocking. Christmas is the reflection of candle flames in a dark window; it is the sense of deep comfort, completeness, and charm a home can have when it is warm and lighted and full of love.

Christmas is all of these things—and it is home-made gifts in a lonely farm house out on the Kansas prairie; it is fluffy snow on the rim of the Grand Canyon; it is a small scrub juniper, hung with red balls and set proudly erect before a Navaho hogan. Christmas is the soft grey fingers of fog reaching in from the surging Pacific and spangling the fuchsias, roses, and tall hedges of geraniums; it is the lighted glory of living Christmas trees in California; it is a ship-load of home-coming soldiers docking at San Francisco.

All these things and a great deal more mean Christmas in America— Christmas, 1945. In it is the flavor of hope, tradition, goodness, and a people at peace. *(Dec. 1945)*

SING NOEL!

It is Christmas and the voices of the noel-singers are everywhere on the air and in the hearts of men. Into man's own dim past music first came when his voice had developed beyond the mere harsh bestial calls of his forebears. Long ago someone sang, and the world ever since has known music.

But man was impatient with the limitations of his voice, and so he worked with growing skill to produce simple musical instruments. He beat with a stick against a hollow log and discovered a drum-rhythm that at first was but an echo of his own hot pulse. One day someone—the ancient Greeks said it was Apollo—blew on a hollow reed and found a new sound. Holes in the pipe produced variations. Several pipes fastened together were even more exciting when the human breath and the skill of questing fingers drew forth strangely alluring melodies. And a harp or lyre first was made of cords strung across a tortoise shell. Music even in remote times had begun to sound out some of its infinite possibilities of delight.

All down the years music had its own meaning to every man. Music was the ancient Hymn to Apollo composed by Mesomedes, the Greek, in 200 B.C. It was the old laments of the Hebrews and the deep tones of the Kaddish; it was the somber monks of the Middle Ages feeling the growth of melody in the Gregorian chants intoned in chilly chapels. It was the part songs and plain songs, and it was the suddenly gay and revolutionary spring song called Sumer is Icumen In of the 13th century—perhaps the first piece of music with sound effects. It was composed for the enjoyment both of the singer and the hearer.

Music is the Gloria in Excelsis and the Missa Solemnis; it is Palestrina groping for melodies never known before, and Bach going on from there to the splendor of the Elijah and the complexities of pipe organ music.

It is Papa Haydn enthusiastically composing more than a hundred symphonies in the joy of musical discovery. Music is Mozart creating his deceptively simple compositions; it is Beethoven walking in the woods and dreaming of a Pastoral Symphony that contained the voices of nature.

Music is all things to all people. It is as much the possession of six kindergartners singing "Here we go round the mulberry bush" as it is that of great musicians playing for cultured ears and educated tastes. It is as much the possession of a mother singing to her child as it is that of square dancers at a barn dance in the Kentucky hills. Music is the folk songs of all the peoples of the world. It is the Ojibway lament, the Cherokee hunting song, the Iroquois war chant. It is the Londonderry Air, Turkey in the Straw, and the Tannenbaum.

Music is old hymns sung in a country church. It is the obvious rhythms of a swing band; the behind-the-scenes tuning up before a concert; the universality of radio music and phonograph music. It is the Faithful Shepherd Suite and a Shostakovich concerto; it is the Ring of the Niebelung, and Carmen with a rose between her teeth. It is the tone pictures conjured up by Scheherazade and Til Eulenspiegel; it is Anitra dancing beneath a palm tree; it is the Grand Canyon Suite and the Afternoon of a Faun, the thunder of Finlandia, the Rhapsody in Blue. It is the color and humor of Petrouchka and the Mikado, the deep drama and stark tragedy of Tristan and Lohengrin; the gaiety of the Strauss Waltzes and the depths of gloom that sound in a Chopin funeral march.

And besides all these things and many more which music is, it is the essence of Christmas itself. Since the first masses were sung in honor of Christ's birth, music through the centuries has become more and more a permanent part of this celebration. During its existence it has grown gayer and gayer until the music of Christmas today not only is the hymns of the church but just as surely is the jollity of Jingle Bells and Santa is Coming to Town. It is Silent Night sung by the children's choir at midnight on Christmas Eve;

it is Adeste Fideles and Good King Wenceslas, and Bing Crosby singing White Christmas to bring tears to the eyes of soldiers from Murmansk to Malaysia. Sing Noel! This indeed is Christmas. (*Dec. 1946*)

A CANDLE ON A CHRISTMAS NIGHT

Now as the dusk of Christmas Eve comes over the snow and the dark hills, over the sea and over the mountains, over the desert and the prairies of America, candles one by one are lighted in homes across the land. The small flames, with infinite meaning behind them, flicker and gleam in that heightened atmosphere which is Christmas.

Archaic though they may seem in a modern world which is well lighted with electricity, candles have a mysterious background which gives them deep importance today. They are a heritage which we seldom take time to analyze, for, like the fireplace in modern homes, candles really are not necessary for illumination; we like to use candles because of that remote ancestral background which is still part of us. And in spite of the fact that we do not need candles, the candle factories report that the sale of their wares today is greater than ever before in history. Now at Christmas the sales reach their peak.

For candles are inseparable from Christmas. Since the earliest beginnings of that festival as a religious period in the Christian church, candles were part of the observances of the church, and they were vital to the ritual of the still earlier Jewish church. No one knows when the first candles were made, but according to ancient writ, it was Moses who, commanded by Jehovah, made a seven-branched candlestick to fittingly bear the holy candles of the temple.

The earliest candles may have been rushes dipped in melted tallow or other fat; they burned with an acrid smoke and a flickering light which nevertheless was better than no light at all. It was candles like these, it is believed, which the early Christians carried into the depths of the Catacombs where secret religious meetings and services were held. Later, candles followed the Christians into the open, were used finally as part of the essential equipment of the church. There were special Christmas candles and the huge Paschal candle which five hundred years ago was burned day and night during the forty days of Lent. The Paschal candle was a tremendous thing which cost a great deal of money; some were 30 to 300 pounds in weight and almost impoverished a small parish to buy them.

The manufacture of candles developed slowly as time went on. For many centuries they were virtually the only light one had after the sun went down, but only the wealthy could afford to burn more than one or two at a time. The tremendous crystal chandeliers at Versailles contained hundreds of wax tapers, each carefully lighted by hand by anxious lackeys, but in the poor peasant's hut there might be only the guttering remains of a smoky candle-end flickering in its own pool of grease, and no more tallow or money to make another candle possible. To save money, many people went to bed at sundown. A candle would last a long time if one lived frugally and went to bed early.

Many kinds of grease have been used for candles. Some gave off a smoky flame and an unpleasant smell that made the eyes smart. Mutton tallow was used for some of the poorest candles. Fine bleached beeswax was used for the best and most costly. For many centuries all church candles were made of pure beeswax because of the religious significance contained in the fact that "beeswax is made by virgin bees." Blessed in the annual ritual of Candlemas Day, February 2, these candles served in the most important ceremonies of the church.

In America candle-making progressed from the desperate need of the early colonists who gathered bushels of little grey-green bayberries to make small green candles, to the vast business of the petroleum companies who today manufacture from paraffin a large percentage of American candles. There still are beeswax candles made carefully by such conscientious concerns as the St. Louis Candle and Wax Company; large and small votive lights for use in Catholic churches; four-foot candles and two-inch candles; candles made in the image of Santa Claus or snowmen or Christmas trees; molded candles and hand-dipped candles; candles for the dinner table and candles to be carried by carol singers in the streets. And there are those out-moded little candles which long ago used to perch dangerously but delightfully on the outspread branches of Christmas trees.

Candles are inseparable from Christmas. Over all the world on Christmas Eve the ceremonies of candlelight are taking place. Everywhere as Christmas Eve grows darker and more exciting, the candles of Christmas sparkle over the land. (*Dec. 1948*)

O CHRISTMAS TREE!

During December they have a new name, those fragrant balsams and crisp Douglas firs, those sharp spruces and drooping hemlocks, those long-needled pines and prickly cedars—they are all Christmas trees.

During the year they live in deep northern swamps and forests; they know some of the wildest lands on the continent. Among peaks of western mountains where the great spires of Douglas firs reach into the sky, the symmetrical trees are sleeked with snow. The air is so crystalline that it seems to splinter into bright bits when a bird calls—when a moose-bird whistles and a white weasel streaks across the dazzle and into a hole beneath a rock.

Trees in sphagnum bogs know the crackle of northern lights on an icy Christmas night, know the blurring of hoar frost on a winter morning, know the thunderous report of sound as lake-ice "talks" in its sleep.

With a rumbling of the old ice breaking up in the sun, spring comes to the Christmas-tree bogs. Arbutus scents the April air and a loon is on the open water. Summer, and in the bogs a vireo sings all day long; the wintergreen bells are open and blueberries are ripe. Autumn, and the birches and aspens blaze with gold; red maples are crimson; robins gather in the bogs and suddenly are gone; geese go over in the night. Now the first snow lightly lies on the spruce and balsam spires. It is late September and time to begin the annual Christmas-tree harvest.

Only the balsam, Douglas fir, and several kinds of spruce are used as commercial Christmas trees in America. Each grows in a special area; their systematic cutting begins in autumn and ends when orders are filled. Although in the past there was much wrongful cutting that destroyed the coming crop and laid waste much forestland, Christmas-tree harvesting today is a business that has the approval of conservationists. Into the swamps and up into the mountains go cutters to take trees only of a certain size; those that are left will attain a fuller growth because of the removal of the crowded trees. The cut trees are graded for size, taken to the factories to be trimmed, and are placed in cold storage until time to go to market. Legally and properly cut trees usually are tagged for identification.

Then when December follows Thanksgiving, the markets of America are full of northland trees—Douglas fir from the northwest, black spruce from Minnesota and Michigan, balsams and red spruce from Wisconsin, Canada, and New England. They are a brief crop, a market that ends abruptly on December 24. Then, in homes over all the land, a heady holiday scent comes from trees decorated with thin glass balls and colored lights, and surrounded by the love and friendship of families at Christmastime. (*Dec. 1944*)

SHINING FRUIT

Joyfully and lovingly the hands of the household decorate the Christmas tree. The ornaments may be simple strings of popcorn and cranberries strung by grandma and the children, paper chains made by the kindergartner, glass balls and lights saved from year to year, and candies and cookies made especially for Christmas. There may be gifts hung on the bending boughs; or candy canes, cookie animals, paper figures, and an angel with spun glass wings presiding at the top of the tree. They are all Christmas tree ornaments and they have their own meaning to the owners of the tree.

For Christmas tree ornaments, in most homes, are not transient things. They are parts of tradition, part of the family and its growth, part of its fun and memories and all its other Christmases. To the outsider, some ornaments may not be much to look at but in the heart of the family they are part of a special, private, Christmas tradition.

Christmas tree ornaments may have had their origin far back in early Roman times when, as part of the annual ritual of propitiating the gods, little masks of Bacchus were hung on vines and trees to make them fruitful in the coming year. As so many Christian customs evolved from pagan ceremony, so did Christmas tree ornaments, after many centuries, come into common use.

In Strasburg, Germany, in 1604, there was what is believed to have been the first Christmas tree, but the kind of ornaments it bore is unknown. It was in Germany later on, however, that the splendid, shining, blown-glass balls of many colors were made for use at Christmas time. Germany fashioned intricate and wonderful ornaments to decorate its beloved Christmas trees— delicate birds with quivering tails, balls and icicles and fairies and angels and stars. Cookies were made for use as ornaments, and the confectioner created sugar ornaments which were painted with vegetable colors, wired to hang, and added their bit of beauty to the shimmering wonder of the tree.

Today's Christmas trees still hold many of the traditional ornaments of the past, as well as new ones which are added each year. Perhaps there are a few very old, tarnished, heavy silver balls brought by grandmother from Saxony; perhaps there are brightly painted glass balls from Japan; there may be some of the glass birds and glass fruit from Germany before the war; some of the transparent, sturdy ornaments made in America during the war; the somewhat battered but still beloved angel which has poised at the tip of the tree for so many years. And perhaps there are some of the amazing sugar ornaments which still are made by a very few sugar craftsmen in America.

It is Christmas, and the Tree once again bears shining fruit. (*Dec. 1949*)

PELZNICKEL AND THE CHRISTMAS ANGEL

Christmas may appear to have become too commercialized in these latter days—too impersonal, too manufactured, with its old charm lost and its original meaning forgotten—yet perhaps these still are only superficial things. They cannot really mar Christmas, any more than the old vinegar-voiced edict of Governor Bradford banning Christmas from the Massachusetts Colony because of the Day's pagan background, could quench Christmas in American hearts.

For Christmas since its beginning has been so closely enwrapped in people's lives that the personalities of the Season alone will forever keep it alive. From the Christ Child and the Christmas Angel to Pelznickel and the Jule-Nissen, from La Befana to Santa Claus, the true meanings of Christmas are made living and human. From its deepest religious meaning to its most humorous and gay significance, Christmas and its old-fashionedness belongs to us.

It all began in an obscure little village in Judea where, it is said, a Child was born in a stable which was only a cave in a rocky hillside, yet to which, tradition says, came kings and angels and wise men and common people with gifts. Yet the feast-day claimed by Christmas actually may have begun long before that, back in the dim days of old Britain where the Druids celebrated the shortest day of the year by conducting rites beneath the sacred oak.

Ever since, there have been personalities which, in each race and in each age, have stood out as symbolic of and part of Christmas in its annual celebrations around the world.

The Christ Child, the three kings, the wise men, the shepherds, and the caroling angels are part of every Christmas pageant. The Cratchit family and their goose, dismal old Scrooge and fat jolly Fezziwig rollick in this special season as gaily as they did almost a hundred years ago. Jule-Nissen, the kobold of Scandinavian attics who rides a goat that butts naughty children, comes dashing about the house; Pelznickel, in Pennsylvania Dutch homes, still snaps his whip under the door-crack to sting the eager fingers reaching for candies he has just thrown upon the floor. There is St. Nicholas and his white horse, Father Christmas bringing gifts, poor old Befana hunting for the Christ Child and leaving gifts for children everywhere, and Tante Aira on her white donkey carrying gifts. And there is Santa Claus who is the American embodiment of all these other gift-bringers. Though some of them in the Old Country tradition are frightening personalities designed to scare children into a proper state of panic before they receive their gifts, Santa Claus has none of this unkind manner. With the gentle and democratic spirit of America itself, Santa Claus brings gifts whether the children have been perfect little angels all year or not. He and his reindeer—one seldom finds one without the other in December—are the composite of those other personalities which, all down the years, have meant Christmas in many countries of the world. (*Dec. 1947*)

THE STORY OF MUSIC BOXES

It was Christmas Eve in the old house. The family had come together from faraway places and now in that electric atmosphere of Christmas Eve, with the tree glittering and sparkling and fragrant, embodiment of all the Christmases that ever were or shall be, there was that closeness of spirit which only families know. It was a time to fill one's heart and throat with sentiment, to make the least thing significant, to express one's affection in loving gifts and foolishly delightful surprises, all the more delightful because they were part of the family and the family was together again.

The old rooms were shadowy in the corners as the lights were turned off so that the Tree could shine and the fireplace could give off that ruddy light which has been part of the family hearth ever since the childhood of mankind. Now the flames made dancing shadows on the walls, reddened the faces turned toward it. And then someone quietly cranked up the old music box that always had been a part of Christmas since the days just after the Civil War, when Grandfather had made the Grand Tour and brought home this wonderful music-maker from Geneva.

It had a rectangular box all of thirty inches long and fifteen inches high, a mahogany case kept well polished even now, so that the inlaid design of roses and ribbons on the top was still beautiful. There was a crank on the side by which one wound up the inner mechanism, and then, as it started, it was good to see the strange steel cylinder with its curious protruding pins roll over and over and let the pins brush past a thin steel comb which somehow picked music off the pins. And as the cylinder revolved and as the music tinkled forth with delicate and painstaking detail, using the "forte-piano" and then "mandoline" to make the tune more expressive, there were silver bees on hammers that from time to time struck bells. The bees moved as if they were alive and very well trained, each one differently designed, each one intent on its work of striking the sweet-toned bells to charm the listener.

It was fascinating. Nothing in modern music could equal it. The children always looked forward to the moment when the music box was wound up and the bees would move about in that mysteriously beautiful box while Silent Night tinkled forth into the Christmas evening, and Adeste Fideles (how the little bees worked on that one!) and old Tyrolean tunes no one knows today.

For years, music boxes have been part of Christmas. In the past of not so long ago they were the only "recorded" music to be had, and so music boxes were not always saved for Christmas, but for all the long winter evenings and for the coming of guests. Mankind for centuries had learned to make music for himself by means of various musical instruments and with his own voice, but not until about 1789, when the first musical watches were invented in Switzerland, was it possible to have music without producing it oneself.

Many changes followed the first musical watch with its tiny spring-wound motor and the thin metal teeth which were struck by the pins of the revolving cylinder pins to make weak music. The size grew; volume was produced; many variations were added; the cases themselves became as elaborate as the repertoire. Next came changeable cylinders so that new tunes could be added. Disks were invented, the forerunner of the phonograph record. There even was an electric music box operated by coins.

But the phonograph itself caused the decline of the music box. No longer was it the only available mechanical music. Its thinner tones were relegated to the attic, or to the front parlor, until, as the years passed, music boxes became antiques and were collected and admired again. Novelties containing tiny music boxes still are made.

Yet today as yesterday, a music box which is a family heirloom is still part of the family and the traditional gathering at Christmas. It is now, when all the old familiar things are brought out to be part of the celebration, that the tinkling carols from the old Swiss music box are most fittingly at home. (*Dec. 1947*)

OLD CHRISTMAS

Christmas first came to Illinois in the early eighteenth century when the French villages of Kaskaskia, Cahokia, Belleville, Prairie du Rocher, and Renault celebrated Christmas as the inhabitants had done in France. There was Mass in the churches, the feasts of Reveillon on Christmas Eve and Reveille on Christmas Day, and the best foods the wilderness could provide, with a few French dainties conjured up somehow by the ingenious womenfolk. The French Christmas was real and vivid in the old, lost villages along the Mississippi.

Later, there came German Christmases, and the Swedish kind, and the Greek and the Polish and the English, and it was a German who set the first Christmas tree along the Mississippi in Illinois. There had been no Christmas trees, it is believed, until 1833 when Gustave Koerner in St. Clair County, yearning for the old, rousing, jolly German Christmas, did something about it. No fir trees grew in St. Clair County, so Koerner secured a small, green-barked sassafras tree, and he and his family decorated it with bits of ribbon and bright paper, polished redhaws, perhaps, and glossy hazel and hickory nuts. They made small candles which were fastened to the twig-tips, and on Christmas Eve the family and their German friends gathered around a little Christmas tree shining with candlelight.

The immigrants who settled in Illinois may have endeavored faithfully to become Americans, citizens of the nation and of the State, to revoke their native language, dress, and customs, yet when Christmas neared, the old, old traditions of this special season of the year came forward and could not be wholly put down.

The Swedish must have their butter-rich cookies, the *sandbakkelse*, and the specially-made *lutefisk;* they must tie a big sheaf of wheat on a pole and put it in the garden for the birds. It would not have been Christmas without these things. Nor could the people who had come from Holland and who farmed the rich black fields near Chicago entirely forego the arrival of St. Nicholas on his white horse and the rascal Black Piet with his bag of candies and the whip which mercilessly flicked the eager fingers scrambling for the sweets. And for a long time the Dutch-American children in Illinois put down their shoes, padded with soft hay, to invite small gifts at Christmas.

The English who followed the early French brought their own customs, too—the ritual of the plum pudding, the hanging of the greens. The English in southern Illinois found mistletoe like that back home in England, green plants set with waxen white berries in clusters in bare elms and oaks; and, if the Illinois holly held its red fruits but dropped its leaves, it was at least a substitute for the proper English kind.

It all made Christmas—the German tree, the French traditions, the English mistletoe, the Swedish cookies, the Dutch jollity, the Carolinian and Virginian celebrations—the Illinois Christmas, a little different in each family, but, nevertheless, just as Illinois combines many nationalities, unified in the spirit of Christmas. (*Dec. 1953*)

CHRISTMAS AT KASKASKIA

It was the year 1700 in the old French town of Kaskaskia, situated on a point of land thrusting into the Mississippi in southern Illinois. Now in the chill early dusk of December, the bells in the church rang out across a wilderness of land and water to call the faithful to Christmas Eve services.

Alone and brave above the great river, Kaskaskia felt itself "an outpost of civilization and culture; in a wilderness peopled largely by unlettered savages, the civilization and religion and learning of the West had found their foothold." As the centuries passed, Kaskaskia vanished from the map, but the old town had played its part in the story of America.

Christmas in the early days of Illinois was not celebrated very extensively as we know it and observe it today. But in the French manner, modified only by the exigencies of wilderness, Christmas nevertheless came to Kaskaskia.

When the evening services were over and the candles still burned before the altar, the people, wrapped warmly against the cold of a December night, went through the snow to their log and stone homes. The fires in the big stone fireplaces were fixed for the night; bed warmers were heated to ease the chill of winter beds. And the children, before they said their prayers and dived beneath layers of homemade coverlets, carefully placed their shoes beside the hearth.

Christmas at Kaskaskia. Two hundred and fifty years ago, what did the Christ Child bring to the hopeful children of that outpost of old France along the Mississippi? No one knows. But in the old records of goods sold in shops, there were many things imported from France, as well as utilitarian items made locally. Perhaps in a boy's shoe there might have been a pair of silver knee-buckles; there might have been a bright Paris ribbon for little sister; there could have been maple sugar candies wrapped carefully in soft paper saved from France; perhaps little white cakes, the *petit gateaux,* which even then may have been loved by children whether they lived in Paris or Kaskaskia.

And on Christmas morning, there was the same shining joy over gifts, meager though they might be, as there always is joy among children at Christmas. The Day, however, was not celebrated with merriment, but with solemn mass at the church. Merry-making was reserved for New Year's, and for Twelfth Night when special cakes celebrated the end of the Christmas season.

Although there may be no records of Christmas at Kaskaskia, more important events were recorded in the long story of the old town.

Kaskaskia saw the coming and going of adventurers and explorers and the makers of history. It saw three flags wave over its hundreds of houses— the flag of France, in the days when the Illinois shore was French and the Missouri shore was Spanish; saw the coming of the British flag, and saw it fall before George Rogers Clark and his American soldiers who brought the American flag to Illinois and left it planted there forever.

But Kaskaskia did not stay forever. Year by year when floods receded, the point of land had grown smaller. The legislature and seat of government were moved in 1818 to Vandalia, for the river was devouring Kaskaskia. In 1880-81 the Mississippi cut across the neck of land and Kaskaskia became an island. Year after year as the floods came, more of Kaskaskia vanished. One by one the old houses slipped into the swirling brown water; fewer people remained to defy the river, though some remained until 1898, and a few lived on the bluffs out of reach of the water. In 1906 a single chimney stood on a bank above the river—and when the chimney fell down under the relentless river's rising current, that was the end of Kaskaskia, whose church bells on a Christmas night once rang across the wilderness.

(Dec. 1951)

CHRISTMAS AT NEW SALEM

All day and all night the snow had fallen in a fine sifting of flakes and the morning of the twenty-fourth of December dawned on a brilliant, whitened, prairie world. The bare oaks in the woods that crowded around New Salem village were a lacework of snow-ridged twigs. Far out over the frozen Sangamon and its valley, a marsh hawk slowly flapped its grey wings and on the hill the breakfast smokes from cabin chimneys spiralled into a high cold sky. It was the day before Christmas, but there was little hint of it among the pioneer folk of New Salem in Illinois. In the early eighteen-thirties many religions and many individuals did not consider it seemly to celebrate in any way the birthday of Christ. Christmas came and went, year after year in the raw prairie village, and apparently there was no celebration worth recording.

But in the tavern—in James Rutledge's house where Abraham Lincoln roomed—there might have been something different. For Rutledge fore-bears long ago had lived in South Carolina where there had been Christmas even in the early days. Perhaps James Rutledge far off here in the Illinois country, far from the winter warmth of the southern sun, far from moss-hung live oaks where the wild pigeons nested—far from terrapin stew and 'possum baked with sweet potatoes—perhaps in him there was a deep-down yearning for Christmas as it was celebrated there. Perhaps he had heard his people tell tales of mistletoe and holly brought in from the swamps, ham and venison roasting in the big fireplaces, and oysters brought up from the coast, and the best cornbread in the world baked by the family cook. Christmas gifts, and Christmas dinner, and dancing and punch that night. Mistletoe over every doorway to catch the unsuspecting, and a great holly wreath on the big front door. But in New Salem there was nothing: No festivities, no gifts, no wide-eyed children tiptoeing softly down the broad stairs before anyone else arose, no mistletoe and holly. No Christmas.

It is not recorded in the scant annals of the short-lived village above the Sangamon, but it might be that James Rutledge talked it over with his wife and perhaps between them they made a Christmas at their house. All during that cold bright December day, Mrs. Rutledge and Ann were roast-ing one of the hams they had put by for the winter, were making a pudding like James' mother used to make, soaking dried corn, making a big supply of corn pone, trying as best they could with their scant larder to imitate Christmas abundance. Perhaps Abe Lincoln cracked nuts, a flat-iron held between his bony knees, and occasionally slipped a fat walnut meat into his mouth, until Ann, with pretended ferocity, insisted that he whistle while he worked, else she would have no nuts for her maple-sugar candy.

The winter dusk closed down early that short afternoon, and it was Christmas Eve, silent, cold, blue, bright with stars, but in pioneer New Salem scarcely anyone was aware of its significance. Without any knowledge of what the night was, the children huddled under the heavy patchwork quilts and slept.

But perhaps that night the sparks flew from the broad chimney of the Rutledge Tavern. Ann was popping corn; the Rutledge boys, munching, were sprawled on the braided rug their mother had made, listening to Abe tell stories—Abe in whose childhood there never had been a Christmas.

James Rutledge and his wife had a contented look on their weathered faces. This was Christmas in the Illinois country. Next day they would invite half the folk of New Salem. Perhaps there would be toasting in the old style; there would be food, and at night there would be square dancing to make the tavern logs shake. Yes, if there was Christmas at New Salem during the stern and work-worn years of the 1830's, it may have been found in James Rutledge's log house on the hill. *(Dec. 1943)*

❈

❈ # TRAILS AND PLACES

❈

❈

THE RAIL FENCE

Symbol of the pioneer and synonymous with Abraham Lincoln, the rail fence has almost vanished from the middlewestern landscape which it once patterned. Its gentle angles provided nesting places for quail and larks; it was an unobtrusive fencing which seemed to be only an extension of the woods itself. The rail fence was an indication that a man had cleared land and had planted crops from which he wanted to keep the varmints out. It sometimes failed to bar the lithe-heeled deer who could sail over most stake-and-riders with insolent ease, devour young corn and beans and peas, and leap out again before anyone found them. Some pioneer farmers built fences ten feet high to keep out the deer, close-railed them together at the bottom to bar rabbits; but they couldn't keep out the climbing raccoons, nor the woodchuck which could dig underneath, as could the fox. A bear or a panther could climb over or knock down the best-laid rail fence. But the split-rail fence was laid up proudly by the pioneer to mark his boundaries, to show that he had come to stay and, to the best of his ability, prevent trespassing. Its shadow on the face of our history remains inerasable and bright.

To split enough rails to fence a twenty-acre field was no job for a weakling. Good, straight, long rails required the efforts of a man who had muscular strength, good aim, steady nerves, a strong back and shoulders, and determination. All he needed besides this enviable equipment were wedge and maul and axe, the former to make the entering crack and be driven home by a crashing blow from the maul, swung high and brought down hard, splitting the log from end to end. More wedges were needed for a large trunk. The halves were wedged and split several more times, the rails finished off with a heavy axe.

Abraham Lincoln had the physical attributes to make him an excellent railsplitter so that, although he excelled at a good many other things and was not at all fond of hard work, it was as a railsplitter that he became famous during his political campaign. There are still a few ancient, weathered rails in central Illinois whose owners swear were made by Lincoln himself; and, since he made more than ten thousand rails to fence prairie fields from Indiana to Illinois, it is not improbable that some might still exist.

During the year in which he and his family lived on a bleak farm near Decatur, Lincoln, working with his cousin, John Hanks, made some three thousand rails for Major William Warnick for which they were paid $2.50 a thousand. He cut 1,500 rails, it was said, just to pay for a home-made suit of clothes; for fence rails often took the place of currency. One of his Indiana neighbors, admiring his prowess in the woods, is quoted as saying: "Abe could sink an axe deeper in wood than any man I ever saw . . . could strike with a maul a heavier blow than any man."

Fences to civilize the wilderness, railsplitting to show the mettle of a man — these were two of the things which helped to build America. *(Feb. 1961)*

THE MILL ON THE PRAIRIE

In the early days of scattered settlement in Illinois, the mill was a sign of progress and of advancing civilization. It brought comforts to people who had had to provide for themselves everything they needed, or else had had to go without. The mill filled two big needs of pioneer settlers. Its heavy millstones ground hard corn into meal and the more scarce and precious wheat into the luxury of white flour. The mill was, besides, the machine which converted raw timber into boards. This was the type of combination mill which was built beside the Sangamon River in 1829 to become the nucleus of the village of New Salem, home of Abraham Lincoln in the 1830's.

These little isolated mills along the rivers gave pioneer women two of the things they wanted most in order to feel civilized—white flour for raised bread and light biscuits, and sawed boards to make a smooth floor instead of rough puncheons or hard-packed earth.

With this sort of progress a reality in the prairie village, a carding mill was the next step forward. It freed women of one more onerous task, that of hand-carding and cleaning the dirty, burr-infested wool of sheep which had foraged in a tangled countryside.

Sheep themselves, in fact, were a sign of progress; for only a few years earlier in Illinois it was almost impossible to raise sheep or have wool because of the wolves. In a decade, the people who now lived in New Salem had witnessed the clearing out of wolves, the success of sheep farming and the coming of a carding mill, so big that it reminded some of the thread mills back in New England and was as noisy in operation.

It was in the spring of 1835 that Samuel Hill, New Salem's most prosperous merchant, built the carding mill. When other businessmen failed in the uncertain fortunes of a prairie village perched on a bluff above an unnavigable river, Sam Hill had always prospered. His was the last successful store in the village; and, at a time when many people were leaving New Salem, he erected his big mill and made a success of that too.

In the *Sangamo Journal* of May 2, 1835, Hill advertised: "The machines are nearly new and in first rate order, and I do not hesitate to say, the best work will be done. Just bring your wool in good order, and there will be no mistake."

People came on horseback, in wagons and on foot with wool done up in sacks or in old petticoats fastened with locust thorns, until the big wool house was full. The machine with its great cylindrical, many-bristled combs thumped and growled all day as the yoke of oxen hitched to a forty-foot wheel tramped on the turntable back of the mill. This moved the great wooden cogs which operated the cylinders. Machinery was still operated solely by animal power. Through these cylinders, then, the dirty, matted wool passed and came out straight, ready to be washed and spun into yarn on the spinning wheels of Sangamon County.

Although the old mills have all vanished, the two at New Salem have been restored with the village. The saw and grist mill on the Sangamon and the carding mill in the village are built on their original sites. The carding mill is complete with wool house, turntable for the oxen, great wooden cogs and a genuine old carding machine installed inside as an example of the early stirrings of progress on the prairie. *(Feb. 1958)*

THE TRAILS AT NEW SALEM

Up on the hill is the village—New Salem as it looked more than a hundred years ago when the young Lincoln lived there. The village maintains an atmosphere of the past. Hens and geese wander in the yards; the log houses are outfitted with authentic pioneer furnishings; and behind the houses are herb gardens and vegetable plots planted as in the old days. It was from this peaceful place that Abe Lincoln, perhaps leaving the press of work, went down the hill to the valley, and took a footpath up into the deep woods on the next hill south. All around the New Salem hill crowded the woods, the heavily forested ravines, covered with big old oaks and the soft, leaf-mouldy earth that comes with long years of undisturbed woodland.

And the path that went up the hill was old, too—perhaps the Indians had made it—and led in rambling fashion toward the top. The school house was up there, and so was the New Salem burying ground. Lincoln may have walked that footpath often.

Today the trail in New Salem State Park is as alive as it was long ago when other footsteps trod the firm earth. Today from the picnic area beside the stream in the valley, where at dusk the whip-poor-wills set up a nightly serenade, the path leads into woods that are almost as untouched as they were in Lincoln's day.

The trail is built for easy climbing; it goes up a steep place, passes the old quarry where New Salem people once dug out rock for foundations and well shafts; over a solid rustic bridge under which a phoebe annually nests, and where chipmunks, with a scolding whistle, skitter out of sight.

The trail leads among the big oaks, up the ridge to the top. On the north the path goes down into a deeply shaded valley, through wild crab thickets that open just enough for a path to enter. Somewhere among the ferns the elusive song of the Kentucky warbler may be heard, or there may be a rare glimpse of a scarlet tanager or a friendly towhee. A little stream moves over a limestone bed, sometimes past boulders, sometimes between overhanging grass banks where self-heal and gerardia bloom in August. In the woods are blue skullcap and tall blue bellflower, great dusty-pink plumes of Joe-pye weed, tangles of yellowing bittersweet, and the delicate sprays of elm-leaved goldenrod.

The trail is one of the delights of a state park which is dedicated to capturing the spirit of the old days. This is well done in the hilltop village, but on the trail, perhaps even more deeply than in the village, there remains the atmosphere of pioneer Illinois.

New Salem State Park: 17 miles northwest of Springfield. Route 125 west to junction. Route 97 northwest to park. This is the site of the old road over which Lincoln rode or walked between New Salem and Springfield. The countryside—fields, farms, houses—still has that old, settled look. There are hills and deep woods just before the park entrance is reached. Return: Take route 97 to Petersburg, route 123 across the Sangamon east to route 29, thence south to Springfield. 28 miles. *(Aug. 1940)*

THE BUFFALO TRACE

By January, the old Buffalo Trace was frozen deeply under snow. The herds of buffalo, which had tramped so heavily across the prairie earth of Illinois that not even spring rains nor all the snows of winter could erase their trail, now grazed all winter long on bluegrass in Kentucky; a few went as far as Virginia and North Carolina. In spring, once more the buffalo in a tremendous herd trotted ponderously back to the Illinois Country.

The Buffalo Trace was more than a highway made by ancient bison whose popular name of buffalo christened their old trail. It was this same Trace which lured Daniel Boone over the Cumberland and into Kentucky, the Buffalo Trace which also was an Indian trail and later was known as the Wilderness Road.

Bison ages ago had found the easiest route over the southern mountains, there at Cumberland Gap, and followed the valley of the Cumberland River north through Kentucky to the Bluegrass, where those that had wintered no farther south than this joined the moving dark horde traveling north. The herds crossed the shallows of the Ohio near the present location of the city of New Albany and followed since time immemorial the customary route over and around the hills of southern Indiana. At Vincennes the

Trace forded the Wabash at the point where in 1830 the Lincoln family crossed into Illinois. The Buffalo Trace cut almost straight across Illinois. The highway of the buffalo is indelibly imprinted on the landscape of Illinois.

The herds pushed westward. They were moving to the lush grass of the Illinois prairies and the broad marshes of the American Bottom around East St. Louis; they surged westward now as directly as if they sensed the waters of the Mississippi and could not get there fast enough.

Mile after mile, year after year, the rumbling herds crossed the Trace. They carved a highway which later was followed by Indians who found it, as did the animals, the most direct way from the Wabash to the Mississippi. Later still, white men used it as the route between Louisville and Cahokia. From 1805 to 1824, it was a route followed by post riders carrying mail across the wet prairie. Then it became a stage route. (*Jan. 1953*)

HUBBARD'S TRACE

In 1818, when John Jacob Astor and the American Fur Company set trading posts at strategic points of the middle north, Gurdon S. Hubbard of Vermont was sent to man the post in Illinois. It was a wild country, that section south of the tip of Lake Michigan, an area of glacial moraines and flowery swamps, a land dominated by the Potawatomi whose numbers were still strong enough and great enough to command respect. Astor encouraged his young men to be friendly with the Indians; they brought in more and finer furs if the traders were friendly. To win even more favor with the native customers upon whom his own success depended, Hubbard married a Potawatomi girl, Watch-e-kee, niece of Chief Tamin. The Potawatomi no doubt beamed and brought in all their best and most glossy pelts.

With his bales of furs, Gurdon Hubbard blazed a trail for his packhorses from his post at Danville to the trading post of Fort Dearborn which later became Chicago. The laden horses of his packtrain stumbled in the muddy ruts of spring and snuffled the dust of summer or struggled to cross the flooding Kankakee when spring freshets put it out of its banks. Later the wheels of his wagons cut deeply into the glacial drift and carved a road which ever afterward has been marked firmly on the contours of Illinois.

The river crossing at Kankakee often presented problems to pioneer travelers on Hubbard's Trace. It was in November, 1830, that he feared he might not make it across with his load and reach his market at Fort Dearborn. The wagon was a heavy, large-box Pennsylvania wagon, just right for a boat. Hubbard chinked the box with snow, over which water was poured. This soon froze and made the wagon water-tight. Into this the harness, blankets, utensils, and goods were placed. The men climbed in and paddled their make-shift boat across. The horses swam in the rushing, cold waters and with wild eyes dodged the floating ice.

Three years earlier Gurdon Hubbard made a wild ride from Fort Dearborn to his home base at Danville. He was a Paul Revere of the Illinois

Country—the Winnebago were rising against the whites, and word had come that Fort Dearborn was about to be attacked. Young Gurdon Hubbard mounted his horse and rode all afternoon and all that night, and reached Danville nearly one hundred and thirty miles away by the next day.

"The Indians are coming!" he cried, and a force of fifty men grasped their firearms and mounted their horses to return to Fort Dearborn with the nearly exhausted messenger. But the Winnebago must have learned of the coming reinforcements, or perhaps they never had intended to attack. They signed a truce and Fort Dearborn and its rescuers celebrated with an all-night drinking bout—all except Gurdon Hubbard who couldn't stay awake for the festivities.

Hubbard's Trace, now well marked as Route One in eastern Illinois, was voted by the State Legislature of 1833-34 as a State Road. From Danville to Chicago it follows the exact route and comes into the Big City as determinedly now as it did when Hubbard's half-wild hogs were driven to market or his fifty packhorses loaded with furs plodded to the fort and followed, as the highway does today, up the busy thoroughfare which became State Street. (*June 1953*)

THE GREAT SAUK TRAIL

When Indians of the Great Lakes region learned from trappers and traders that there was considerable profit to be had from furs, the Great Sauk Trail came into existence. The Sauk in their stronghold at Rock Island brought in furs which they had collected from their traps all winter, pelts which were prime and thick and glossy; and when great quantities had been accumulated, groups of braves set out with their packs of pelts. The route was almost straight east across Illinois, thence over upper Indiana, and into Michigan to the trading post of Detroit where the furs were sold.

In consequence, the Sauk Trail became one of the best traveled and most definite of trails in the northern part of the state. It was used by Black Hawk, for years the leader of the British band of Sauk, who led his people over the trail and onward to Fort Malden, Amherstberg, Canada, there to receive annuities from the "British father," for services in the War of 1812. Even after the Sauk were sent out of Illinois after their terrible defeat at the Battle of Bad Axe in 1832, their old trail continued to be the path which led men from Rock Island's young village to the growing settlement of Fort Dearborn, later to become Chicago. The last Indians to leave Illinois (Potawatomi) left by the Great Sauk Trail in 1837.

The years went on and the Indian trail became a road, the main route of covered wagons going westward into Iowa. There went trappers and traders, missionaries and soldiers, all that restless surge of westward-going pioneers seeking homes elsewhere. Many of them crossed the Mississippi at Clark's Ferry to Buffalo, Iowa. This great influx of people caused early land speculators to dream of a great city on the site of the village of Andalusia nearby. Elaborate maps and plats of the city-to-be were intended to halt some of the thousands of westward-going travelers on the Sauk Trail. When the bubble burst, the tide of men still moved westward near this point on the great river.

The Sauk Trail grew more renowned. Men of the gold rush used it. Abraham Lincoln is said to have traveled a distance over it. Abolitionists from New England, hurrying west to Kansas, used the Trail as their quickest route. Negro slaves escaping from Missouri to Indiana and Michigan traveled by night along the route of the old Indian fur trail.

Today the Great Sauk Trail has lost the character of the path which was beaten clear by the moccasined feet of Indians carrying furs to Detroit. The rumbling wheels of Conestoga wagons are gone forever. There are no frightened slaves slipping through the protective darkness along this route. The old path no longer is clear on the map, although the modern highways crossing Illinois in part still follow the old trail. From Rock Island to Geneseo on Route U. S. 6 the highway evidently keeps to the original path. Beyond that it is vague, although it may pass through Troy Grove below Mendota, and just south of Joliet. Routes 52 and 30 apparently follow the old trail eastward through Chicago Heights. Six miles eastward, the old Sauk Trail and its modern counterpart cross the boundary of Illinois. (*April 1953*)

ILLINOIS AND THE TRAIL OF TEARS

Andrew Jackson hated Indians, and his successor in the White House, little Martin Van Buren, was eager to follow in the precepts of the great Jackson by also hating Indians and doing his bit to get them out of the growing union of States. No State, he argued, waving his white hands in indignation, could achieve proper culture, civilization, and progress in safety as long as Indians were permitted to remain. And so it happened that in 1838 the Cherokees were sent away in a mighty exodus from their ancestral lands in the Great Smoky Mountains of North Carolina and Tennessee, and from Alabama and from Georgia which was, perhaps, the greatest stronghold of the Cherokee Nation.

The Cherokees were civilized Indians; perhaps they were more civilized than some of their persecutors. The Cherokees had had the advantage of possessing a great teacher in Sequoyah, who created for his people an alphabet by which every Cherokee could learn to read his own language. Most of the Nation were devout Christians; they possessed fine ministers of the gospel, teachers, and leaders.

The deadline came. Soldiers ousted the stunned people unceremoniously from their homes, gathered them into stockades, and started them on the long, weary trail westward to a new homeland in Arkansas and Oklahoma territory. Everyone had to go—everyone, the blind, the very old, the very young, those who were born on the trail itself, the strong and wise, the weak and mentally deficient, the grief-stricken women, the wailing children, the tight-lipped men. Georgia wanted no more Indians lurking behind the white settlements. The vastnesses of the Great Smokies, too, must be cleared out; but the Smokies were a wilderness and some of the Cherokees stayed so well hidden in ancient forests and laurel-covered heights that no white soldiers could ferret them out.

Because of the distress and misery suffered in the stockades, the Cherokees requested permission to move under the direction of their own chiefs, promising to guarantee discipline.* Thirteen detachments of the homeless and hopeless Cherokees, each under the leadership of a native conductor, started off in the autumn of 1838. Hundreds died along the way; thousands, finally, perished. They climbed the Cumberland Plateau and passed through Nashville, and went north through Hopkinsville, Kentucky, and crossed on Berry's Ferry, formerly Lusk's, over the Ohio to Golconda, Illinois. The cavalcade of wagons, carriages, horsemen, and plodding people seemed to never have an end, so many thousands were there always coming, and they often met unkindness and cruelty along the way. Illinois was not hospitable to the refugees. A large group of the migrant people once cut wood and pitched tents in three different spots before they were allowed by farmers to rest there for the night.

And when the Trail of Tears led the Cherokees through southern Illinois, they came at last to Union County where the ridges rise high from the Mississippi flood plain. There they found the Mississippi flooding and choked with massive ice floes. The people could not cross. Spread out along the trail in smaller camp groups, 8,000 Cherokees camped for two weeks while they waited for the ice-filled river to clear so they could cross to their new lands beyond. It was a terrible winter, even for southern Illinois, and disease struck heavily. In those two desperate weeks of helpless waiting in an unfriendly, frigid, and wintery land, two thousand of the weakened Cherokees died and were buried near that old camping place.

The town of Wetaug commemorates a group of Cherokees who camped for a while during that winter in southern Illinois. A marker indicates the spot where the great gathering encamped more than a hundred years ago. It is reached on highway 146 near Ware in Union County, Illinois, not far from Union County State Forest. For many of the displaced people, the Trail of Tears ended for them in Illinois. (*Jan. 1954*)

* Thompson, Scerial, "The Cherokee Cross Egypt," *Journal of the Illinois State Historical Society,* Winter, 1951.

THE BLUFFS ROAD

There is a part of Illinois, a comparatively small section of the Illinois River valley, where the work of the post-glacial period stands today as a monument to that ancient efficiency. The receding glacier once sent torrents of water down the main river valleys—down what is today the Mississippi, the Ohio, the Illinois—and created huge flood plains that are occupied by the smaller streams of today. In some places vast lakes spread out over the country. In the Illinois river valley there was water from the hills to the west to the hills on the east.

Here, when the waters receded, vast stretches of mud-flat were left, where myriads of water-birds came down to feed. As the prevailing western winds blew year after year across the growing waste of drying mud, the yellowish dust and the sand that the glacier had dropped were carried and deposited on the low outcropping of limestone bordering the one-time eastern boundary of the lake. Year after year, century after century, the yellow-brown soil piled up, packed down, finally formed pyramidal hills of great size—great, that is, in contrast to the prairies which stretched in all directions beyond. The hills, with their bottom slopes grading into each other, were composed of a soil called loess which stands in vertical cuts for long periods without washing away.

Today the hills still stand, and the old burial mounds on top still give up the bones of a prehistoric people and their possessions, preserved in that queer, packy, brown soil which gives bones a reddish patina. These were the people somewhat loosely called Mound Builders, who later were succeeded by their descendents now known as Indians.

Today, perhaps a trifle more worn, a trifle less steep, the bluffs lie in a wide curve east of the Illinois river, and a graveled road, hewn out of the sides of the hills, midway between top and bottom, takes the traveler into the heart of this unique country.

The road goes west out of Arenzville, a small, Central Illinois hilltown with something of the flavor of New England in its quiet streets and old houses. The town lies well away from any paved highway, but can be reached by taking route 67 west of Virginia, and turning south on the "blacktop" road just east of Beardstown.

The bluffs road goes down the hill and across a creek just west of Arenzville and follows the curve of the range of hills which lie like huge, supine animals, covered in winter with the tawny, sun-burnt prairie grass. There are big prosperous farms astride the road and broad fields in the bottoms, a vast, flat patchwork of greening winter wheat, bleached corn-stalks, and rich black soil. A far-away edge of trees means the river. On the hills that tower above the road stand heavy forest, terraced pastureland, a scattering of native red cedars.

In summer countless satiny barn swallows swoop across the road or perch on the wires. In winter brilliant cardinals flash into the weeds. Big grey marsh hawks beat slowly back and forth low over the winter fields. Flocks of ducks move out of the western sky, and in the horseweeds tree sparrows tinkle and chant. Perhaps an eagle soars inland from the river.

Winter and summer, the bluffs road has a strange and haunting charm. It is always different, always a pleasure, from its beginning at Arenzville, to its end at a junction with route 100 east of Meredosia and the river. (*Dec. 1940*)

THE FRUIT HILLS

Spring comes earlier in southern Illinois than in the central and northern counties; and so folk who live to the northward may have a foretaste of spring late in March or early in April merely by following U. S. Route 51 to Carbondale and beyond, down into Little Egypt. On the way, spring seems to grow, as if one moved bodily through the calendar. Peach trees may be bare and cold in the north; past the middle of the state they may be studded with coral buds, but in the southern tier of counties the small trees are in full, crisp, pink bloom. Violets by this time have burst into bloom; spring garden flowers are at their best; forsythia and iris are blossoming; leaves visibly increase on the trees. The pear trees blossom; the redbuds change from a dull purple-red haze to bright pink-purple; the willows drape fragile golden greenery along the streams. Magnolias open their waxen, rose-purple and white cups and fill the air with perfume.

Past Carbondale the south is at its loveliest. Mile after mile over the high hills extend the orchards, acre after acre in pleasant, methodical rows. They start at the edge of the highway and pass up and over the horizon. Here is spring. No matter what happens to spoil the magnolias and peach trees in the north, the traveller will have seen spring. The hills are high and full of color; the air is warm; mockingbirds sing along the fences. Down in the cypress swamps a haze of pale green comes over the ragged trees; vultures are back and sail in vast, slow sweeps over the cottonfields.

Here in Egypt the Old South maintains its hold. Here are the gracious, balconied houses, the southern magnolias, wild holly, tupelo, and winterberry, and even, rarely and accidentally, a wisp or two of southern Spanish moss. Resurrection ferns upholster the trunks of great trees; mistletoe grows in dark bunches in the treetops.

The Mississippi winds its never-settled route down and around the tip of Illinois and joins the broad Ohio at Cairo. Further inland the Cache River bottoms, once the biggest swamp north of Virginia, long ago provided a hiding place for fugitive slaves and renegades. Little Egypt lies just across the rivers from Kentucky and Missouri, and in spirit is much like them. It all but seceded from the Union when the War Between the States found southern sympathies here. But Illinois somehow stayed together and southern Illinois became the buffer between North and South. At Cairo, Grant had his headquarters, and here troops were loaded and unloaded, prisoners brought or exchanged, slaves helped to safety. Today southern Illinois is still more southern than northern, still a land apart.

Perhaps this is because it is set away from the rest of the state by that high range of fruit-hills, a spur of the Ozarks, blossoming pink and white. Suddenly out of the flatland the uplands rise to the heights, and between Ullin and Carbondale the country is a vast upheaval of hills. The fruited ridge of Illinois is rocky and wild, high and rugged, the unspoken boundary between north and south, where spring comes early and peach and apple paint a splendid landscape and fill the air with the scent of blossoms and of April. (*March 1941*)

OXBOW COUNTRY

Prairie streams are a cantankerous lot. Instead of following their ancestral channels, as rock-bound rivers do, the prairie rivers sometimes leap out of their old banks and cut a new channel. There is no certainty from one year to the next about a prairie stream's route. It may be the same as it was ten years ago, or it may be very different, and the country through which it now flows may wear a bulldozed look and the raw appearance of having gone through a minor cataclysm. They all do it, little Bear Creek or Sugar Creek or Elk Creek, the Sangamon and the Illinois, and the Mississippi most freely of all.

It is the larger rivers in their moods of self expression which have made the oxbow country. This is a loose term; still, there must be some designation of this area. The prairie rivers usually travel in winding fashion down the state; they seldom flow very far in a straight line, but continually turn and twist on themselves, so that a boat must go many times the distance it might if the stream was straight and to the point. In time of flood, the larger rivers sometimes burst across the neck of one of the bends, cutting a new channel, and when the waters go down again and summer comes steamily over the land, the old channel has become a curving lake which is deserted by the river. Because of the shape, the old channels left when the river cuts a new one are called oxbox lakes. Such a lake may last a long time. In its quieter waters lotuses sometimes spring up and in a few years may fill the lake so that there is no water left. When it becomes too dry for lotuses, they die, and soon the area is full of smartweed and horseweed and wild sunflowers and willows. And that is the end of the oxbow country in that particular spot.

But sometimes the lakes last longer. There is a certain amount of inflowing water. Fish live here and frogs sing lustily every evening in spring. The clicking of cricket frogs on a summer night reaches deafening proportions, and in autumn the barred owls and horned owls "hoo-hoo" in a weird chant. The trees along the lake are usually huge old soft maples and sycamores, and here may nest the great blue herons and night herons and the owls themselves. Raccoons sleep all day in hollows. Sometimes the great red and black pileated woodpeckers chisel huge rectangular boxes in the trees, and crows gather in noisy roosts for the night.

The oxbow country is a wild land, cut off from the more familiar course of the river. It stagnates as a backwater land and reverts, more often than not, to a wilder wilderness than it was before. It has a stark look in winter—gaunt trees, snags of stumps in the shore water, ice forming around the edges, muskrats smacking their tails among the ghosts of lotus stalks, shy teal feeding on the submerged lotus seeds, and canvasbacks further out. Perhaps geese come here, and an eagle may have a perch on a lofty dead sycamore that died when the river, that wild day in spring long ago, changed its course and made a lake. (*Nov. 1948*)

THIS IS THE ILLINOIS PRAIRIE

The prairie lay in the sun, a vast, open barrier between the security of the East and the winning of the West. It was the product of coal-forest, glacier, and earthquake, damp, black soil covered for miles with waving thick grasses, many of them six to eight feet tall, and with occasional vast islands of forest in the sea of green. It had once been the bottom of post-glacial marshes, and something of that old character clung.

As the summer came on, white orchids and wild roses bloomed for miles, the scent of ripe strawberries was heavy in the warm sun, and there were prairie clover, rattlesnake master, blue spiderwort, golden acres of mustard, pink trefoil, and wild onion all in blossom. It was no wonder that the explorers noticed these flowers on the old prairie. There were none like them back home in the well-settled East.

Late summer, and the prairie was yellow with rosin weed and prairie dock, with millions of sunflowers and tickseeds, and with always the waving tall grass of the wet prairie. A certain prairie grass, today known as Andropogon, is recognized by its coppery pink stems that stand brightly above the snow on those few spots where prairie soil remains untouched.

Only scant areas of the prairie have never felt the bite of the plow. Much of this original area is found along railroad right-of-ways, especially where the highway parallels the railroad. The famous Bates Experimental Road west of Springfield shows an excellent example of untouched original prairie.

This indeed is the last stand of the prairie. Here are the prairie plants, the virile grasses, still holding their own yet now only a remnant of what they once were. In this narrow strip of land, however, a surprising number of prairie animals and birds also make their home. Here is the burrowing crayfish, the striped ground squirrel, the grey spermophile, and hordes of grasshoppers and the sun-loving insects of the prairie. Birds are characteristic. Not robins and thrushes and Carolina wrens, but the sun-loving birds which sing when most other birds are silent in the heat. Here is the indigo bunting, the meadowlark, the dickcissel, yellowthroat, goldfinch, grasshopper sparrow, and field sparrow, most of them nesting on or near the ground. The prairie horned lark, killdeer, upland plover, and vesper sparrow have adapted themselves from the short-grass prairie to the plowed fields and well-cropped pastures. And over it all sails the intrepid, marsh hawk whose ancestors knew the wet prairie which once lay here undisturbed.

"To make a prairie it takes a clover
And one bee,
And revery.
And revery alone will do,
If bees are few."

                              Emily Dickinson. *(June 1940)*

THE ILLINOIS PRAIRIE

Now the remnants of the Illinois prairie are bright with the sunflowers native to its deep, matted, black soil, and once again the question of why these plants are here comes forward to be answered. The Illinois prairie— why was it here, and why were there so many plants in it native much farther west and south.

It happened between 2000 and 4000 years ago, but background for the prairie took place long before that. A forerunner was that time which came near the end of the pleasantly mild Pliocene Age. The climate was changing.

Years grew progressively cooler. There were cooler summers, shorter summers; colder winters, longer winters; snows which had not time to melt . . . and the Pleistocene Epoch arrived with the growth of ice caps in the north. It was the shorter summers which evidently had the greatest influence in producing the coming Ice Age. The deep snows which had become a common thing in the cooling north had no chance to melt very much during the short, chilly summers. The snow packed deeper, many feet deep, and the lower parts changed to larger crystals, and the lowermost parts became ice—glacial ice. Pressure of each winter's snows on top started movement in the lower sections. The snowfields in the north became a moving glacier. And still the snows fell and still the shortened summers were not warm enough to halt the moving ice.

The Pleistocene lasted a million years. In that time there were four major glacial periods with pleasantly mild, interglacial periods between. It was a time which influenced Illinois tremendously . . . influenced the shape of the landscape . . . influenced the kinds of plants which grew there . . . influenced those which grow here today.

Life existed almost in the shadow of the glacier. The temperature was not excessively low; abundant moisture both from the melting ice edge and the climatic humidity, the heavy rains and snows produced by the atmosphere attending glacial ice, made a climate which, south of the glacier, fostered living things. The wall of ice looming in the north was always there during the glacial periods. Not far south of the moraine being deposited by the melting ice there were low, evergreen-leaved plants of the tundra (cranberries, cottony sedge, Labrador tea, crowberry), and beyond that were dwarf willows and low birches. The next zone of plants growing in the cold, wet boggy soil contained tamaracks and black spruces, and, as the land grew drier and the climate farther away from the glacier was milder, the bog trees and flowers gave way to pine and hemlock forests, and then to deciduous trees. As the glacier moved south, forests and tundra were destroyed. As the ice melted backward, the plant zones came back in sequence. In the absence of the ice during interglacial periods, Illinois was heavily forested, sometimes with balsam and spruce and white pine, sometimes with deciduous trees.

Illinois was essentially a forested state; its climate was that of forest country.

But when the last ice sheet retreated into Canada and came no more into Illinois, and when Illinois once again was forested, something happened. Illinois then was a moist land filled with shallow lakes created by glacier water. Vegetation had grown around the rims of many of these lakes until they were marshes. But now that change took place which caused the prairie in Illinois. No one knows the exact date, but it is believed to have occurred comparatively recently, between 2000 and 4000 years ago. A great drouth at that time came over the northern hemisphere and sent endlessly hot winds blowing over Illinois. The broad, marshy lakes grew more shallow, and the marsh plants were replaced by a new, foreign vegetation. Spartina grasses came in—Spartina, the prairie indicator. Prairie plants from the southwest appeared. Oaks from southwest of Illinois replaced the beeches and maples and pines on Illinois hills. Still the hot winds blew. The marsh soil became black, dense, matted with roots which did not decay. Prairie land had developed in Illinois.

This kind of soil and its peculiar vegetation apparently was out of place in the climate of Illinois, which was tempered toward supporting deciduous forests. Now because of the heat and drouth, large areas in Illinois lost their forests and for miles across the glacier-smoothed landscape the prairies took their place. Prairie plants, principally certain grasses, legumes, and composites, blossomed in the deep black soil, and Spartina, ten feet tall in the wettest places, waved its plumes in the hot winds. That was the prairie. It would remain virtually unchanged until the steel plows came and broke the ancient postglacial soil. Prairie soil when it was plowed lost the qualities which made it prairie soil and changed into black farmland where corn and soybeans grow luxuriantly today. (*Sept. 1950*)

WET PRAIRIE

There are few spots more significant of the past than the chance locations of wet prairie in Illinois. These are relics; they remain like living fossils in a world not part of them.

Once there were miles of wet prairie; it dominated much of central Illinois in particular and extended far south and north in the state, in large areas dominated by the plants, animals, and birds which were an integral part of this particular kind of landscape. It was especially the plants which were indicative of wet prairie—it was these, the tall marsh grasses, over which a man on foot could not see, and in which a man on horseback had a hard time following a trail.

When cultivation came to Illinois, the wet prairie departed. Tiles were laid, ditches dug; water was drained. The dry sod was burned and plowed.

It was an extraordinarily heavy sod, one made up of a foot or so of densely matted grass and other roots, generations of them which did not decay. Trees did not grow here because tree seeds when they germinated could never penetrate that tremendous texture of living and dead roots in the black prairie soil. But now when the moisture was gone and the sod was dry and the steel plows came at last, the wet prairie became extinct. It was gone utterly and completely, as utterly and completely as the mammoths and mastodons were gone. Yet not quite. Here and there—not much, just a little, a corner triangle where several roads met, a spot beside a railroad embankment, a never-plowed section between cornfield and country road— bits of the wet prairie clung to the present. They are there today.

The wet prairie is descended from a swamp and the swamp from a lake; hence, the wet prairie has water-loving plants. Moisture remains around their roots—moisture which began back in postglacial days when the ice left broad lakes which became swamps. Here today are the fountaining narrow leaves and eight-foot-tall plumes of Spartina grass, always the sign of wet prairie: it is the signpost. There are sedges with brown tops; there are the stout plants of Sullivant's milkweed which is distinguishable from common milkweed by having broad blue-green leaves conspicuously veined with pink, with a great thick pink midrib. There may be psoralea with its purple pea flowers, and some of the tall silphiums whose place is rightfully on the dry prairie. And there may be cattails, showing even more than the Spartina does that this is kin to a marsh. And there very likely will be a pair of redwinged blackbirds shrilling on a nearby road guard or wires, and there may be a nest down in the dense sea of Spartina leaves or sedges. Prairie crayfish burrow in the black soil.

Multiply this little spot by hundreds of miles like it; multiply the grasses by millions of plumes of Spartina higher than a man; multiply the birds by hundreds of pairs of redwings and hundreds of nests in the sedges. Multiply the milkweeds and the prairie crayfish and there comes into focus a picture of the wet prairie as it once extended for miles through Illinois. That was a long time ago, long before steel plows and railroads and highways. The wet prairie was here when the pioneers of Lincoln's time came up from Kentucky, but it was not many years after that that the primeval prairie began to wane, to disappear. All but those relicts in road-corners and along tracks, remnants of wet prairie, placarded by Spartina and made musical by blackbirds. (*Aug. 1949*)

ILLINOIS, 1776

It was July 4, 1776, in the Illinois country. It was hot and humid, and the fever-and-ague season was getting underway in the cabins along the Mississippi and the Wabash. No one here knew what was happening in Philadelphia that day. News was a long time traveling to the wilderness west of the Alleghenies, and it mattered very little anyway to the people of the Illinois Country that this day in July was to become vitally important in history. They did not know that Thomas Jefferson's Declaration of Independence, after many days of wrangling, finally had been voted for by the delegates of the thirteen colonies. Illinois had had no voice in the matter; it would not become one of the United States until forty-two years later. On July 4, 1776, Illinois was a British possession and was part of the vast Northwest Territory. It was generally considered to be an unpleasant malarial wilderness peopled by degenerate savages, apathetic French, bored British army personnel who wanted to go home, and a few traders, missionaries, and others.

Illinois in 1776 still was almost the same as it had been since the earliest days of the Indians before Columbus' discovery. There had been little cutting of the forests, little change in its appearance. Southern Illinois was chiefly heavy forest, both on the hills and in the wild bottomlands. North to what later became Peoria and Rock Island, it was a vast prairie covered with tall turkey-foot grass in the dry places and with waving Spartina in the marshes, with great islands of forest standing green on the summer prairie. North and east the prairies spread in an almost unbroken stretch, except for forests along the rivers and a wilderness in the northwest hills where the Sauk and Fox Indians had their strongholds.

By July the prairies were bright with yellow Silphiums and sunflowers, with coneflower and blue spiderwort. In the bison herds small calves followed their mothers along the well-trodden trails to the mudholes and river shores. Prairie chickens led their families of small young chicks trailing through the tall grass and, with a bravado acquired in a few short weeks in the prairie world, catching fat grasshoppers. Wild turkeys in the forests clucked to their young and guarded them from foxes at night.

The summer night was quiet in 1776. For miles upon miles there were no people; only the owls talked, and there were whip-poor-wills, the endless chittering of insects, the yowling of a panther in the hills. There were few white settlements—only the French at Kaskaskia, Cahokia, and Chartres, some at the trading posts at Chicago and Massac, a few at Galena, trappers' cabins scattered lonesomely here and there. In those days Kaskaskia along the Mississippi across from Sainte Genevieve was the capital. After the British had taken over the Illinois Country and the French civil government was removed, the British had been slow in sending their own officers. Even after a lieutenant governor was appointed for Kaskaskia to administer affairs of Illinois, he drew pay for six years and never appeared at his post. In 1776, morale in Illinois was low.

In Philadelphia, Benjamin Franklin and Thomas Jefferson and the others mopped their brows and wished the session could be finished before the heat got the better of them all.

In Vincennes, General Henry Hamilton was completing his plans to send the Indians against the settlers on the frontier. Shortly, the calm in Illinois was to be shattered. Illinois cabins would be attacked day or night, the people killed or carried off, cabins burned, scalps brought to Henry Hamilton. The general paid for scalps, white or Indian. The year 1777 was to be known as the Bloody Year in the Illinois Country; 1776 was the prelude.

The champion of Illinois, George Rogers Clark, meanwhile, was off defending Kentucky and begging the Virginia legislature to make Kentucky a county of Virginia as protection against Indian attack. Presently destiny would send him to Kaskaskia and Vincennes where he would do more than any one person to free Illinois from foreign rule and Indian marauders.

But this still was 1776, a dull year. Perhaps the only industries operating at that time were the tanneries near Fort Massac along the Ohio, the salt works along the Saline River, the lead diggings at Galena. Leather, salt, and lead—they were three significantly vital products which soon would play their part in the coming struggle of Illinois in the American Revolution. As yet no one was much concerned about the war. The malaria season was causing more discomfort than the prelude to freedom. No one knew or cared about that priceless parchment which at that moment was being signed in Convention Hall at Philadelphia. All that came later. *(July 1948)*

THE WINTER ROCK

Midwinter, and Starved Rock is alone; the charm of winter is missed by those who visited the Rock in June. Here in January there is a vastness, a quiet majesty, a greater sense of timelessness of rock and water than summer offers. The canyons echo with a single bird-call; the Rock itself stands somberly above the ice-choked river where mergansers sit like penguins on the floes. The aged, gnarled cedars on the cliffs are the only touch of color, and they are almost black. Nature may be gentle in summer, when so many people walk the canyon trails that no bird or chipmunk knows privacy, but in winter it is as wild, as aloof from human contact, as it was a thousand years ago. A heavy fall of snow stands unmarked by any human foot—deep, pure, and light, just as it fell, flake by flake, in the night. Now the sky has cleared to a brilliant, clear blue that shines in contrast to a white world, and up against the color sail white gulls, like moths, on black-tipped, immovable wings. An eagle comes flying over the Rock, passes it, soars over the river and the forests to the south.

There are no trails in the snow. We must make our own path. It is as if we, first of all white men, had found this new land and now explored it for the first time. We climb the Rock, look out from the top—out across the valley to the hills beyond, and then descend south on the steep slope. Trees are motionless in the clear, cold air—air that, without wind, loses the sensation of cold. It is exhilarating, exciting to breathe, but it is not cold.

The blueberry bushes that jut and sprangle from the rocks are brilliant in the snow; their red twigs and little coral buds gleam in a blur of color. A chickadee hangs upside down on a witchhazel bush, whose seed capsules are empty now. A downy woodpecker drums loudly in the silence; a brown creeper squeaks from a tree-trunk, and in a tangled cedar kinglets flit about, puffed in the winter air, oblivious of cold.

On the sheltered, sunny side of a stream, where the roots of a white pine grip the overhanging bank, the snow has melted. The earth is soft and moist, and the shallow water runs clear and amber-colored over the sand. And look! A robin runs on the warm shore, pecks under leaves and into the earth for food. A robin, in January!

The path rises sharply above the stream, frozen now in the shadow. Around the bend where rock walls rise high, there is the suggestion of a path, knee-deep in unmarked snow, which leads into the silent halls of French Canyon. A gull screams overhead, up beyond the pines at the top. And at the far end of the canyon there hangs a great, many-colored sheet of ice, an ice-fall where water has been.

The dripping water freezes slowly in a multitude of separate icicles, which fuse, merge, yet stand distinct and apart from each other. The colors of iron in the water, and the reflection of the sky, and the green pines above, bring out an illusion of rainbow beauty in the ice. It is pale green; it is pale yellow; it is white; it is russet, with icicles of tea-color, lavender, a suggestion of blue, and brown, and red. The great mass hangs against brown walls upholstered with pale green-white lichen powder and green liverworts. A squirrel coughs on the upper rim, and with a scattering of bark under scurrying claws, runs up a pine, and flings itself in one mad, magnificent leap to a tree on the other side. Then silence again—that ageless quiet of trees and snow and rocks. This is Starved Rock in winter. (*Jan. 1941*)

THE DESERTED DOORWAY

They came to the Illinois Country for many reasons and from many places, all those folk who were impelled by the urge to travel with a few of their precious possessions westward away from the settled places, west to Illinois. Some came by the Wilderness Road and the Buffalo Trace from the stony hills of Kentucky to the rich bottomlands of Illinois. Some came by flatboat and some by keelboat from West Virginia and Ohio, from New England and New York; some came by Conestoga wagon from Pennsylvania and Maryland; some on the little black-smoking railroads which were pushing out to Illinois after the '50's together with the immigrants from Europe.

For many reasons, by many people, Illinois became inhabited. And there were successes and there were failures. There sprang up many towns which lived for a while and then died. Some perished so completely that nothing marks their passing. New Salem disappeared. Sangamo Town disappeared. Nauvoo — Nauvoo *almost* vanished.

Part of this old town beside the Mississippi, the section lying in the bottoms, is almost as dead as the ruins of Egypt, but the upper portion of the town survived a varied history and is alive and prosperous. The long-empty houses of the lower town, however, depress the visitor with a nameless feeling of personal disaster. These were fine houses, prideful houses, homes which once sheltered families.

The Mormons drained the fever swamps in the bottoms and by strength of will and muscle had laid out the largest city in Illinois. Nauvoo was a community of 20,000 in the 1840's when no other town in the young state had attained such size and prosperity. Yet seven years later the fine brick houses were locked and deserted; and the people, having lost the religious freedom they thought they had found, sadly left their city and the strange temple on the hill and went to set up a new civilization in Utah territory outside the United States. The old town in the bottoms lay uninhabited. Even when the Icarians settled in the upper town and later were supplanted by others who made it a permanent settlement along the Mississippi, the lower town, as if too dreadfully haunted by the past, was little occupied. Today it is part of a state park. The empty doorways, mutely locking tragedy behind the blank mask of their weathering wood, stand along the broad streets more than a century after their owners went out and never returned. (*Sept. 1953*)

TEMPLE ON THE HILL

Higher and higher the leaping flames soared into the black sky, and now with a roar that was heard by the watchers across the river in Iowa, the limestone walls of the Mormon temple fell in a calcined heap. The flames went down, finally, and the stones, still hot after several days had passed, were all that remained of what had been the most magnificent edifice in Illinois.

It was October, 1848, and the Mormons, sent away from Illinois and forced to abandon their city called Nauvoo beside the Mississippi, were on their way to lands outside the United States—to Utah—when word came that the Temple had been destroyed. Hatred and lack of understanding of the Mormon people and their beliefs had culminated in a wilful firing of a Temple which had cost almost a million dollars and uncounted hours of cheerful labor given as a tithe by men of the Nauvoo community.

In 1839 the Mormons had come into Illinois in search of a place in which to build their city and live in peace. The Prophet, Joseph Smith, had heard about Galland's bog, up along the Mississippi north of Quincy and Keokuk, where the river flowed in a great crescent past a broad point of swampy land. Back of it rose a majestic hill, wild and wooded; in the bottoms was a small trading post and village called Commerce. There once had been an Indian village here, but now the Indians were gone. Land which no one else wanted was Joseph Smith's goal. He and his people bought Galland's bog and proceeded to drain it, lay out streets, build houses. There were epidemics of malaria, but finally the new city of Nauvoo rose along well-planned city blocks. In the days when Chicago was small and Springfield, the new capital, was a muddy village on the prairie, the city of Nauvoo had a population of 20,000 people who knew a higher standard of living than the majority of those who had come out to populate the raw state of Illinois.

On the hill looking far out over the city and across the beautiful river to the green shores of Iowa, the Temple grew. Limestone for its walls was quarried not far away in the bluffs. Fine timbers were hand hewn. There were three floors with many windows, a basement housing the baptismal font held by stone oxen, and a tall cupola holding a statue of the angel Moroni. Extending two stories high were thirty stone pilasters. The base of each was a stone bearing the figure of a crescent moon of great size. The capstone of each pilaster was a figure of a sun with a cryptic face surrounded by rays and topped with two hands holding trumpets. Above the sunstones were stones bearing stars.

And then the Mormons who erected it, after having used it only for a few months, were compelled to depart into the west, and the Temple was destroyed. A year later there came the French Icarians, a communal society who believed in a town based upon the common division of labor and possessions—"each one according to his ability." Under Etienne Cabet, these French people planned their town on the ruins of the Mormon city, built community buildings for sleeping, eating, and instruction. The Icarians were fascinated by the ruins of the Temple, and with great expense and work they began to build it up again.

Alfred H. Piquenard, who later was to design the Illinois state capitol building, was then a member of the Icarians; he was sent north to arrange for timber to restore the Temple to its old grandeur. But when the Temple was only partially rebuilt, a tornado swept across Iowa and the river and struck the Temple on the hill. And the roar of falling walls could be heard three miles away. Once again the Temple lay in ruins. The Icarians abandoned the project. They used some of the stones to build their community school house and other buildings, and the spot once occupied by the Temple lay full of weeds and debris. When the Icarian plan would not work and some of the community migrated into Iowa, there came into Nauvoo German immigrants who carried on the culture of wine grapes which the Icarians had bequeathed them. Blue cheese and wines—these are the products of peaceful Nauvoo today. The vineyards spread along the hills where once there was an Indian village, a Mormon city, a French communistic colony, and the present population which is largely descended from all these.

But there were portions of the Temple which remained undestroyed— the capstones and base stones, the stones of the sun and the moon. Still carrying their mysterious symbolism, some of them remained. Records of the whereabouts of most of them are meager, but it is known that in the hotel yard in Nauvoo there is a moon stone, and two more occupy the burial place of Joseph and Hyrum Smith and Joseph's wife, Emma. A well-preserved sunstone stands in Quincy, and another is in Springfield.

It was in 1870, when the new state capitol was being built, that samples of limestone and sandstone were sent to Springfield from various parts of the state for possible use in the new building. As a sample of Sonora quarry limestone in Hancock County, a sunstone was sent here, and perhaps because of this, much of the limestone used in the capitol building eventually came from that source. For a long time the old sunstone, still with its strange half-smile, was propped against the north side of the State House. Then it was hauled to the fairgrounds where it was placed at the west end of a small lagoon near the main entrance to the fairgrounds. A few years ago when the lagoon was removed, the sunstone was placed upon a concrete block and there it stands today, alone and without a marker, with no identification and in imminent danger of being toppled and cracked. During the days of the Illinois State Fair it is submerged in the sideshows and concessions.

Yet it is still a living, vivid reminder of days that are past, days in the story of Illinois which may have gone by with tragic finality, but which, in their vividness, must live forever. (*Sept. 1951*)

SANGAMO TOWN

Briefly the towns of men linger on the land. Some began as villages of great promise, and quickly died; others with weak beginnings grew great. And some, though they faded away, are remembered forever.

New Salem in Illinois was one of these, and another was old lost Sangamo Town on its hill above the river. Both were part of the life of Abraham Lincoln and the story of the Lincoln Country.

Stories are deeply bedded in the land on which Sangamo Town, seven miles northwest of Springfield, rested for a short time. Some 250 million years ago there was an ocean here, along whose shallow shores there lived myriads of small snails, clams, and corals. As these died, their shells drifted to the seabottom and there, over millions of years, blackish limestone formed in which the shells and bodies were fossilized. Finally the seas went away. After a very long time there was a swampy fern forest in the region which laid down a thin layer of coal.

Time moved on. There were eons of change. Glaciers came out of the north, engulfed the region, and retreated. Now broad lakes lay in the level lands; the Sangamon River, wide and rapid, perpetually gnawed at its hills until the river bed was down to the old layer of black limestone.

The Carolina wren sang along the wild shore, and a great blue heron, early in the morning, came silently along the sunlit river and stopped on the rocks to fish. Soft maples and giant sycamores grew along the shore, and up the slope were oaks and redbuds and hosts of spring flowers.

Indians hunted here. The Kickapoos may have come from Kickapoo Town to the north, and there may have been others, for many arrowheads were left on the uplands. Then the Indians went away and on a hot June day in 1824, when the Illinois Country still was raw and uncompromising, a new village was incorporated on the hill above the river. The village was called Sangamo, or sometimes Sangamo Town, and four years later it was said to be more pretentious and to have more true promise than the ugly little village of Springfield seven miles away.

Sangamo Town was located on the hill above the rocky section in the river where fossil snails and corals forever weather out of the limestone. This place was known as Roll's Ford because in the early days of Sangamo Town one Pearson Roll owned land on the other shore and used the rocky bottom as a sure-footed crossing for wagon or horse. From the ford, a winding road went up the hill to the village, where there was a grist mill, a cemetery, a carding mill, a doctor, several merchants, a public square, and streets. A sawmill beside the river stood on a jutting point—the only sawmill for miles around.

It was because of the mill and the abundance of good timber that a young man named Abraham Lincoln, with two companions, came here by canoe from Decatur, in the spring of 1831, to build a flatboat for Denton Offut. Offut wanted a good, solid, large boat to haul hogs and other produce down to New Orleans.

Lincoln and the others worked for six weeks on the flatboat and camped in a shanty on the river bank. Lincoln was cook, though sometimes he deserted and went to dinner in homes of the villagers who liked to hear his stories and his comments on current politics.

When the boat was finished—80 feet long and 18 feet wide—most of the villagers gathered at the shore to watch the launching. A good crowd climbed aboard among the squealing hogs and the piles of barrels, and rode downstream as far as Lemon's Bend, 2½ miles below Sangamo Town.

But at New Salem a few miles away, the flatboat stuck on Rutledge's mill dam, and before the craft could proceed, Lincoln had to bore a hole in the bottom to let the water out. The flatboat eased off the dam and went on to the Mississippi and down to New Orleans.

The days of Lincoln and of flatboats on the Sangamon have vanished. The faint mark he left on Sangamo Town was not enough to keep it alive. The river one spring washed away the sawmill; the log houses fell down, and the streets and gardens filled with cockleburs. Less than ten years after the village was incorporated, Sangamo Town had vanished.

But today along the Sangamon there still is a bed of blackish limestone that provides a ford across the river, and the fossil snails still weather out and lie in the flats. A Carolina wren still sings along the wild and wooded shore, the heron still comes at dawn to fish at the ford, the sycamores still grow white and huge. Still, up the wooded hill there winds the ghost of a wagon trail that may be all that visibly remains of Sangamo Town—the trail that evidently went from the village to the sawmill, and to the ford where Pearson Roll used to cross when the river would let him. (*Feb. 1946*)

GREEK CLASSIC ON THE PRAIRIE

It was raw, undeveloped prairie, the Sangamo Country, a slough of mud in spring, hot, dusty, and weedy in summer, deep with snow in winter. The earliest settlers who came here were rough pioneers and trappers; few stayed very long in one place. But in the first quarter of the 19th century there came Kentuckians, not all of whom were cabin people, who were determined to rise above mud-chinked cabins and bring culture to the prairie.

In 1818 Illinois was made a state. Not long afterward the Kelley brothers from North Carolina built a log cabin near Spring Creek, and that was the start of the ugly little village called Springfield. Other mud-daubed cabins were erected round about, and, for want of a better place, the circuit court was held in the Kelley cabin. In 1821, the first log-cabin courthouse was built at a cost of $42.50. The raw prairie crowded around the village.

When the state capital, after much political controversy, was moved from Vandalia to Springfield, there was need for a building that fittingly would house the Illinois judiciary and law-makers. Clearly, Springfield was past the log-cabin era, had outgrown the rude brick courthouse that had followed the cabin courthouse of the 20's.

On a hot July 4th in 1837, while the ladies in their full skirts fanned themselves and small boys scampered about in the dust and set off powder caps to scare the girls, a limestone block was set as a cornerstone in the Springfield Square. Meanwhile all that summer the state offices and records were moved by ox-cart—there were no railroads—from Vandalia to Springfield, and the legislature and supreme court held forth in three of the drafty Springfield churches.

Some ten miles south of town in the region of Cotton Hill there was activity in the small limestone quarry near Sugar Creek. Laboriously, blocks of stone were dug out and shaped, loaded on ox-carts which slowly and with much screeching of heavy wheels plodded on mud roads to the Village Square. Here a new building was rising. At a dollar a load the brown limestone blocks came to Springfield and there, with a care and skill unknown to cabin architecture, a structure designed in Greek Doric style stood up proudly on the prairie. It stands there today as one of the few American examples of this type of architecture.

The tall Doric columns soon weathered to that rusty brown of limestone native to the Springfield region. During the time when it was the State Capitol, the building heard the words of Abraham Lincoln, Stephen Douglas, and Judge Logan; it was here that Lincoln's body was brought one spring day in '65, to lie in state before he was buried on the hill in Oak Ridge Cemetery. The old Capitol stood ageing, and when the new Capitol was built, the old building was used as the county courthouse. In 1899 it was raised eleven feet to make an additional story and, at the expense of some of its classic lines, to give more room for offices. Years went on. The limestone from Sugar Creek grew browner and more pitted with time.

As it stands today, its original stones are sturdy, its classic Doric columns still as dignified as when they rose up surprisingly from the raw prairie and brought beauty and distinction to the muddy streets of Springfield. The columns are weathered; to look at them without the distraction of their surroundings, they resemble the ageless Greek classicism of Old World ruins. Since 1841 they have been a landmark on the prairie, a milestone in the progress of Illinois culture. (*April 1944*)

⊛

⊛ RIVERS

⊛

⊛

SYCAMORES OF THE SANGAMON

The Sangamon is a river-personality that has taken uncounted lives and hid the bodies; it has vicious whirl-pools and eddies which perpetually harass the brown surface of the water and make navigation dangerous. It is deep here, shallow there, sometimes with a rocky base, sometimes all soft, bottomless mud, again with a bed of sand where the water runs clear. This is the Sangamon and the sycamores are a part of it.

Ages ago the Sangamon was part of that vast postglacial chain of rivers which, forced all out of proportion to their present size by the great surge of flood-waters from the melting glacier, rushed seaward across a thawing land. In those days the Sangamon was very large and swift. It caught up great quantities of sand and gravel from the burdened glacier, here and there dropped great pockets of debris, and then, changing its route, left lakes and gravel beds in Illinois. The Sangamon knew the tread of mastodon and mammoth; on its shores the giant beaver with its great yellow teeth cut down poplar trees; herds of musk-oxen drank here, and prehistoric drum fish and turtles swam in the waters. Sycamores probably were here even then, for they originated in the Cretaceous Period several million years before the Glacial Age.

Today the Sangamon, rising in east-central Illinois, rambles beside its white-limbed sycamores and passes through deep forests in the flood plains of the old river. In this rich, alluvial soil the sycamores still reach enormous girth and height.

At Decatur the Sangamon is enchained by a system of dams to make Lake Decatur. Then westward the river suddenly narrows as it again crawls somberly between muddy banks, and near Springfield it passes the sandstone cliffs at Carpenter's Park. Here for ages the river has gnawed away the

95

sandstone, and years ago the winds from the west blew the sand in high dunes above the river hills. Along Route 66 the old dunes now lie today. There are Indian flints in many of them and in other fields near the river, and sometimes there are burial mounds, for this was Indian country.

Northwest of Springfield the river makes a U-turn beneath high hills, past sand banks, and flows over the dark bed of limestone which made a pioneer ford for wagons travelling from Springfield to New Salem across the valley. Roll's Ford was on a well-used pioneer route, and Sangamo Town, one of the first Illinois villages, came into existence in 1824 on the hill above the ford; in those days its builders felt it would rival raw little Springfield a few miles away. Today, however, there is no trace of Sangamo Town. It is gone. Only the old wagon road, blurred by time, still winds down the hill and through the woods to the brown river.

The river moves on past sycamore shores, below old New Salem hill with its restored village of Lincoln's time. An old grist mill is soon to be reopened at its former location on the river bank, not far from where the now historic flatboat load of hogs stuck on a sandbar and caused a good deal of mental anguish to one Abe Lincoln.

Now through sand country, past high dune hills, past loess bluffs that rise up from Oakford to Chandlerville, the river at last moves off through swamps into the broad valley. Out there the Sangamon, still accompanied by sycamores, merges with the Illinois River moving south to join the Mississippi, and, eventually, the Gulf. (*March 1942*)

THE MISSISSIPPI

Near the blue waters of Lake Itaska in northern Minnesota a clear little stream runs out of the woods. It runs so far and picks up so much water along the way from rivers that drain into it that when it finally reaches the Gulf of Mexico 2,553 miles away, the stream is more than a mile wide. It has left the crisp coolness of Minnesota and basks like a great muddy alligator in the somnolent heat of the Gulf country.

The river has had a great influence on Illinois and its people. It touches the state first at East Dubuque, where gnarled rocky headlands stand on either side of the river, and forms the western boundary of Illinois. Limestone bluffs rise higher southward; here are the cliffs of Palisades State Park. The river passes Rock Island and the old fort on Campbell's Island where Black Hawk's people were fired upon.

Then comes the jutting peninsula of Nauvoo, where once there rose a Mormon temple, followed by the communal life of the French Icarians. . . on, past Keokuk dam, past Quincy, past Hannibal, past Tom Sawyer's cave in a nearby hill . . . past the Illinois apple country. Then there is the great loop past the village of Golden Eagle where a mysterious man who once lived there in a cave was thought by some to be the Lost Dauphin, son of beheaded Louis.

Here comes the Illinois River, and on a bluff near the juncture, a lime-stone cross marks where, it is said, Father Marquette climbed up to see the meeting of the Rivers. Nearby is Pere Marquette State Park.

Downstream the river grows more powerful. Past the white cliffs of Grafton, Elsah, and Alton, home of the mythical Piasa bird, past the Alton dam. Then there comes the flood of the yellow Missouri from the paint country of the West. In the Illinois bottomlands stand the Cahokia mounds. And the river goes on, past the rising bulk of the Illinois Ozarks, past the lost city Kaskaskia, which the river partly has swallowed, through heron-haunted swamps, through wild goose country, to Cairo, tip of Illinois. Here the Ohio swells the great river. Ever wider, on it goes, to lose itself beyond the cane-grown delta and disappear in the Gulf of Mexico. This is the Mississippi.

The river was known by white men since 1541, when DeSoto claimed the lower part for the King of Spain. Much later, Marquette and Joliet canoed down the Mississippi from the mouth of the Wisconsin to the Arkansas; in 1682 when LaSalle paddled down the Mississippi to the Gulf, he claimed it as part of the French territory of Louisiana. Eighty-one years later, England took part of the river away from France.

Events moved on. The American Revolution freed the river of English rule . . . negotiations with Spain eliminated Spanish ownership . . . from Napoleon in 1803 the entire Louisiana territory, with the Mississippi thrown in, was purchased, and then the river belonged to Americans. In 1832 Henry Schoolcraft, nosing about among the Minnesota lakes, found the source near Lake Itaska.

The river has known many eras. There was the time long ago when perhaps only the birds knew it, and in the sky followed it on the great flight trail called the Mississippi Flyway, which connected the nesting and wintering grounds. In another era the Mississippi was a route of human migration, as along this broad stream the prehistoric Mound People probably came north and lived for a long time.

Exploration followed the coming of white men. With the opening of the middle west, river travel became a cheap and practical means of transport over long distances. Paddle wheelers opened the Steamboat Era as a colorful chapter in American history. Most of the river towns grew up at this time.

Later there came a lull in river traffic, but now once again paddle-wheelers travel up and down the Mississippi. Some are show-boats; others push enormous flatboats and barges loaded with freight. Coast Guard boats cleave the water, and sometimes there is a submarine. This is the Missis-sippi. This is its part in the story of Illinois. *(Oct. 1943)*

ALWAYS THE RIVER

It is always there, forming our boundary, defining our reaches. Here, we say, at the edge of the Mississippi lies the edge of Illinois, for the

river leaves no doubt as to definition. It is, besides, a geographic line marking the boundary between East and West. On its eastern shores, westbound
pioneers felt their hearts leap in anticipation and fear, in hope and trepi-
dation. Behind them lay the surety of the East where men and women,
plowing and cutting and building, had moved with history toward the
sunset, toward the Mississippi, the jumping-off place, the step into a great
beyond whose promise was wondrous but whose future was unknown.

There was always the river. It carved out the western shores of Illinois
and carried into itself the waters of streams flowing into it from far places.
The Wisconsin brought down yellow-brown sand and the amber liquid of
peat bogs and cedar swamps. The Rock River united Wisconsin with
Illinois and entered the Mississippi, while the Illinois River poured its way
down its own ancient valley. And the Missouri and the Cache and the Kaskaskia and the Ohio and many more: they made the Mississippi. The little
rivers were filled by creeks and rivulets draining swamp and cornfield and
hill-country ravine, and the little rivers braided their routes across Illinois to
become one with the biggest river of all.

Men used it, built beside it, farmed in its bottomlands, paddled canoes
and flatboats and keelboats and steamboats and towboats on it. Men pulled
out snags and deepened the channel, set buoys and lights, dredged the
shallows and strengthened the banks. They tried to corral the river into
narrower and more man-prescribed limits, and then cursed when the floods
came and the Mississippi rose as a Leviathan unchained and gnawed through
the levees, surged over the banks, drowned out the cornfields and stood
six feet deep in the living rooms and kitchens of farm houses in the bottoms.
Cattle and hogs and wild rabbits, possums, coons and foxes waited on the
high places, saw the waters rise higher, to narrow the scope of their haven.
The tree climbers took to whatever trees were close, and the others swam,
if they could make it, to still higher ground.

There was always the river. It would rise and it would drop, and, like
villages on the slopes of Mount Etna and Mount Vesuvius, people and
animals would come back and trust that there wouldn't be another disaster for a little while. Yet, knowing the river, they knew it would come
back, one day; but, knowing and loving this mud-monster, they could
not stay away from it.

Once again, the silt-crusted bottomland fields are plowed, land so rich
that if three out of four crops are flooded out, the fourth will usually pay
for the lost ones. Farm families scrape the mud out of their carpets and
pick cornstalk hurrah's nests out of fences and orchard trees. Pastures grow
green again and cattle and hogs are turned into them, and the raccoons
hunt for frogs and clams along the stagnant backwaters left by the flood.

And the Mississippi grinds its way in its powerful course on the other
side of the levee, on the other side of the willows, in the bottoms below
the bluffs. It was there yesterday and it will be there tomorrow, and today
it carves out a little more bank-mud, churns a new eddy, deepens a channel,
shoals a crossing . . . the river, flowing forever to the sea. *(Sept. 1960)*

THE LITTLE RIVERS

To the traveler, a small river means just another bridge to cross and a quiet stream beneath, for the little rivers of Illinois are slow and sluggish except in flood. To the local resident, the little rivers are a means of watering stock in the river pastures, a source of high water and flooded fields in spring, a place to fish and a place near which to hunt. The little rivers are insignificant; they are only crooked lines meandering across a map, a bridge upon a highway, an item in a newspaper. Yet they are a part of Illinois and have played a vital part in its history.

It was down the rivers both great and small that the first explorers came into the Illinois Country late in the seventeenth century. Before that, the Indians knew the rivers well and used them as highways through a country noted for its murderous tangles and its dangerous open spaces. A river, however small, was a smooth road to travel through rough country. It was only natural for the white men, faced with the disillusioning greatness of the Illinois jungle and the dreadful open sea of its prairies, to launch canoes on the rivers. The Fox River in northern Illinois was one of the first of the smaller rivers to help the white men. It was a link in the complex journey from Green Bay on Lake Michigan, where ships from France put in, to the Mississippi, the Illinois, and back again. One by one, after that, the little rivers of Illinois showed the way to its wealth and possibilities by means of the watery highways.

Later came the settlers. Many of them came by flatboat from the Cumberland and the Tennessee, into the Ohio, up the Wabash, into the Little Wabash and the Embarrass, or around to the Mississippi and the Illinois, up the Sangamon, or the La Moine, the Plum, the Green, or the Rock. And there the settlers built their cabins and from these cores grew villages. And more often than not, it was a mill beside a little river that formed the beginning of a settlement. The mills along the rivers were one of the first, if not the first, arguments for settling down—here was good water, pleasant land, ample wood, and a means of livelihood to be gained by grinding corn and wheat for the neighborhood, as well as sawing lumber to make new houses. A little river made all these things possible.

Up some of the little rivers there even came river traffic from the greater streams, but the smaller rivers usually had too shallow and treacherous a bottom and too many curves and angles to permit very large craft navigating very far. Yet Lincoln piloted the Talisman to the Springfield landing of the Sangamon, and there were great, unwieldly flatboats launched down many a small river at time of flood. They carried a load of hogs, or barrels of flour and corn, or lumber, and more than likely a junketing load of young people off for a good time while the high water held.

There are rivers which nobody but the natives ever heard of before, nor cared about, and there are those that are known wherever Illinois history is known. Aside from natives of Ogle County and travelers on U.S. 51, perhaps few others ever heard of the little Kyte River, but the equally un-prepossessing Sangamon is known from America to New Zealand, wherever the story of Lincoln is known, and the Spoon River, a minor stream, is part of English literature and American tradition.

They are many and their names are often odd, drawn as they are from Indian lore of the region, or named for early settlers, or from experiences which were too vivid to be forgotten. There is the old Fever River in Jo Daviess County, known now as the Galena River, which knew the excitement of the lead diggings and the bloody times of wars with the Sauk and Fox. These tribes also hunted along the Apple River, and the reaches of the Pecatonica, the Sugar River, and the clear-flowing Rock, which is called the Hudson of Illinois. These northern rivers contain the clearest water of the Illinois rivers; most are muddy and impossible to see into, but the northern streams, although not completely clear, are much more refreshing to the eye.

There is the history-strewn Fox River which has known the villages of the Potawatomies and more primitive peoples, the canoes of the early French, and later the clatter of mills along its shores. The town of Aurora is built on either side of the Fox, whose islands are part of the city. The Chicago River has known much human tampering, from the time a hundred years ago when it was tapped by the Illinois and Michigan Canal which connected the river with the Illinois and thus changed its flow, so that traffic could go directly from the Great Lakes into the Mississippi and thence to the Gulf.

Not far away is the beautiful Des Plaines which to Chicagoans is one of the best known Illinois rivers because of the forest preserves and recreation areas along much of its length. But the Rock, the Des Plaines, the Chicago, the Kankakee, and the Fox are large and important as compared with some others which travel across the Illinois map, and this tale deals with little rivers. There is the Edwards River, and the Kishwaukee, the Iroquois, the La Moine, and the Mackinaw, and the Vermilion. There is the muddy, dour little Spoon River below the Dickson Indian Mounds in Fulton County. The Kaskaskia near Champaign is a thread of a stream which grows wider and more important, and finally enters the Mississippi at the point near which stood the first capital of Illinois, the town of Kaskaskia. In the early 18th century, George Rogers Clark knew the Kaskaskia as LaSalle knew the Fox. So did the French and the Indians, and the bison that drank there, and the malaria mosquitoes which multiplied in its marshes. And there is the Embarrass (pronounced Em'-bar-rah') near Charleston, a tributary of the Wabash, which may also have known Clark's men. It flows near the spot where Abraham Lincoln's parents built a cabin in Coles County, and into the Wabash near Vincennes, where Hamilton, the Hair Buyer, had his headquarters until Clark captured the town and sent the general East to explain his misdeeds.

The rivers of the south are full of mud and history. The Big Muddy is a yellow-brown stream running through the Mississippi bottoms, along with the Little Muddy which is just as brown and thick, and the Little Wabash with its wandering Skillet Fork. There is the Saline with its somewhat salty waters which find their flavor from the ancient salt wells which the Indians and early settlers knew as sources of valuable salt. And the Cache runs through cypress country and Indian country, down to the tip of the state at Cairo.

From north to south and from east to west, the little rivers are a vivid link in the long story of Illinois which began so long ago that no one knows the true beginning, and they continue to link the present with the days to come. *(Sept. 1948)*

RIVER-WITHIN-A-RIVER

The channel of the Mississippi is a river-within-a-river. Invisible on the surface, it weaves its own unpredictable way back and forth across the Mississippi, following a deeper cut on the irregular bottom than does the rest of the water. The endless problem of the navigator is to determine where the channel is today, this hour, this minute: where, exactly, it runs close to the bank, where it follows the middle, where it cuts over to the other side by an almost invisible but vital crossing. It may change sides half a dozen times in as many miles and must be followed carefully except during high water when most of the river becomes a safe, deep channel.

Down on the murky, mysterious bottom of the Mississippi there lie deep canyons and high hillocks. These and other obstructions very likely determine where this river-within-a-river runs, but why it changes so frequently and so unpredictably is something which no man, perhaps, will ever quite understand. He will try to figure it out; he will perhaps wreck his boats, may curse the Mississippi as an impossible River of Perdition. Yet he knows that usually the channel cuts close to the outer curve of a loop or bend because the force of water is faster there and silt consequently drops near the inner bend to make the water shallower. He knows, also, that the channel is so easily misplaced, even today when he follows between the carefully located red and black buoys, that without constant attention to the look of the river, the inscrutable rightness of the channel, he may find his boat foundering on a shoal, ramming a sunken barge, or nosing up into the trees of an island or towhead.

The heights and depths of the river bottom are caused by natural obstructions, such as rocks and ridges, massive sandbars and gravel bars, as well as by heavy, octopus-armed snags which will never float again, by wrecked steamboats and river equipment, and other impedimenta which have found their last resting place in the river. Around these lumps and hummocks and masses, in the deep pits and valleys, the swift current of the river shoves and swirls and seldom runs straight.

On the surface, these swirls may show as strange, polished, boiling spots surrounded with churning ripplets catching the sun, or by crazy, erratic leapings and twirlings of the agitated water. Sometimes an eddy that begins to boil around an obstacle grows wilder and broader and stronger, churning around and around, carrying drift and small boats if it catches them. It chews out the nearest bank in a circular sort of hollow, the earth crumbling away under its onslaught. When a big eddy begins to cup down in the middle like a full-fledged whirlpool, strong men are downright scared and get out of reach with their boats as fast as possible.

And then the peaceful-seeming river may turn smooth as glass on a calm day. It may be gray as ice when there is weather brewing and the wind has not risen or slashed into angry waves frothing with high-flung foam when the wind hits, while flying sand and rain obscure the shores so that the river looks like a stormy ocean. It can calm itself just as quickly after a squall. It may look pale green and smell of the sea, or it may be liquid amber, or red as paint up in the iron-mines country, or clear as air, or earth-gray and thick with mud boils, or it may look like coffee-and-cream and smell of willows.

From hour to hour, the river changes. Each day will be different from all others in the manner in which the Mississippi shifts another sandbar a little way downstream or gnaws madly with slashing force into a caving bank and topples live trees into the water. It will toss chunks of brown foam like floating bread on the current, to show that another bank has gone into the maw of the Mississippi. And the river will bring down more driftwood, old black driftwood wallowing every which way, big as telephone poles and deadly to boat propellors, or small enough for terns and dragonflies to hitch a ride—driftwood plunging and tugging and lolloping, or sliding easily, silkily, downstream, goal of all Mississippi driftwood.

From source to mouth, the river is endlessly changing, endlessly different. Over shoals and reefs, over rapids and bars, over rocks and snags, over ripples concealing deadly obstructions, over its uneven bed, for 2,552 miles, these things determine the character of that strange river-within-a-river, the channel of the Mississippi. (*July 1956*)

TOWBOATS PASSING

Long, quiet, aloof, the towboat moves rapidly down the channel of the big river. The mellow whistle has all the mournful and exciting cadence of a fog horn on the ocean; there is that pulse-quickening quality of drama and splendor peculiar to marine craft and marine life. For the rivers have a life of their own, and a particular sphere of that life passes by on the quickly moving, gigantic towboat. Loaded with oil or coal, it slides down the channel of the Mississippi and around a bend which hides the craft from view. Wistfully, wishfully, the eyes of those on the muddy shore, or on the green levee, or on the tall white cliffs, follow the towboat and its tremendous barges.

When, in 1811, steam first came to the river, the arterial waterways of America—the Mississippi, the Tennessee, the Cumberland, the Missouri, the

Illinois, the Ohio, the Big Kanawha, the Monongahela, and the Allegheny—became busy routes for the packet boats. There came a day when the packet boats were all that was elegant and splendid; they were passenger boats, conveyors of mail, foods, and other supplies to the towns and plantations, and carried crops from the plantations to the markets. The river boats were a vital force uniting the remote parts of a railroadless land. The packets came to a reluctant end, however, late in the past century when the railroads proved they could carry people and goods cheaper than the river boats could. The packet boat was too small to transport great quantities of goods. But when the packets were doomed, men who loved the river and its ways discovered the towboat system, and made it work.

The towboat does not pull; that would take too much power. But it can push many times its own weight, so the towboat pushes—and that is the secret of its success. The boat itself, 100 to 300 feet long, is like a compact house built over a throbbing engine. The boat is as complete in its housekeeping arrangements as any house, but is more shipshape and better organized than many a house on land. Twenty-five to thirty men and women live on a towboat and work seven days a week, yet after their time off on land they are eager to get back on the towboat and start off into the endless reaches of the shining river. On the towboat the food is good, the talk is agreeable; the river is somehow an isolating influence from the problems left on shore.

The towboat pushes a string of barges which are tied closely together so that they navigate as a single vessel. Navigation is not easy on the river, not for any vessel; and for a mammoth tow often as long as an ocean liner to find its way skillfully between bridge pilings and around tight bends, through shallows and sandbars and shifting crossings, through currents and eddies and slack water in that unpredictable river, the Mississippi, is an accomplishment credited to the pilot who knows the river and to the engineer who guides the boat. A 750-horsepower diesel twin-screw pusher can transport barges carrying the equivalent of several shiploads of cargo, or coal, oil, sulphur, or steel to fill 450 railroad cars. River transportation, though slower than by rail, is cheaper, and the rivers are busy places today. One day in October, 1949, sixteen towboats passed the old river port of Elsah near Alton.

River traffic waned during the first World War. Up to that time river boating had been dependent upon the seasons. The towboats and barges traveled with high water and trusted that the high water wouldn't run out from under them before they got to where they were going. Flatboats and barges traveled in spring and fall, and prayed for a flood crest. Dry periods kept the boats tied up to shore and the rivermen scowling .

It was in 1920 that Congress authorized and established the Federal Barge Lines to revive, explore, and develop freight transportation on the rivers. The Ohio was the first to be surveyed and dams were built to control the water level; the Mississippi above St. Louis, and the Illinois, were next. The lower

Mississippi cannot be dammed and is a constant annual source of difficulty and anxiety to the engineers, coast guardsmen, and river boat pilots who find it impossible to predict what the cantankerous river will do next.

The dams stabilized the channel depth and brought back river traffic which reached an all-time peak during the late war. Now it has dropped somewhat, but every day still the long, quiet barges move in their aloof world of the middle of the river, past the cotton country, past the white cliffs of the Illinois shore, up to Minneapolis or Chicago or Pittsburgh. The barges, lashed together to form a single vessel, are guided by a towboat sturdily pushing, maneuvering through locks, till the home port is reached. (*March 1950*)

BIRDS AND NESTS

HUMMINGBIRD

When the first red flowers bloom in Illinois, the ruby-throated humming-bird arrives, visits columbine, honeysuckle, and bergamot all summer, and goes back to Yucatan when the last red salvia succumbs to frost. He came speeding north at the rate of 500 miles a day, swooped like a low-zooming bullet in the trough of the Gulf waves, and now, the only one of his kind east of the Mississippi, he builds a tiny, lichened nest high in a tree.

Hummingbird eggs, two to a nest, are just the size of a navy bean, and the young at first are no bigger than honeybees.

Hummers in the tropics are odd creatures. Some have beaks longer than their bodies. Some have sickle-beaks for probing into curved blossoms. Natives of Trinidad, who used the hummer's silky feathers for royal robes, called the island "Iere," Land of the Hummingbird. *(May 1939)*

BIRDS BEFORE BREAKFAST

It was April 25th, and over the Mississippi and its lowlands lying below old Fort Kaskaskia and enveloping Kaskaskia Island, a dense spring fog lay massive and immovable all night. The newly leafing willows were drenched in moisture which dripped with small wet sounds from leaf to leaf and to the curled old leaves on the sand. The urgent, melancholy sounds of towboat whistles came like strange spirits of the river talking, as some boats attempted to navigate the white confusion. They were using their radar, the scanners endlessly revolving, recording on the radar screens the whole aspect of the invisible river and its shores. Yet to push through a murk, which at four o'clock in the morning was so dense that no pilot, even with his powerful arc lights turned full ahead, could even perceive the outline of his first barge, was obviously a risk. Many tied up. The wet willows along Kaskaskia Island tethered two big tows, waiting for morning and a possible lift of the fog.

105

Even before the sun was up, there came a stirring of the whiteness, a wreathing motion in the veils of mist. There was a visible lightness coming to the upper levels, a gilding of water particles with unseen sunlight.

And as if at a signal, birds awoke in the willows and sang to the coming dawn. Perhaps in the density of moisture suffusing the air, the songs had something of the enlarged quality they have in a woods full of fluffy snow; there is an echoing of sounds, magnifying the volume.

At any rate, the boat crews, due to be called at 5:30 a.m. for the 6-to-noon watch, were wakened half an hour earlier by some of the loudest mockingbirds, brown thrashers, catbirds, yellow-breasted chats, orchard orioles, white-eyed vireos, redwinged blackbirds, song sparrows, cardinals, and Carolina wrens to be heard anywhere in America! Against their will, and in spite of burying heads in pillows, the men woke to that concerto of song coming through windows and doors. Here with a vengeance were birds before breakfast!

Outside, a suffusion of glorious golden-pink light was dyeing the mist with an other-worldly glow; and the fog was picking up its skirts from the hurrying brown water, higher and higher, now drifting in great, loose, smoky swaths across the bottomlands. From the heights of the pilothouse, the captain could look out across an undulating white blanketing, as if he were on a mountain-top looking across a mist-filled valley. And then as the sun climbed over the trees and burst full on the fog-filled river, the blanket broke, the veils vanished, the whiteness dissolved and in a few moments was rising as clouds into a magnificent blue sky drenched in spring sunshine.

And still the birds sang, though now the concert did not seem so loud. It was still an ecstasy of spring music by some of the best songsters along the river.

As the boats were on their way at last, twenty-seven great white pelicans went north. Their broad, black-tipped wings had a nine-foot spread, rowing the air in a magnificent rhythmic flight. The yellow pouches were drawn in to rest on the curving necks. In the dense fog the pelicans had gathered for the night on a great sandbar downriver in Dogtooth Bend, and now with the coming of sunlight, they were on their way. And to the men on the river, the big birds were a stirring sight. It wasn't every morning you saw *such* birds before breakfast! (*April 1958*)

AND NOW THE LURE OF BIRDS

March, and the day has come to look for new arrivals among the birds, to time the coming of new robins and meadowlarks and bluebirds as they fly up from the south. Over all the country there are folk with an enthusiasm for birds who now are watching the changes which spring brings to bird life. These people make up the bird organizations which have risen in most American cities. Bird clubs are mixed groups with varied aims, yet they are all, men and women and children, bound up in the common interest which centers in birds. In winter large audiences hear nationally known lecturers who show extraordinary films of wild birds in their haunts. Colleges and universities have added ornithology to their courses to satisfy a growing demand for the subject. There are people everywhere who like birds and who, with field glasses, spend pleasant hours in woods and fields. Some even make it their life work, either in research or in the fields of art and literature. The lure of birds has captured a large part of America.

Some feel that in birding there is both relaxation and exercise, an escape from work and worry; and whether it is relaxation or exercise depends upon the energy of the individual. For birding may mean sitting placidly under a tree and watching birds go about their daily lives, a method from which have come some of the keenest of bird observations. Thus, physical disability or bodily weariness need not handicap birdwatching. Another form of the same pursuit is found in the energetic birder who tramps miles, explores swamps and forests, or builds a bird blind forty-odd feet up in a tree in order to photograph an owl's nest. A birder may be as lazy as he pleases and still see and enjoy birds, and conversely so with surplus physical or mental energy that needs to be worked off in constructive channels. Some bird people make a careful and detailed breeding bird census from April until September, and compile their reports for a national magazine while others, from the pantry window, may watch the progress of the current robin family. Either way, birding reaches the greatest good in the individual.

Yet there are still other reasons for enjoying birds. Birding in general is just hard enough to be interesting yet easy enough to be exciting to the beginner. There is the spirit of the gambler in most people, and it is this, some say, which leads them out on the chance of seeing something new. The old familiar birds are reward enough, yet there are those thrilling times when something new does come along. It is these ecstatic moments which whet the appetite for more, which lead bird people on and on to ever more rewarding fields.

Yet perhaps the greatest reason of all is one which is hardest to put into words. It is the spiritual uplift which comes from the sight of a wild bird in its own haunts, with the complement of trees, sky, and flowers to make the perfect, unforgettable picture. It is an antidote for war and worry. Birds make no demands; they are there when they are wanted, yet they seldom intrude. The exuberant, quick life of a bird pulsing behind its delicate feathers, the wild, living look in the eye, the fleeting moment when it shares its life with a human being, the unconscious humor and pathos and human parallels— these make up the real meaning of the lure of birds. (*March 1943*)

GREAT BLUES ALONG THE RIVER

A dim gray shape, silent and powerful and big, flaps through the early spring mists above the Mississippi. A mile or so downstream, there comes another. A third gray shape has swerved to drop down on a muddy shore. Slowly working their way up the Mississippi, the great blue herons have come back to Illinois.

All winter they fished along the lower Mississippi. In coastal marshes and quiet bayous, where the supply of fish and frogs is constant around the year, they found plentiful food. Then, with thawing in the north and a gradual procession of spring up the watercourses, the herons left their wintering grounds. By May, there will be great blue herons well distributed in the fish-and-frog country, from the Gulf of Mexico to Lake Itasca—2,552 miles of four-foot, fishing birds.

To old willow woods and cottonwood thickets on towhead and river shore, the herons return to what remains of last year's massive nests. Great blues, as most herons do, prefer to nest in colonies. Their huge cradles, too large and bulky even to fit into a bushel basket (if any heron were so minded to try such an outlandish thing), are skillfully balanced in the shaky tops of willows, soft maples or cottonwoods not far from the river. Two or three large, stained, bluish eggs are laid in the hollow of each mass of sticks.

How an adult bird which, unfolded and on its feet is over three feet tall, can compress itself to squat properly upon a wobbly nest perched high in a wind-shaken willow and can brood the eggs until they hatch; and how the scrambly young can survive up there until they can fly is a question which only the willows, the river and the herons can answer.

While the young are in the nest, they grip the twigs with their scrawny feet. They gulp partially predigested whole fish from the mouths and throats of their hardworking parents.

Although the young are large, they are virtually helpless. They also have a well-developed ability to fall out of their nests, and few birds manage to do so as thoroughly, as disastrously or as fatally as young blue herons. They lean over the edge too far and suddenly topple, flapping at all angles, to the ground. If the fall is broken by branches or by the spring-wire padding of wild cucumber vines and nettles below, the surprised, disheveled youngster gathers itself together in injured dignity and, with a wide-eyed and somewhat puzzled look, limps off among the willows. Some of these lost ones may eventually reach the river shore and find food for themselves.

The fate of most of the unfortunates, however, is never very happy. Many of them will starve to death. Others of these helpless birds will have a more merciful death when discovered by some predator such as a fox or dog because, in spite of their size, they have not yet developed the ability to fish for themselves.

But along the marshy shores of all the waters of the Mississippi's drainage basin there always seem to be enough herons. Today, once more, out of the mists of March they come. They swerve, bank and lose altitude to come down on mud flats which have not known their giant footprints since last autumn. (*March 1958*)

BIRDS ALONG THE SANGAMON

It is an old river that carries the mud of a thousand fields along its route, a river with boiling spots that look as if they were stirred violently from below, a river full of hidden snags and many curves. Along much of its length grow the forests, among the last and among the least touched of the Illinois woodlands. Here live birds that are characteristic of the Sangamon. They are as much a part of it and its strange personality as the giant silver maples on the banks and the raccoon tracks in the mud.

Early in the morning when dew is wet on the nettles and trumpet vines and rests on the webs that formed overnight across the crayfish chimneys and among the mallows, a silent bird floats on broad wings upriver. It is the great blue heron coming home from fishing in the brown waters; its throat is full of fish to feed the noisy young in a platform-nest somewhere near the river.

Over the sunlit maples soars a red-tailed hawk; the sun catches coppery glints on the broad, spread tail. A killdeer excitably yipping flies along the water to a convenient mudflat, runs about with lowered head, clucks and screams, leaves neat three-toed tracks in the morning mud and pricks a pattern among the raccoon tracks.

As sunlight comes to the open river a darting flock of swallows catching insects dashes by, dipping beaks in the water to send a shower of drops over their backs.

Morning moves on. A Carolina wren skips among the tangled tree roots that clutch the eroding bank, stops long enough to sing a loud song, flits in and out of the roots. From a willow stub that leans at an angle over the water there comes a flash of orange-peel gold and blue-grey, the prothonotary warbler. In June there was a nest with white eggs in a hollow of the stub and in a few weeks more the warblers will be on their way south. But all summer long the prothonotaries are birds of the river, birds of the Sangamon. Although only a short distance through the woods a traveller might not be aware of the presence of the river, the song of the prothonotary would tell him that it was near and lead him to it.

All day long as the heat grows, the monotonous songs of the redstarts are sung incessantly in the old trees. At noon a kingfisher comes rattling along the river and flies on around a curve. The great blue heron comes back to fish on the muddy shore, and the flight of a cooper's hawk across the river from woods to woods silences the small birds for a long, pulse-stopping minute. Then a wood thrush somewhere in the shadowy, mosquito-filled woods begins its late afternoon song, and as sunset gilds the river and shines in late yellow light behind the maples on the west shore, the birds that sang in the morning now sing again.

Dusk, and there are whip-poor-wills all about. They, too, are seldom found far from the river. They seem to be everywhere as their voices fill the woods.

And now it is dark night with stars in the water and a sky full of them— Vega, Arcturus, Hercules, Corona; Antares red in the south, the neat pattern of Sagittarius rising in the southeast. Insects jingle in the dewy pasture beyond the trees; tree crickets are in the maples; the night is full of sounds. And then there comes the deep-throated hooting of an owl, the barred owl, calling in the darkness. It is a full, rich, resonant, exciting call, the owl by the river. It is part of the picture of the ancient Sangamon and its birds. (*Aug. 1944*)

HIGH ADVENTURE

Now in January the bird man looks reflectively down his lists—his monthly lists, his year's list, his life-list which contains all the birds he has ever seen and positively identified—and remembers those momentous and matchless dates of discovery. Here indeed is a record of high adventure.

There is that day in November when, among the mallards and scaups on the open lake, a new bird swam and dived, and was a horned grebe. There are those green-eyed cormorants madly diving and fishing in a small pond when the hickory shad were swarming; the breathless majesty of the first great blue heron rowing its enormous grey wings across the misty water; the excitement of those first egrets in a sunny marsh—egrets like unreal white creatures from another world. To the individual who compiles a life list of birds, it becomes a concise record of his birding adventures.

In it he remembers the honking of geese lost over the city, picked out like silver birds by the lights below; snow geese settling like a snowdrift in a field of winter wheat; the first time a green-winged teal, found dead in a marsh, was examined in its perfection of golden green head and speculum, and russet breast. It is the first sight—and all those thereafter—of the painted glory of a wood duck; the first old squaws on a choppy lake; the goldeneyes at their laughable courting antics.

The list marks that first bald eagle flying above a great river; the first time a duck hawk flashed low over the water and scared the scaups into a flurry of fear; the first king rail, like a cautious brown hen, leading a quartet of tiny black Easter chicks along the mud. There is that wonderful flock of golden plovers floating on set wings against the broken blue and white of an April sky, and the fluting of their strange, exultant calls as they drifted on the wind; the sounds of woodcocks nasally calling in the dark spring night of the dune-marsh; that first upland plover gawking from a telephone pole; the amazement in using strong binoculars on a flock of miscellaneous sandpipers, and finding half a dozen kinds on one mudflat; the eerie keening of gulls on ice floes; the flights of terns along the airlanes from the Gulf to the Great Lakes.

Birding marks that day when the yellow-billed cuckoo was first distinguished from the black-billed; the rainy spring day when a barred owl, hooting mellowly, followed the birder's inadequate imitation, flew soundlessly out of the swamp forest to perch above his head, and looked down with large, questioning brown eyes. It is that day when the long-eared owl's nest was found in a blossoming haw tree; it is the roaring of chimney swifts pouring into a chimney; the tremulous sound of whip-poor-wills; the first amazing pileated woodpecker, huge and gaudy, in a hilly wood. It is that moss-decorated nest of a phoebe plastered against a cliff; that first glistening barn swallow over a summer field; a violet-green swallow following a flock of tree swallows along the Mississippi; the day the tufted titmouse followed a whistle and came into focus at last.

To the maker of such a list, old delights return with the names before him—that ridiculous, tilt-tailed marsh wren spilling song in the swamp; the first mockingbird tootling at two o'clock in the morning; the first kinglet that danced a nuptial dance in the sunshine and flashed a ruby crown; the pursuit of an unknown voice in the hedge and the materialization of Bell's vireo; the whole long list of warblers which, like rare gems, spring after spring, were discovered. And the Canada warbler that was almost that rarest warbler of all, the Kirtland's, but wasn't.

Down the list—those gay bobolinks in a wet clover field, how tinklingly they sang; the Baltimore oriole that turned out to be an orchard oriole; the impossibility of the scarlet tanager, each spring still impossible, still breath-taking; and that summer tanager as rose-red as a ripe pomegranate. Then came the January day when there were evening grosbeaks, yellow as a winter sunset, eating box-elder seeds, just as the books said they did; the purple finch colored like a ripe strawberry against the snow; the charming nest of a towhee hidden among the ferns; that queer, flat-headed bird that was a grasshopper sparrow; the day there was an Oregon junco among the slate-colored juncos; the white-crowned and white-throated sparrows piping in the April rain; the brightly cold night when, beside the moonlit, frozen stream, a song sparrow sang as warmly as it might in May.

All these are the rewards of birding. The list, growing with the growth of the individual, becomes not only a check list of personal discoveries among birds, but a guide book to high adventure. (*Jan. 1947*)

PRAIRIE LARKS FLYING

At last there comes a day when winter steps back and a hint of springtime is in the air. It is not really spring—not yet. This is only the foretaste; this is the prelude. But today there is sunshine, thawed earth, blue sky. The twigs of the maples along the creek seem redder and more alive than they have been all winter. The sycamore trunks are whiter, the willow twigs more golden. There still is some ice in sheltered places, but now the water of the little creek runs almost freely and makes a pleasant noise as it dashes over the stones.

Music and motion and sunshine: these are the heralds of spring. For a long time there have been so few of them—hungrily now the ear, the eye, and the senses absorb it all. Where there still is snow in the woods, green things wait beneath its shelter for the moment to grow. Mosses are bright as living emerald, and on tufts of *Catharinea* there are hair-thin, gleaming stalks topped with ruddy spore capsules. Algae on the north sides of trees gleam fresher.

But the thing which suddenly brings springtime closer—the thing which changes the whole aspect of February—is a faint tinkling in the sky. There appears to be nothing. The tinkling is a sweet, scattered voice sounding here and there remotely over the blue. The voice is from birds—the prairie larks are flying.

The prairie horned larks spend the winter from Illinois to the Gulf; they walk about in quiet flocks in stubble fields and glean bits of grain and weed seeds. In the early days of February the larks start north. They are the first birds to come through Illinois on the northward migration, first to head into the teeth of the north while the wrath of February and the deceit of March still lie ahead. Some may go as far as Manitoba to nest; others may stay in Illinois fields. Now on a February day that nevertheless contains the essence of spring-to-come, the larks are on the wing. Scattered, tinkling, almost invisible, they pass over town, over woods, and over fields.

The prairie horned larks are quiet, dust-colored birds that live in open country. There are black markings on face and throat; a pair of small black feather horns stand erect on the head when the bird sings from a clod of earth or a beanstalk. There is often a wash of pale yellow on the white throat; the tail is black beneath; the eyebrow is white. Horned larks are ground birds that walk with a long stride, and they almost never perch in trees. The nest is made on the ground at the edge of a field.

Now in February, as the breath of spring becomes more and more pronounced, the prairie larks fly north. (*Feb. 1946*)

BLUE JAY TALK

A blue jay is a bird of considerable character and vigor and has a fluent vocabulary which, with his bright blue feathers, dominates the winter woods and gardens. A blue jay is a master showman.

Having as his goal an ear of corn on the feeding tray, he bobs up and down a time or two on a tree branch across the yard, as if he had steel springs in his black legs, and he makes small joyful gurglings in his throat without opening his beak. With a rustle he unfolds those magnificently patterned wings of wedgwood blue, black and white, and he swoops. His is no ordinary patterning flight; any sparrow could accomplish that. He swoops down and then veers up in a splendid curve to the rim of the tray. He bounces up and down again, and this time his voice comes out strongly as if in a gratified chortle.

According to Mark Twain, "Whatever a bluejay feels, he can put into language. And no mere commonplace language, either, but rattling, out-and-out book-talk—and bristling with metaphor, too—just bristling!"

The blue jay on the feeding tray expresses himself, then bends his elegant crested head to lift a grain of corn from the ear. The grain doesn't come out. It is firmly affixed to the cob. The jay gives a stronger tug, a slight twist, then a sterner twist. The grain stays.

The bird says things under his breath; then they come louder, as Mark Twain commented: "A jay can outswear any gentleman in the mines. You think a cat can swear. Well, a cat can, but you give a bluejay a subject that calls for his reserve powers and where is your cat?"

The jay in question dances up and down on those spring-steel legs and utters whatever it is that frustrated jays utter in such trying circumstance. He leaps over the ear of corn and attacks it from the other side. The cob rolls over on his toes and the bird dances back from this dangerous thing, expressing himself with more than an edge of sizzling irritation.

"And as for command of language—why *you* never see a bluejay get stuck for a word," said Mark Twain. "No man ever did. They just boii out of him!"

Not wasting time on his sentiments when work is to be done, the jay leaps on top of the corn, takes hold of a grain, leans back on his heels, twists, pulls, and the grain comes out and the jay topples over backward with a blue flutter and a squawk. When he opens his beak he drops the corn, of course. And a cardinal departs with it.

The blue jay lets forth a raucous screech of exasperation, but he is not one to be foiled forever. He attacks another grain, but this time he doesn't topple. He has his prize. He flies with it to the nearest tree, puts the grain carefully between his feet, a pair of toes holding it securely down, and whangs at it with mallet-blows of his beak to get at the germ, letting the hard, flinty endosperm fall to the ground.

The jay goes back for more corn. He repeats the successful operation six times, flying back and forth between tree and food with each grain; and then, having had enough, he gives a tender fluting whistle, and is on his way. Up in the tree he pauses to yell, "Jay, jay, jay!"

Yes—"there's more *to* a bluejay than any other creature. He has got more moods, and more different kinds of feelings than other creatures; and, mind you, whatever a bluejay feels, he can put into language . . . ." and certainly, in life as in literature, he leaves no doubt as to the state of his emotions! (*Dec. 1960*)

(Quotations are from "Jim Baker's Bluejay Yarn" from *A Tramp Abroad*, by Mark Twain.)

". . . AND SWALLOWS IN THE SPRING"

Weeks ago when the first maples came into bloom and when crocuses performed small miracles on muddy lawn and garden border, the first insects promptly appeared. There were early bees around the February maple blossoms. Bees tumbled about in the golden luxury of crocus pollen and came away dusted with it and with their pollen-baskets heavy. The first over-wintering flies came out; small spiders ran about over brown leaves of the sunny forest floor.

And almost as soon as the first flowers opened and the first insects were in the air, the first insect-eating birds had come back. Among the earliest were the purple martins, those big, dark, glossy, energetic swallows whose presence is synonymous with sunny skies in summer. The sky itself, simply a route to somewhere else when traversed by the majority of birds, becomes a place of music and motion against a backdrop of clouds and sunshine when the martins take over. The sky is their domain. Contact with earth is brief, for martins are on the wing during most of their waking hours. Here is no humdrum flight, no routine beating of wings—the swallows cut great parabolas across the sky and send down a throaty twittering almost like exultant laughter.

They come so early, often by the end of March, that sometimes the unseasonably warm south wind which brought them here collides with a cold front from farther north, with violent winds and storms as a result. There is a sudden drop in temperature following a meteorological fracas of this sort, often falling from eighty degrees to twenty-five overnight, with ice forming on ponds again. Flying insects vanish. And the martins, still twittering, cut arcs across the cold, bright, polished morning in search of food. Too long a cold spell may result in many martin casualties.

Purple martins, our largest swallows, spend the winter in Brazil. For months they live far from cold snaps or from any dearth of insects there in the broad valley of the Amazon. With them also winter our cliff, barn, and bank swallows. Yet lush though the Amazon country must be, the swallows depart in early spring and come far northward to nest and rear their young in a land but newly replenished with insects.

Martins once nested in hollow trees. Indians enticed them to live near their villages by putting up poles from which hung hollowed dry gourds. It was evidently an easy transition for these adaptable birds to live in the often elaborate martin-houses put up for them by modern man. Here occasionally they have difficulties with the usurping starlings and sparrows and may at times desert their old home for some other neighborhood. Sometimes, too, an area which once knew numbers of martins is suddenly without them, the result of a severe storm over the Gulf of Mexico or a late blizzard which intercepted the migrant birds.

Yet, in spite of casualties, year after year the martins return. High atop their miniature apartment house or lined up on the nearby wires, the big glossy-purple swallows sit about and twitter and gurgle, and then, on powerful wings, leap into wind and sun and sky to exult in vast circlings in the upper air. They are part of that annual April excitement—of returning life and hope and joy—embodied perhaps most of all by the sight of swallows in the spring. (*April 1961*)

QUAVER IN THE NIGHT

Thin as water running over a stone, tragic as loneliness, full of melody as an oriole, the voices of young owls sound in the summer night. Sad, quavering, running up and down the minor scale, the voices contain a sound of melancholy out of keeping with the pleasantness of June. And then, in the middle of the most mournful trill, there may come a laughable break in that voice, a youthful uncertainty which betrays the inadequacies even of owls. Somewhere in a dark, full-leafed tree beside the street or in the woods, three or four young screech owls may sit impatiently side by side, clawed feet sidling back and forth a bit, waiting for the parent owls to bring a mouse or other bit of food to satisfy their gnawing appetites. For some time the young screech owls have been out of their nest hole but they are not yet capable of hunting for their own food. And so they wait, and when the parents come, there is a fussing and a whining of voices which continues until each mouth is too full for sounds to come forth. Mouse after mouse may be stuffed into the young owl until, for lack of room inside, the tail of the last unlucky rodent may dangle from the beak until digestion makes room for more.

The voice of the screech owl is a matter of controversy. To many people it is decidedly disagreeable; to others it is even a thing to fear because of ancient superstitions surrounding the calling of owls. But to others, numbering among them Thoreau and Burroughs and most of the other nature men, the calling of all owls, and in particular the melodious, mournful quavering of the screech owls, are among the most delightful sounds out of doors. (*June 1948*)

HUNTER IN THE NIGHT

The mouse was aware of the owl before the owl discovered the mouse. The latter had been following its secret paths under the garden ferns, had gleaned corn from the bird-feeding stand, had frozen suddenly at the sound of the heart-stopping wail of a screech owl quavering through the darkness.

The mouse had lost four of those born with it in the same nest under the garage. They had foraged together when they were newly on their own, then had ventured alone in untried ways, and one by one four had disappeared when the owl was about. The mouse had little memory and no sentiment. But it knew that now in the autumn night it was terribly alone in the shadow of the ferns, that a hunter was out there, and that it was a long, dangerous way back to the safety of the haven beneath the garage.

The mouse in its nervousness twiddled its whiskers, tested the air for scents. The ears cocked forward like twin gray shells, trying to locate where the owl was now, but the sound of the wailing seemed to fill the night and there was no location to it, only an immense sensation of dread. The mouse sat up and hastily wiped its paws over its face and whiskers.

It knew the owl was close now. There had been no sound of its coming, but the intangible vibrations of perfectly silent owl-wings had sent small velvet shock waves into the cupped ears of the mouse, then had ceased, suddenly, as the owl paused in a juniper above the ferns.

The mouse knew the menace was there, knew that safety lay in keeping completely still, but its nerves broke under the strain, and, with a curiously wobbling, panicky gait, the mouse tottered out from the shelter and headed blindly toward the garage.

Lightly, the owl dropped. The curving beak pinched the base of the skull so that the mouse died almost at once. On broad, silent wings the owl was wafted upward again into the juniper to where the moon was sending a broad, illuminative beam that spotlighted the little red-brown hunter and its meal.

Of all the owls in America, the screech owl is the one most often using the modified haunt of cities as its hunting and nesting ground. As a mouse-catcher, it finds a ready-made life-zone often abundantly stocked with some of its favorite food. (*Sept. 1960*)

GULLS FLYING

Gulls are a part of the world of water, international birds to whom the sea is home.

But the freshwater gulls, identical with some of the sea gulls of both coasts, are as much a part of the inland waterways as their kin are a part of the salt seas. In winter there are gulls on most open water from Lake Michigan and the lesser lakes down the Mississippi to the Gulf, but in spring they fly north and most of them nest on the purple lava rocks along the Great Lakes. There, over the cold blue waters of Lake Superior and over the sparkle of Lake Michigan, they flash white wings and sleek bodies against a bright summer sky.

On bare rock, one or two mottled eggs are laid—laid in a cranny where they cannot roll off or be blown off, or on sandy or rocky islands where so many gull eggs are deposited that it seems impossible that their rightful owners would know which was which. But during the nesting season the rights of gulls and their territorial boundaries are rigidly enforced, and the penalty is bloody wounds or death. The time of greatest danger from infringement comes when the downy young gulls, able to waddle about but as yet unendowed with the perception of adult gulls, ramble over the invisible boundaries of neighboring gull families. Immediately the innocent intruder is fiercely set upon by adults and usually is flogged and pecked to death.

But at last the surviving young are grown. Crowds of adult gulls, snowy with grey-blue backs and wings tipped with black and white, are joined by dusky, full-grown young. They sit about on the rocks or wait passively and with little conversation along the roofs of fishhouses or piers or jetties. They gather by hundreds around the fish-packing houses along Lake Superior where motor-driven launches bring in the lake trout for immediate cleaning and icing and shipping. The gulls sit about and wait and watch. Occasionally they change places on roof or pier, or thrust forth a belligerent head and utter defiant keening notes and catcalls.

But when two men bearing a tub full of fish remains emerge from the dark coolness of the fish house and walk to the shore where a single great wave breaks on the rocks, the gulls about-face, their wings lift, and the instant that bloody mess is tossed into the surging water the gulls have risen as one bird. In a tangle of wings and bodies and shrill cries, they sweep across the sky and drop down to the water to snatch up the morsels. In a matter of minutes, every scrap of fish has been taken from the water. The gulls circle once more and then move out to sit like a flock of white ducks on the bay. On the single curling wave a fading patch of blood is all that remains of the manna thrown to the gulls.

These birds are the essence of the waters. Lakes, rivers, oceans, none would be the same without the salty, tart character of gull voices and bright gull wings. (*July 1951*)

THE WAY SOUTH

In October, the geese dallied among the bent-over pipeworts and crowberries along James Bay. Mornings, now, had a sparkle of frost on the bending sedges, and the cranberries in the muskeg had already grown dead ripe; they rolled off their thready stems when the geese nipped at them.

The days were brilliant and crisp yet unseasonably warm with a south wind that blew gently for days from another land. The geese were restless. There was much gabbling among them, a shrill honking and bugling, a flapping of powerful wings with their strong, hard, newly grown feathers. There was a daily exercising of wings, a running into the wind, rising in small flocks to make a circuit of the sky, and back again. Across the tundra country of upper Canada, a landscape patterned with innumerable pools mirroring sky and wings and little else, with the chill silence of James Bay beyond, there were thousands of long black necks with white cheeks lifted above gray bodies. Waiting. Waiting. The geese marked time until there came the signal which would spur them to flight.

The weather changed. Clouds boiled out of the south and the landscape lay immersed in rain and mist for three days. Then the western rim of the low pressure system lifted and the clouds and rain moved off to the east. That night the sky cleared to a bright darkness full of cold stars, northern lights flaring pallidly below. At dawn the geese were alert and were feeding with an intentness which had not marked their earlier days around the bay. They talked less and in lower tones; there was less wing-flapping, a greater earnestness in picking up cranberries and crowberries.

Late in the afternoon the signal came, and the flocks rose with a great rumbling of heavy wings. Lifting powerfully into the windy sunset, they climbed, gaining altitude with each push of wing and lift of body. Family groups, largely, stayed together, the oldest bird in the lead, cleaving the way through the resisting air, the wind on their tails. Each bird in the pattern opened an air channel for the wings of the bird just behind, each one traveling in the slip-stream of the bird ahead. In great V's, long lines and the staggered design of the echelon, the geese traversed the highway of the upper air in perfect accord and timing. When the lead bird had had enough of leading, he dropped back a notch or two and another bird took his place, others along the line changing position, while the leader rested in the gentler air-push of the wings ahead.

The geese flew high all night, steadily, their calling guiding each other and the flocks nearby. They came down at dawn in a great marshland to feed and rest, stayed several days, and again on a north wind they were on their way. Some, daily, were shot. Indians in the tundra took some; hunters along the Mississippi and near the Horicon in Wisconsin took others. But one November day, with a wild bugling, thousands of Canada geese dropped down onto the waiting levels of Horseshoe Island in southern Illinois where they would spend the winter. They would linger until March, when a soft south wind and an urgency in the air would send them skyward again, bound for the still frozen wastes of the tundra and the great ice of the James Bay country. (*Nov. 1960*)

EGGS WITHOUT NESTS

There are in the world a number of birds which lay their eggs and rear their young successfully without the benefit of nests. To these birds a stretch of sand, a litter of shells, a pebbly shore, or a shale road are perfect nesting places.

For eggs which are laid on bare ground or on other exposed, harsh places without any nest material to shelter them or soften the hardness of the surroundings, are protected by their form and color. The eggs on a sandy or shell-covered beach are sand-colored and are mottled so that they are exceedingly difficult to discover. Even after the discovery, they are easily lost if the finder glances away and back again. They seem to disappear in full view. It is this protective device of coloration which makes it possible for the population of terns, gulls, and many other shore birds not only to survive but to maintain their numbers.

Eggs which are laid on stony places look like stones. The eggs of a killdeer are pebble-like; they hide, as the tern's eggs do, in full view—two to four pointed eggs laid in a hollowed place among stones. Miraculously the eggs laid even in well travelled roads usually escape destruction. The parent bird, nervous and excitable, shrilling its incessant calls, flutters up from the eggs when danger comes near, and, pretending injury, flops and flutters away to draw attention from the eggs. When at last they hatch, the young birds, long-legged, downy as little brown and white Easter chicks, run almost as soon as they have left the parted shells. For this sort of "nest"—or lack of one—does not afford shelter to young and tender nestlings. These hardy ones must be able to run as soon as their down has dried. Off they go, along the shore or into the fields, and leave in the expanse of shore or road the mottled shells of eggs which, by their own invisibility, for so many days were kept from harm. (*May 1946*)

THE NEST IN THE BARN

They built the nest of mud pellets picked up from the pasture pond, and plastered the bits securely against a rafter of the barn, to make a nest both durable and safe. Like polished navy blue and orange fish, the barn swallows flashed in the sunshine and swooped in and out of the barn, across the feed lot, past the watering trough, across the sloping pasture, to the muddy pond where the cattle drank. Then, down to the mud, a brief hobbling about on inadequate feet, then up again on wings that were as powerful as the feet were weak, back with a single mud pellet for the growing structure in the barn.

The barn swallows came back in April. They posed and preened on the wire fence, their long, forked tails slim and keen and decorated upon the curve with jewel-like white dots. The wings, back, tail, and head all were that glistening satiny dark blue; the breast was a dark, ruddy apricot that shaded to a pale yellow below.

These, perhaps most elegant of the swallows, are found, in forms which are virtually alike, over most of the world. They are the familiar swallows of the Southwest Pacific, England, the European continent, and Asia. They all have much the same habits and appearance as these American barn dwellers.

When the eggs are laid in the feather-lined nest—chicken feathers picked up from the barnyard—the parent birds take turns brooding them in the sometimes sultry atmosphere of the barn. When the young hatch and fill the nest with eager bodies and hungry mouths, the adult swallows work from dawn until dusk to catch insects in the air. (*June 1947*)

THE NEST IN THE WOODS

Without the slightest movement of the head or body, and without flicking an eyelid, the ruffed grouse sat on her eggs, while sharp rustling sounds pattered across the fallen leaves of the springtime woods. And the weasel, coming home with a mouse dangling like a limp rag from her teeth, passed within three feet of the grouse on her nest among the leaves and did not know she was there.

The weasel's sleek body undulated over the ground without any appearance of touching it, streaked into a tunnel in a rock pile, and was gone. Still the grouse did not blink or move. And the blue jays cruising in a raucous gang through the trees a few feet above her head did not see her there. The night before, a fox had come close but had failed to smell her presence, and she had held on to her nerves and had sat tight.

And then the rustling of the weasel's footsteps ended, and its rank odor faded, and the jays went on through the morning woods . . . and only then did the little hen relax on her nest. She stretched a wing over an extended foot, and then the other, and then stepped neatly off the nest. Like a small brown chicken she strolled through the woods in search of breakfast.

Fifteen creamy-buff, round eggs lay in a hollow of the leaves under the shelter of a broken basswood and its tangle of young sprouts. Vulnerable to every danger in the woods, the eggs gleamed in the sunshine, yet as soon as the hen came back and spread herself over them, both hen and eggs became invisible. Protective coloration in the wild is surely no more effective in any creature than it is in the ruffed grouse or partridge, a bird still to be found rarely in northern Illinois but commonly northward to the tree line in Canada.

The bird is brown, yet each feather has a pattern of gray and buff and black, breaking up its contours. One may stand only a few feet away from the brooding partridge and be quite unable to make her out against the similar coloring of the leaves.

But this is not the whole reason for the strange fact that neither the keen-eyed, keen-nosed hunters, the weasel and the fox, nor the hunting jays and crows, knew that a grouse was there. In a wonderful protection for a ground-nesting creature, nature seems to provide that while the grouse is on her nest she is scentless. Apparently deodorized at this crucial time of the year, she can depend upon this quality as well as the protective coloration to enable her, most often, to bring off the downy young successfully.

As soon as they are hatched and dry, the little brown puff-balls go running off into the woods. The parent tries to keep them together, directs them with clucks and calls. They freeze into a nothingness under the violet leaves and ferns, and most of them usually escape the hungry creatures coveting them. By autumn the young are fully grown, colored like their mother. The young males do not acquire the broad, banded tail, crested head and ruffed neck of the adult male until the following spring. (*May 1960*)

THE WINTER NEST

Deserted, forgotten, seldom or never to be used again, the old nests of last summer remain on bough and in bush. They reveal the presence of resident birds which, all summer long, were cannily inconspicuous in where they had hidden their nests and were feeding their young. With the falling of the leaves in autumn, the old habitations are startlingly revealed, some so close to house or doorstep as to seem impossible of concealment.

On a winter's day, one may become an out-of-season nest hunter. Numbers of robin nests in town were built over sidewalk and street; take a robin-nest census for a glimpse of the population. A dangling old sock of a nest was once carefully woven by a Baltimore oriole. Perhaps half a dozen untidy nests of English sparrows clutter a single tree, or the fallen-apart structure of a rose-breasted grosbeak remains among sycamore twigs, while a small knot on a horizontal bough materializes as a hummingbird's nest. The small woven basket of a vireo is hung below the fork of a twig. In lilac and syringa bushes are the bulky nests of cardinal, brown thrasher, and catbird, that of the cardinal more easily identified than the others because thin strands of grapevine bark are usually arranged in the cup.

These old abodes are something to be looked for on a winter's walk in town or in the woods. They are mute evidence of the inhabitants of a region. They are at the same time something of an indication of the birds which may be found there next summer, for birds customarily nest in the same general area, often in the same bush or tree, year after year. These old nests, capped with snow in every blizzard, are guides to next season's birding. (*Dec. 1965*)

NEST AGAINST THE SKY

When the leaves fall, the well-concealed nests of summer are revealed mockingly against the winter sky. There are nests a few feet above a busy sidewalk, one close to the back door, another in the trellis vines, still another boldly in the crotch of an elm. There are large nests and small, each one so well hidden all summer that few were discovered until now. Of those occupied nests which were discovered while still in use, many soon afterward were ravaged and left empty, for although the study of nests and eggs may be a fascinating one to bird students, it is not a good thing from the standpoint of the birds. In spite of the fact that the careful person who finds a nest may leave it unharmed, he may not be the last to find it. Along his carelessly mashed-down trail through the grass a black snake may travel straight to the nest, and there dine on eggs or young. Or a fox may sniff the man-tracks and in curiosity follow them to the nest. The spying eyes of crows and jays may watch the discovery of the nest and mark the spot to be robbed at a later time.

But an old bird nest is one of the almost useless things in the woods. It is true that some are used again—perhaps by the white-footed mouse that roofs an old nest and fills it with plant down for a winter bed. Sometimes the hawks add to their old nest high in an oak and use the same structure over and over again; the eagles and ospreys do this for years. But the majority of birds do not return to the nests they built the year before. These are outworn beds, shaky, soggy, soiled, often infested with mites or lice. A nest is used for one brood and then deserted; by the time winter is over, the snows, winds, and rains have made it still more unusable.

Now in winter is the time to collect nests, to dissect them and pick them apart bit by bit to see how they are made. Here are character-quirks which are insights into bird personalities and actions. Here is the cowbird's egg embedded in the fibers below the main part of a yellow warbler's nest—unable to eject the alien egg, the little warbler simply built a floor above it. Here is the nest of the Baltimore oriole that picked yarn ravellings from the yard, the goldfinch that collected tags of sheep-wool from the barbed-wire fence, the wood thrush that nested in a park and used paper napkins in the nest structure, the phoebe that decorated its mud cup entirely with knight's plume moss. There may be the house wren that determinedly used old nails for bedding material, the chipping sparrow that fancied short hairs from the neighbor's spaniel to use in a cupped grass nest, the nest of a shrike with a mouse-skull embedded in it.

Nests reveal the painstaking skill of birds in using raw materials to create a solid bed for eggs and young. A marvelous sense of balance and a nicety of twig-laying, even in the most fragile and unformed nests, provides a safe place for eggs, brooding birds, and young for a period of many weeks. The more carefully built nests show family skills and an instinctive schedule of work that proceeds from foundation to lining, and a sense of timing that brings the nest to completion at the time when the eggs must be laid.

All this is visible in these winter nests which now are capped with snow and at the mercy of the elements. (*Dec. 1945*)

❀

❀

THE NIGHT SKY

❀

❀

STARS IN THE EAST

There are, of course, stars all over the sky, but on a winter's night perhaps there are none as bright, as full of stories nor as intense with sparkle and color as the stars of the east. These are the rising stars, the constellations which will dominate the sky all winter, moving over the zenith, sinking, finally, as spring approaches, into the oblivion of the west. The summer stars are there now, the last of the constellations which put light and form and meaning to the summer sky. Some have already vanished, but there still are the white stars of Cygnus, the Swan, which, as the Northern Cross, stands upright in the far northwest. Blue Vega of Lyra is still in the northwest, and so is the orange-pink of Arcturus with the kite-shaped form of Bootes arranged above it.

In the south lie the strange, pallid constellations which belong to the southern hemisphere—Cetus, the Whale, with white Mira, a variable star; the Southern Fish and Fomalhaut; Capricornus, the Sea Goat; and dim Aquarius.

The north contains its usual constellations. They are always there, but positioned differently with the seasons, and all revolve around the Pole Star, Polaris, in the end of the handle of the Little Dipper. Around this strangely important little guide-star twirl Draco, the Dragon; Cepheus, the King; Cassiopeia, the Queen; and the concise form of the Big Dipper. In December the Big Dipper is low on the northeastern horizon with the two end stars of the Dipper's bowl pointing forever to Polaris. In twenty-four hours, the Big Dipper makes one complete revolution around the Pole Star.

But it is to the east that one's eyes turn on a winter's night when the air is cold and the sky so clear that it would seem that human eyes could penetrate farther than ever before the depths of the universe.

The winter panorama of the night, accented by the flowing Galaxy, the Milky Way, lying from northwest to southeast, contains constellations which

122

are among the easiest to identify and some of the most thrilling to know. Taurus, the Bull, is worth the price of admission—Taurus with its ruby-colored eye, Aldebaran, snapping fire in the brisk chill of December, with the misty star cluster of the Pleiades above it, and the dramatic V-shape of the Hyades using Aldebaran as one tip. Northward is pink-yellow Capella with its own star group, the Kids, and there are the three stars of Aries, and the great Square of Pegasus high in the sky and already sliding toward the west.

Out of the east rises the drama of Orion. As it emerges from the horizon's mists, it sets the sky ablaze with red Betelgueze and white Rigel, the glittering Belt, and the magnificent Sword, while lower still, flashing blue fire and white sparks, with red glints and ice-green glitter, rises the brightest of the stars, Sirius.

Perhaps only one body in the sky will take one's awed eyes from this eastern spectacle, and that is the planet, Venus, which, in this year of 1955, is the Evening Star in the west, the Christmas Star. Not until October did it return to the west, where it will remain, huge and softly glowing, for many months, long after the magnificence of the stars of the east have given way to the inexorable return of the summer constellations. (*Dec. 1955*)

THE SILVER RIVER

Across the sky tonight flows a shining river of stars, the Great Galaxy, the Milky Way. It actually is a circle of stars which we see only as part of a circle, that part which stretches from one horizon to another. There is always a part of the Milky Way visible in the sky.

The Milky Way is the rim of our universe. We are as if situated on the edge of a vast saucer in which we and our solar system are insignificant specks somewhere near the middle. Our sun is only one of the lesser suns making up the millions in the Galaxy. They are all so distant and in such numbers that they blur in the heavens and appear to make clouds of stars—create the Silver River to which men have looked for thousands of years.

There are many names given to the Milky Way, names far more meaningful and many far more beautiful than the one by which we know it. The Chinese called it the Silver River or the River of Heaven, and saw in it a counterpart of the Yellow River of China. They believed that if one traveled far enough on the Yellow River, he would eventually reach its source in the Galaxy, in a celestial land where the peaches of immortality grew. One need only to eat of the magical peaches beside the Silver River to attain the immortality of the gods. The Hindus believed that their holy Ganges sprang from the Milky Way, which was known as the Bed of the Ganges, just as the Egyptians believed that the source of the Nile was among the stars.

The Norse knew the Milky Way as the sky bridge across which rode Odin, the Thunderer, the bridge down which the Valkyries galloped to carry to heaven the bodies of warriors slain in battle. And there was a medieval Christian myth which stated that the Milky Way was a bridge which connected earth with heaven, by which angels could come and go. The Greeks knew the Milky Way as a great heavenly street along which stood the palaces of the gods.

Beliefs were greatly varied, depending upon the peoples who looked at the skies and pondered their meaning. For although in many early myths and beliefs of diverse peoples there is a definite parallel of ideas, there were few parallels when it came to explaining the Milky Way. The Polynesians called it the great blue shark; certain American Indians called it the pathway to heaven, lit by campfires of weary travelers going to the kingdom of Ponemah, land of the hereafter. And the Mongols, Tibetans, and Siamese told of a great white elephant which lay in the celestial sea and breathed so heavily that the emanations of his breath became the Milky Way itself which swirled across the sky and changed with the seasons. And the Pawnee Indians matter-of-factly called it a cloud of dust kicked up by a buffalo and a horse racing across the sky.

The same Milky Way—the same Silver River, the same celestial elephant's breath, the same blue shark, the same road to Valhalla—which the ancients knew and which has fascinated every tribe of men since the beginning of time, lies across the sky tonight. In the autumn night the Galaxy begins in the northeast where the pink-gold star, Capella in Auriga, rises low, and the Milky Way spreads in a white veil up over the sky, punctuated by the brighter stars of constellations around it, and passes down into the southwest. The Milky Way is in the sky every night of the year but its exact position among the constellations varies with the changing seasons. *(Oct. 1949)*

THE PLEIADES

Ornament of the glittering winter night, the Pleiades are seen at their best in December and January when the sky is purple-black, the air sharp, and the constellations are splendid. In winter the stars seem to give off electric sparks of red, blue, green and white.

High in the east tonight is the star cluster called the Pleiades. It is in the upper part of the constellation of Taurus, the Bull, and is one of the most renowned and best loved star groups. The Pleiades rise like a small sparkling cloud of light which, when examined more carefully, takes the form of a miniature dipper. It is as if some celestial jeweler had reproduced the Big Dipper itself in miniature and had set it carefully in the sky, all by itself, so that its beauty might be best appreciated. It rises above that V-shaped star cluster, the Hyades, which is arranged like a flock of flying geese or a speeding arrow, not far from the red star, Aldebaran, the eye of the Bull. This year the planet Jupiter, large and white, also occupies a place of prominence in the eastern sky, located in the nearby constellation of Aries.

The Pleiades have always held a place of importance and mystery in the story of mankind. They were the Seven Sisters of the Greeks and were worshipped by the Aztecs, the Peruvians, the Japanese, the Hindus, and the

Egyptians; the Chinese knew them four thousand years ago. Among many early people, a propitiating memorial service for the dead, corresponding to All Hallows' Eve and All Saints' Day, was held each year when the Pleiades rose in the east. It was as if some monumental catastrophe had once occurred at a time when the Pleiades were ascending and had affected people over much of the earth.

To the Greeks, the Seven Sisters were known as the daughters of Atlas and Pleione, daughters who wept with such grief at their father's great burden in supporting the earth on his shoulders that the gods transported them to the heavens. They are named Alcyone, Merope, Celaeno, Taygeta, Sterope, Electra, and Maia; six of them may be seen with the unaided eye, a test of eyesight used by the Indians. There is, however, a legend which tells that once seven Pleiades could be seen. One, Merope, mysteriously vanished. There is now a lower-magnitude star in the cluster which, some astronomers believe, may have once shone with greater brilliance. If this change in its habits occurred within the memory of early man, then indeed it might have been observed that one of the Pleiades faded away and the legends of the Lost Pleiad began.

The cluster appears small, yet the diameter of the group is believed to be some thirty-five light-years—the incomprehensible distance of approximately 210 trillion miles. Great clouds of nebulosity make the whole area of the Pleiades appear to be enveloped in glowing light.

In the great cosmic movements of the stars, it has been discovered also that the Pleiades, like a flock of birds, are all moving in the same direction, as the Hyades themselves are moving, toward that red star, Betelgueze, in the nearby constellation of Orion.

So vast a movement and so tremendous a group as this miniature cluster actually cannot be truly comprehended. It is enough, perhaps, just to stand in the backyard on a winter's night, breath coming in a frosty cloud, mittened hands steadying binoculars, while the lovely Pleiades rising above the neighbor's roof glitter through bare maple twigs, gems placed with a jeweler's skill upon the December sky. *(Dec. 1964)*

"FALL FROM HEAVEN THE BRIGHT STARS"

In the summer skies of 1862 there came a comet which was watched by astronomers. Its orbit was plotted. And then the comet disappeared and never was seen again. No one is completely certain as to what happened to that lost comet, but it is believed that it disintegrated, blew up, went into pieces, and the vast stream of particles remaining after this event continued to follow the same orbit as the extinct comet.

Not long after the discovery of the comet, the August sky was suddenly marked with silver streaks of meteors, not just a few as the summer sky always shows, but dozens, hundreds in a night. "The hot stars down from heaven were whirled," and astronomers and laymen spent their summer evenings on their backs on rooftop and lawn and hilltop, watching the northeast sky, where the constellation of Perseus rose after midnight, and counted meteors. At first they were very abundant, but after years of the meteor showers had passed, the average count in mid-August became 69 meteors an hour.

The comet of 1862 was not a particularly important body, but its meteor showers, called the Perseids, have streaked the purple velvet of the August night for many years and are among the most noted of the meteor showers. Each year as the earth moves through part of the great stream of metallic particles from the comet, there is a nightly display which is at its best from August 9 to 14. They are sometimes called "The Tears of St. Lawrence" because they begin on St. Lawrence's Day, August 9.

Every night, however, has its meteors. Some are short and swift, some are large and slow, some are fireballs or bolides that explode in colored fire. Usually meteors burn out before they reach the earth; that is the wonderful safeguard of the earth's atmosphere, for friction with the atmosphere causes the lump of meteoric metal or stone, hurtling darkly through space, to ignite. Most often it burns out without striking the earth. Sometimes, however, one is too large to be completely consumed, and with a bang and a blinding flash of light, it strikes the ground. One such, the Tilden meteorite, fell in Illinois in 1924.

Astronomers have calculated the distances and speeds of meteors. When they are observed in the sky, they are believed to be about 75 miles away. They usually vanish at about 50 miles distant; their speeds range around 27 miles a second, though some are believed to streak through our atmosphere at a hundred miles a second.

Meteors come from outer space, yet they are closely related to the earth's own substances. No foreign material has been found in a meteorite, but such commonplace items as iron, nickel, cobalt, silicon, and magnesium make up the meteoric body. Usually the crust of the meteorite is fused and pitted from the great heat which burned it as it fell through the atmosphere.

Since the beginning of man's life on earth, he has observed those bright flashes in the night sky. More than a thousand years ago the ancient Icelanders in their classic Edda wrote:

"The stony hills are dashed together, the giantesses totter;

The heavens are cloven, the sun darkens;

The earth in ocean sinks;

Fall from heaven the bright stars

And towering fire plays against heaven itself."

(*July 1949*)

THE MOON IN ECLIPSE

On November 17 when the moon, the earth and the sun come into exact line with each other, and when the shadow of the earth is thrown upon the moon shortly before midnight, we have an eclipse. Since the beginning of the human race, men have had their own interpretation of this astounding yet natural event. Men began by being afraid. They came at last not only to accepting the eclipse but of using it to predict omens and further their own ends. Today, we observe it scientifically and without a great deal of wonder.

But when earlier men, without the slightest warning or knowledge of what actually was taking place, suddenly discovered that something—witch, demon or monster—was beginning to devour the light of the moon, the effect was quite different from our own calm acceptance of the phenomenon. Among most primitive peoples, the general idea was that some sort of fearful creature was going to make off with the moon during an eclipse. Consequently, the best way to preserve that vital orb—or the sun during a solar eclipse—the Creek Indians believed, was to make a great racket to scare off the attacker. This was most easily accomplished in the greatest volume by thrashing all the dogs in the village. Their howling and barking, said the Creeks, would surely frighten away the sky-dog which was menacing the moon or sun. And, as anyone could soon see, the ruse worked; pretty soon the sky-dog went away and its prey shone as brightly as ever.

On the Northwest Pacific Coast, the Indians said that a huge, hungry fish, perhaps a killer whale or a halibut, tried to swallow the moon at certain times because the moon was made of a jelly-like substance, very tasty. The sky-fish coveted this morsel and periodically tried to make off with it. Here again, noise was the remedy.

Everywhere among early people the effect was much the same; something was destroying the sun or the moon. And because man could not visualize his life or the earth without these two vital beings, he was terrified and in a panic. The medicine men and shamans were begged to do something—to bring back to the sky its luminous gods. So the wise men, who were probably as frightened as everyone else but had to conceal it, devised elaborated charms, spells and incantations. Drums were beaten, sacrifices were burned in sacred fires, prayers were said. And, since the exorcism was deliberately lengthy, the eclipse eventually began to go away and everyone in devout relief knelt to thank the gods and the wise men for their beneficence and skill in chasing away the demon. Today in certain remote parts of the world, primitive men still beat drums to scare away an eclipse. In the calm light of scientific observation of the November 17th eclipse, there is, in the dim background, still the anguished thudding of tribal drums.

Celestial phenomena, even in the light of modern wonders of the world and man's bold exploration of the skies, are still totally uninfluenced by man and his ways. We can no more cause an eclipse to happen, nor can we command one to go away, than the Creeks could actually stop an eclipse by beating their dogs or the Haidas their drums. We have nothing whatever to do with lining up the sun, earth and moon in the vastness of the heavens so that the earth's shadow neatly blots out the moon. An eclipse is still an astonishing event, one upon which we must look with an unending awe from our own proper niche in the universe. (*Nov. 1956*)

CELESTIAL FIREWORKS

When the rosy light preceding the rising sun appeared gloriously across the east, the Greeks called it the coming of the Goddess Aurora. But when, at night in northern lands, men saw a strange and eerie rosy glow, bands of many-colored lights, and ghostly veils moving back and forth across the sky, they called it the Aurora Borealis—the northern dawn.

But it was not dawn, and they knew it. This strange manifestation came several hours after the sun had set and it might last all night, or might disconcertingly flicker away and leave the sky dark and star-sprinkled again, the sprawling constellation of the Great Bear unadorned, the North Star again plain as the mariner's guide.

Because the flickering lights and awful magnificence of the Aurora Borealis were mysterious and unexplainable, early men believed they must be related directly to the spirit world. The Celts called them the "merry dancers." Indians knew them as ghosts of warriors dancing forever back and forth across the north.

Although the Arctic knows the most glorious display of the Aurora Borealis or northern lights, the northern tier of states may often have magnificent displays, most of which, however, lack the shimmering, iridescent, incomparably blue arch of light which is a feature of the Arctic show. One of the most awesome arrays to have been seen in Illinois appeared in September, 1957, alarming the uninitiated with the fear that there was a great fire somewhere, or that some atomic blast had enflamed the universe. At that time, visible even in mid-state, the entire sky was filled with moving and flickering cherry-colored lights, like red smoke.

At other times, it may only be a white glow low in the north; or a procession of undulating ribbons and veils of pale green or pink; or long white beams, like searchlights, playing back and forth.

The ancients were not the only ones who were baffled in trying to explain the source of this fearful phenomenon. Early scientists could not do it, though most of them made valiant guesses. When called upon to present an explanation—after all, encyclopaedias, dictionaries, and curious children demanded an answer—it was somewhat vaguely stated that the Aurora Borealis was caused by the Midnight Sun casting reflected prismatic light upward from Arctic ice fields. Even Webster's Unabridged Dictionary in 1946 called it "a luminous phenomenon supposed to be of electrical origin." And so the most tremendous display of celestial fireworks granted to the dwellers of the earth went unexplained until only a few years ago.

Then at last, through cosmic research, the causes were made more clear. Now we know that as violent explosions occur on the sun, vast fountaining jets of protons and electrons rush outward. These speed out in all directions at velocities of some 3000 miles per second. Those that come into our atmosphere meet and collide with the molecules and atoms of the earth's magnetic field. This head-on collision produces a glow which is very much like that made in neon tubes, in colors which are determined by the kinds of particles involved.

Thus, blue lights are caused by nitrogen atoms, green by atomic oxygen, and the glowing red made by quantities of atomic and molecular oxygen. What determines why there is more of one color-producing material than another? What causes the great solar storms and their atomic explosions? There are still many more questions to be answered on the subject of the northern lights.

Yet, as we stand in the cold darkness of a winter night, when the stars are fairly crackling in the rarified atmosphere, and we watch the leaping clouds of glowing red, or the eerily moving processions of pale green specters, or long white celestial searchlights probing to the zenith, all with no sound, no commotion, no ado, only orderliness and vastness and the silence of cosmic space, we need no further explanation or reason. This is the glory of a universe untouched by man. (*Dec. 1959*)

EXPLORE OUTER SPACE TONIGHT

Let the astronauts, in their own way, and the moon-rockets in theirs, explore outer space. Tonight we, with a pair of binoculars, may explore outer space and discover marvels which do not need the help of great telescopes nor of space craft to be brought to our eyes. These celestial discoveries may not appear as large as when seen through a Palomar telescope nor as intimately as some astronaut may one day succeed in seeing them, but the personal gratification in finding and bringing closer some object in remote space is very great. Use of binoculars is more suitable, perhaps, for the earth-bound, who still prefer that outer space be kept at a comfortable and properly awe-inspiring distance.

The moon itself shows an astonishingly detailed topography when observed with a pair of binoculars of no great strength. The lunar heights and depths are best seen when the moon is about three-fourths full, or several days on the wane. At these times, sunshine is coming at a slant over the moon's face, so that the ranges of mountains lying along the line of shadow are picked out in high relief. Steady your binoculars—sit down and rest your arms on your knees—and examine with awe this dramatic landscape of the moon.

These mountains are very high, very stark, extraordinarily sharp and un-eroded, for here there is evidently no wearing away as we know it on earth. Without rains and snows and winds, rocks remain tall and sharp. Moon-mountain peaks, however, may be changed or knocked down by some catapulting meteorite, dozens of which may strike the moon everyday.

Elsewhere in the sky, the wonders of outer space lie just beyond the power of the unaided eye. With only binoculars you may see far more than you saw by looking up unaided to the glittering, star-filled sky. The Milky Way alone is a revelation of wonder, the Pleiades a glory. High in the east or already at the meridian, this twinkling cluster of stars, shaped something like a tiny, jeweled dipper, is, with magnification, far more than the seven stars which the ancients named the Seven Sisters.

Below the Pleiades, low in the southeast, there rises Sirius, a brilliant blue-white star under Orion. Now look at its unbelievable, scintillating, blue-purple-green-white-red glitter on this winter night. It is like no other star. Look at the constellation of Orion itself. Find the three stars in the Belt. They are lined up neatly at a slant in the southern sky. To the right below the Belt there is a small blur of stars called Orion's Sword. In this blur there lies the great spiral nebula of Orion. The binoculars see it as a white fuzzy spot, but this is in reality an entire galaxy of inconceivable size, believed bigger than our whole universe. Another great nebula is found in Androm-eda, which is high in the north. A blur, then another little oval, fuzzy light-spot, a window into the mystery of outer space which man still has not attempted to explore with more than mind, mathematics, and telescope.

While you are looking in the north, find the Big Dipper. Look at the star in the bend of the handle, then find the smaller star just above it. To be able to see the "Papoose on the Squaw's Back" was a test of good eyesight to the Indians. The Arabs called the two stars Alcor and Mizar, the Horse and Rider. But neither Indians nor Arabs knew that your binoculars might find an even smaller star lying between the two.

The planet Jupiter is still bright in the western sky. With binoculars you may see its moons, tiny pin-points of light arranged on one side or another of the planet. Their positions change as the nights pass. Although Jupiter has nine moons, only four may be seen without a strong telescope. These moons of Jupiter were Galileo's first discovery when, in 1610, he turned the first telescope to the sky—man's first entry into the mysteries of space. It was through avidly watching the moons of Jupiter, night after night, and observing their eclipses, that it was discovered that light needed time in which to travel.

Man has come a long way from that first telescope and Galileo's astound-ing discovery, yet on a winter's night, with only a pair of binoculars or bird-glasses, some of that same thrill and awe awaits anyone who does his own celestial exploring, for his own inner satisfaction, in the orderly, exalted wilderness of the sky. (*Dec. 1962*)

THE WOODLAND PATH

ADVENTURES DOWN THE WOODLAND PATH

He stepped proudly and a little pompously down the woodland path, his black and white tail blowing a little in the spring breeze, his beady black eyes roving over the ground. It was spring, and the skunk was pleased with life. A shiny brown beetle crawled across his path; he paused, picked it up, cracked the shell in his teeth, spit out the gritty parts, and ate his find. Then he went on, while the new flowers of the crab-apple trees sent perfume into the air, and a phoebe caught mosquitoes over the trail.

If you met him coming toward you down the woodland path, the chances are that he'd pause a brief moment, and then turn off into the bushes until you'd passed. Or, if you were polite, and stepped aside so he could pass, there'd be nothing more than an exchange of woods-courtesy. But if you came with dog and gun, or if you bristled up and flung a stick at him, something very different would very likely happen, and it wouldn't be pleasant.

The skunk would pause in dignity in the path, as if to give you one more chance to cease such incivility and go on your way. But if you persisted, and your dog barked and strained to tear him limb from limb, the skunk would pat his forepaws sharply in the path. Then he'd slowly turn his back on you —but not to retreat. Slowly the tail would rise, and then—and then you'd wish you'd never seen a skunk, or ever walked that woodland path. The odor which he throws is vile and choking, penetrates hair and clothing, and leaves a recollection that is hard to obliterate, a resource which has given the skunk a reputation for evil doing which is none of his fault. *(May 1940)*

$*$ $*$ $*$

It was June, and there was a new nest in a haw tree beside the woodland path. A long, lean, cinnamon-brown bird with a keen yellow eye watched the path as she brooded the five eggs spattered with brown. Clean, perfect eggs, laid now as the culmination of the year, the climax to all the long miles of migration, the hunt for territory, the mad singing on pleasant April days. Now it was June, and the eggs were laid.

The brown thrashers had spent the winter in the far south, perhaps in the palmettos of southern Florida, or in a walled garden in Charleston. But with the first hint of northern spring, the thrashers moved north, a little way at a time, jaunting along night after night, and staying during the day in a garden or in a berry tangle along a country road.

Then one day early in April, a long brown bird came down on an old rail fence beside a thicket, and poured out a rapturous, tumbling song that for splendor and beauty was unequalled on that April day. A song that bubbled with innumerable mimickings and improvisations from that versatile throat, with each phrase repeated twice over to fix its magnificence in the listener's mind.

Days went by. Days of courtship, of ardent song. And then in May a nest of thin twigs was built in the protected fortress of a haw tree along the woodland path, not far from the open pasture where the sun was hot. And in early June the eggs were laid.

Now the thrasher sang little; brillance of song was dulled by the heat of summer, and by the the constant, harried search for food to fill those clamoring beaks of young thrashers in the nest. Not until next April would song pour out again so splendidly. Not until another spring would a long, cinnamon-brown bird with a snapping yellow eye claim sole thrasher-rights to that particular bit of woods. (*June 1940*)

$$* \quad * \quad *$$

Take the woodland path to its end, past the thicket in which the thrasher's nest still clings, to where the path merges with the park or golf course. Here lives the eloquent ground squirrel—not a gopher, as he is often called, but a squirrel who prefers to live in holes in the ground instead of in trees, which, after all, is merely a matter of preference. Here in complicated runways he stores seeds and grains, makes a comfortable bedroom, and has at least one back door in case Danger, four-legged or two, chases him into his front door and camps there until he comes out.

The thirteen-lined ground squirrel or spermophile—which means he's a seed-eater—is a small, sand-colored, sleek-backed little squirrel with a sparse tail, big eyes set rather high in his head (the better to see you, my child), and thirteen stripes (count 'em) down his back. The stripes are broken into little squares, unlike the five smooth, sleek stripes down the chipmunk's back.

The ground squirrel, secure in the sunny grassland, claims rights of priority to the park and golf course, and seems to resent the presence of golfers on the tees. And why not? His holes were there first—and if by accident a golf ball rolls into one of his burrows and effectively stops it up, the golfer shouldn't complain. The righteously indignant ground squirrel sits up like a picket pin, jerks his abbreviated tail, presses his hands to his heaving chest, and coughs out some of the most piercing, vindicative, and shrill reproach to be heard in the animal world. (*July 1940*)

The woodland path came down the slope, through the cool blue-green shade of deep woods, into a sudden blaze of summer where under the August sunshine, the pond lay bright and hot. Water lilies were opening, and dragon-flies, awakened from the lethargy of cool dawn, zipped back and forth in the reviving heat. A sandpiper peeped, flew on bowed wings to the muddy shore, and at the movement a black turtle on a log nearby moved its head with a rapid flick of alarm.

The turtle was ruler of the pond, perhaps the largest creature that lived in it—he, glossy black of shell, a glimpse of red and yellow on his wrinkled skin—he, the painted turtle. The log was his by undisputed right; the August sun was pleasantly warm to his cool blood.

Around him the water lily leaves, grown lush and thick now in the latter end of summer, crowded in great green masses, and among them were flowers with waxen white petals and a cluster of quivering yellow stamens. Lilies like these once were adored for their serenity, their soul peace, in Egypt, in Greece, in Persia, in China, and in India; they were "Stars Fallen Into The Water" to the American Indians, the Throne of Osiris to the Egyptian. And the turtle—perhaps the turtle didn't even see them, but only knew of lilies by their rubbery stems down in the water, where tadpoles wriggled past, and where a thick growth of tiny plant and animal life used the stems as abiding places.

August—it means ponds like this one, full of cattails and lily pads. It means hot sun and blue-green shade, water lilies, and a flat, glossy black turtle basking in the sun. (*Aug. 1940*)

*   *   *

The woodland path comes out of the trees and into a blaze of sunshine in the marsh, where, over the trackless cattails and mallows, slim birds wheel and circle, cut keen parabolas in the air, or suddenly swoop down to rest on telephone wires. Miles of wires are lined with birds—with twittering, restless swallows, thousands sitting side by side in immaculate rows, or taking wing again in the endless search for insects.

The swallows finished nesting weeks ago, and came away to the swamps for a final whirl of gaiety, dining, and community fun before they all head south for the winter. Swallows—the bank, rough-winged, barn, and tree swallows—gather in the lowlands as early as mid-August, and wait for the southward call. Meanwhile they moult and grow fat for the long, exacting journey into another continent. Once long ago folk thought that swallows simply dived into the mud of ponds to hibernate with the frogs; their presence near water, and their sudden disappearance easily explained this theory, but now it is known that they fly fast and far, and that they spend their winter thousands of miles away.

Sometimes there are mixed flocks. Sometimes they are all one kind. There may be the little brown bank swallow with the brown band across its white chest; the rough-winged swallow distinguished by the smudge of brown-gray on the not-so-white chest; the dark blue and orange satin barn swallow whose movements are all exquisite, whose colors are unequaled. And there is the neat tree swallow that nests in abandoned woodpecker holes in river lowlands and swamps. It is pure white below and steel-blue or shining green above, or brown in the females and young. Tree swallows are the first of the glad-voiced clan to come early in spring, the last twittering flocks to leave in autumn. *(Sept. 1940)*

* * *

When milkweed silks are flying off into the trackless blue October air, and when that air is so full of ripe scents and pungent possibilities that a walk is like wine to the senses, there come drifting orange and brown butterflies, Monarchs, heading south. They are scattered everywhere, fluttering over corn fields, probing the nectaries of purple New England asters beside the road, gathering by dozens among the trees. Sometimes thousands of butterflies are scattered over the sky, which, as is told so vividly in the October issue of *Reader's Digest,* in some places is actually darkened by the flitting, bronze and copper throng.

The Monarchs which come through Illinois may have left Canada a few weeks before, or they may have been hatched from the jewel-like chrysalids hung on milkweed stalks in Illinois pastures and fields. They pick up additions all along the way as they fly, and move on to the south to spend the winter. In spring they come back again, more tattered, more weather-beaten, and fewer in numbers, than this glistening delegation that flutters through October.

The Monarch butterfly has an interesting race history. A native of tropical America, it comes north to lay its eggs and die. Several batches of Monarch caterpillars hatch and spin their chrysalids in a summer, so that by autumn the parent butterflies of springtime are all dead. Yet back goes a lazy, drifting flock, unerringly southward to the tropics where they, like all their migrating ancestors, spend the winter. No one can explain how the Monarchs find their way, nor why they gather in such flocks. But it is enough to see them in October, orange and brown, brilliant against a blue sky, a part of leaf smoke, color-ful trees, and the delight which comes with a walk in October. Monarchs even come into town, and on any autumn day there may be an orange butterfly caught in the stream of city traffic, blown about by air currents and hurrying cars, tossed high, then low, yet always flitting on, on to the south. *(Oct. 1940)*

* * *

There is snow in the woods, snow in the fields, and in its tell-tale album the small woods-creatures write their autographs. Here are the bold prints of a crow, the skippings of white-footed mice, the lace-work of junco tracks, the gambolings of rabbits. There must have been dozens of rabbits, hundreds of them. Their tracks make rabbit lanes, rabbit roads, arterial highways made by furry feet of rabbits going somewhere, coming back. Main roads are crossed by others at a neat and precise angle; only a few tracks wander from the beaten paths—the footprints of individualists that prefer to go their own ways. And after a night of winter moonlight, the snow in thickets and corn-fields is so interlaced with lanes that the tracks themselves are blurred. It is in winter that we really begin to see the extent of the cottontail population.

Rabbits are the fuzz-tailed comedians of the woods, leaping humorists that, with a sidewise fling of strong hind-legs and a twitch of roguish ears, scamper in a blaze of moonlight, and then head for garden or cornfield. Last summer's cabbages are well-gnawed by the end of winter. Around each stalk as it juts from the snow there is a neat ring of pressed-down snow where rabbits sat to dine on what was left of cabbage flavor. Leftover nubbins in the field are chewed; fruit trees in the garden are gnawed for the sweet inner bark just above snow-line. Rabbits—dancing, furry-footed clowns that trample whole highways in their own domains—inject a bit of humor into any picture, take away some of the burden of winter, lighten the seriousness of bitter cold. (*Jan 1941*)

*   *   *

In winter the woods are occupied only by those hardy creatures that can withstand the rigors of cold and hunger. Squirrels sleep fitfully in their leaf-nests, and then scamper about to hunt unforgotten caches of nuts and acorns salted away last fall. Rabbits have a gay time of it; they dine well. White-footed mice set a lace-work of little tracks around rattling weed-stalks. Foxes make a bee-line for unwary bird or rabbit, and the ravenous shrew and the blood-thirsty weasel hunt out the warm blood of sleeping bird or mouse.

All these animals are self-sufficient in winter; they seem to enjoy it. But others slumber peacefully through the long, cold winter. They sleep beneath the snow-drifted woodland path, under rock piles, or in tree-holes and tree-stumps—placid sleepers undisturbed by cold.

Some of these occasionally awaken and step out for a bite or a stretch—the raccoon, the muskrat, even the chipmunk. But the skunk, the ground-squirrel, the opossum, and the woodchuck like to stay long abed, curled up in a compact ball, tail over nose, fast asleep until the warming fingers of spring prod them into hungry wakefulness.

Upon one of these sleepers, however, a solemn duty has been imposed. The woodchuck, or groundhog, is the only American animal with a national holiday named in its honor—apparently for no good reason, for the groundhog is one of the winter's soundest sleepers. It seldom fulfills the legend which states that on February 2 the groundhog must leave its warm bed, scan the sky, and predict the weather for the next six weeks. It is all a legend, zoologists say—yet perhaps it may be hard to explain the presence of tracks, one February day, around the entrance to a woodchuck's hole. (*Feb. 1941*)

Suddenly across the woodland path a slim body moves over the fine grey dust and into the grass. "The grass divides as with a comb"—and the ribbon snake is gone. Here is one of the neatest of creatures, one of the cleanest, least pretentious, and most compact. It walks on its hundred ribs and goes about catching insects and crunchy beetles from April until frost tightens the lock on the cold earth and seals the snakes in their winter quarters.

The ribbon snake, one of the garter snake tribe, is a harmless reptile whose shining scales overlap in a neat, precise pattern; the body is painted length-wise with stripes of black, yellow, and brown; it is never slimy. The head is oval and shades off into the body. This is one of the distinguishing marks that indicates as plainly as words that this is not a poisonous snake, and that its bite, should it be provoked, is nothing more than a prick. The non-poisonous snakes are all one piece; the head is not triangular nor distinct from the body. The body tapers neatly to the thready tip of the tail.

The snake pauses in mid-path, raises its head and tests the air for signs of danger or disturbance. The orange tongue, tipped with black, flicks in and out —not in arrogance or menace, but inquisitively. Then, if all is well, the ani-mated ribbon moves off among the grass and leaves, where it is camouflaged by that nice touch of nature which makes creatures invisible in their chosen environment. (*April 1941*)

∗　　∗　　∗

Out of the loose, rich, leaf-moldy soil of the bottomland woods, out of cool slopes and along streams and in ravines, spring up the early mushrooms— inky caps, mica caps, morels, and gyromitras. Of them all, the morels are most famous—queer, hollow sponges on brittle white stems. "Sponge mush-rooms," many call them.

They have been often confused with the false morel, the robust, deceptive gyromitra. This is a big semi-solid fungus, the stout stem pure white, and corded as if it were made up of a group of half-fused stems. The cap is red-brown and deeply convoluted, yet not pitted as is the morel's thinner pale brown cap. The almost solid center of the gyromitra is chambered and tun-nelled through and through. Compare the two and their dissimilarity is striking; see the one and it may be confused with the other.

Many people eat the gyromitra with apparent relish and no after effects. Yet behind its innocent and morel-like attitude stands the record of more than 150 deaths from the helvellic poisoning contained in the gyromitra's juices. Authorities are still puzzled about this inconsistency of the gyromitra, a mush-room which may be eaten safely by a thousand persons, and yet may kill one. It may be that the age of the mushroom is the deciding factor; perhaps it is the food with which it is combined; perhaps it is the way in which it is cooked. Nevertheless, and in spite of its undoubtedly excellent flavor, the gyromitra should be shunned as food. (*May 1941*)

ANIMAL STORIES

IN THE FOOTSTEPS OF THE DEER

It is half past five on a misty, cool morning in a northern forest. The chipmunks and red squirrels, awake since dawn, now set up a whirring and a fussing and chattering as a yearling black bear, oblivious to their racketing, heads down the sandy road for his private path into the forest. All around him the forest is awakening to the daylight. The creatures of night are ready for rest, the creatures of daylight are ready for activity. And in that in-between time, that crystalline period in the day which is neither night nor morning but a suffusion of both, the creatures of that moment move in calmness and in confidence.

As mists steam off the bog, the tamaracks and spruces are pearled with fine droplets of water. The hummocks of muskeg are misted as if with frost, and the deer trails through the sphagnum show where the deer have walked during these early hours of not-quite-day. Now on the sandy trail above the bog the sharply pricked hoof marks are unhurried and do not show the deep jabs which indicate deer on the run. These were made by ambling deer— and there, down the sandy trail where lately the bear walked, are three deer. They walk in leisure, snatch mouthfuls of wintergreen from the roadside, pause, move on. A doe and her fawn up in the woods graze noisily, as if there never could be danger in the world; the dawn hour gives them great confidence which will leave them when the sun is up.

An osprey shrills. Loons, commuting between lakes, fly over and send down their wild yodeling cries which are part of this wild northern country. Birds in the woods are awake. Chickadees flit, talking, in the pines. There is the lazy song of a black-throated green warbler, the song of a mourning warbler in a pile of slash, the incessant singing of vireos, the *kit-kit* sound of a winter wren, the baby-talk of a red-breasted nuthatch, and, in the distance, always the loons.

The trail dips down and crosses the swale where white violets of utmost fragrance bloom in June. A deer moves noisily in the cutover. A barred owl, not yet asleep in the balsams, hoots a few resonant tones before the sun comes up. And then there comes a loud "tunk-tunk-tunk!" on a dead aspen stub. There—a pileated woodpecker. It is huge and black and gaudy, a tremendous bird which digs and hammers with gargantuan strength upon the tree. The chips fly. The pile of chips on the ground already shows some size. The beak of this bird is a massive chisel which can dig strongly into a living hemlock or pine, and it delves into the soft dead aspen wood as if it were putty. The pileated woodpecker, emblem of wilderness, shining black with long rakish red crest accented with white on the long neck, opens its black capes of wings to reveal white patches and silently drifts off among the pines up the slope. The bird is gone, but the pile of white chips is evidence of one more creature which has worked here during the dawn hour when magic is in the woods. And onward, past the old tree, past the clump of orange mushrooms among the pearl-grey reindeer lichen, past the indian pipe beside a stump, past the bright green beds of ground pines up the slope, go the footprints of the deer, on, into the broad day. (*July 1950*)

A DEER ON THE RIDGE

The young white-tail stood poised on the crest of the ridge. His sharp tracks had pricked the light snow all the way from his bedding-down place in the swamp to the top of the hill. He stood there, very still, only his nostrils moving as he took in deep, knowledge-filled breaths of the wind coming up from the valley. He stood like an iron deer in a Victorian garden, noble and strong and just a little bit unreal in the winter landscape. And then with a sudden whistling he wheeled, kicking snow, and rose in splendid, high-heeled bounds over the hazel bushes. His plumy tail, flung high, was gray on top and white below, the white hairs standing out in an aura. Leaping, the buck was gone.

He was out of sight, but the grandeur of his wildness on the ridge remained as if in a visible memory. A jet plane went over in a high burst of sound, was gone. The voice of a Diesel engine called, and the distant rumble of train wheels came and went, far away down the valley. Beyond the second ridge a four-lane highway carried thousands of motor cars at high speed on their separate errands to their separate destinations. Although an ageless curl of smoke came from chimneys in the valley, there were tall television antennae standing like gaunt trees under the chimneys themselves. It was today, 1963; but, there had been a wild deer on the ridge.

As if today had never been, the deer took memory back into an era in which his kind were abundant and free, unhampered by fences, unendangered by highways, when the only fear they knew was the cougar's leap, the wolf's attack, the Indian's arrow, or the pioneer, with flintlock musket, who was out to track down meat for the table.

That was the world of the deer; they belonged in it; they fit. If they were struck down at times, then their attackers not only fed themselves on succulent dark venison but prevented an over-population of the deer so that the survivors themselves had enough to eat during the long, hard winters.

There are many deer in Illinois today. There are more, it is believed, than there may have been since 1830-31 when the Winter of the Deep Snow destroyed thousands of them. The deer had not been able to get about in the drifts, or else they fell helplessly on the crust and were pulled down by the wolves. The deer population waned rapidly after that. Civilization came into Illinois. Farms were fenced; cities were built; there were fewer and fewer deer. But they were still living and multiplying in Wisconsin and in the Missouri hills and bottomlands. Reintroduction in the past half-century has brought them back in numbers into Illinois. There now are thousands. All too often they are killed on highways. Now and again one becomes confused and comes into a city, usually managing to create a good deal of havoc by jumping through a picture window or crashing into a store-front before being captured or shot. After fifty-seven years of no deer hunting in Illinois, the first open season began in 1957, when more than two thousand were taken.

In spite of the fact that large wild animals are occasionally troublesome to farmers and a danger on highways, the return of the deer is one of the strange and undeniably heart-warming occurrences among native creatures. We think we have subdued the wild. We regret having caused extinction of passenger pigeon, heath hen, or Eskimo curlew; we wish we could have it to do over again and do it better, knowing what we do now. But some wild things have refused to be exterminated. The sight of the deer on the ridge is a timeless glimpse into a far past which is our ancient heritage. *(Nov. 1963)*

THE HOUR OF THE BEAR

He came slowly and with dignity down the trail over the Hog Back Ridge and like a shadow moved among the pines. Now was the Hour of the Bear and on soft feet he came through the twilight.

He was a yearling black bear who lived somewhere over in the Big Woods and each evening he made a circuit of feeding places, chiefly to garbage pits near forest cabins. By day he foraged in the blueberry patches or in the tangles of wild red raspberries on the hills. He was cautious; he was wary. He had been shot at too many times, shouted at too many times, to take chances now. He was a young bear, unused to the world, and he still must have been somewhat taken aback at the reception his unobtrusive visits created. He confined his attention to the garbage pits; he bothered no one, wished to cause no disturbance, wanted only peace. But folk were afraid of him. Some threatened to shoot if he came near. Mankind for too many years has read tales of wild bears and been conditioned to the reflex of fright in the presence of a bear.

It was also the instinct of the bear to feed himself. In late summer and autumn all northern animals must eat heartily, must build up their fat reserve to meet the coming onslaught of a severe winter. There must be food, and often the bears augment their diet of fruits and acorns and beetles by visiting that source of supply, the garbage pits.

Now as the sun set in a brilliantly clear northern Wisconsin sky, there grew an electric feeling in the air. As that tremendous crystalline silence of the north closed down through the forest and over the hills, there came that positive assurance. Bear! Tonight he would come.

It was twilight when the slow black form materialized on the crest of the wooded ridge and angled off through the pines to the deer trail above the bog. He was not coming straight this time. He was wary. He had been alarmed too much lately. He moved with no undignified speed or awkwardness, but each movement had its velvet meaning, each spot where his big black feet were placed was a planned place. No twig snapped. The ferns parted silently as he went through. He paused, threw up a massive head, listened. He was grace itself, a smooth black shape among the blacker trees, his alert ears and senses keyed to any breath of danger. He stood still for so long that he might have been a stump rooted there for a hundred years; and then he moved on again, circled the quiet cabin, was lost to view for a moment or two in the hazel bushes, then appeared on the far side of the cabin and came closer, closer . . . paused again and snuffed the air, loudly . . . moved to the sand pit and with a last look at the cabin, descended ponderously into the pit.

There were the eager sounds of slurping as he lunched on melon rinds. Tin cans were nudged about and morsels which the busy chipmunks had missed during the day were retrieved. Now and again the black head rose above the pit to eye the cabin. With a sudden heave he was out again. He moved darkly to the stump where the chipmunks fed during the day, and with a huge munch he engulfed a sugared doughnut which had been put there for him to eat. Still watching the cabin, the yearling paused for a long, tense moment. Then he noticed two people who stood there breathlessly watching him. He had missed their scent before and now it smote him in the face. He flung up his head, his ears alerted, twitched forward; he snuffed, then— whoosh! With a tremendous, expelled breath the bear tore for the high country, and the crackling of branches and snapping bushes along his route told where he went. It had been too peaceful for him; he had been uneasy all the time and now the scent of people came at him like a tangible thing. His great soft feet carried him racing for the safe distant darkness of the Big Woods.

The Hour of the Bear had come and gone. There, briefly, had lingered one of the last members of the wilderness fraternity, the bear. Garbage pit, watermelon rinds and doughnuts notwithstanding, here was some of that nearly lost primeval animal life which still in many places lives as it used to live in Illinois in the days before Columbus. *(Oct. 1950)*

BATS ON THE WING

Of the bats in this region, the red bat is most abundant. It is the small flyer in the sunset sky, a flitting shadow over ponds, the bat which sleeps hung up by its claws in bush or tree. The golden-red fur of the four-inch body glints in the sun. The wings, which are folded compactly when the animal sleeps, look impotent and weak, but when spread they may extend to eight or ten inches and have a tremendous power of flight. These are not coarse, leathery wings stretched across a bony framework; they are thin, fragile, silky skin which is almost translucent in the sunlight. The skin is fitted across elongated fingerbones in the bat's modified forelegs to make a structure admirably capable of sustained flight.

In these remarkable wings, and in the expressive head of the bat, there centers the greatest interest. The small face has personality. It is fierce, but in spite of a diminutive and uncompromising ferocity it is not an evil face. Yet because of the centuries of superstition which have made of the bat an unpleasant thing to be shunned, often the peculiar beauty of this small creature's face goes unobserved. The ears are delicate, intricately shaped, large, and are very highly sensitized. Hearing, not eyesight—though a bat can see—guide the animal in its jagged journey through darkness. By means of a sort of radar system, the bat avoids obstacles in its path. The mouth has well-shaped jaws; there is a red tongue and a set of fine, sharp teeth which are fitted for holding and chewing insects caught on the wing. Young bats, too, have this same queer elfin aspect. They are born in summer, sometimes two, occasionally four, and are fed for several weeks on their mother's milk. For a while she carries them around with her as she flies; when they grow too heavy she leaves them on a tree trunk while she forages for food. In a short time they become independent and join their parents in flying after insects.

Then on a day in late summer, in that quiet, listening time when it is neither night nor day, when a star or two is out, yet the light of the sun has not been entirely blotted up, bats flit against the twilight or come down and swoop by dozens over the pond. Insects in these places are abundant in summer, but as autumn nears and there are frosts, the insect quota daily lessens.

Now the little red bats from all over Illinois, feeding as they go, begin to move in numbers across the daytime sky. At the time of bird migration, small mammals follow the sky route of hawks and thrushes, south for the winter. As autumn moves onward, no more jagged bat-wings trace invisible pathways across the pond or among stars. Not until spring brings back the migrant birds will there be bats in the sky. (*Sept. 1945*)

LAST NIGHT'S MICE

Last night the moon rose late and dim. It shone pallidly over a dark world in which there were small rustlings and thin voices, the rustlings and voicings of the creatures of an autumn night, moving about their business.

For night is the world of many wild things. It is a cloak for their movements, a shelter as wide as the sky and as broad as the dark itself, in which the timid ones, the tasty ones, the hunted ones may nourish themselves. Night was made for the little things. The dark was made for mice.

Last night's mice were busy ever since the cloak of twilight seeped up from the earth and finally blended with the last glow of the sky. They had hunted at intervals during the day, then had napped, now were ready again to hunt. Meadow mice uncurled from their grass nests in tangled tussocks or down in the ground, and ventured into the arched tunnels through the grass which extended in a maze across the pasture. The floor of these tunnels is beaten hard by the pattering of many hurrying feet.

From above, the grass-highways are scarcely visible, even in daytime; at night they are twice as hidden. They convey the rotund, brown-black meadow mice from nest to foraging grounds without showing themselves to the menaces which wait for small running things.

But beyond the tunnels' ending lies the whole broad terrible world of night. It is a night where owls hunt, where foxes prowl, where shrews forage, where a plume-tailed skunk waddling past may take a meal of mouse, or a raccoon on its nightly walk between den and pond may chance upon *Microtus*, the meadow mouse. There are so many creatures which relish mice that it is a wonder that any survive. Yet there are always plenty of last night's mice on hand to carry on next evening.

Now in September the mice are harvesting the drying seeds of grasses and other plants to store in underground burrows. Sharp yellow teeth cut down tall stalks in order to get at seeds high in the air. Bulbs of wild onion, tubers of hog peanut, the roots of dandelion, blazing star and sunflower are dug up and stored. Plains Indians, it is said, took advantage of *Microtus's* harvesting ability and frequently unearthed the store rooms which often contained half a dozen quarts of edible roots, bulbs and seeds.

But *Microtus* does not confine his foraging to wild foods. He often does considerable damage to alfalfa, grain, orchards and gardens. In normal concentration, this mouse damage is usually not too high; the large numbers of predators relishing mouse dinners take care of many of the hungry ones. But about every four years, the meadow mouse population takes a sudden spurt. Nearly six times more mice are produced in a season than usually. In Victor Cahalane's "Mammals of North America," he states that in 1907 there were an estimated 8,000 to 12,000 mice per acre in Humboldt Valley, Nevada. Destruction was terrible, yet neither poisons nor predators eventually ended the epidemic of mice, but rather disease. Four months later, scarcely any could be found.

In Illinois, although *Microtus*, the meadow mouse, follows the same sort of cycle, there is seldom too great a supply. The busy mice dwell in pastures and meadows, make tunnels, hunt by day and in the darkness, and try to avoid the hawk in the sky, the fox in the field, the snake squirming into the burrow, all of which are trying to reduce by a slight ratio the number of last night's mice. (*Sept. 1957*)

SHADOW IN THE NIGHT

In the twilight a shadow flits in a long swoop from a high tree toward the ground. When it almost reaches the ground there is a sudden swerve and the shadow is lost against a dark tree trunk perhaps a hundred feet or more from where the flight began. The shadow has floated as if disembodied and weightless, as if some whim of night sent part of itself to merge with the dusky woods. But it was a flying squirrel, not a shadow, which has started on its way through the forest.

It is a tedious route, perhaps, but to the little squirrel it is the way it knows, the best way to travel from tree to tree across the dangerous forest or through a town. The little animal may have been sleeping all day in an old woodpecker hole high in an oak, wakening at sundown. It thrusts its white and brown head from the hole and blinks its large, luminous dark eyes against the last glow of day. In a flash the animal is out of the hole—it can come in and out of a hole one inch in diameter and do it with ease—and poises on a limb many feet above the ground where it may sit for many minutes polishing and grooming its fur and wiping its whiskers. And suddenly it is not there.

In its leap the flying squirrel spreads its legs widely and thus stretches taut the loose membrane of skin and fur connecting hind legs with forelegs. These loose folds of skin act like little "wings," buoying up the squirrel in its leap through space. It is not truly flying, only gliding, yet it can control to a great degree where it goes and where it lands. It may glide almost 150 feet, may seem about to plummet to the ground, when a quick flip of the tail halts the glide and aims the animal at the tree trunk ahead. The maneuvering of tail, flanges and body contrive to send the little squirrel in almost any direction it chooses except back up to the perch it has just left. With a thump the flying squirrel hits the tree, and clings. It is perfectly still so that any enemy eyes which saw that long glide cannot detect an animal on the trunk. Then the squirrel races up the tree to another high limb, and launches off on another long glide. If the trees are close enough together so that the animal may run like other squirrels through the upper branches, it does this; but to bridge gaps between trees, it has perfected the long glide and seldom or never comes down on the dangerous ground. In the trees, the flying squirrel travels faster than any other animal. "Flying squirrels," said Dr. C. H .D. Clarke, "are like coiled springs . . . they leave the observer blinking in amazement at not having seen the jump."

As a nocturnal animal, the flying squirrel has the large eyes which many creatures of the night must have in order to get about and find their food. It eats the usual varied diet of squirrels—seeds, nuts, small fruits, mushrooms, the blossoms of maple, as well as insects, birds' eggs, and young birds. It is less than a foot long, including the flattened brown and white tail, and weighs no more than three or four ounces. It is often found in town, where it may enter attics to sleep by day, take over a martin house, or enlarge the opening of a wren box and fill the interior with nesting material. Friendly and agreeable among each other, the adults like to gather together for slumber, and as many as fifty individuals have been found together in one hollow tree.

Three or four young are born in late spring. By the time they are two months old they are out of the nest and trying short glides, but not until their first autumn have they acquired their parents' ability to leap into space across long distances between trees. *(Sept. 1962)*

RED SQUIRREL

The red squirrel raced along his private route through the branches, sending them bobbing under his swift passage, then leaped with a thump to the cabin roof. With what seemed unnecessarily heavy feet to the sleepers below, the little squirrel ran up to the peak of the roof and paused there, tail lashing in a fury. A self-appointed alarm clock at half-past five in the morning, the squirrel churred and whirred and chattered and ground his teeth, and flung his tail about in what appeared to be a fine display of temper.

Below him, placidly ignoring the racket, a late-returning skunk waddled past the cabin and disappeared into the ferns. The squirrel, with a parting tirade and a grand flourishing of tail, ran across the roof, rattled down a window screen, thumped on the feeding stand, now quite empty after a night of forays by raccoon, flying squirrel and skunk, expressed his feelings loudly, and bounced to the ground. Hastily but with seemingly excellent memory, he dug up a cone cached there in July, raced with it to a stump and sat neatly upright, tail against his back, holding the cone in his forepaws, to tear it apart and get out the seeds. For a while, the squirrel was too busy to be noisy.

But most of his waking hours and sometimes at night when he is roused by moonlight or dreams to bark and whirr, the red squirrel is one of the noisiest animals in the woods. Most forest creatures seem to prefer quietness. Birds sing for their own purposes, but the mammals find safety in silence, all but this squirrel who seems to scorn caution. He is the self-appointed watchman, notifying everyone and everything of the approach of any stranger. And if no visitors come to the woods, he lets off steam anyway.

Containing all this temper and noise is one of the neatest and handsomest little animals to be found in the American woods. A northern animal in the midwest, though more southern in the Appalachians and western mountains, the red squirrel is the smallest of our tree squirrels. His big eyes are rimmed with white. He has snowy paws and underparts, and a beautiful copper-red color on tail and upperparts which glints in sunshine or is accented magnificently against snow. The red squirrel *(Tamiasciurus hudsonicus)* is now gone from Illinois. He is not to be confused with the big fox squirrel *(Sciurus niger)*, occasionally called red squirrel in some parts of the state. Scarcely bigger than a chipmunk, he is, nevertheless, able to hold his own with the larger members of the tribe.

Although he stakes out a claim on most seeds and nuts in his territory, he is not solely a vegetarian. A hungry carnivorous animal at times, he may be discovered sitting on his haunches, avidly tearing apart the bloody carcass of a young bird just taken from a nearby nest. It is part of his nature, part of his squirrel character.

A bundle of furious energy, leaping, arguing, sassing, racketing through the trees, the little red squirrel in his splendid copper color and his indomitable disposition of independence and challenge, is a delightful and important part of our northern woods. They would seem hollow and astonishingly empty without him. (*Aug. 1960*)

THE SEPTEMBER CHIPMUNKS

Listen! Around tree trunks, over humpy roots, through the crackling dryness of autumn leaves, there goes the bustling sound of small feet. The chipmunks are working hard, and the woods are full of small, scampering mysterious little noises. There goes another—and a plump brown chipmunk, tail audaciously outflung, cheeks stuffed with seeds, dashes off to its hole in the ground.

The chipmunk is a small striped squirrel that spends most of its time in a search for food, or in digging home burrows in rocky places or under tree roots. Down in one of these complicated underground hallways are sleeping rooms and storage chambers, the latter for those seeds and nuts which the chipmunks are now gathering. The bounty of September is welcome fare. The hard basswood seeds are neatly halved and the meat eaten; hazel nuts are hastily monopolized and stored away; the sweet, white oak acorns are often garnered, and so are the seeds of panic grass, wild plum, wild crab, and apple. Even mushrooms are eaten. And when a camper drops a prune seed along the trail, the first chipmunk on the scene hurridly stuffs the prize in a cheek pocket and races off to dine in gluttonous solitude. The debris of picnic spots is closely examined and small edibles carried away in furry chipmunk cheeks—or prudently eaten on the spot.

The chipmunk feels safest on the ground, especially when one of the doorways of the home burrow is well within reach. However, in time of extreme danger when the hole is too far away, a chipmunk will run up a tree and from a perch of vantage will scold the intruder below. A chipmunk has a most surprising voice for one so small and one so apparently meek. With wren-like violence, a loud, irritated barking is shrilled from an angry chipmunk —perhaps one who has been annoyed in his calm contemplation of a choice prune seed. (*Sept. 1941*)

EXPLORING FOR SNAILS

These are the snails, the quiet ones. Perhaps it was, in part, about such as they that an old philosopher once said: *"The more things thou learnest to know and enjoy, the more complete and full will be for thee the delight of living."* To become acquainted with the snails and the places in which they live is to know one more small part of a complex and fascinating world. For you cannot find and learn about a snail without at the same time learning about the bit of woods or water in which it lives.

A snail is a soft yet muscular, boneless body encased until its death in a coiled shell. Some are hatched from eggs laid under dead leaves, others from eggs laid in water; some are born alive. A snail moves about on a single foot, the muscular grey part of the body that extends from the shell. Silvery mucus flows from this foot, and, in the case of the land snail, paves a gentle route about the woods in the search for food. Snails are scavengers; hundreds of sharp teeth arranged on the long tongue rasp into and devour small dead things as well as greenery. Land snails have eyes placed on the ends of two long "horns"; two shorter tentacles are used as sensory organs, but the water snails have only one pair of tentacles with the eyes at their bases. When the snail is alarmed, the tentacles are drawn into the body and the body itself is contracted by powerful muscles into the shell. There the snail lies, motionless, until danger is past.

But now it is a warm spring day—it is almost summer, for leaves are on the trees and in the hilly woods the mayapples bloom under their broad umbrellas. The rocky wooded hillside slopes to the level bottomland with its thick covering of soft leaf mold; out beyond in the sun is the brilliance of a shallow pond, and still farther away flows the river. These all are the haunts of snails.

Some live on the hillside and hide under damp leaves or among cool stones. Here are the flat, coiled, brown-striped shells of *Haplotrema* and the pale brown *Polygyra* with an ivory rim around the opening of the shell, a white tooth-like projection on the curve. There are many kinds of *Polygyra* in the woods; to learn them all is to know many pleasant days among the trees.

At the foot of the hill there is a log and under it are more snails. Some have tiny, amber-colored, paper-thin shells—these are *Zonitoides*. Under the log may be the remains of a cache of well-gnawed hickory nuts and hackberry seeds, with a half dozen empty and broken *Polygyra* shells which were cracked and the contents eaten by a deer mouse.

The snail population changes from hillside to log to the edge of the pond. There may be the thin brown shells of *Succinea* among the shore plants, and in the water are small oval *Physa,* the common tadpole-snail which populates most shallow waters. Among the stones are *Helisoma* with wheel-shaped, algae-coated shells.

Beyond in the river there are others which are like none to be found on land, nor commonly in the pond. They are the large, striped *Viviparus* and the greenish *Campeloma,* and that ancient type, the slim, top-shaped *Pleurocera* that crawls among the river rocks.

These are the snails, the lowly ones. To know a few of them is to know one more phase of life out of doors, one more link in the miraculous whole which is the world. (*May 1945*)

SAGA OF THE BEAVER

Back of the tall, long dam laid by beavers across a northern river, a beaver-made pool lies smooth and quiet in the sunset. Tall dead trees mark mutely the beaver's industry, for once this was a wooded place along the river, and the trees died when the water rose. Now it maintains that two-to-three-foot depth which is necessary to insure food and protection to the beaver colony. Suddenly a resounding splash—a beaver slaps the water in a great dive. Another, in a long submarine swoop from the water tunnel of the den which is heaped against the bank, comes up and breaks water. Beaver kits inside the den cry plaintively like hungry kittens. Quietly in the twilight the beavers go about their business.

In them one may see the strong, wise engineer, builder of great dams and strong lodges, the animal which through no choice of its own determined much of the history of the north in America. Beaver fur . . . that was the driving urge which sent men and nations into wildernesses and wars to gain a beaver fur monopoly.

The Indians of America had known the warmth and desirability of beaver furs for hundreds of years before white men suddenly became aware of them. Then in 1600 the first fur-trading post was set up in Canada. That was the beginning—that was the inception of a new way of thinking in North America and in Europe. For here in the wilderness of the New World lay wealth to make men rich. So explorers gave up the idea that by going west across America they could find China. Nicolet's fine robes, brought along to impress Chinese mandarins when he should land on their shores across Lake Michigan, impressed the Winnebagos—and instead of gold, the Winnebagos had beaver furs. LaSalle's fur post near Montreal did a bigger business in beaver furs than they had dreamed of doing in gold and silks from the Orient. Champlain gave up hunting for the short cut to India and on his last and longest trip into the American wilderness in 1615 gathered beaver furs instead.

France began the trade. In the search for greater and greater quantities and in an effort to force a monopoly in the beaver trade, the French were compelled to colonize, to push westward into unexplored country. The English coveted beaver pelts and organized the Hudson's Bay Company, whose shield and coat of arms today still shows the beaver supreme in honor. For the beavers—those quiet, industrious animals swimming about in the last glow of sunset on a placid spring day in the north woods—the beavers precipitated the Seven Years War and its echoes in America, took Canada away from the French and put it into the hands of the English, sent Lewis and Clark exploring westward to open the fur-traders way to the Pacific and ever richer sources of fur wealth, sent John Jacob Astor and his fur company up on the Columbia River, guided the fabulous fortunes not only of Astor and the Hudson's Bay Company, but of many others who grew rich from trading in beaver skins.

For one main purpose, to get beaver pelts to sell at a high price abroad, the major trails, towns, exploring parties, killings, discoveries, and commerce took place in northern America.

And so, with all this taking of hundreds of thousands of beavers in the wildernesses of the north, the animals began to grow scarce. In many places they were wiped out completely. Although the trade in beaver slackened with the change in fashions in hats and the difficulty of sewing the skins, colony after colony became extinct. The southern part of the range was almost entirely lacking in beavers by the early twentieth century, but many have been stocked in protected places and have begun to come back as they were in the old days. In Jersey County and southern Illinois, beavers have become naturalized as they were before the greatest fur business in the world put a price on every beaver's skin.

It is almost dark. But still the water is silver, and the even wake of ripples spreads widely into the dark shadows of the trees as a beaver dives and puts a period to the saga of his tribe. (*April 1951*)

RECORDS IN THE MUD

Clear and sharp, the hand-like tracks of the raccoons which had fished along that shore were criss-crossed in determined paths upon the firm dark mud. There where the water during the long hot summer days had subsided and left a bare area of wet earth, where the old stalks of lotuses still held seed pods and tattered leaves, the raccoons and other animals had imprinted a record of their wandering.

The raccoons had come to catch crayfish and frogs—and fish, too, if one came into the shallows and could not escape that scooping paw. Monkey-like, the raccoons' hands could catch and grasp and rend; the coons ate anything that was edible.

Muskrats were here, too. Their footprints in the mud were less than half the size of the raccoons' tracks, and were pricked like small stars everywhere in the mud. Among them were heaps of crayfish shells left by the raccoons, or fragments of lotus roots eaten by the muskrats themselves.

There were tracks of herons in the mud; great blue heron, green heron, egret. They all had come along here to fish and had left their marks. And crows—they often came to pick the flesh of dead fish. And there were the small tracks of woods birds which came to the water's edge to drink and bathe. The stories all were here, printed in the mud as if they were printed in a book. They were a natural cuneiform writing in which the one who knows may decipher much that went on here in the hours when people were absent and only the wild creatures dominated the shores.

The tracks of birds and mammals, even those of spiders and insects, are a part of the unified picture of the wild in which all things have significance. The dusty road, the sandy lane, the muddy shore, the soft snow, all provide a recording device in which everything which walks here leaves its imprint. The best time to see wild tracks is early morning when the slanted sunlight picks out the curves and contours of the marks and makes them clearer. Early in the morning the tracks are fresh and have not been marred by man-made tracks or by shifting dust or sand, or the melting of snow.

Tracks are comparatively easy to photograph: let the shadows pick out the forms of the tracks; photograph them with a portrait lens or as closely as possible without one. There in the mud or on the shore the tracks form an interesting pattern, a fascinating story. (*Sept. 1950*)

HOLES IN THE GROUND

Holes are fascinating doorways to an underworld which lies directly beneath our feet, a world of ants and moles and night-crawlers, a world which man only shatters when he attempts to examine it.

Holes which attract the most attention from mankind are those with an entrance diameter of about an inch or more. "Snake holes," these are called, but they aren't. At least, the snake didn't make the hole himself; he only borrowed it in a moment of danger, slid into its protective dark depths, and waited until it was safe to emerge. A snake is not constructed to dig a hole in the ground. He would need a nose like an augur to make a hole as big as his body several feet deep in the ground. No, a snake doesn't dig his own holes; something else did it for him.

One of the most energetic diggers of "snake holes" is the silent crayfish. It spends a good deal of time in the water, but not all of it. Around the pond and along the river, often far away, the crayfish digs a well which promptly fills with seepage water. Around the mouth of the hole he usually piles up the grains of earth which he dug out, to make a sort of mud chimney. In dry weather the crayfish puts a mud cork in the chimney and there below ground, in a nice dark little pool of cool water, the crayfish sits in comfort and waits for rain.

The ground squirrels with their maze of underground burrows in open country are other busy diggers of holes often used by snakes. Larger holes are made by muskrats that burrow in banks of lakes or creeks, tunnels that go far into the earth where a den is made and the young born. And there is the woodchuck with his deep cave, the chipmunk, the mole, the fox, and the skunk, all of which dig holes in the ground.

Even birds make holes. These diggers prefer a fine upstanding clay bank along a road or above a body of water. Here the kingfisher with his shovel-feet digs a burrow straight into the bank, and hollows out a room at the end where the eggs are laid. Often in the same clay bank the bank swallows in mysterious fashion dig quantities of small holes little bigger in diameter than their bodies, and make nests at the ends.

Smaller holes belong to the denizens of earth and air. Into the soil burrows the cicada-killer wasp where she brings a paralyzed cicada as food for her young. Other wasps dig into the ground; so do yellowjackets. So, in fact, do many insects—the ant lion, the burying beetles, the cicada, hawk moths and June beetles, and many more. And there are the worms that live in the soil and which sometimes come out of their small, neat holes. In grassy places there lives the big night crawler, an earthworm with almost the proportions of a young snake, huge and pinkish, that comes out at night. It is a swift thing; with a zip it pops back into its hole.

And there are ant holes, too, neat holes with their little mounds of fine earth-grains around them like miniature volcanoes. Underground, the burrow branches into many passageways with rooms for the young, for storage, and for sleeping. They are efficient burrows, perhaps the most wonderful of all the holes in the ground.

These are some of the makers of holes in the ground . . . tunnels that not only provide shelter for many wild things large and small, but bring air into the earth and prevent packing and stagnation. Holes have their purposes; they also have their element of mystery and surprise. *(July 1943)*

THE YOUNG RABBITS

It is spring—it is Easter—there is a nest of young rabbits under the dogwood tree.

One morning the dry grass, which had been heaped concealingly over the nest, moves as if under its own power as the infant rabbits push blindly over each other. Six of them, like small, sleek chipmunks, muzzle each other, seeking their mother. She comes back periodically, usually at night, to nurse them, but most of the time she leaves them alone. They are safer under the covering of dry grass than if she were there to attract attention to the spot. The miracle of birth and infant survival in a land dangerous to rabbits takes place all over again.

By the end of the first week the young grow restless. One has its eyes open. A day or so later all but one can see; they look more like rabbits now, with small, crisp ears and bodies covered with close brown fur. Before the second week is past, the hollow is filled to overflowing, and one day three of the rabbits slip out and are quickly and irretrievably lost under the arching leaves of the violets. By the next morning the other three are gone, and nothing now will induce them, skittering with shy liveliness, to go back to the one-time safety of the nest. It is this moment in the life of a cottontail rabbit which perhaps is most dangerous of all. The world is full of hungry creatures to whom a baby rabbit just out of the nest is the most delicious morsel to be had. Snakes, foxes, rats, hawks, owls, cats, dogs, all are potential enemies. But in spite of their weakness and softness and expendability, there is always a percentage of baby rabbits which survive and reach an age of greater self reliance. They must know how to get away from danger or to "freeze" beneath a leaf and rely upon its concealment, their own immobility, and the kindness of shadows to hide them.

It would be a far more solemn world if there were no more cottontails dancing in the moonlight or feasting on forbidden tulips and garden peas, no more bunnies hightailing it over the hill as the hiker comes along, no more rabbit tracks crisscrossing the new-laid snow on a winter morning, or, at just the right moment, leaping with a flash of white out of the garden when a very young child is earnestly hunting Easter eggs. *(April 1950)*

❀

❀ # PLANTS AND FLOWERS

❀

❀

"THE MUSHROOM IS THE ELF OF PLANTS"

Although mushrooms have been eaten by prince and peasant for several thousand years, no one seemed to be very sure about what these things were —whether they were plant or animal, or manifestation of the devil, or something akin to witches and fairies.

In the old days mushrooms were called toadstools; later this name was given to those believed to be poisonous, but today the word "mushroom" is accepted for all of them.

People throughout the centuries have braved superstition for a fine dish of stewed mushrooms. The ancient Romans paid high prices for them, but believed that any which grew near a serpent's hole or near rusty nails undoubtedly were poisonous. There were other elaborate and untrustworthy means of knowing mushrooms, some so unreliable that at least one Roman emperor died of their poison. Many another person afterward mistook the wrong kind for an edible sort, or ate a specimen which someone told him was edible—and it wasn't. It was simpler to try the silver-spoon method or the peeled-cap method, neither of which was worth much, because disproving these rules, many a deadly kind did not tarnish a spoon, and the cap of many a poisonous mushroom readily peeled.

Actually there are very few poisonous kinds. Though some are deadly— deadly with the finality of murder—others may cause a severe illness. Still other unreliable sorts have a bad effect upon certain individuals. It all adds up to the great need for caution in picking and eating any mushroom, yet properly identified fungi are as safe to eat as most other known foods. As with many another dish, mushrooms must be fresh and unspoiled at the time they are cooked.

Although there are no rules which will distinguish all poisonous from non-poisonous and edible sorts, the deadly Amanita mushrooms are known by a cup-shaped base which sometimes is hidden underground. The graceful, inter-

151

esting, often colorful Amanitas are to the mushroom world what a rattlesnake is among reptiles. And there is no known cure for Amanita poisoning.

All these deadly and edible specimens belong to a low form of plant life which grows from a tiny reproductive body called a spore. These are produced by millions in gills or pores under the mushroom cap, or inside a puffball, or in the corrugations of a morel. When the ripe spore flies on the wind and lands in a moist, favorable location, it sends out a tiny white root-like body which branches and expands in the soil or inside a dead tree or piece of dead wood until there is a network of delicate white mycelium. By and by, sometimes not until the next year, minute bud-like bodies swell from the mycelium threads, grow larger and larger, but remain beneath the surface of the ground until they are almost fully formed. Then in damp weather they burst through the soil and grow quickly—they truly seem to spring up over night.

Here in the mushroom world are some of the strangest and most interesting forms to be found in nature. When they are fresh, they have a transient perfection unlike anything else in the world. Mushroom flesh is cool and interesting to the touch and smell, colored delicately or brilliantly. There are odd shapes, fascinating textures, earthy odors. No matter if they aren't all edible, these are like flowers, curious and beautiful, ornaments of woods, fields, and lawns. *(July 1944)*

THE LIFE OF AN ORCHID

The orchid in a florist's shop is surrounded by a strange aura of mystery. Its beauty is not quite understood. The crystalline petals seem too fragile to be touched, yet many a Cattleya or lady's slipper will live for weeks without withering. Behind it always is the unforgotten background of jungle which is part of the orchid's personality.

On a great mossy tree in the Costa Rican mountains, the ripe seed pod of a Cattleya orchid bursts and a million powdery seeds fly into the breeze. Not many of the million find a suitable place in which to germinate, but one, perhaps, falls into the damp lichen-growth on a high branch, and here in the warm moisture the seed swells. As this occurs, the spores of a fungus that lives among the lichens enter the softened seed and surround it with a jelly-like substance. Into this protective jelly the tiny orchid-life sends out an almost microscopic root and a single seed-leaf. And that, for a long time, is all.

Dry seasons and wet seasons come and go. In a year the orchid may be only an inch high, but it has increased to three little leaves. Development is incredibly slow as year after year the plant increases in size. Water-seeking roots dangle in the moist jungle air; other roots cling to the tree itself and absorb salts and minerals from decayed vegetation among the lichens. In direct or indirect sunlight, the orchid leaves manufacture food. The plant, therefore, is not a parasite; the orchid only uses the tree as a resting place and actually derives no food from it.

The years go on. Seven to twelve years after the seed germinated, the plant puts forth a slender green bud encased in a sheath. And on a dripping tropic morning when the calls of the quetzals are loud in the trees, a glistening, translucent trumpet spreads its wine-red, fluted lip to the dim jungle sunshine. An exotic, rich perfume comes from the flower.

Now that the orchid blossom is in full bloom, only one kind of insect may fertilize it. If none comes in time, the flower dies and makes no seeds. But now as a bee enters the Cattleya's delicate lip, his thorax lightly brushes against a sticky gland which immediately fastens a mass of pollen on his back. He climbs backward out of the flower and goes to the next Cattleya where the pollen mass which he carries sticks to the flower's stigma. Within a few hours after the orchid thus has been properly pollinated, its function has ended and it withers and dies. The purpose of all the long years of growth has been fulfilled. As the microscopic seeds begin to form, the life cycle of the orchid is complete. With a few individual variations, this is the procedure followed by all orchids.

Tropical orchids have played a part in man's experiences. To delve into the relationship between orchids and man is to probe the legends of jungle villages and the romance of discovery and adventure. In many native villages certain orchids were held sacred and in high honor; many a white man lost his life in trying to obtain some of these forbidden flowers.

It was Cortez who discovered the vanilla orchid in Mexico, and some of the early Spanish priests used the holy ghost orchid to explain a phase of their religion. Very little was known of tropical orchids, however, until explorers, outfitted as if for big-game hunting, went into the snake-infested jungles and brought forth, not jaguars and anacondas, but dancing-girl orchids, butterfly orchids, rare yellow Cattleyas, green lady's slippers, and the glistening white holy ghost orchid itself with the snowy dove in the center. Out of Burma they brought blue moth orchids, tiger orchids from Siam, white moths from the Philippines, leopard Cymbidiums from China, and the delicate Laelias and Dendrobiums. Many, when they first were shown to European botanists, were claimed by them to be impossible; no real blossoms could look like these. But they were true orchids and they were all strange, all elusive, all sought for and obtained by skirting danger and courting death.

Meanwhile men, not content with the marvels wrought by nature in the orchid family, spent years in hybridizing and producing new varieties. A hybrid moth orchid displayed in the New York Orchid Show in 1928 was priced at $10,000, which is believed to be the highest price ever put on a flower. Forty-two years had been spent in selection, hybridization and care to produce two exquisite blossoms whose like never had been seen before. Many a time, however, nature has produced a hybrid which men labored for years to produce artificially.

All these tales and a great many more lie behind the delicate rosy-lilac petals of a Cattleya orchid. Yet the mystery of the shining self-lit petals, the alluring, powerful scent, that listening look, that silent gaze, that indefinable splendor of the orchid flower still remains unsolved: the orchid still is an unknown personality. *(May 1944)*

TIGER LILIES

Down a half-forgotten lane where dark Norway spruces droop long boughs to the tall grass, the tiger lilies bloom again. The old house nearby is falling into ruin; once it comforted a family, saw people come and go, saw them go at last for good. The spruces have grown tall and old, and now they shadow the garden. Storms beat the old house, sparrows roost untidily behind the shutters, a tree-frog lives under the back steps. All the human life of the past seems gone beyond recall.

All but the old garden. Here the loving hand of a gardener still is visible. No matter how much the grasses overrun the place or weeds come in, the human touch is still here.

When the pioneering woman of the past came west, she brought along little slips and twigs and seeds; these didn't take very much room, she insisted when the man scouted such notions. And she who was starting out to make a new home in the wilderness went out that last day and dug up some of her lily bulbs, took a sprout from the lilac, from the yellow rose, somehow found room for them in the crowded, creaking Conestoga wagon. And when they came at last to the place where the new house was to be built, the growing things were tucked in first of all.

Now that the people have gone away, the ancient lilac bushes still grow in a thicket; the Persian yellow rose still weights down the fence. And under the spruces the tiger lilies bloom. The firm, salmon-orange petals, spotted with purple, curl back, the six long waxen white stamens curving forward and tipped with quivering anthers of orange-brown pollen. These are flowers that link a brave present with a brave past.

Still in forgotten gardens the tiger lilies bloom. *(July 1944)*

TREE-TRUNK BOTANY

It is an old tree, a big tree, hoary with the years that have added ring after ring in silence and in darkness inside the structure of the wood.

For a long time the rough bark has been host to a large assemblage of plants. Generations of lichens have grown here for no one knows how long. Little curled and crisped lichens are grey-green, some a powdery gold. Some have black edges; some have scarlet fruiting cups; others have black tips and chalices, and still others have leathery grey-green cups and three-trumpeted cornucopias, all in miniature on the big tree. There are a few dry, small mushrooms that have found a footing, and small and insignificant though they seem, it may be these which will spell the doom of the giant tree. These others will stay on the bark and harm nothing; the roots of the fungi go deeply and drink the strength of the tree, until it becomes a decayed shell which a storm will topple.

But now the tree is still tall and fine. On it are mosses, some tight and dark, others, the knight's plumes, feathery and ferny. And here, too, are the leathery resurrection ferns. In cold weather the fronds shrivel, but during a January thaw they grow green and soft again, and magically revive with only a little moisture.

The old elm in the Mississippi bottomlands stands silently in the January woods. High in its lacework of twigs there grows a great cluster of green mistletoe, and on the trunk, the bark all but hidden, are the fairy gardens that appear fresh and green all winter long. (*Jan. 1943*)

FACE OF THE FIELDS

A hillside covered with green grass, a field upholstered with clover, a woodland community complete from mosses to trees—this is the good land. This is Nature controlled and in order; it is a situation which, if unbroken, can last indefinitely. Under this ancient and ageless supervision, few species exterminate each other; hills seldom erode; a body of water does not lose a balanced community of plants and animals. Nature itself, when stabilized, is endless.

Consequently for a long time men in America considered the wealth of this land to be a boundless wealth. When in a few years of reckless cultivation a field was worn out, it was easy to move to another place and start over again in the rapid process of ruination.

Not until comparatively recent times when the facts became evident, when much land lay ruined, stripped of top-soil and vegetation and eroded into miniature Grand Canyons which could support few living things, were the simple laws of soil conservation brought into focus. The land owner now knows that he constantly can renew his land by putting back into it the things he takes out; by contour-plowing to hold water instead of letting it run off; by checking erosion that already has begun. He can put in check-dams across gullies, and in a single season will see how the soil has piled up instead of running off; he can plant cover crops to hold the soil of eroded land until other plants can get a roothold.

For Nature abhors a bare place on the earth. The process of covering up has taken place unceasingly ever since the bare rock emerged from primeval seas; even on rock, vegetation eventually will grow. Algae come first; these simple pioneer plants need only a place on which to lay a thin slime of green. This is very little, yet it is finally enough to enable lichens and thin mosses to catch hold. The mechanical action of frost, rain, and sun together with the chemical action of generations of lichens break down a very thin portion of the resisting surface, break it down into something into which the largest mosses and liverworts can sink their tiny roots. After centuries that multiply into thousands of years, the decay of plant material mixed with decomposed rock particles grows and becomes soil which holds moisture and minerals and is rich and sustaining. There are ferns, there are spring blossoms, there are tall trees and the generations of saplings and seedlings growing up to replace the old ones when they die and return to the earth. Here are all the living things which depend upon each other in an endless cycle.

To maintain the unbroken fabric of vegetation—to plow so that the soil stays in place, to plant so that the soil is not devitalized, to check erosion and prevent its starting by the simple means of keeping the rootcover, the grass-cover, the woods-cover on the land—is one of the obligations of man to his world. He is repaid a thousand-fold by the greenery, the life, the myriad goings-on of living creatures, by the endless supply of things in a well-regulated life community. Ample reward indeed is the pleasant face of the fields. *(June 1945)*

WHITE MAN'S FOOT

Few of our native plants are weeds. Plants which come into newly broken and cultivated soil are, with a few exceptions, all foreign plants. Take them one at a time: dandelion, chickweed, orange hawkweed, wild carrot, wild lettuce, mayweed, oxeye daisy, burdock, Canada thistle, wild parsnip, white and English plantain, mullein, jimson weed, gill-over-the-ground, most of the mustards, shepherd's purse and peppergrass, most of the smartweeds—they are naturalized from Europe or Asia. Some have been here a long time. Frederick Brendel, in his *Flora Peoriana*, records many of them prior to 1852. A great many others came with the earliest pioneers into Illinois. These weed plants came with immigrants from Europe and were carried with emigrants out of the settled places and into the wilderness.

It was this notably speedy characteristic of foreign weed plants to come immediately into newly plowed lands of the American frontier which prompted the Indian name for plantain—white man's foot. For, said the Indians, wherever the white man comes and sets his foot, this plant springs up and remains forever. It was true—wherever a white man put in his plow and turned the virgin sod or broke the ancient humus of the forest land, the mark of his foot sprang up as weeds and grew and spread and throve.

The white man's weeds went with him out of the East and into Ohio and Kentucky and Indiana and Illinois. Suddenly weeds were there, growing and reseeding by the following springtime. It may be that some seeds, slow to germinate, traveled in wool or in bales of hay, in bedding or among fodder, or in garden seeds, and as soon as they fell to the ground and were moistened, they grew. Some escaped from gardens. Many species sprang up along railroad tracks and either remained in colonies in the ballast, or spread into cultivated fields. The white man's foot had been there and had left its mark.

It was strange, to those who took the time to observe and record, how suddenly certain plants appeared among the native flora. There were the sandburs (Cenchrus) which suddenly sprang up in the Sangamon River country in the 1830's, it was said, after strangers had camped and bedded down their horses. The sandburs must have been in the hay. Ever afterward, said the old settlers, there were sandburs, increasingly pestiferous, in the sand country. By 1852 there were black mustard, shepherd's purse, purslane, stamp-weed, wild parsnip, great mullein, hemp, and several grasses new to middle Illinois. By 1860 there were sow thistles, butter and eggs, motherwort, and hound's tongue. Ten years later, chickweed appeared on the scene; so did moth mullein and campion. About fifty years ago or less, the little Peruvian weed, Galinsoga, appeared in the middle west after a long journey from the New World to the Old World and back again. Native of South America, Galinsoga appeared in Europe, then came with immigrants to the United States in 1856. Strangely, the travels of plants follow in the wake of the white man's foot, not only in the past but continuously, wherever changes take place in a landscape in which the native plants are never as forward as plants from other lands. *(July 1951)*

LICHENS, THE PIONEERS

Lichens grow on bare rock, on tree trunks, on drouth-parched earth where little or nothing else will grow. In the unwanted places, lichens thrive. They are no strangers to hardship. They developed in trying times, evidently were created in a necessity which came of primeval poverty. They came about as a combination of two plants in the lowest order of plants, the Thallophytes, yet were quite unlike each other in appearance or habit.

No one knows exactly how or why it happened, but it did happen—an alga with green coloring and a little whitish blob of fungus, which had no chlorophyll, combined forces. Perhaps neither one was doing very well at surviving alone. In a sort of botanical alliance called symbiosis, the alga was enabled to live more successfully by mingling its cells with the tangled hypae of the fungus than it had on its own. The fungus, unable to make any food for itself and having had to live as a formless little saprophyte—perhaps the dead material it required as food was scarce at that time—found a reliable source of nourishment in the alga's chlorophyll. Together they built up form and substance as a plant which was neither fungus nor alga, but lichen. The fungal mass held moisture. The algal cells made food. It was and still is a successful union which has lasted since some of the earliest days of life on earth and seems to be in no hurry to end or change. With this combination of power and resource, lichens in their many variations and forms have proved they can live in almost any situation on land.

They are the pioneers which contrive to subsist today on the uncrowded, barren, unwanted, hungry areas of the world, finding sustenance and anchorage on such unlikely habitats as bare rock, tree trunks, dead branches, or sterile soil. They are abundant yet inconspicuous until a rain revives their dryness and they spread and take on color, like deep-sea growths come alive again.

Changing their brittle dryness, the once-shrivelled, charred-looking lungwort lichens in rain take on a fresh, green, spinach-like look. Dog lichens, like small, tattered pieces of blackened green paper with white undersides in sharp contrast, freshen on moss banks. The lovely rosettes of gray-green Parmelias on bark and rock look newly minted. Cladonias in the miniature forests of moss hold up their gray, powdery, cup-in-cup arrangements of fruiting bodies, the pyxie cups of the woods, while the scarlet caps and knobs of British soldier Cladonia are magnificent small spots of color against the gray-green of the lichen mass—ancient color as bright as the tanager which sings in the rain. *(July 1960)*

A BANK OF MOSS

Against the bosom of the winter earth the emerald hue of moss is bright, and sometimes in cold weather it is the only spark of living green. During a period of winter mildness the mosses in protected places stand out as they never did when summertime was on the land and green things flourished everywhere. Moss makes a footing for other plants, a carpet for woodland banks, a decoration for tree trunks, a cover for a log, a cushion for a ledge. No other plants cover so completely or so well; the mosses are one of the best of all to hold moisture and prevent soil from washing. They perhaps were the first of the soil conservators in the days when the world was young, and still they continue their silent mission.

To the casual eye, moss is moss, a velvety green cushioning in shaded places. But at the eye-level of a beetle the moss is a vast forest peopled with slim-trunked stately trees; it is a jungle of interlacing vines; it is a bed of stars bearing long-stemmed apples. One by one, to the discerning eye, a few of the multitudes of mosses are discovered—there are over a thousand species in America, a dozen in the most ordinary small Illinois woods. Although more kinds in greater variety and lushness are found in northern woods where moisture, shade, and acid soil produce some of the most striking mosses in America, they do not all require such an environment. Some grow on stones along a stream; some are on dry bark and bare rocks. Some make odd pin-cushions on the north slopes of roofs, and still others poke up between bricks in a pavement and give a gentle, velvety ornamentation to the stern contours.

Wherever it grows, moss has a secret, little noticed life. It begins with a powder-fine spore which falls on a damp place and grows into a delicate green network that stretches hungrily over the soil. After the thready network or protonema grows for a while, it puts forth a tiny green bud which develops into a stem and leaves—this is one moss plant and the bank of moss contains thousands of close-set plants of this sort. Down in the middle of a leaf-cluster the reproductive bodies form. Sperms swim in dew or rain that gathers in the cup of leaves and fertilizes the egg. From this, some time later, there grows a long thin, thready stem topped with a capsule which varies in size and shape with the kind of moss. When this is ripe, it is filled with dry powder-like spores which are ready to be released on the wind to start a new colony or perpetuate the old one. Spore capsules usually are noticeable things; they are one of the best marks by which to identify the mosses. Some capsules are round, some long and slim, others shaped like a heron's head, some like little pepper-boxes.

The moss plants themselves vary from the foot-long pale green or white stalks of the spongy sphagnum that fills peat bogs in the north, to the common dark green Ceratodon between the city's bricks. There are the green-white cushions of white moss or Leucobryum; the little trailing vines of Mnium and Georgia mosses; the fern-like Thuidium and the beautiful golden knight's plume, Hypnum. There is tree moss or Climacium that stands up an inch or more on a brown stalk and is tufted with stout green branches; there is the wind-swept appearance of broom moss, Dicranum, the stars of Catharinea, the big seed-like capsules of pigeon wheat of Polytrichum, and many more. *(Jan. 1945)*

FERNS IN THE ILLINOIS WOODS

Compared with the fern-strewn woods, bogs, and roadsides of New England and Wisconsin, Illinois hides her ferns in scattered places here and there. Almost always they must be hunted; they are the more highly appreciated because of their scarcity.

Around the swampy margins of northern Illinois lakes and bogs are stiff clumps of royal ferns. Back a little distance in the damp woods are the fountaining fronds of cinnamon and ostrich ferns, often with the stout leaves of skunk cabbage beneath and, in spring, sometimes the glow of marsh marigolds among the unfolding crosiers. When the sun is hot on the northern Illinois uplands, the ferns in shaded boggy places grow tall and lush.

On sandstone cliffs whose surface under the slow impact of years powders off in a fine, wet, crumbling that is held together by a film of blue-green lichens, there are the neat masses of polypody ferns, the spreading tufts of evergreen woodferns, and woodsias. Here the long slim arrow-leaf of the walking fern, bending to touch the moist sandstone, starts roots and tiny new leaves at the touching leaf-tip and makes a new fern.

Away from the coolness of the sandstone country a great palisade of dry limestone follows along the east shore of the Mississippi almost the length of the state; here in small crevices are ferns. There are tight close mats of brown-green, densely downy little plants, the woolly lip fern. In dry weather the hair-fine little fronds curl up as if dead, yet when wet weather comes they uncurl and spread their mats across the limestone. With the lip fern often grows the purple cliff brake with its leathery, shiny dark leaves and its wiry purple stems. And in the south where northern Illinois is forgotten and there are cottonfields by the road and buzzards over the cypresses, the dense colonies of resurrection fern, a polypody, cover the broad arms of swamp elms. These ferns, too, dry and curl in a drouth and revive as soon as moisture comes. On the hills are groups of ebony spleenworts. They are part of the unique picture of southern Illinois.

But throughout most of Illinois there are few rocks; the old glaciers effectively pared and carved and rolled the state to a semblance of smoothness, and oak-hickory or maple woods on low prairie hills and ravines predominate. It is in these woods in springtime that the delicate little fronds of brittle fern uncurl. They are everywhere locally abundant, yet frail, and often by midsummer when the weather is dry, they have disappeared. In bottomland woods is the curious three-parted grape fern and in woods where there are shady ravines and the rich soil of centuries of decayed oak leaves, there are the mahogany stems of maidenhair, neat Christmas ferns on a slope, triangular beech ferns in a damp hollow. In a damp place there may be the coarsely cut fronds of sensitive fern which vanish with the first frost.

These are the common ferns of central Illinois, these of the oak woods. Occasionally where there are outcroppings of rock or some unusual condition in certain woods, some of the northern ferns appear, but this is not common. For a fern, no matter what the kind, is typical of a certain environment. It is part of that grouping of plants which forms as a result of a certain set of soil qualities, moisture, and climate—cinnamon ferns to the bogs and lip ferns to the rocks—it is as simple as that, this ecological pattern of our ferns and Illinois. (*Sept. 1944*)

CLIFF DWELLERS

The vertical world of the cliff country has its plants and animals which dwell in a concise haunt of narrow ledges and shadowy walls. It is the habitat of a limited group of living things whose way of life is comfortable; in an area in which many plants and animals would starve or perish of hardship, a few find it a cherished, sheltering homeland.

In Illinois, the limestone and sandstone cliffs are found most often along the rivers where water, long ago, cut down through rock layers to expose them to weathering, and in many places produced cool and secretive canyons. Parmelia lichens plaster fanciful gray rosettes on bare rock; golden crustose lichens paint sunny, hot stone surfaces. Mosses grow in more shadowy, cool niches; and in the slow annual growth of these ancient plants a small amount of soil is developed in which later generations of moss as well as certain other plants may grow more plentifully.

Here also the probing, wiry roots of ferns penetrate for a support, for moisture, and for the meager amount of nutrients produced on the cliff-sides. On bare, dry river bluffs, the purple cliff brake hangs its dark, compact fronds; tufts of little lip ferns expand in moist weather or curl up when dry. In shadier canyons and on cool cliff walls are ferns which prefer moisture and dim light —bulblet bladder ferns, woodsias, ebony spleenworts and Christmas ferns, and the strange, groping, triangular fronds of the walking fern.

And where these cool ornaments of the canyon walls embroider the rocks, snails may creep along and leave a slimy trail. Spiders hang their nets. Chipmunks and wood rats skitter on their private business along the narrow ledges.

The chipmunks may have their burrows in the woods above, but they come foraging on the ledges, or sometimes store nuts and acorns in little caves, but the Illinois wood rat is almost solely a creature of the ledges. These are its domain and its special world, and perhaps no other creature knows its route so well along the devious pathways of the cliffs. (*June 1960*)

THE DECORATED LOG

There is a purpose in every creature, animate or inanimate, in the vast economic plan of the world. In our woodlands, some of the lowliest of creatures play a mighty part in preserving a balance of life through disposing of the remains of death. Decay may appear grim, yet if all dead plants and animals remained in the forms they had in life, no forest could hold them.

But in the orderly plan of nature, the end of a plant, as small as a moss or as great as an oak, is a signal to the clean-up squad, the fungi, to begin its work. Rot weakens the tree's fibers and a wind brings it down. Lying on the damp ground and absorbing wetness from earth, rain, and snow, the saturated wood cells break down. Fungus spores enter the wood, send out mycelium which takes food from the dead tree, further breaking it down, and from the mycelium come forth buds which push to the surface and materialize as mushrooms—brackets, honey mushrooms, pear puffballs. Generation after generation of fungi live on the dead tree whose body long since has been reduced to a sodden trunk half sunken into the woods earth. Year after year the decaying wood grows softer and at last it has become part of the earth itself, enriching it and providing nutrients for other trees and plants to grow, while the fungi, their work done, attack other fallen wood to the same end. (*Nov. 1953*)

THE LIVING ROCK

There where the sandstone canyon is cool—there where the trickle of a spring keeps the earth moist, and where in wet weather a little waterfall comes scampering and tumbling down the rocks—the rock itself has begun to lose its identity. It no longer is uncompromising, lifeless stone. Now it has taken on a patina of life. As in the beginning of the world, when the bare rocks began to break down enough to support a bit of greenery, the sandstone has become a garden.

The rock itself is not as hard as it used to be. The surface has begun to loosen a little from its archaic moorings; it is not as firmly cemented as it once was. Heat, frost, rain, wind, all have contrived to disintegrate a small, thin layer of the rock. Now when the spores of algae, lichens, liverworts, and mosses happen to fall there, their tiny, thin, root-like parts thrust out for anchorage and find a cool, sandy soil which is a perfect place in which to grow.

Mosses live there. So do the thin rosettes of lichens and the tiny plants of the alga called *Pleurococcus,* like bright green paint. And there are masses of dark green liverwort plants which thrive in the moisture of the trickling spring and the shadows of the cool canyon.

Liverworts are related to mosses but they do not resemble them. A liverwort usually has a flat, leafy growth which extends in a medallion on the rock or on moist soil, and from this spring the reproductive parts. In the liverwort known as *Marchantia,* which from a purely interested viewpoint is one of the most decorative of miniature plants, the reproductive parts are neat umbrellas that stand above the leaf-like bodies. Upon the latter also are cup-like gemmae in which asexual spores are formed. *Marchantia,* found in Illinois woods, is part of the life which transforms rock to life and color. (*May 1947*)

WHITE SNAKEROOT

In woods and woods-pastures in late summer bloom the fuzzy white flowers of snakeroot. When much is dry and sear, the fresh green leaves of white snakeroot maintain a cheerful, deceitful candor which foolish cows accept as excellent herbage.

Thus it happened long ago, when the first pioneers in Illinois turned their cows out to graze in woods-pastures, that illness mysteriously came, and the country doctor could seldom cure it. Milksickness. It felled alike the hearty and the weak. The poison of the snakeroot leaves eaten by cows was disseminated in milk, was drunk by men, women and children and was the direct cause of many pioneer deaths which at the time were unexplained, but which the continued presence of the snakeroot today reveals.

In 1818, Abraham Lincoln's mother died in a wilderness cabin. Milksickness, said the stolid neighbors as they helped Old Man Lincoln bury his wife just as he had helped them bury their own dead. In 1814, the little town of Hindostan Falls, Indiana, was almost completely wiped out of existence by the lurking presence of snakeroot in the woods.

White snakeroot (*Eupatorium urticaefolium*) is still a common weed. It is still dangerous, still poisons milk in sections where the weed is permitted to grow in parched cow-pastures. (*Aug. 1939*)

THE CANYON

Long since, the stream that carved through the sandstone subsided to a trickle that now only becomes a torrent in freshet-time; it still carves, but fitfully. The layers of cool brown sandstone through long years have taken on a soft patina of lichens in the light crumbling of the stone itself. In this shallow roothold are damp mosses and, in crevices, ferns. White pines on the heights lean over the top of the canyon and shut out the sunlight; it comes through in a soft green glow. Witch hazel bushes grow under the pines and there is a shawl of Canada yew draped over a ledge; the dangling vines of Virginia creeper reaching with tendrils for a place to anchor, clothe the pitted surface of the rock with starred green leaves. And in the cool dampness of the canyon walls are tufts of blue harebells on slim wiry stems; they dangle their flowers in the soft canyon air that contains the breathing of pines and ferns.

Outside the canyon are hot, wide cornfields, level prairie, open river.

Although on the prairie not more than half a mile away there grow the sun-loving plants of Illinois, in the canyons are delicate northern or mountain plants—harebells and saxifrage, walking ferns and partridge berry, blueberry and dwarf cornel. Even the pines and the yew are northern; their extreme southern limit in Illinois is here in the cool sandstone canyons of Starved Rock, in this oasis of northern atmosphere set in a hollow in the prairie. (*Aug. 1944*)

PINK MOCCASIN IN MAY

Now it is spring in the northern sphagnum bog. New pale needles have come in clusters on the tamaracks, new silvered needles on the spruces. The mayflower blooms; arbutus scents the air; bunchberry beds are a dancing flutter of white. The hermit thrush has come back to nest and sing, and the white-throated sparrow, nesting in the tangle of alder along the open lake which borders the bog, whistles from the new tip of a balsam. It is May in the north and the moccasin flowers bloom.

From a spongy hummock of pale green sphagnum there appears a glistening point of green which becomes a pair of corded, downy, oval leaves. These spread apart so that a waxen bud may grow, day by day, until it stands erect on a firm and downy stem. Daily the bud takes on color until at last it stands there in its perfection, a pouched, rose-colored, veiny blossom with twisted brown sepals and a glint of golden light. The moccasin flower has bloomed in the secret places of the bog.

Like other orchids, the moccasin flower—the Whip-poor-will's Shoe of the Cherokees—has that aloof, secret wonder which few other flowers seem to possess. It is a member of a proud race; it is unlike other flowers, almost it is not like a flower at all, but the embodiment of something supernatural. It is not to be passed carelessly nor is it to be picked—then the wonder is shattered, the spell broken.

This picture of an orchid in a bog is rare in Illinois. A few wild orchids remain, but never again will there be as many as in the days when the wet prairie lay in the sun and acres of white lady's slippers danced in the wind; when yellow lady's slippers grew in great golden colonies in the woods; when there were thousands of pink moccasins where the Gary steel plant now stands. Today they are all but gone, and some are extinct in Illinois. Part of our heritage of beauty is lost.

For too many years there was too much picking; when an orchid is picked, most of the plant comes with it and then the root dies. This, combined with the inevitable expansion of cities and the increased grazing, draining, and plowing of land, has helped destroy most of the large orchid communities in Illinois.

In a northern bog the pink moccasin stands silently and luminously on its hummock of golden-green wet moss. Growth is slow in orchids, mortality normally very high. The triumph of this perfect blossom on a day in May is the magical fulfillment of a seed that was allowed by all the forces of nature and man to grow. In it is the hope of more wild orchids in the coming years. (*May 1945*)

INDIAN PIPE

Like a creation in white wax set among the ferns and mosses, the Indian pipe on a late summer day puts a special quality of excitement in the woods. Devoid of all color, the strange, brittle-looking pipes stand motionless and unreal. It is as if they were spectres from another world, ghost plants of the forest made tangible through some alchemy of summer. The Indians may have felt this same wonderment at sight of Indian pipes and explained their presence by saying that wherever an Indian sat down for a smoke, and wherever he knocked out the white ashes from his pipe, there the plant called Indian pipe sprang up.

Indian pipe is a saprophyte, not a parasite, which means it lives on dead material in the ground (not on other living things), usually dead wood buried in the rich, soft humus of deep woods. From this there rise the curled-over white stalks with their pipe-like blossoms. These are composed of many white, overlapping scales surrounding a chaste, vase-shaped pistil and dark stamens. The stems are pure white with a few alternate white scales upon them instead of leaves. For the Indian pipe has no true leaves and no particle of greenness. Occasionally there is a hint of pale pink or red in flower or stem, but usually it is that stark ice-white which, as the plant ages, slowly blackens. At first only the scales and parts of the flower are tipped with accents of ebony. Then slowly the ripening flower stands erect and the whole plant turns black.

Indian pipe is in the family of the Heaths, Ericaceae, in the company of pyrolas, blueberries, wintergreen, cranberry, rhododendron, and many more which require a specialized acid soil. Of them all, perhaps, Indian pipe is least exacting in its habitat and is found more commonly than other Heaths in Illinois woodlands.

It comes at a time when little is in bloom in the woods. Now it is August and September. The sunflowers and goldenrods and asters blossom along the roads and over the uplands. In the woods the clear red berries of spikenard ripen. The clubs of scarlet seeds of the jack-in-the-pulpit and dragon arum ripen until they mark flaming accents in the woods. It is a time of ripening, of seeding. Yet now on the dark, leaf-strewn mossy bank there has sprung up that cluster of white wax pipes. They are as aloof and strange and wild as the pipe of an Indian which had been forgotten in the woods—wraith-like as the vision of a flower. *(Aug. 1950)*

MAYAPPLES

When late summer moved with dryness and heat over the oak woods of Illinois long ago, just as it does today, possums, pigs, and pioneers all used to know where to go to look for the lemon-colored fruits of mayapples. Ever since April when the new, stiff, bronze-green shoots with their carefully furled leaves opened their umbrellas, people and wild creatures kept track of progress beneath those green canopies. Everyone knew that the roots were poisonous; no one dared eat the mandrake root, not unless a granny-woman who knew "yarbs" dug the roots and tried them and prepared them just so and administered them in case of dire illness. Nobody gathered the leaves for spring greens either. Mayapple plants were avoided; not even cattle ate them; but in late July and August the fruits were ripe.

The fruit, like a small lemon, pale yellow, thick-skinned, filled with silvery pulp and seeds—that was what folk had been waiting for. It was picked carefully and a hole bitten in one end, and that smooth pulp was sucked out, a cool confection that slid down like some refreshing beverage.

They are ripe today, and to those who like them, the mayapples taste as good now as they did to the possums, pigs, and pioneers who sought them out in the old days, and to James Whitcomb Riley, who said:

"And will any poet sing of a lusher, richer thing

Than a ripe May apple, rolled like a pulpy lump of gold

Under thumb and finger tips; and poured molten through the lips?"

(*Aug. 1954*)

TIME OF VIOLETS

And so spring comes again and there are violets. In meadow and on prairie, in woodland and in swamp—violets again. It is as much proof as anyone may require to know that the orderly procession of the months and days and seasons has gone its allotted round, that the sun is back in the north, that spring is here again.

The trumpets of the spring may blow a loud halloo in the souls of men, but the sounds which are made are small and often thin. Some are not heard with ears—the sound made by daffodil leaves thrusting aside the particles of earth to stand in the sun, the push of air under bluebird wings, the portent in the splitting of a frog's jelly-coated egg, the velvety sound of violet petals opening. There are the louder sounds of trumpets—the sounds of wild geese flying high, the pipe of Hylas in the marsh, the nasal calls of woodcocks over a wet meadow, the fighting of flickers on a cottonwood branch, the faint snap of a phoebe's beak to catch a stonefly fluttering past . . . stoneflies above the first blue violets of the spring.

Spring does not come with a clash of cymbals shouting "Look! Spring!" It comes quietly and softly on night rain, moves on the soft footfall of rabbits over new grass, is visible in all the newly growing, swelling, singing, blossoming things.

So spring comes again and there are violets. Now in April they are everywhere—along the grassy bank of a country road, in the pasture beside the creek, up in the woods where spring beauties whiten the slopes, in the marsh where redwings sing, in city gardens and in little parks. Perhaps no other emblem of the surety of spring and the timelessness of earth is so needful to the land as violets on an April day. (*April 1951*)

A TIME FOR BLACKBERRIES

July and August are wild blackberry time in Illinois. It is a pleasant, warm season when the juicy black globules ripen under the summer sun— globules which, in spite of the surrounding fortress of thorns, nevertheless are taken as part of the summer's annual provender by many creatures other than man. Man comes with his pails and pans and picks blackberries for pies and jellies and jams and wines, but during the quiet hours when people are not in the berry patch, the animals and birds come there to dine.

The berry-eaters come—the robins and catbirds and brown thrashers, the bluebirds and grosbeaks and waxwings—to eat ripe blackberries until beaks are stained and the birds sit about in rapt satiety with no room for more. Chipmunks from the nearby woods come to the upland pasture or along the country lane to visit the blackberry patches. Not just for the flesh are the berries gathered—the chipmunks prefer the hard seeds inside. The bobwhites come; they, too, eat blackberries for their seeds.

The blackberry tangles themselves are a specialized sort of environment in which certain mammals and birds find haven and a way of life. Since long before Br'er Rabbit and Peter Rabbit made a mad dash to safety in the Dear Old Brier Patch, blackberry bushes have provided shelter for many a rabbit and wood mouse and chipmunk. Few foes except the lean and sinuous weasel can follow game among the thorny canes.

Birds live, too, in the realm of blackberries. Brown thrashers and cardinals nest here. And always the Bell's vireo, quiet and small, builds a neat, tight basket which is swung from a cane so securely that often the old nests of other years last through still another season among the haunts of blackberries. (*July 1951*)

"CHICORY BLUE"

From June through late summer, many an Illinois roadside is a lovely bright blue as the morning sun opens millions of chicory blossoms. For miles they margin the highway shoulders so that the passing motorist is aware of a blur of azure which seems unending and a part of the summer morning. By noon, unless the day should be cloudy, the chicory flowers are closed. Next morning, however, a whole new river of blue again flows through the prairie landscape.

During that first period of bloom in June, the mowers often clip off all growth beside the highway, shearing away the blue blossoms with brief finality. But chicory is a persistent plant. Kin to the dandelions and other fluff-seeded composites, it has deep taproots which can be killed only by poison, perhaps, or by out-right digging.

Therefore, in a few weeks after the mowing, there are new chicory stalks, a new crop of sky-colored, two-inch blossoms of exquisite beauty which will continue, after repeated mowings, without discouragement until that greater mower, autumn frost, cuts them down for the winter.

Early in the history of settlers in America, chicory (*Cichorium intybus*) came to our shores. No wild prairie landscape had known its color before that time; no New England upland had its glory. From Europe it was brought as a cherished salad plant by the English who called it succory, and by the French who knew it as *chickoree*. The latter dug the long taproot, dried, ground and roasted it, and from the dark brown residue they brewed a bitter black coffee. When the French came to New Orleans, ground chicory roots were added to Brazilian coffee to make a "high roast" of utmost blackness, bitterness and strength.

From the east, chicory spread westward with the settlers, as well as on its own account, as the fluffy seeds scattered on the wind into fields and pastures and along the new roads which were patterning a continent.

Everywhere it went, its clear blue color became a bright addition to the landscape. That blue, in itself, is so marked a color that, in Europe long before, this particular shade of sky-color became known as "chicory blue." The plant is considered a common weed in Illinois—a weed only, perhaps, because it is so common. The lovely blossom is so abundant that it need not be cherished as some rare and exquisite garden flower. (*Aug. 1956*)

FRUIT OF THE MUSKEG

"Muskeg," the Algonquins called it—a sphagnum bog filled with hummocks of moss. And in the muskeg grow wild cranberries, ripe in the cold winds of the North Country. The bogs freeze, but the cranberries grow sweeter with the coming of frosts, and some still are edible when spring reluctantly comes to the North.

Perhaps of all the native American fruits which have become popular on the American dinner table, the cranberry has remained aloof in its original habitat. It is as stubbornly an isolationist as any of our plants. It will grow only in its chosen haunt, and unless one has a sphagnum bog in his backyard or on his farm, he will never successfully raise cranberries. For a bog is a localized sort of terrain, not to be found everywhere. Common in the northern parts of America, the bog is the product of the old glaciers and has not yet reached its ecological climax. The water deep in the bog seems as cold on a warm summer day as it must have been when it accumulated from the melting glacier. The cranberry bog began as a lake which may have formed when a pocket of ice, some 25,000 years ago, melted and remained there as a body of clear, cold water. Many, many years later, when plants of the north were growing on the shores of the lake—when swamp spruces grew on the brink, and balsams and birches and white pines stood farther back—moss along the wet shore began to extend into the water. Generations of plants expanded, and as the sphagnum moss and other mosses grew in the water, a boggy rim was formed. For centuries this rim steadily pushed into the lake until at last there was only a central pool of open water in the middle of a wet bog. The sphagnum was dense enough to support other plants, the acid-loving bushes of bog laurel, rosemary, Cassandra, the wild orchids, the buck-beans, the sundews and pitcher plants, and cranberries.

The bog could bear the weight of a man, but with each footstep the unstable substance of the bog rocked and quaked and threatened to engulf him. At last the open water was filled with moss. Still it multiplied, and since there was no more room to expand laterally, the sphagnum began to push upward until it developed hummocks of solid moss three feet high. This, as the Algonquins called it, was the muskeg. It was no longer as wet as the quaking bog, but between the hummocks, where the deer pressed down their trails, the standing water was icy even on a warm day.

Over the hummocks of muskeg grow wild cranberries. The tiny vines are thready and bear alternate, tiny, oval leaves. In June the delicate stems bear pink, recurved flowers, and all summer long the little green cranberries grow. By autumn they are carmine jewels studding the pattern of the sphagnum.

For many years all cranberries eaten by the inhabitants of America were gathered by hand or with special cranberry scoops, by pickers who had bent backs and wet feet—from the wild bogs of the northern states. Since colonial times, cranberries were used as a welcome food; ten barrels were sent across the Atlantic to King Charles II, as a special gift from the New World. It was only comparatively recently that cranberries came under cultivation in bogs systematically flooded and maintained to produce a good crop—though still it is a crop which is produced under the cranberry's own terms. There still must be a sphagnum bog and cold water full of bog acid; there still must be the specialized conditions which are summed into one Algonquin word: muskeg. (*Nov. 1949*)

CATTAILS

In the glowing days of autumn, acres of cattails in shallow bays and marshes are filled with tall, vertical, tough, ribbon-leaves and sturdy clubs of seeds. They are one of the emblems of autumn, a sign that the growing season is at an end and the time of seed dispersal is at hand.

Cattails *(Typha latifolia)* are found almost everywhere in the temperate zone around the world, wherever shallow water and a mud bottom provide their chosen habitat. In Europe they are known as reed-mace, but the species is exactly the same as the familiar cattail of Illinois bottomlands.

The cattail is a child of the wind. Its leaves are built to bend but not break, to present narrow edges to the heat of the sun. The pollen is dispersed by wind and so are the seeds, and because of this often wasteful means of dispersal the cattail is one of the most prolific of plants both in pollen production and seed production. When the clubs of flowers blossom in late spring— stalks bearing a velvety green section of minute pistils, with a closely set, velvety yellow zone of stamens above—one head may produce 175 million pollen grains which are carried on the wind to fertilize the pistils. When this is accomplished and the stamens fall away, the pistils grow into the familiar dark brown head of the cattail, with a bare stretch of stalk just above the seeds to mark where the stamens once were.

There may be 300,000 seeds in one head. Each seed is tufted with a bit of amber fluff which bears it lightly on the winds of autumn. These seeds and fluff were used by the Indians for padding inside mittens and moccasins in winter. The Indian name for the cattail was "fruit for the papoose's bed," for the fluff was used to line the papoose-carrier in winter.

The cattail has always been a multi-use plant, perhaps because of its universal abundance and its downright practicality. Not only the seeds and their fluff have been used by Indians as well as modern man. The long, tough leaves, built to flutter in a wind but not break, buttressed inside with air spaces and braces like those inside an airplane wing, have had many uses. In pioneer times, barrels were calked with them, and they were braided or plaited for rush-bottomed chairs and settees. The prehistoric Indians of the Mississippi Valley used them as mats for the sides of their houses, for sleeping mats, and for thatch. The Indians long knew the uses of the roots, which are starchy and were cooked and eaten as we eat potatoes. They were sometimes dried and ground into flour, a nourishing flour with something of the quality of corn-starch and second only to potato flour in minerals present. A jelly was also made of the roots. The pollen was made into cakes and eaten as a special delicacy.

In autumn, the marshes are full of ripened cattail heads standing above millions of green or brown ribbons of leaves. Down among those leaves, the redwinged blackbirds last spring wove old leaves into nests. Among the cattails the marsh wrens also built their globular nests of marsh grass, and sometimes the male wrens built several extra nests just to keep themselves busy. Grebes nested on mats of cattail leaves and rushes which were often afloat in the marsh, and the muskrats cut down the waterproof leaves to add to their mud houses. A place of many uses, of song and activity and sunshine, the cattail marsh on a day of September quietly stands waiting for winter. *(Sept. 1962)*

"NAIL DOWN THE SAND"

Before sand can become soil it must have plants. Moving sand is forever unstable. Not until certain hardy, determined plants put down long taproots and spreading lateral roots can any other vegetation grow. Plants follow a succession of growth—the pioneers on the outer beach, the first low willows and cottonwoods managing to develop behind a small dune formed back of the pioneers, and, in their shelter and a bit of decomposing plant matter, grasses, gentians and Equisetums grow.

Slowly, back from the open beach and far from the sand-blasting wind, real woods take hold, and the longer they persist, in what once was sand but which has now a layer of topsoil and humus, the deeper the woods-earth grows. But before there can be anything of the sort, the pioneer plants must first begin to secure the sand.

One of the first plants to come into open sand is *Artemisia*, a wormwood with silvery basal leaves and deep roots. American beach grass and certain sedges come up, and around their bases the sand heaps itself, forming just a little shelter from the wind for something else to grow back of it. Another early plant to come into moving sand is the silvery cinquefoil, a member of the Rose family. Its roots travel long distances beneath the surface, down where the sand is cool though it may be broiling hot on the surface. Here and there the roots send up more plants, and at the same time there are long, strawberry-like runners which put down roots and make plants. Very effectively the little yellow-flowered cinquefoil is "nailing down the sand," holding it until other plants come in and help to populate it still further. *(July 1959)*

SIDEWALK BOTANY

When a naturalist yearns for far places and new sights yet cannot get away from the city, it is possible to partially assuage the longing by trying something new—a sidewalk safari in search of plants. Customarily unnoticed except by the tidy home-owner, the plants occupying cracks in the sidewalk provide a source of collecting and a means of learning the names of plants hitherto ignored. These specimens are as interesting, often as difficult to identify, and as challenging to find as those to be found in far-off places.

It is not the pristinely new and well-kept sidewalk which yields the specimens. The extreme temperatures of Illinois summers and winters, besides, seem to conspire against perfect concrete. Just as these forces since the beginning of time have slowly cracked and disintegrated the rocks of the world, so do our sidewalks suffer the same fate. Then, just as into the crevices in rock faces, there come small plants with long taproots. In prostrate growths characteristic of high mountains and rocky shores, the sidewalk plants are soon well established. Given the time, their growth, coupled with heat, cold, and years, may eventually destroy the civilized pathway made by man along his streets.

Here is a plant habitat which approximates the hardships to which plants in punished places have long adapted and endured. The sidewalk is a place of burning heat, dryness, wind, sudden flood, extreme cold, ice, and the constant menace of passing feet, tricycles, and lawn tenders. On old sidewalks in shade, especially those kindly old red brick walks remaining in some towns and villages, there may be plants which are found in cool, shadowed ravines.

Nature has always had to adapt to changing conditions; otherwise, its unadaptable creatures died. The sidewalk, like the bleak mountain top, is a place for plants which require little for survival and are exceedingly tenacious of life. Nature, in fact, forever an opportunist, seems to be ready with a plant for every kind of place and for every occasion.

Many of the sidewalk species came from Asia, Africa, South America, or Europe. Their seeds may have come in ships' ballast and other debris which spilled on waterfronts. The seeds sprouted and sent taproots into sand or rocks, and, through the years, slowly moved inland to neglected spots unused by other plants. Since most of the sidewalk plants are small and inconspicuous, they get a rooting before anyone notices. A little carpetweed with its rosette of tiny leaves and pretty white flowers may seem fragile, but its grip on the earth is difficult to dislodge. As with most plants in the cracks, the long taproot extends narrowly down to the cool, damp earth below the concrete, then sends out lateral roots which have an astonishingly firm hold on their domain.

Walking for a dozen blocks may net more than two dozen species growing in the cracks. There will be knotweed, *Polygonum aviculare,* several kinds of low *Amaranthus,* carpetweed, *Mollugo verticillata,* purslane, *Portulaca oleracea,* as well as white clover, hop clover, alsike, black medic, shepherd's purse, dandelion, yellow oxalis, and perhaps three kinds of plantain. There may be three-seeded mercury, *Acalypha,* the low common mallow with lavender flowers, perhaps pineapple weed, several kinds of prostrate spurge, *Euphorbia,* known by its milky juice, various grasses, and perhaps some elm and maple seedlings.

The old red brick sidewalk in shaded places may have tiny plants that grow on rocks in shadowed ravines—several kinds of mosses, perhaps liverworts, lichens, tiny ferns, and green, paint-like algae called *Pleurococcus.* In addition, animals are to be found on any sidewalk safari—ants, a beetle, earthworms after a rain, a caterpillar or two, butterflies, a bird, a toad. In the once plastic surface of the concrete there very likely are the tracks of cat, dog, robin, and human being. *(July 1966)*

SPRING IS DAFFODILS

Springtime, to be complete, must have daffodils, just as June must have roses and October red leaves. Daffodils are the springtime made tangible in crisp petals, slim stems, spears of leaves, and a special sort of blossom-perfume which means only daffodils.

They grow quickly from plump, brown-skinned, white bulbs that, planted the autumn before, made a rapid growth of brittle white roots and short leaf-tips before winter closed down. With the coming of warm weather, the daffodil shoots leaped into the sunshine, sent up sheathed buds, bloomed. Before anyone is aware of springtime, the daffodils announce it.

The daffodils are only one of the narcissuses and are known by their long trumpets and six spreading calyx parts which are yellow or white, or charming combinations of the two. The jonquils most often have several flowers on a stalk and have short trumpets.

The narcissuses were named for a vain Greek youth, Narcissus, whom Echo loved and for whom she died. Therefore Narcissus was punished by the gods—he fell in love with his own reflection in a forest pool, and pined away in his desire for the lovely image. Narcissus died, and in his place beside the pool grew a beautiful, scented flower which sprang up every springtime beside pools and in gardens—daffodil, narcissus, jonquil, flowers of the spring. *(Mar. 1947)*

A STORY OF LILACS

On a weedy embankment above the rutted lane, a massive lilac bush puts forth leaves and purple blossoms when springtime once again is on the land. The house and the people who built it and lived in it are gone, but the ability of the lilac to withstand the impact of centuries enables it to mark where human habitation used to be.

Lilacs were one of the first, if not the very first, flowers to be planted around the newly built cabins and farm houses over most of young America.

Lilacs were planted in a garden in Portsmouth, New Hampshire, as long ago as 1750 and they still grow and blossom there each spring. Jesuit fathers brought slips to the mission at Mackinac Island in the Straits of Mackinac late in the 17th century, and even they continue to live and bloom. George Washington planted lilacs at Mount Vernon; Jefferson planted them at Monticello.

For unknown centuries the lilac has been dear to human hearts. Perhaps some of this affection unwittingly may go back to old Europe where peasants believed that a lilac bush close to the house would keep away lightning. Long after this was forgotten by lilac-lovers, the crisp perfection of the pinkish-lavender, four-petaled flowers continued to be part of civilization's spring-times. The flowers were enhanced by their perfume—there never has been anything quite like the perfume of the lilac tree in bloom after an April rain, or lilacs scenting the soft May night with a quality which is both nostalgic and exquisite to the senses. The common lilac is believed to have originated in the Balkan mountains; the so-called Persian lilac actually came from a remote corner of the Chinese wilderness. Silk caravans carried plants to Persia where the Persians called the flowers "nilak," or "little blue flower," and the name by which we know it today grew out of the Persian.

Today the numbers of lilac species reach well into the hundreds. Some are large flowered, some small flowered; some are sweet scented, others ill-scented; some bushes are a dozen feet tall, others are low and graceful. The flowers of some are almost pure pink; there are doubles, bi-colors, whites, and infinite variation in shadings of bluish, lavender, and purple.

Yet perhaps none are as deeply loved and as much a part of our ordinary life as the common lilac which once grew unknown except by birds in the Balkan mountains. It is this which, lovingly wrapped in wet moss and layers of cloth, was brought along in covered wagons into the Middle West. Almost any of the precious plants in the garden of the old home could be left behind, but not the lilac which perhaps the great-grandparents had planted long before. Now a shoot of the old bush was planted in the Illinois soil and a new bush grew. It watched the family increase and saw it fall away; it provided great bouquets for weddings and rejoicings and funerals. And when at last the family was gone and the old house fell into decay and finally was lost in the encroaching weeds, the lilac bush remained. The brown thrashers nest there every spring, and each springtime the delicious scent of lilacs once more floods upon the April air. (*April 1949*)

A STORY OF THE HYACINTH

With the coming of early springtime, the stiff, glossy sprouts of bulbs planted last autumn push through the cold, wet earth. Now come the crocuses, daffodils, tulips, and the fragrant, waxen spikes of those Old World lilies, the hyacinths.

When the hyacinth's flowers are done, the curving green leaves, standing for several weeks in the sunshine, manufacture food which is finally stored in the bulb, and by summer all evidence of hyacinths has vanished. The bulbs lie dormant all summer. But with the autumn rains new white roots spring from the bases of the bulbs. The first new spurt of growth comes to the tiny leaves and flower buds which have formed inside the bulbs. All winter they remain in a state which is ready to grow when spring arrives.

This blossoming, drying, and subsequent revival was the apparent reason for the legend of Hyacinthus, from whom the flower took its name. In the days of the ancient Greeks there was a myth concerning Apollo and his friend, the fair youth Hyacinthus. When Apollo, the Sun, accidentally killed Hyacinthus by an unlucky throw of the discus, the blood of the slain youth seeped into the earth. From it sprang a flower known as the hyacinth. In this case, it was not the hyacinth which we know; legend states that it may have been the martagon lily, the iris, or the gladiolus. The European hyacinth was given this name later. The legend, however, personified the annual scorching of the summer earth by the sun, and the renewal of plant life when moisture comes. In Peloponnesus, the Festival of Hyacinthia in midsummer embodied this same event. It began with a period of mourning for lost flowers and ended with rejoicing in the assurance of renewed life on earth. And the spring hyacinth today embodies this same assurance when winter gives way to milder days. (*Mar. 1953*)

A WORLD OF IRIS

Out in the broad, open sunshine of the marsh, where redwings carol and a hawk slants low over the acres of cattails and sedge and cutgrass, there are slender, silken, dark blue buds which open wide in the morning of a new day. It is May, and the wild irises are in bloom. They are transient flowers, but each stalk has several buds, so that there are blossoms for many days as summer moves into the marsh. Pearled with dew, crisp and fragile, ancient among the flowering plants, the iris flowers open. They follow the typical pattern of the family—six flower parts, three turned up, three down. They are a splendid blue tinged with lavender, with purple and white veins and opalescent stamens, accented with a delicate, pale gold, brush-like "beard" on which visiting insects may leave pollen brought from other irises. In the acres of marsh, in the multitude of blue-green spears of leaves, the wild iris of the Middle West, *Iris versicolor* (or *I. shrevei*), blooms.

Irises grow wild in North America, Asia, Europe, and on the North African shores of the Mediterranean; they are as varied as their habitats, as unique to the lands they occupy and as much beloved as any flower in the world. In North America, irises range from the low *Iris setosa* of the Gaspe Peninsula and Alaska, to the miniature, jewel-like, crested iris which grows along forest trails of southern Illinois, of the Great Smoky Mountains and the southern Appalachians; from *Iris virginica* of the Lake Superior country to the common wild iris of Illinois; from the remarkable species of Louisiana— the terra-cotta red of *Iris fulva* which grows around New Orleans, and in swamps of southern Illinois, to the magnificent blues and purples of large

Louisiana irises in the Cajun country and remote cypress swamps along the Gulf. There are wild irises from the Rockies to the Sierras, from California to Canada. Not only have these been collected for American gardens, but plant explorers have dug into the remote corners of the world to bring back others—from Manchuria and Japan, from China and Korea, from Tibet and Kashmir, from Turkestan and Bokhara, from Persia and Greece and Spain, from central Europe and North Africa.

Of them all, perhaps, the tall bearded iris is the best known, most commonly grown, and, if one may pass judgment on a flower, most beautiful and varied in form and color. Bearded irises were grown and cherished in European gardens even before the sixteenth century. As the hybrids of two European species, *Iris pallida* and *Iris variegata,* the bearded iris produced many variations which became familiar in gardens here as America became settled. France did much hybridizing and in 1841 listed more than one hundred distinct species known as diploid hybrids. After 1900, however, much intricate hybridizing of irises took place to produce the magnificent blossoms of tetraploid hybrids which are the pride of flower shows, the envy of gardeners, and the lure of floriculturists who still endeavor to produce finer and greater variations.

Yet, basically, these floral triumphs may be no finer than the wild irises themselves, except for size and stranger color combinations. A wild blue iris on a day in May, when the marsh is a-sing with birds and the sky full of sunshine and wind and clouds, perhaps is still a perfect flower which no man can improve. *(May 1955)*

A ROSE FOR THE WORLD

Pale pink, five-petaled wild roses, fragrant with the essence of early summer, grow in a prickly tangle along railroad tracks and in upland pastures. Great festoons of ramblers, Paul's scarlets, silver moons, and Doctor Van Fleets, beds of hybrid teas and polyanthas, hedges of *Rosa hugonis,* banks of the white froth of *Rosa multiflora,* the sweet, pale-pink old-fashioned cabbage roses in an old farm yard, a spiny, cantankerous Persian yellow rose in the eloquent spot where a pioneer cabin once stood—these all mean June.

Casually, the buds of roses open. They are fresh and new as the morning of the world. They spread their unique perfume to the sun and the butterflies. It is June in Illinois and our roses bloom, but over the whole northern hemisphere, from China to England and from Sandwich to Seattle, other roses bloom. Although England claims the rose for its national emblem, the rose belongs to the world.

The rose is believed to be the oldest cultivated flower; it was grown because people liked it and for no other reason. Rose culture, therefore, marked a high point in man's own culture, for only among people with time for the gentler pursuits are roses grown. Two thousand years ago in Athens it was crowned the Queen of Flowers and it has been reigning ever since.

Even before that, Solomon spoke of the rose; so did Isaiah and Homer and Sappho, and Herodotus in 450 B.C. spoke of King Midas's rose garden where there were fragrant roses of more than sixty petals.

Since wild roses seldom or never attain sixty petals, it is to be assumed that even in those remote days there were gardeners who painstakingly developed double roses from accidental doubles found in the wild. Gardeners down the ages have continued in that pursuit, until today's roses are marvels of perfection.

In Queen Elizabeth's time there were only about a dozen roses grown in England, among them the Damask rose, the flower brought back by the Crusaders from Damascus; there were the ancient cabbage roses Pliny knew, moss roses, the Austrian yellow brier, the York and Lancaster, and the *Rosa mundi,* and several more. But when the trade with the Orient opened, roses which had been grown in China and Japan for thousands of years came to Europe. France had a favorable climate for roses, and here the rose hybridizers did some of their best work, but it was not until the time of the Empress Josephine in the early 19th century that rose culture really made great headway. The Empress liked roses, and in her extensive gardens at Malmaison she ordered planted every rose known which would grow there—and there ultimately were 250 species. She encouraged the hybridizers, and in making roses fashionable, Josephine started a trend which to this day only increases with the years.

The family in which the rose finds itself contains some of the most illustrious and most useful plants the world has ever known. In the Rosaceae there are the apples, plums, pears, peaches, strawberries, cherries, raspberries, blackberries, and spiraeas, the haws, and many more. Supreme in beauty, however, the rose stands alone. There is no flower like it, none more highly developed for the pleasure and inspiration of mankind, nor cultivated for that purpose for a longer time by the loving hand of man. *(June 1948)*

THE LILY FROM TIBET

High in the mountains between Tibet and China, there where a narrow trail skirts the precipices and leads men and mules down to the outpost of Singpang Ting, forty mules stepped lightly and carefully over a man who lay quietly across the trail. A rock slide had crushed his leg; another slide might destroy the entire train of mules if they waited for him to be carried out of the narrow path; there was no place for them to turn out and wait in safety. So the man laid himself across the mountain trail and the mules stepped over him and went on their way. And when they had all gone, the Chinese bearers came and tenderly but inadequately splinted the leg, and by painful, forced marches they carried him down to Singpang Ting. And so it was that the man who discovered the regal lily, and brought it to America, was rescued from almost certain death in the Tibetan mountains. With him in safety went several thousand lily bulbs, packed in moist peat, and with him they traveled finally to the coast and from there to America.

The story of the regal lily, which now in June blossoms in gardens over much of America and perfumes the warm air with a scent which less than fifty years ago was unknown by white men, goes back to those wild mountain vastnesses of the high country between Tibet and China. There the valleys were filled in summer with thousands upon thousands of large white trumpets, washed on the outside with pinkish or lavender, and with six long curving stamens thrusting into the sunshine. But not until the plant explorer, Dr. E. H. Wilson of Boston, discovered this lily was it known to civilization. Out of China had come many splendid flowers — peonies, roses, chrysanthemums, bleeding hearts, hollyhocks—but not until 1910 was the regal lily discovered in its hidden valleys.

Here the winters were cold and the summers were hot. The lilies grew along streams and on mountain sides, in moist places, in dry places, in full sun or in partial shade. When Ernest Wilson came into that valley on a day in June, his botanist's mind catalogued carefully the assets of this glorious lily, this queen of lilies, *Lilium regale,* as he named it. Yes, the American climate was hot in summer and cold in winter; its gardens were moist or dry, sunny or shady: this lily might do well.

His first shipment of bulbs was sent out painstakingly by muleback along the mountain trails and eventually reached the coast and the experimental garden in Boston. But they did not grow. Disappointed but determined, Dr. Wilson went back to the mountain valleys between China and Tibet and this time he judged the digging time better. He packed his bulbs so that they would not dry out; and finally, jubilantly, with several thousand of the precious bulbs, the party started back to civilization.

It was then that the rock slide caught them and crushed Dr. Wilson's leg. Yet, though his leg remained forever crippled, his enthusiasm for regal lilies was greater than ever. For his lilies grew and bloomed and multiplied until that original several thousand bulbs was increased many times to ornament the gardens of America. Regal lilies blossoming today are descendants of those original bulbs brought in 1910 by mule train and a man with a wounded leg over a trail in the Tibetan mountains. *(June 1951)*

SUNSHINE ON THE WHEAT

Broad and burnt-gold and endless, the wheat fields stretch to the sky. There are millions of heads of bending grain, millions of stalks drying in the sunshine, millions of roots nourished in the soil of the field and now drying, too, their work done. It is June, high summer, and wheat is ripe over the landscape of Illinois. The scent of its ripeness is a rich aroma which is akin to the pleasant toast-color of the fields.

The field of wheat is part of the year, and to understand the field and the golden stalks is to understand something of man and his development on the earth. Now the annual cycle of wheat fields reaches its climax. Last autumn when the earth was plowed and planted with winter wheat, the new green blades soon sprouted. In the autumn rains, they grew as a luxuriant lawn which put an aspect of freshness and newness and greenery upon the face of a year which was waning and whose growing time was largely done. But in November the wheat was growing. In January the wheat was growing. Now it needed snow to cover it from the blighting effect of extreme cold, but in the past winter, extreme cold in most parts of Illinois failed to come, and so the wheat blades continued to grow a small amount as the weeks went on; the wheat was green and alive. With the coming of actual spring, very late in this year of 1950, the wheat fields really began to grow, and rapidly, it seemed, after all the quiescent months, millions of green plants shot into the good sunshine of late May and early June. In a burst of growth and burgeoning of seed heads, the wheat suddenly was fruiting.

Green, tall, waist high in most fields, the wheat heads fattened and then, as hot weather baked down upon the grains, began to ripen to that rich brown-gold color. Now over all the landscape the pattern of wheat fields is a splendid accent against the dark greens of corn and soybeans. Bright is the color of the wheat as an indication of the richness of the first great harvest. Warily, watching the weather, fearful of high winds and sudden storms, the wheat farmers are cutting and threshing their wheat. Daily the big combines move over the fields and leave behind them acres of yellow stubble bristling with the sheared-off ends of wheat stalks. Truck loads of wheat go to the elevators.

The story of wheat as it is told in Illinois is essentially the age-old story of wheat since its earliest known cultivation nine or ten thousand years ago in the "Fertile Crescent," the region including the Delta of the Nile River and the Tigris-Euphrates Valley in Asia. In the "Crescent" an ancient village site, Jarmo, has been found revealing the earliest known farmers. Methods of wheat farming today may be different in their outward manifestations of machinery, storage, and shipping; but it is basically as it always has been— plant the seed, watch it grow, protect it from pests and diseases, pray for favorable wheat-harvest weather, cut the stalks, remove the grains, use the straw, send the wheat to points of storage or consumption. For ten thousand years or more the process has taken place over much of the world.

It was wheat, that food grass, which helped to civilize man. As he learned to cultivate grains to feed his family, he discovered at the same time those ancient important principles that underlie civilization—the usefulness of the tamed ox, the plow, the wheel, the cart, and the use of waterpower. Wheat and civilization—there in the Fertile Crescent about 8000 B. C., and centuries later successively in the Indus Valley, in China, in Central Europe, and at last in England.

The ancient grass which was the ancestor of wheat was the forerunner of a food which would be used throughout the world, but the ancestor itself is lost. It is believed to be extinct in the wild, although scientists still hope to find wild wheat growing in some secluded spot near the Euphrates or on the hills of Syria.

Wheat was used for bread as early as the Swiss Lake Dwellers in Europe; stone-hard remnants of ancient wheat bread have been found in the ruins of villages. In early Roman times, wheat selection was carried on to improve the crop, yet in all the thousands of years in which wheat was a major crop in the world, little change in planting and harvesting took place until after 1865. Now the invention of threshing machines and combines made possible the cultivation of wheat on a larger scale than ever had taken place in the world. Today wheat is planted from the heights of Tibet at 10,000 feet to the mountains of Ecuador, from the delta of the Nile to the prairie fields of Illinois. Variations in the wheat species have produced hard and soft wheats which are used in various types of flours, and spring and winter wheats adaptable to the climate in which they are grown and to the uses to which they are put.

Broad, bright, gold-brown, the landscape of Illinois sparkles with sunshine on the wheat. *(June 1950)*

THE STORY OF WATER LILIES

Now it is midsummer, and every morning on the pond the water lilies open wide their scented, waxen petals to the sun. Each morning now their ancient tale is told again. The story is a strange chapter in the drama of the world, a tale that is fascinating in its half mystical, wholly amazing qualities which made of the water lily a god, a motif, and a religion.

Long ago in Egypt the Nile was broad and its shores were marshy; in these sedgy areas grew multitudes of blue and white water lilies which were called lotuses, and which became a vital part of the Egyptian plan of living. The tropical blue water lily standing erect above the Nile was queen of all Egypt.

This was the flower of which people said: "From the lotus the gods are born." They thought of the water lily as the counterpart of that original cosmic lotus which grew from the Nu, a dark and watery abyss, at the dawn of creation. Long before there was either sun or substance of earth, Tumu, the Mighty, voiced across the eternal waters the words—"Come unto me," and immediately the mysterious lotus of the cosmic world unfolded its petals, and Horus, the sun, appeared at the edge of the open cup. The father of the sun was Osiris, god of the dead, who reigned in the Land of Amentet. To him came the souls of the dead who must first pass a huge blue lotus which grew in a stream in front of the throne. Because this flower was so essential in judging the souls of the dead, it became the symbol of soul peace, soul purity, and good life.

Because the lotus was such a vital part of the Egyptian way of life, art was dominated by the flower, and the temples of Karnak, Luxor, Edfoo, and the Ramaseum, and many others, were constructed around the lotus motif. Their lotus-bud columns were among the most beautiful ever created. Each represented a cluster of stems tied below the base of a group of buds which formed the capital or top of the column.

Just as the blue water lily dominated Egyptian life, so the pink Indian lotus dominated the Hindu religion. Here the flower symbolized the world, the Meru, residence of the gods. It soon became both the sacred flower of India and the emblem of royalty, and the Ganges became known as the Lotus Clad. An ancient Vedic law stated: "The lotus embodies the sacred fire of spirituality. In it the Hindu sees the symbol of the triumph of spirit, as the hard seed sends its lovely blossom of fulfillment into the sun."

From food for the soul, the urgent demands of the body made the water lily and the lotus into physical food for the hungry peoples of Egypt and India, as well as in America. Here the yellow moon-lotus, called Chinquapin by the Indians, gave its seeds and roots to be ground and made into bread long ago. Yet, with a far-off Oriental heritage in their blood, the American Indians looked upon the water lily as a star fallen into a pool, called the lotus the goddess of the swamp.

There are several reasons, perhaps, why the blossoms of water lilies with their floating leaves and the tall-stemmed lotus with its erect leaves were so deeply loved and worshipped in such a large part of the world. First of all is the odor, which in water lilies ranges from a delicate tea odor to the overpowering, fruity fragrance of the *Victoria regia* which can almost intoxicate with its strength. Then, too, there is the absolute beauty and symmetry of the flower. The color is often rich, yet it is always delicate; the petals are almost translucent, with an opalescent, sparkling, unreal quality. Lastly, the manner and place of growth of lilies and lotuses is different from that of other flowers of great beauty. In a habitat of mud and water, they are infinitely pure and clean.

These are the water lilies. Behind them lie portions of the drama of the world, fragments of the mystery of mankind. *(July 1945)*

LOTUS LAND

In midsummer the Illinois River and its adjoining lakes become a land of pale yellow lotuses blossoming, acre upon acre, slantwise through the State. There are lotuses in or near most of the Illinois water-courses—along the Mississippi, in the lakes north of Chicago where they are perhaps most famous, and here and there, few or many, in unexpected swamps and ponds throughout Illinois.

Something of the sense of worship devoted to lotuses in India, Egypt and the Orient is to be felt in the presence of the Illinois lotus, the Chinquapin of the American Indians. Late in spring the rolled-up, red-brown leaves push out of the mud, and as they emerge in the sunlight they become a soft, silvery green. The convoluted, crinkled, twirled-up leaf slowly spreads wide in the warm sunlight and becomes a big leaf platter, slightly cupped, with a depression at its center where the stem joins from below. Here almost every summer morning a few drops of night dew roll down the slippery leaf surface and come to rest mercury-like, in a glistening globe of water, where insects might come down to sip, and where more than one prothonotary warbler, flashing orange-peel gold in the sunlight, darts down for a drink.

By the time the leaves have spread to their usual width of a foot or more, a big egg-shaped bud comes pushing up from the mud, is encased in several layers of corded scales and sepals, and finally stands almost five feet high from its base in the lake. Early one morning the sepals fall away and the delicate, enormous flower, pale yellow and sweetly scented, opens at last. The center is made up of a large, flat, pepper-shaker pistil in which the seeds form. Around it cluster dozens of shivering, lightly poised, dusty yellow stamens. Rows of big oval petals are arranged around the magnificent center. A lotus is in bloom.

Today, from mid-July until September, the lotus is the outstanding blossom of Illinois, and often may be seen in great numbers along the highways. From Morris to LaSalle the Lotus Highway is Route 6; from Ottawa to LaSalle, Route 71; from LaSalle past Bureau Lake and Lake Senachwine, both crammed with lotuses, it is Route 29 all the way to Peoria. Between Peoria and Havana, Highway 24 passes mile upon mile of lotus-clad country—blossoms by the thousands, especially in Banner and Beckstead lakes. And from Havana to Grafton at the mouth of the river, Route 100 in midsummer acquires new beauty in the Lotus Land of Illinois. (*July 1941*)

A FLOWER FOR NOVEMBER

Above the plaintive cheeping of the garden's last forlorn cricket that hides beside a stone and feels the chill of winter striking deep within his horny coat, the chrysanthemums bloom. Like the witch hazel which seems to require a frost to do its best with its late autumn blossoming, the chrysanthemums seem intended by Nature to occupy that uncrowded niche of flowering at the closing of the year. They are part of that scent and sound and atmosphere which is peculiarly November's—against the patterning of autumn leaves and in the ice-box chill of the long, misty, frost nights, they thrive.

The chrysanthemum maintains a sturdy personality which has given it a place in man's appreciation of beauty since those ancient days when Confucius, then the "keeper of herds and lands" in the province of Shantung, wrote, "The chrysanthemum has its yellow glory." That was in the year 550 B.C. Long before that, however, there were little wild yellow chrysanthemums growing on the hills of Korea, tiny single blossoms with a weedy growth and trailing stems. An Oriental gardner with a discerning eye and a knowledge of horticulture took this wildling and began the first of a long series of experiments and improvements which have resulted in the hundreds of delightful varieties of chrysanthemums today.

Between A.D. 365 and 427, a Chinese horticulturist developed the chrysanthemum to such new and unparalleled beauty that the city of Chu-hsein

(Chrysanthemum City) was named in its honor. It became the official flower of autumn in China, and perhaps was the flower most frequently used by artists in all types of artistic expression. The Japanese in A.D. 386 acquired seeds from Korea and developed new colors and forms in the chrysanthemum, even a blue variety which is lost today. By 910 the chrysanthemum was chosen as the national and royal flower of Japan, and the royal crest from that day to this has been the conventionalized, sixteen-petaled chrysanthemum.

The flower was deeply loved and revered in the Orient, but elsewhere it was slow in gaining popularity. The record goes thus: 1754, the first chrysanthemums introduced to England; plants lost. 1795, brought again to England. 1824, an established florist's flower and one which at last was being planted in gardens and greenhouses. 1842, at the end of the war in China, the first pompons arrived in England, but were not well thought of at first. Folk preferred large blooms.

And in 1847 the first chrysanthemums came to America. Only the little pompons were used in gardens, for chrysanthemums were flowers of the year's end, and in the northeast it was cold, often snowy, and downright impossible for garden flowers. It is said that in New England our determined, flower-loving grandmothers protected their chrysanthemums from cold by covering them with red flannel petticoats at night, and so this type of covering became almost traditional for chrysanthemums.

Meanwhile, breeders both in America and abroad were working on chrysanthemums which would bloom ahead of that last gasp of a chilly November. The anemone-flowered, quilled, daisy, spoon, single, and pompon types were developed as the popularity of the huge, top-heavy exhibition chrysanthemums began to wane. In the past 35 years there have been greater advances in the development of beautiful chrysanthemums both for the garden and for the florist than Confucius ever visualized in the old Chinese sort with its yellow glory. Tough, lovely, early flowering, easy to grow in a sunny garden spot, oblivious to all but the hardest frosts, today's chrysanthemums, the flowers of November, serenely watch the fading year. (*Nov. 1947*)

FINAL FLOWERING

Late autumn—and the final flowers of the year open their blossoms to short, sunny days and long, chill nights. Some are aftermath blooms of plants that normally blossomed in spring and summer. Others, however, have waited during a full growing season before blooming. The witch hazel, a large shrub, is one of these—witch hazel, our final flower. Hardier than chrysanthemums, impervious to all but the most severe frost and ultimate freeze-up, the witch hazel casts its exciting, lemony fragrance upon the cool air of October and November.

The timing of most flowers is hinged upon the fact that before a plant may bloom there must first have been produced a certain number of leaves. The requirements differ in each plant. Certain leafless parasites and saprophytes, of course, do not follow this rule. Leaves manufacture food whose sugars and starches create energy which spurs certain cells into growth as flower buds, and then hurries them into bloom. In the earliest flowers of spring, these requisite leaves and the manufacture of food came the year before. The energy in the stored food lay quiet in bulbs or roots during autumn and winter, and woke to vigor early in spring.

Light-hours, or photoperiod, are a key factor in blossoming time, but the fact that we have the same number of hours of light in April as in October will not make the witch hazel open its flowers in spring instead of autumn. You may catch some of the violets opening again in October, but not witch hazel in April. It must have the whole long summer's sunshine, cast meagerly through the upper levels of the woods, to make plant food. The tiny flower-buds in tight clusters develop slowly all summer. With them are the enlarging clusters of hard seed pods.

Each contains a pair of small, missile-shaped seeds which were begun last autumn when the 1960 crop of witch hazel flowers scented the chill, late-autumn air. The green pods are so hard that not even a knife-blade can be very easily inserted.

Witch hazel seeds ripen in late autumn, at the same time that new flowers burst forth with long, thready, pale yellow, twisted petals. In the cold, dry air, the pods grow more dry.

After several nights of chill and frost, the pods contract suddenly. Their spring-action mechanism yanks open a seam across the pod and two shiny black projectiles are catapulted at a great speed and with much force into the woods. They may be heard rattling on dead leaves and against tree trunks fully twenty feet away.

Only a few of those fast-flung seeds manage to germinate. Many are no doubt frugally garnered by the wild mice and chipmunks, to be put away for winter's use when snow piles high around the bases of the witch hazels, whose new seeds for next year are only just begun. (Nov. 1961)

❀

❀ # TREES

❀

❀

THE TREES

When De Soto tramped across Florida to the Mississippi; when Jolliet paddled a canoe from Quebec to Arkansas; when John Smith sent reports back to England about the amazing plants and animals of Virginia, the great American wilderness was all a vast and wonderful expanse of greenery and life. It stretched from the Atlantic Coast to the Pacific, with only the broad openings of the Great Plains and desert and watercourses to break its expanse. There were, it is believed, at last 937 million acres of virgin forest in America when the first white people came here.

Today, only a little more than five percent of that acreage is left in forest, mostly preserved in national parks and forests.

The early settlers found trees of unbelievable size and extent, immediately put them to use, or else simply cut them down to get them out of the way to make space for farms and towns. The first cargo sent back from America to England in 1603 is said to have been sassafras bark, to be used in medicines. American white pine logs were going to England by 1605— they made spectacular ships' masts. Live oak in southeastern United States was invaluable in ship-building. What must have been the earliest move by the Congress to protect any tree in the United States came in 1799 when a grant provided that 350 acres of live oak forest were to be set aside for ship-building use only. The area was increased to more than a quarter of a million acres by 1845.

The trees! Everywhere there were trees, and few people in the world ever had or would ever have again the opportunity to see, use, and enjoy so many different kinds. At least 1,182 species were native to the continent, more than to be found in any other place on the globe, except in India.

As men moved west—everywhere there were trees, and more trees. When Daniel Boone stood on Pinnacle Mountain, he looked with awe into the unbroken green wilderness of Kentucky, to the great unknown of the Mississippi Valley and the far west, and then he moved down, cut a trail, and started a settlement. The people who came behind him began to hew and build, and soon there was a cutting of forests from Maine to Minnesota, and beyond. In Michigan, during lumbering and clearing times, great fires of burning trees and slash flamed continuously for more than two years.

But lumber was only one of the tremendously varied uses of trees. Eventually even the great waste piles of slash, sawdust, and stumps were used. From trees came the sweets of maple syrup and sugar; the yellow dye of osage orange; the wax from Douglas fir bark; the plant mulch of ground-up red-wood bark; the tanning material from hemlock and oak bark; the resins, turpentine, the fruits and nuts and seeds of many trees. And the wood itself, different in every tree, immensely versatile, became the baseball bat and the television cabinet, the woodwind instruments of the orchestra, and the piano, the violin and the guitar. Wood made houses and boats and desks and pencils and salad bowls and railroad ties and wagons and airplanes, and furniture, fans, and newspapers. By grinding up and chemically treating wood in making paper, other uses for pulpwood and waste were found, besides paper for boxes, newspapers, and bags, uses which have turned our present age into an age of synthetics based on the solid presence of the trees. For from wood pulp and chemicals come many of our plastics, cellophane, rayon, photographic film and much more, ever since the first plastic, celluloid, was made in 1870, to the still untapped possibilities of the future. The future, as in the early days, still depends upon trees.

They are indeed useful, but, as Thoreau somewhat sadly remarked: "Is it the lumberman, then, who is the friend and lover of the pine, stands nearest to it, and understands its nature best? No, it is the poet, who loves it as his own shadow in the air, and lets it stand."

Lincoln Barnett said: "Nature has fashioned the loveliest of earth's adorn-ments—the ever-changing woodlands." And a thousand years ago in Portugal, the old prayer of the trees may be our sentiments today:

"I am the heat of your hearth on cold winter nights, the friendly shade screening you from the summer sun and my fruits are refreshing draughts quenching your thirst as you journey on. I am the beam that holds your house, the board of your table, the bed on which you lie and the timber that holds your boat. I am the handle of your hoe, the door of your homestead, the wood of your cradle. I am the bread of kindness and the flower of beauty . . . Ye who pass by, listen to my prayers and harm me not . . ." (*Sept. 1963*)

THOSE WHO KNOW A TREE

A tree is many things to many creatures. To birds, mammals, and insects of woodland areas, the tree provides life, shelter, food, and home in a manner in which creatures of the treeless plains, the desert, and the meadows above timberline never know. For those who have never known a tree—its widely anchored root system, its rough bark, its massive trunk with its fibrous wood, its innumerable twigs and green leaves, its flowers, its fruits, its winter buds—

there is no special need. But take away a tree and a chickadee is lost, a squirrel is homeless, a burrowing beetle is frantic and without shelter, a caterpillar has no food, a butterfly no sleeping place, a flycatcher has no horizontal branch on which to place a nest, the oriole has no pendulous twig, the chipmunk no small cave-like shelter between the roots.

In winter, the basic form of a tree stands out plainly, and because of this a great many of its functions in the animal world are clearly revealed with the going of the leaves. In the case of the big American elm on the cover, its trunk sloping gracefully and firmly into the earth where the roots extend broadly in all directions, almost as extensively as the branches and twigs spread against the sky, a great many animals during the life of the tree have known it intimately. This tree must be very old, as elms go. Nearly five feet in diameter, it is doubtlessly between one hundred fifty and two hundred years old. In its life, many a fox squirrel has sat on that curving bough, back braced against the trunk, to gnaw patiently through the thick shell of a walnut. Many a blue jay has hidden acorns in crevices of bark.

Behind another shred of bark there is, on a winter's day such as this, a thin, dry creature, wings folded together, body as if dead. It is far from dead. Even though this is midwinter, scarcely anything about this elm is dead. Sheltered by the tree, the mourning cloak butterfly survives deep cold, and, on a mildly thawing day in late winter, may emerge to flitter casually in the thin sunshine and then retire again with the coming of night and cold to the protection of the tree. Other insects are using the tree, as insect generations have used it for many years—beetles and their grubs, caterpillars, ants, bees—there is a hollow, higher up, where bees have a nest full of dark wild honeycomb.

It is an old tree in which many a raccoon has slept, tail over nose, in a comfortable crotch. When the tree was young, buck deer polished their autumn antlers against it and a bear may have brushed past. Many a woodpecker has explored the rough bark, and many a Carolina wren, prospecting along the creek, has poked among the roots clinging to the overhanging bank. For many years, crows nested high up, until the horned owls appropriated the nest for their own.

It was none of these creatures, however, which changed the tree in any noticeable manner, but man. Not modern man, but, long ago when the tree was young, an Indian may have bent that south branch as a trail marker, so that it grew as we know it today. There is no record of this event, any more than there are records of the crows and butterflies and deer, only the scant mute evidence of those who have known a tree. (*Dec. 1955*)

THE WINTER TREE

It stands in its strength, revealed in its power—the oak on a winter's day. Each tree at this season shows its true form and character; each species thus is distinctive because of its manner of branching and growth. As at no other time, the trees appear as they developed—splendid woody structures built with botanic engineering which keeps them upright, impervious to most storms, able to live longer lives than most other plants. Fibers are cells which give them strength and become part of the wood. A complex system of cells act like pumps and form a tube system which carries water up from where the roots take it out of the earth, sending it up in a great invisible fountain into the smallest twigs and into each leaf. From here some of the moisture is transpired into the air or is condensed as dew or, eventually, becomes rain. Food materials which are produced in the leaves are conducted down another system of tubes into the trunk. All summer the tree is a great factory whose intricate system of pumping and transporting is unequaled by other plants. Although all the mechanics are hidden, the great woody structure which contains them now stands exposed.

The leaves which had their vital part to play in keeping the tree alive with food have served their purpose for this year and have fallen to the ground—leaves which are broomed about by winds, dampened down by rains, and softened, decayed, and assimilated into the earth at last. Around the tree is created a rich, thick humus which is full of minerals, aiding the welfare of both the tree and the other plants growing there and directly influencing the animal populations as well.

Wrapped in bark which is a necessary insulation, the trunk holds its inner mechanism intact. The tree is dormant until springtime starts the sap to moving, sends it up into the smallest twigs to trigger enzymes in the winter buds and brings forth leaves and flowers.

The strength, shape, and longevity of a tree are not achieved by chance. They are the result of millions of years of plant evolution, of trial and error—trials which, if they turned out to be errors, caused extinction in forms unfitted to survive in today's world. With annual problems of temperatures ranging from thirty degrees below zero to well above a hundred, and with a massive, upright form which must withstand the twisting of winds and the drying of sun and air, the tree today is a marvelous plant, and in winter it shows its true self.

Abraham Lincoln expressed admiration for trees in winter when he said: "I like trees best when they're not in leaf and you can study their anatomy. Look at the delicate firm outline of that leafless tree against the sky. And there's the profile of the tree in its shadow on the snow."

As far away as it can be seen, the tree in winter can thus be distinguished by its outline, its profile, and its manner of growth. Oak, elm, maple, walnut, hackberry, willow, poplar, ginkgo—they are as distinctive in winter as the profiles of people. To know a tree in winter thus is to really make its acquaintance forever. By the time the bark is identified, the twig arrangement distinguished from other species, and the winter buds known without question, then the incidental growth of leaves and flowers and fruit only verifies and embroiders the knowledge. A rewarding personal plan of enrichment is to learn the trees of one's community; it is astonishing how many kinds inhabit towns and how distinctive they are in their winter condition. (*Nov. 1964*)

PERSIMMON IN THE SNOW

Persimmon trees are black against the blanketing of snow. The dark bark is broken into even squares—a simple mark of the persimmon tree's identity —and the small twigs make patterns flung against the wintery sky. Here and there upon a twig remains a ripe, round, stemless fruit—a soft, sweet, dull orange-colored fruit which may become the food of winter robin, hungry opossum, or autumn hiker, depending upon which gets there first.

In May the persimmon is covered with delicate, small, white bell-like blossoms that show a plan of four. Until autumn, the oval, blue-green leaves hide the fruit; then it becomes a glowing pink-orange with a whitish bloom like that on a Concord grape. It is then that the persimmon appears to be edible but is not; tannin in the fruit produces an astringent sensation which puckers the mouth and disillusions the hasty eater. Time and, usually, frost make the persimmon soft and custardy inside; the thin, delicate, pale skin holds together the brown seeds buried in the half liquid, golden pulp.

Now late in the autumn the persimmons begin to drop to the cool, leaf-strewn earth, and often in falling they burst open where they lie. Pigs in woods-pastures know the whereabouts of these trees and linger in their neighborhood when the fruit is falling. Grey opossums at night climb hand-over-hand up among the bending twigs to pluck the fruit, eat it, and toss the seeds to the ground. And in November, people gather persimmons to make a delectable pudding to serve cold with cream. In the old days there also was fermented persimmon beer which was something very special at the slab cabin in the hollow or down the creek.

Persimmons have been known and eaten since colonists first settled in Virginia and found, that first autumn, the ripe fruit on the checker-barked trees. Captain John Smith commented, "Plumbs . . . which they call Putchamins . . . if it be not ripe, it will draw a man's mouth awrie with much torment, but when it is ripe it is delicious as an apricock," and spoke perhaps from personal experience. Here was something new, something typically American. As early as 1629, when a ship went back to England loaded with strange new foods and trophies of the new land, persimmons were sent along.

Meanwhile, over the southern and central parts of America, persimmons every autumn were eaten by Indians, who sometimes dried them or made the pulp into sweet little cakes. Wild persimmons helped early explorers in Illinois survive the hunger that was ever-present; these were sweet morsels in a land where little was really sweet.

All during pioneer days in the southern half of Illinois, the persimmon was a fruit to take away some of the monotony of corn pone and fatback and beans; during the coffee blockade in Civil War times, the seeds were ground and used as a coffee substitute.

Persimmons are native only to the southern half of the United States, to Mexico, and to China. In the latter place the huge Oriental persimmon is a major fruit which only recently has been grown in America. These exotic gold-orange fruits have little casual resemblance to the wild persimmon which is as American as rail fences and popcorn. As a part of the picture of November, the last few dead-ripe persimmons cling to bare black twigs until claimed by hungry denizens of the winter woods. *(Nov. 1945)*

A PAPAW BY THE RIVER'S EDGE

Through the leaf-ripened woods of autumn flame the papery pale golden leaves of papaw trees. In a habitat where shade all summer has been dark and green—there in the river bottomlands where tall sycamores, maples, and elms monopolize the sunlight that cannot penetrate their broad canopy—the papaw trees have flourished. They are slim, small trees with magnolia-like, tapering leaves, thin leaves that live without the toughening influence of full sunshine. The papaw trees since springtime seemed almost invisible here in the forest greenery along the river.

Last spring, however, when April was upon the land, the papaws blossomed and were suddenly important in a woods where as yet the leaves had not appeared. The ground was carpeted with sweet william and anemones, with spring beauties and the purple of the lowland violets, and folk came here to hunt for succulent spring mushrooms, the spongy brown morels. In the thin April sunshine, the fuzzy black, round buds of the papaw trees expanded, turned bronzy green and showed parts arranged in threes around a tight, hard, round center. Then the flower changed still more until one day the April sunlight shone through silky, translucent, three-parted, purple-red flowers that hung on slender twigs. The globular centers of golden-green stamens were open to the bees, and the flowers emitted a rich, fruity, almost tropical odor. On the twig-tips the pale green leaves, folded neatly down their centers, slowly unfolded, so that by the time the flowers had shrivelled, the leaves were well on their way to covering the trees. All summer they were there, thin and green, hiding the forming fruit.

Now it is autumn in the Illinois country and the papaw fruits are ripe. In the bottomland forests along the Mississippi, along the Illinois and the Sangamon and the Kankakee, along the Wabash, the Big Muddy, and the Cache, the papaw fruits are ripe.

It was in these same forests that the Indians knew the richly flavored, custard-filled, ripe papaws when autumn came to the Illinois country. They were called *rassimina* by the Iliniwek, to whom this was an important and much sought-after fruit. *Assiminier,* the French called them, from which *Asimina,* the present botanical name, much later was derived.

The early settlers in papaw country apparently were of two minds concerning this autumnal fruit. Some praised it highly while others said it might be eaten only in the case of direct necessity. To some it was overly rich and cloying; to others, who liked tropical flavors, it was a taste of the Indies. It was called the "wild banana" by those who knew what a banana was and "papaw" because someone from the south thought it resembled the tropical papaya, or papaw.

Now these oval, heavy fruits with their brownish-purple skin covering the yellowish, creamy flesh in which the big brown seeds are embedded, are ripe in the bottomland woods where Indians once gathered them. Their delicate flavor is heightened by a light frost. Although papaws may be prepared in several ways, including a spread-for-bread which pioneer mothers in desperation conjured up, papaws are best known and liked by those who walk the woods and eat a papaw as it is found—a ripe, autumnal fruit picked from yellow trees along the rivers. (*Oct. 1946*)

TREES AND THE SYMPHONY

From the very beginning, there were, somewhere in the world, certain trees whose wood, carefully prepared by men and fashioned into strange instruments, might produce tones which no other creature or thing could utter. Far away and long ago, when men had begun to discover their world that lay in manifiold mysteries all around them, an innate craving for music caused the creation of musical instruments. Many of these were made of trees.

For a long time, the bodies of woodwinds were made of the heartwood of old coconut palms that grew slantingly in the sand and sun along the tropic seas. No one knew why some musicians contracted skin irritations until it was discovered that in this wood there was a resin which causes skin poisoning. And so the instrument-makers sought a better wood.

After many tries, they found that grenadilla wood was perfect. Mozambique ebony, it is often called, or African blackwood. Far out in the deserts of Mozambique in South Africa, and on the island of Madagascar, the ebony trees grow in conditions in which few trees could survive. The wood is purple when cut, but later it turns black when oiled and cured. Curing takes five to ten years, and by that time the wood is so hard that it will almost ruin the cutting edge of a lathe. The finished grenadilla wood is the nearest to a warpless, crackproof wood that has yet been found. And the clarinet or oboe made from it produces the finest tones that are possible within the range and character of those instruments.

Mahogany from Africa and the Amazon makes drum shells and pianos; the sounding boards of pianos are made of basswood, often called the artist's tree; walnut is used for tambourines; the bars of marimbas and xylophones, and castanets are made of Brazilian rosewood which produces a brilliantly resonant tone when struck; castanets themselves originally were a pair of chestnuts clacked with the fingers; drumsticks are made of snakewood from Dutch Guiana or hickory from the United States.

Violins, complicated and sensitive structures of wood, are made possible by trees from many parts of the world, from the balsam fir in northern Italy from which the finest rosin is obtained, to the Brazilwood tree, inland from Pernambuco, Brazil, whose thin red heartwood makes the best violin bows. Nothing finer for the purpose, it is said, ever has been discovered. The Stradivari and Amati violin makers in Italy found that the Norway spruce or the

Swiss pine were unequaled for violin tops. Long afterward it was discovered that through the wood of these high-altitude, magnificently straight-boled trees sound travels faster than through any other wood. Though they did not know the reason for their choice, the old craftsmen had chosen the perfect wood for a violin.

The baton is poised in that breath-taking moment—then drops in a sudden downsweep and the music begins. And behind that glorious burst of sound stand the trees, from Africa to America and from Mozambique to Pernambuco, that make so much of that music possible. *(Oct. 1947)*

❀

❀

TO EAT AND DRINK

❀

❀

THE AMERICAN GARDEN

In the days when there was wilderness from the Virginia pines to the cypresses of Monterey, there were gardens in America. They helped build the continent, for even then gardening was an anchor-stone which kept nomadic men in one place and which, in giving them an assurance of food supply for at least part of the year, planted the foundations of a home. And since an agricultural people seldom knew the need for war, gardens fostered peace.

Long before historic times, Indian fields were planted with four grains of corn and a fish for fertilizer in each hill. Elsewhere in the land, the Indians after their own customs planted gardens every spring, cultivated them, and harvested crops which differed with the region, the soil, the climate, and the people. Sweet potatoes were grown by southern Choctaws, peppers by the Cherokees, pumpkins by the Illini. In the rich black loam of Mississippi bottomlands the Indians, according to the custom of their ancestors, planted corn, beans, and squash and with flint hoes tilled the fields. In the southwest country where water was scarce most of the year, an early form of irrigation was developed by the Indians so that there would be good crops of the small white tepary beans. The Papagos and Pimas had cultivated the tepary since prehistoric times; it was one of the principal foods of the ancient and little known argicultural people of the southwest.

Here in the hot, dry, dramatic desert, soil for gardens often was carried in baskets to the tops of the mesas where wild squash and pumpkins were cultivated, and corn and teparies and melons were grown. These were crops that held desert dwellers to their homes. Some even had peach orchards planted in the desert from seeds brought by the Spanish.

The Indians passed on their knowledge of American fruits and vegetables to newcomers who landed dubiously but determinedly on American shores. In addition to the squash, corn, beans, cranberries, blueberries, wild grapes, strawberries, and sweet potatoes bequeathed them by the Indians, people from

191

England and Holland brought with them the staple foods of the Old World. Almost at once the early colonists planted fruit trees and gardens, and thereafter the roots of these people were firmly set in New World soil; they and the American garden were rooted here forever.

Ever since when spring comes on, gardens have been planted throughout the land, planted lovingly and with reverence and gratitude. There are the pocket-handkerchief gardens in city backyards, window-box gardens and gardens along railroad tracks, vegetables planted in flower borders, steep garden patches of mountaineers in the Smokies, the collards-and-okra gardens of the South, gardens in sand and clay and in chemical solution. Certain parts of the continent are noted for garden specialties—watermelons and peaches of Georgia, and the potatoes of Aroostook, Maine; Michigan celery and Fort Pierce pineapples; globe onions from upper New York state, and cabbages south of Chicago; vast cornfields in Illinois and Iowa, and cauliflower of the Catskill country; Colorado muskmelons, Virginia spinach, Ontario rutabagas, Texas broccoli, Louisiana strawberries, oranges from Florida and California, pomegranates and figs from the Carolinas, cactus fruits and dates in the desert, extra-large lima beans from the Santa Clara Valley.

Not for centuries, however, were garden products available out of season, nor very far from where they grew, but with the coming of long-distance transportation and the invention of refrigerator cars, fresh fruits and vegetables travelled to where they were most needed. Let the north freeze when winter comes; the sunny fields of the Rio Grande, the coquina fields of Florida, and the fertile valleys of California send northward and eastward endless carloads of garden-fresh foods.

The war-time garden is closely linked with these great fields and with the little gardens on the mesas, the spotty cornfields of Massachusetts Indians, and with the cabin gardens on the prairie; they still provide that primitive connection with the soil. When spring comes and the mellow earth again is ready to be planted, a garden supplies an ageless need in man, his need for an assurance of things solid and permanent and consoling; the soil is his certainty of life. It is this which connects the earnest American gardener with a long line of ancient tillers-of-the-soil who for many ages have worked American earth. *(May 1944)*

THE KENTUCKY COFFEE TREE

In the days of the Civil War, when commodities were scarce and the blockade on coffee prevented many Americans from having their morning cup, a great many substitutes were tried in the search for something to take the place of coffee. There was an old-time brew made of burnt bread and water, which at least looked like coffee, and there were bitter chickory coffees which many people became so accustomed to using, especially in the South, that many never returned to the more expensive true coffees of South America. There were many other more or less futile attempts at coffee substitution, for in those days, as it may be soon again, shipments of coffee could not pass through the war zone. Here in the Middle West the pioneer families that lived in cabins out on the prairie, or at the edge of forest land bordering the rivers, had little money but much ingenuity. From the forest, source of much of their livelihood, they found a coffee which, though it probably tasted little like the real thing, nevertheless formed a substitute during the hard war years.

In the river forests were tall, rough-hewn trees that were like pioneers in appearance—stern, straight, and earnest. The bark was flaky and rough, in hard, curved plates firmly attached at one point to the trunk. The twigs were stiff and blunt, not tapering or feathery like elms or hackberries. When a twig was broken, a bright salmon-orange pith lay in chambered sections to further identify the tree. For months—all winter and far into the spring—this tree stood stark and leafless, as if it were dead of the too-rigorous prairie winter. But suddenly from the blunt twigs in spring came buds concealed in the bark, from which grew large compound leaves almost a yard long. They had a long central stem and side branches, all bearing small oval leaves. When the tree was in leaf it was a ferny, airy thing which now showed its relationship to the locusts. There were clusters of greenish-white flowers, followed by a pod or two in each cluster which developed and grew, until in autumn there were heavy, hard, thick pods of polished mahogany color. As the leaves turned yellow and dropped early in the autumn, the clusters of fat pods here and there on the tree hung black against the sky. By and by the pods fell, and when they were pried open, inside there was a sticky, greenish-yellow substance with a sweet taste, and imbedded in it were several marble-sized brown seeds of utmost hardness. Somehow, a few of the coffee-hungry pioneers contrived to mash or grind these rock-like seeds, and brewed coffee from the resultant grains. What it tasted like we do not know, nor how widespread was its use. There was probably no cane sugar in the house for sweetening; not only a war blockade but the pinch of circumstance allowed none of the luxury of refined white sugar in any but the houses of the well-to-do. Coffee was sweetened with sorghum, perhaps with maple sugar. It was a day of sub-stitutes, a time when a man might not be able to buy the things he wanted or needed, but by means of his alert brain he could contrive to find substitutes in his wood lot, in his fields, in the skill of the gnarled fingers of his frontier wife.

Today the coffee tree still grows in woods and forests lands along the rivers, and the pods, long untouched as a source of a doubtfully flavorsome beverage, ripen and fall, a silent reminder of the privation of the past. (*Sept. 1942*)

TEA IN THE WOODS

Ever since men hunted and camped in the American forests, they found around them many sources to supply the makings for a cup of tea. Simpler and more economical to make than coffee, tea was an acceptable substitute when coffee was unobtainable or too costly. Wild tea, besides, was the defiant answer in Revolutionary America when China tea was burdened with exorbitant tax applied by the unpopular English king. For a long time only Tories drank China tea; patriots went to the wild for substitutes and found them in dittany, New Jersey tea, wintergreen, catnip, and many other herbs or tree leaves. No one needed to depend upon the imported product; it was revelatory of the American spirit of defiance and independence that folk found excellent substitutes which were not only all-American but tasty brews besides.

A man on a long hunt into the wilderness could always provide for himself a refreshing hot drink so long as he had a cup, a kettle, and some fresh water. In fact, any sort of kettle would do—a tin cup, a stew pan, a shot cannister, anything that held water and could be placed over a small fire. Thus the wild teas of America were part of our early pattern of living.

The efficacy of some teas was learned from the Indians. Other teas were experiments in time of need. There were occasional mishaps when misguided experimenters tried Jimson-weed leaves, poke root, or buckthorn for tea. The first two were poisonous, the third a violent cathartic. But, in the main, a man or woman could locate a tea for almost any need, as a stimulant, a soothing potion, a medicinal remedy, or for a purge.

The season began with sassafras tea. It was the proper brew for winter's ending, was calculated to "thin the blood" after a winter diet of salt pork, cornbread, and hominy. Sassafras tea was made by boiling the bark from the roots or broken pieces of the orange roots themselves. If one lived in the north, he could make tea of leaves of wintergreen, Labrador tea, or snowberry which remained green all winter. The thick dark leaves were broken in pieces and boiled until the preferred flavor was obtained. The scale needles of arbor vitae or white cedar, when boiled, made a delicious tea which was rich in vitamin C, a remedy for scurvy. Needles of hemlock made a tasty drink. This was not the lethal hemlock tea which ended the life of Socrates. His was a potion made of poison hemlock (*Conium maculatum*) which is in the parsnip family.

Thoreau was one who agreed that tea made from hemlock tree needles was delicious. In his expedition in the Maine woods, he wrote of trying a different kind of tea at each evening's camp. The Indian guide knew many. Thoreau commented: "Asking for a new kind of tea, he made us some, pretty good, of the checkerberry [wintergreen] (*Gaultheria procumbens*) which covered the ground, dropping a little bunch of it tied up with cedar bark into the kettle; but it was not quite equal to the Chiogenes [snowberry]. We called this Checkerberry-tea Camp."

The common plants of Illinois are not evergreen; hence few need to be boiled, but rather to be steeped in boiling water until the desired flavor is obtained. Fresh leaves and flowers often do well; some kinds improve in flavor when dried before steeping. Drying may be done on a baking sheet in a slow oven or hot attic, or on a screen-wire frame. When completely dry, the leaves or flowers should be packaged in pliofilm bags or in glass jars with screw lids. Some plants that are recommended as excellent wild tea are alfalfa leaves and flowers, red clover blossoms, flowers of linden or basswood, and elderberry flowers; leaves of mint, catnip, pennyroyal, sage, shredded persimmon leaves, New Jersey tea, bergamot, the chopped, dried seeds or hips of wild roses, and those mentioned earlier—wintergreen, snowberry, hemlock, and arbor vitae. *(June 1966)*

THE STORY OF BREAD

In the story of bread we read the story of civilization. No other food, perhaps, is so old or so interesting; none other has played so vital a role in the story of man. Bread! Bread! Bread! It is the cry of all the hungry peoples of the world, a cry against the injustice of man toward man. And today from the tall white grain elevators that rear up proudly from the Illinois prairie, there pours a golden stream which shall become bread for the world's hungry.

Long ago in the doorway of her smoky cave the Stone Age woman, her rough hair hanging about her face, knelt before a hollowed-out rock and with a smaller stone in her hand pulverized wild grain or acorns into coarse meal. Then she took a clam shell full of water, moistened the meal, and shaped it into a cake; this she baked in the ashes of a fire. Here was the earliest loaf of bread.

The greatest improvement over the hard, flat, gritty primitive loaf came ages later when the Egyptians discovered yeast in the fermentation of Babylonian beer. With yeast and finer wheat grown in the rich valleys of the Nile and the Euphrates, there grew the first large-scale manufacture of a new, light bread.

With the growth of industry in Roman times, when every village had its bakery and its flour mills, bad labor conditions arose. Condemned criminals and old slaves, worn-out horses and donkeys that were blinded or lamed, were sent to wear out the rest of their lives in the mills. To be condemned to the bakery or the flour mill was equal in horror to being condemned to the galleys. Here was only pain, toil, and utter hopelessness.

When the ancient city of Pompeii near Rome was dug out of the ashes of Vesuvius, flour mills and bakeries were found just as they had been used until the moment when death struck. In the ovens of a bakery in the dead city, eighty-one carbonized loaves of bread were found where they had burned when the deadly gasses from Vesuvius killed the baker and his helpers, smote the donkeys turning the mill stones, and left the burned bread for a future civilization to find.

The feudal period drew a dark veil over Europe. In those days the kind of bread eaten indicated a family's social standing. Until the nobility by force took over the monastery ovens, white bread first was used only in church services, and the royal family alone ate fresh bread. The nobility, one step lower in the social scale, had day-old bread on their tables. The gentry ate two-day-old bread, while scholars and the clergy were allotted loaves that were three days away from the oven. Slaves and peasants ate four-day-old bread that probably had weevils and was mouldy on the edges.

As years passed, bread-making became a high art. Yet because of wars and bad wheat crops, famine in Europe and Asia always has been close at hand. And because a hungry people are quick to revolt, Holland knew a Bread-and-Cheese riot in 1491, and the failure of the French wheat crop in 1788 hastened the French Revolution.

Today there is still need for more bread in a hungry world. It is still a vital food whose value lately has been increased by enriching flour with essential vitamins. In America where it is manufactured on a tremendous scale, any man, no matter what his station, may buy a ten-cent loaf of oven-fresh white bread for which a duke in feudal times would have given half his lands for the right to eat. *(Nov. 1942)*

DRAMA OF THE SALT LANDS

Long ago when Illinois was young—so long ago that it was not even a state, but was part of the Northwest Territory—one of the important industries of the new United States of America was developed in the Illinois country. Since very early times, the whole world had been concerned with the problem of where to get salt; now in the newly formed nation, one of the first concerns of Government was to locate salt deposits and lease them to enterprising citizens. Thus the salt trade perhaps was the first big business in Illinois.

For in the southern part of the state there is a river called the Saline, which contains salt. In the same region are deep salt springs which have a high brine content, springs that were known by the prehistoric people who lived there for many centuries. In the region of the salt springs these ancient tribes made large clay vessels to use as evaporating pans for salt; the water was carried to a sunny hilltop and poured into porous shallow containers where summer sunshine evaporated the water and left a residue of darkish salt. Early tribes of the Mississippi Valley came many miles to trade with the salt people. Then by and by they all vanished. When later Indians came, they, too, built up a salt trade in southern Illinois. Soon the French brought more modern methods to the business, but continued to use the Indians for labor. In 1800 the English took over the trade. When in 1818 Illinois came into the Union, the salt lands became Illinois property and the business continued to grow.

Men in many trades came to work here—woodcutters and haulers to bring firewood for the long, covered ditches which were the furnaces; firemen to feed the fires; kettle-hands to man the huge 100-gallon salt-water kettles; coopers to make barrels into which the salt was packed; and salesmen, time-keepers, boardinghouse keepers, freighters, hoop-pole merchants, and all the riffraff and hangers-on who were attracted to the boomtown region.

But times changed. Great salt wells in Pennsylvania came into prominence. The tremendous natural evaporation works of Great Salt Lake were discovered and utilized; the salt mines of Louisiana were discovered. In a few years the old salt business in Illinois vanished completely. Yet the old salt wells are still there; the remnants of furnaces and kettles, even some of the prehistoric remains are visible. Here the mark of the past is not erased.

It was a brief chapter in a story which is almost as old as mankind. Ancient man along the coasts knew and used sea-salt; early civilizations boiled seawater and made crude salt which became a very early item of trade. A lack of salt influenced human migration, caused wars over salt lands; it became an almost sacred object and a binding oath. The Covenant of Salt was known in the Bible—to eat salt with another person made him a brother and dissolved enmities; it became an inviolate bond.

Salt to inland people either was unknown and its use uncraved, or else it was one of the greatest and costliest of luxuries. To honor it, the ancient Romans and Greeks created magnificent silver and gold saltcellars which had the place of highest honor on the table. By the time of the Middle Ages, it was the custom to seat the nobles and their guests above the salt, and the commoners and retainers below. It became an indication of caste which survived for many centuries.

During all this time, salt was brought over the earliest caravan routes from the salt-oases of the Sahara; it came by donkey-back over the Via Salaria in Italy to the land of the Sabines; it was taken on human backs from the salt mines of India even before the time of Alexander. Salt-taxes and salt monopolies helped create some of the misery and distress visited upon man by the inhumanity of man; salt in retribution was sown by conquerors in the devastated fields of the conquered. Throughout human history, salt moved as a potent instrument in shaping the world and the things that happened to it.

Salt came to be one of the most important items in all the things discovered by man. It was a preservative long before any other method was used to preserve perishable foods; it cured hides; it became necessary in refrigeration, in the manufacture of glass and soap, as a flux in metallurgy, and as an important item in essential chemicals. It is vital today in all these fields and in medicine, and continues to be a constant part of every meal, an accessory to every dining table. Like so many other ancient stories of the world, the story of salt touched a finger of destiny in the Illinois Country and left its imprint there. *(June 1945)*

CABBAGE AND THE COMMON MAN

A stout, well-rounded head of cabbage in a garden stands for some of man's greatest triumphs over his endless battle against hunger. The cabbage is symbolical of the fat-of-the-land, a symbol also of food that was developed to feed the common man so long ago that no one knows its entire story.

For this rotund member of the mustard family, with its strange kindred forms of cauliflower, kohlrabi, broccoli, kale, and Brussels sprouts, goes back to prehistoric man on the white chalk cliffs of Britain that still rear their sheer bulk above the stormy English Channel. On these cliffs ages ago there grew a flattish plant with bluish-green leaves that hugged the chalk slopes.

No one knows who took this wild plant and began the series of changes under cultivation which resulted in the present forms of cabbage. No one can be sure, but it is known through ancient Greek writings even before Pliny's time that cabbage heads were grown in Greece and were an important item of food for the poorer classes.

It is in this respect that cabbage has played its most vital part in the world's history. Cabbage has come closer to the common man and his destiny than to kings. For bread and cabbage were an old diet of the very poor. Each nationality whose poor and middle classes lived largely upon it had its own ways of preparing it for food. In Germany and the Low Countries there was sauerkraut—fermented, salted-down raw cabbage that incidentally preserved the precious, anti-scurvy vitamin C far better than did the boiled-to-death fresh cabbage. There was cabbage soup in France; sweet-sour cabbage in Scandinavia; boiled cabbage in England; fried cabbage in China. It was a favorite vegetable in ancient Egypt, and was in general use as a food in Europe long before the Indo-Europeans migrated westward.

It was very likely that this wide use of cabbage, especially raw or krauted, prevented a greater mortality from scurvy and other vitamin-deficiency diseases in the days when folk considered fruits and vegetables a source of little nourishment. Captain Cook on his voyages into the Pacific carried sauerkraut as a remedy for scurvy, and in a day when crews generally were debilitated by this disease after a month or two at sea, he kept his men strong and healthy.

From the early prehistoric community on the English chalk cliffs to a modern ship's crew eating sauerkraut off the tropical shores of Pago-Pago, the cabbage has played its silent part in feeding the world. Bulky and coarse though this vegetable may be, in its destiny strange stories lie, wherein man himself may read a portion of his own curious past. *(Oct. 1946)*

A STORY OF CORN

Last spring when the earth was plowed and disced and harrowed, corn was planted in long rows across the fields. The grains sprouted, sent up single pale green blades, grew rapidly, until endlessly and straight the rows of corn marched to the open horizon. Each plant was a huge, light-weight grass; its pith-filled stalk was reinforced with fibers against storms; the base was braced with anchor roots from all sides. To conserve moisture in hot, dry weather, the long narrow leaves rolled into cylinders. As summer moved on and the sun beat down, the fields were cultivated to break up the soil and kill weeds, and in the hot, moist air of Illinois the corn grew in great strides. "Knee high by the Fourth of July"—head high three weeks later. Tassels in the wind, pollen falling, one pollen grain to each silk to insure a well filled-out ear. Then the silks turned brown, the ear grew, bent down as it ripened, until the husk split to show golden grain inside . . . this was the life of corn.

Corn has grown in Illinois soil for many centuries. Before that, so long before that no one knows when or where—though it may have been in Peru or Mexico—a new plant was discovered and grown by prehistoric people. From them the later Indians acquired the knowledge of its uses, and by the time Columbus came to the New World, maize or corn was a staple crop. With a fish for fertilizer in each hill, Indian corn grew easily and almost without care. For centuries it was part of Indian food and ritual and was buried with their dead. It was the early generosity of the Indians who gave corn to the improvident people of Plymouth which saved the lives of the Founding Fathers during the first harsh winter in America.

All through those early days, and during the period when men and their families pushed westward, built a log cabin in a clearing and lived off the corn patch and the forest, corn was part of the daily American diet. There was hominy, and there were samp and mush, grits, Indian pudding, Johnny cake, corn bread, hoe cake, batter cakes, popcorn, dried corn, and succotash. And there were the tender, milky ears of green corn that were just right for roasting or boiling in summer.

Year by year, corn as it played its part in American history, became more and more highly perfected for its role in the world. Long since, it had been developed from small, gnarly ears of original Indian corn, but many years were to pass before men came to know some of the potential values that lay in ear and stalk. They did not guess that from it would come a sweet syrup, a cooking oil, and starch, that it would produce even, enormous ears, nor that it could be fermented to make alcohol. They did not know that from corn alcohol would come explosives, liquors, and plastics to create strange, modern things to be used throughout the world, nor that there would be canned and frozen corn that would preserve the delicate quality of the fresh ear. Since the early years of corn growing, it has been planted from the stony mountain slopes of New England and the Appalachians to the irrigated fields of the far west and the hot, dry lands of the Navahoes, and there are bottomland cornfields that extend unbroken for miles, a deep-green, dramatic lake of corn that grows to feed the world.

From root to tassel, corn is truly and sturdily a part of Illinois and an integral part of the American tradition. *(Sept. 1943)*

THE CHINESE PEACH

Once long ago in the blue hills of China there grew a slender tree which, as August brought a haze to the valleys, bore a fragrant, pink-cheeked, yellow fruit. On many hills in China these pleasant fruits flourished. Birds came and ate of the fruit; early men ate eagerly until the sweet juice ran down their chins. Much later this fruit became known as the peach.

No one knows when the peach became one of the important fruits in China, but it must have been a long time ago, for it was found in Chinese gardens and Chinese legends a thousand years before it was known in any other part of the world. The oval fruit with its red cheek was a Chinese symbol of long life. It was an appropriate congratulatory gift; it was one of the fruits of immortality. The Peach, *Yu,* was believed to prevent death, but if not eaten in time, it at least preserved the body from decay until the last day of the world. "Whosoever eats of the peaches of Mount Kouoliou shall obtain eternal life."

As centuries passed, the peach was carried out of China and into Persia. From there, perhaps, it reached Greece and, later, Italy. The old Latin name for the peach was *Persica;* this is evidence of the region from which the Greeks and Romans acquired the peach.

Peach trees spread throughout the warmer parts of Europe. Many centuries later when the Spanish explorers came into America, they brought peach seeds and left trees growing around the early Spanish settlements in Florida. As early as 1600 there were peaches ripening in America. Some years later they were a part of the cargo sent over to the people of the Plymouth Colony, and soon from Duxbury to Jamestown there were young trees bearing peaches superior to the insipid fruits the English had known at home. By another century, the seeds were carried by explorers, settlers, and Indians to almost every part of the two American continents.

A great many kinds of peaches were developed from that first wild tree in the remote Chinese hills. One of the most popular of all, the Elberta, was produced from a North China type combined with a Persian peach. In the hills of southern Illinois, one of the largest peach-producing areas in America, the Elberta is queen.

It is a long way from the Chinese hills to the hills of southern Illinois, yet here are some of the same growing conditions. The peach does best when the orchards are planted on land that is higher than the surrounding countryside, for the elevation above sea-level is very important. Some do best from 150 to 200 feet, others from 800 to 900 feet above sea level. Planted on the upper slopes, they escape the frosts which settle with the cool air to the bottoms, and in this way the early blossoms often miss destruction. In the April sunshine the slim-twigged peach trees in their orderly rows put a blush of pink upon the Illinois landscape, put forth leaves, set their fruit, and now in the August heat the fruit is harvested. It has been coming into the markets since July. Out of Cobden and Anna and Centralia, out of the vast orchards of the Illinois Ozarks and the relatively more level lands northward, comes the peach crop of 1945. In these Illinois hills are the proud descendents of a fruit which, for a longer time than most fruits have been known, has been eaten with pleasure by people of the world. *(Aug. 1945)*

WILD GRAPES HANG HIGH

A great fibrous vine, muscular and stout, putting out groping tendrils to fasten around convenient twigs, carrying upward a dark, fragrant surge of green leaves, the wild grape ascends to the tree tops. The bottomland forests along the rivers of the Middle West are a favored haunt of wild grapes and, seen from the river itself, the bank often presents a solid tapestry of their leaves. They reach for sunlight, spreading their leathery width toward the light while they effectively shut sunlight away from the inner woods. The tangled competition of many vines characterizes these river shores—not only several kinds of wild grapes but the raccoon "grape," the trumpetvine, wild yam, wild morning glory, bindweed, man-of-the-earth, poison ivy, catbrier, Virginia creeper, coral honeysuckle and Japanese honeysuckle, climbing rose, ground nut and many others. River bottoms are the chosen haunt of vines. But of them all, the wild grapes are perhaps most abundant and develop tremendous perennial growth.

For although wild grapes may also grow circumspectly enough along a fenced roadside and offer fragrant fruits for autumn gathering, a river bottom grape seems impelled to go up to the light. The roadside vines have all the sunshine they need. In the deep woods, light is feeble. Perhaps only about ten percent of all the sunlight falling on the forest strikes ground level. So the grapes climb. They use trees for support, energetically stretch up to where light filters through the upper canopy. There, far from the reach of foxes, bobwhites or human beings, clusters of small wild grapes are produced.

The climbing opossum finds them easily and feasts until his white whiskers are stained purple-red with juice. The migrant robins gather; so do thrushes and catbirds and brown thrashers, their beaks blood-colored from grape juice. Wood ducks leave their ground-foraging for acorns and seeds to come to the tree tops where wild grapes are plentiful. In the days long past, millions of passenger pigeons feasted there on wild fruits and so did the Carolina paroquets. Grapes which by chance were missed hung on the vines and froze when cold came, remaining there for wintering robins to find on a bitter January day.

Wild grapes were the first native American fruit to be known by Europeans. The early Norsemen, those sea-faring Norwegians who had ventured from their colonies in Iceland and Greenland, had come by chance to northeastern North America. It was autumn and wild grapes were ripe, probably the large fragrant globes of northern fox grapes. To men in need of wine, this was an important find. But although the presence of wild vines in Vinland did not encourage the Vikings to settle permanently in the new land, others who came after them used wild grapes. When John Smith was hunting out the natural resources of the Jamestown colony he found the luscious scuppernongs.

Gray's *Manual of Botany* lists a dozen species of wild grapes (five of which are found in Illinois), with a number of variations and subspecies. They range from the almost black, bitter, seedy chicken grape to the fragrant, brown-purple, marble-sized fruits of the muscadine and fox grape. The river-bank or frost grape, *Vitis riparia*, is called *raisin sauvage* in French Canada, and is most often used in the Middle West for wild grape jelly. This is a delectable confection containing all the fragrance and flavor of the wild fruit combined with a rich, dark purple-red color. Some species have the delicate whitish bloom of the Concord grape, while others are glossy and black.

Those which ascend far into the upper balconies of the forest often possess very old, durable lower trunks nearly four inches in diameter, immensely strong and covered with a reddish-brown bark which strips off so easily that the cardinals and catbirds like to pull off shreds of this soft material to use as a lining for their nests. Abraham Lincoln at New Salem, long ago, cut a length of wild grape vine to use as a surveyor's chain.

It was when Europeans were vainly attempting to grow European grapes in the more difficult climate of America that horticulturists discovered how luxuriantly wild grapes grew, apparently undisturbed by blight or insect pest. Thus, when Ephraim Bull in 1849, in Concord, Massachusetts, contrived to make a successful cross between the wild fox grape and the large, sweet Isabella of Europe, he produced the first really American grape, the Concord. It possesses the sweetness of the Isabella and the tang, the whitish bloom and the hardiness of wild grapes festooned in the American river bottomlands. *(Sept. 1959)*

ILLINOIS HARVEST

Once again the granaries, grain elevators, corn bins and storage bins are filled with the harvest from Illinois fields—with great yellow ears of hybrid corn a foot long; with a pale gold torrent of soybeans; with the rich stream of wheat, rye, oats, millet, the fruit of the prairie country. But not all of the Illinois harvest can be contained neatly into the grain elevators and bins, nor can we list our crops as coming solely from vast fields made possible by the glacier's scouring and man's ingenuity at large-scale cultivation. There are some other less well-known crops which, at year's end, have been gathered here and there in Illinois.

In southern Illinois, below the uplift of the Illinois Ozarks, fat white bolls of cotton are still standing in fields, waiting for the late picking. Tobacco, hemp, peanuts and sweet potatoes, all southern crops, have been harvested with fair abundance in an area considered northern. The commercial harvesting of pecans took place in October along the Illinois and the Mississippi, while the unofficial harvest of these sweet, rich wild nuts, once the chief autumn food of Shawnee and Hopewellian along the rivers, is a prize to be gathered by squirrel and chipmunk, jay and hiker for months to come.

The pecan, once called the Illinois Nut, is still one of our choicest crops, while other nuts are picked up by those who like the flavor of wild harvest above anything cultivated. For black walnuts are ripe now; and butternuts; and hazelnuts in their ruffled hulls; while the iron-hard hickories, only awaiting a sharp blow from a hammer (or between two rocks, Indian style, or between hammer and flat-iron, pioneer-style) to reveal sweet meats.

The fruit crop, part of the great harvest of Illinois, is not confined alone to apples on the hills of Calhoun and Pike counties, or to grapes on the slopes of Nauvoo, or to the peaches of the South. There are the wild persimmons of Illinois, one of the sweetest of fruits and well known to the Indians and their predecessors. Persimmon loaves made of the dried flesh (usually with seeds included, which made this delicacy a hazard to the teeth) were a specialty among the river Indians. Some of them, long ago, presented persimmon loaves to De Soto as a special gift of honor.

Wild persimmons for the gathering; and papaws, if you are lucky enough to find them before the possums get to them first. And red haws, wild crab apples and wild grapes—these, in earlier days were cherished for the beautiful, distinctive jellies to be made from them and placed with pride on the housewife's shelves for use in the winter.

Our harvest is endless. It supplies birds and animals with the multitudes of ripened fruits ranging from grass seeds to the fruits of wild cacti in the sand country; from ground cherries to hackberries; from basswood seeds, neatly halved by wild mice, to lotus nuts devoured by ducks, as well as all that great scope of our prairie-nourished products which supply men and the wild things with sustenance and pleasure.

This is the great banquet of thanksgiving which began with the wild strawberries and asparagus of springtime and whose stored bounties will last until strawberries ripen once more next year. (*Nov. 1960*)

❊

PATTERNS

❊

❊

❊

THE SHAPE OF THINGS

The forms of life are basically constructed of nine designs. These are often combined as composite forms which sometimes include all nine of the designs, sometimes only a few. The nine plans are (1) the sphere and spheroid, (2) the circle and ellipse, (3) the cube, (4) the cylinder, (5) the spiral, (6) the undulate, (7) the pyramid and triangle, (8) the lattice, and (9) the frond. Identifying the world's shapes with these designs becomes a fascinating game.

A beautiful example of what can result when all the forms are put together in one unit of life is seen in the spruce tree and the balsam fir. There are many more, of course—look for them—but these are outstandingly simple examples.

The tree is a *pyramid* (7) in form. Its root system and boughs are arranged in *fronds* (9) that spread outward from the *cylinder* (4) of the trunk, around which the branches rise spirally. The *spiral* (5) is also seen in the arrangement of rows of scales on the flowers, in the cones, and in the way in which the needles are set around the twig.

The outline of the fir or spruce is *undulate* (toothed, notched, or wave-edged) (6). The resin ducts frequently are *cubes* (3), the needles are attenuated *cylinders* (4), some of the wood fibers are lattices (8), and the cells in wood and needles are *spheres* or *spheroids* (1). The shadow of the tree makes a *circle* under it (2). The combination is the tenth form, the *composite*—the complete tree in its grace, dignity, power and beauty.

There is certainly nothing haphazard in this design. We need not know its component parts, its botanical details of flowering and fruiting, the lumber-man's evaluation in terms of board feet and waste, the wood-boring insect's one-track interest, the finch's preoccupation with its nest up high in the tree, the porcupine hidden in a crotch, the scars on the bark which a deer made when he polished the velvet from his antlers, or the claw marks of a bear. We can appreciate the tree without knowing any of these things, or even knowing the name of the tree itself, though to many of us this is as essential as knowing the name of a friend. But the recognition of order and the resultant beauty in the form of a thing stems from this awareness of the powerful, complicated simplicity of nature which combines forms with colors, textures, and life, to produce the creatures and landscapes of our world. (*Mar. 1961*)

THE MAGNIFICENT HEXAGON

Part of the gratification to be found in discovering the mechanics of natural forms is to see how simple shapes are combined, either to produce greater complexity of form, or to insure greater overall strength. One of these is the triangle, the simplest form to be produced by a minimum of lines enclosing a unit, other than the circle. But what nature did after the development of the triangle is wonderful to behold.

Three triangles may form a trillium flower, a wild ginger blossom, a papaw flower, or a larger triangle—if the points are arranged outward. But take three triangles and arrange them with the points inward, just touching, and there is achieved only a loose form, a windmill effect which, with the least motion or revolution, will fly apart into space. It has no stability. By filling in the gaps with three lines, however, the loose triangles are thus connected to make six; and with this is created the wonderful hexagon, a six-sided figure of tremendous strength, versatility, and usefulness. It is one of the most efficient forms when arranging a quantity in a given area. There is no waste space; each side of each hexagon forms the side of another.

The hexagon has been utilized in structures built by insects, bryozoans, and certain plant cells, as well as in snowflakes and the hexagonal system of crystals. In the latter, three lateral axes of equal length intersect each other at sixty degrees; perpendicular to them is a vertical axis which is longer or shorter than they are. Quartz crystals are formed in this pattern; so are secondary hexagonal prisms. Since quartz is called the most abundant crystal in the world—most sand grains are made of quartz—then the hexagon and its many variations is surely one of the most abundant forms in nature.

The hexagon evidently was admirably well suited to withstand pressure in colonial organisms, such as the corals. With six sides of six triangles, the central partitions often eliminated, pressure from seawater as well as from the surrounding members of the colony was equalized. The individual cell was at the same time strengthened by those surrounding it. It could not be crushed as the triangle, the square, or even the circle or cylinder could be, efficient though these forms are in many situations. The bees and wasps, in building colonial nests and honeycombs, use the hexagon, a form which has not only withstood both the pressure of the surrounding cells filled with liquid or with young grubs, but the pressure of time and change. The hexagon for ages has been the perfect shape for honeycomb, coral, for wasps' nests, for parenchyma cells in leaves, and as the unit of structure in the wonderful compound eye of insects.

Thus, as a paper wasp today in summer, 1961, chews fencewood and makes liquid paper from which is built a new colony of thin, hexagonal cells, there is created the identical form which is found in the fossil honeycomb coral which lived in the Silurian Age some 450 million years ago. They and all the snowflakes, the sand grains, the amethysts; the fresh-water bryozoans in an Illinois lake; all the wasps making paper cells, and bees building hexagons out of wax—they are all united in the common denominator of form: the structure which resulted when six triangles came together and made the magnificent hexagon. (*June 1961*)

THE STAR IN THE APPLE

In the world of nature and in the world of man, the number five is a magical and mystic figure. It is a figure which appears repeatedly wherever we look and wherever the mind of man delves after the world's great truths. Our personal world is geared to five. Five is the number of fingers we have, and the number of toes and senses, too. We find the five-pointed star as a recurring pattern which is as old as the earth. It lies in the center of a crinoid segment that lived four hundred million years ago, and in the even older blastoid fossil called Pentremites with its star-shaped top. We find it in the delicate, five-fingered "hands" of a lizard, in the starfish, on the top of a sand-dollar, in the star-anise seed, in the leaf of sweet gum, in the starch-stars of the calcium-bearing alga called Chara, in the earth-star mushroom. We find it in all the five-parted flowers of the world, in their five-parted calyces, their five-chambered pods—in all these; and there is also the star in the apple.

To find that hidden star, cut an apple crosswise, half way between stem-end and blossom-end. The star is made by the five seed chambers or carpels, with their oval seeds. In cross section, the carpels form a perfect star. It is the symbolic star of nature which recurs everywhere, often in unexpected places. We truly live in a star-studded world, even though the true stars in the heavens are not star-shaped at all, but spheres.

The five-plan of the star was noticed and its mysteries pondered deeply by ancient philosophers and teachers. Pythagoras in Greece used the six-pointed star as a secret symbol for his followers, the Society of the Star. King Solomon's six-pointed star became the mystic Solomon's Seal—two interlocking equilateral triangles, one dark, the other light, to symbolize the union of soul and body. This figure was used as an amulet to guard against fevers and disease. In our own woods grows the plant called Solomon's seal which has a rootstock marked with rough approximations of that ancient star design. It is also the pattern of the Jewish Star of David.

Perhaps it was this symbolism and mystery of the star of Pythagoras and the star of Solomon, or the teachings of both, which prompted the wise men in Asia Minor, some two thousand years ago, to follow a new star which they discovered in the eastern sky. This, they knew, must be more than an ordinary star. Wise with the wisdom of the old philosophers, they set out to learn what mysteries it portended.

Five is everywhere, and not only in stars. It was the number of some of the great movements and ideas of the world. There were the Five Blessings of the Chinese—long life, wealth, tranquillity, love of virtue, and a peaceful end. There were the Five Books of Moses, the Five Classics of Confucius, Napoleon's Five Codes, the Five points of Calvinism, Russia's Five-Year Plan, the Five Nations of the Iroquois, and the Five Civilized Nations of the South.

Wherever we look, fives and stars meet our eyes. It is not only hidden inside the apple. It lies in the form of its flowers and at its blossom-end; in all fruits and flowers of the Rose Family; in more kinds of flowers than any other number. And nature cunningly produces variations on the theme of the simple star. The Pea family altered the star to the sweetpea shape. The Mint and Figwort families formed a tube but kept five divisions of the trumpet's opening. The Composites elaborated on flower design by adding ray florets, yet the seed-producing flowers are five-parted. The disk of a large sunflower may hold a whole galaxy of tiny, perfect, gold stars.

The star is a crisp geometric figure. It is clean-lined and beautiful, as all pure geometrical forms are. It is produced from the pentagon, a five-sided figure, by placing on each flat face the base of a triangle. And so the star springs to life, is part of life, is an inescapable symbol of mysteries which man has never really fathomed. Five . . . five . . . five, the world silently states, in figures and forms and stars for all to see, or hidden, sometimes, like the star in the apple. (*Dec. 1961*)

THE WAVE

Waves on a summer shore, the flight of a goldfinch over willows, the motion of fish through a sunny pool—all these are proof of the undulate form in nature and its multitudes of examples. The undulate—the wave—represents motion as many creatures employ it in their flight, their swimming, their running, their growing; few creatures follow a direct, ruler-straight course. Everywhere in nature the undulate is in action, intangible as the flight of a bird which leaves no more mark on the air through which it has bounded than the perch leaves a mark in the water behind it, yet is as tangible as the frozen impression of wave action on ancient beaches, solidified in the sandstone records of past waters. The wind, forever gnawing at the loose dunes, carves patterns in undulating curves as the prehistoric waters of the Mississippi carved the limestone cliffs between Grafton and Alton to form a massive, undulating wall.

To see the forms of nature is to see nature as with a sharpened vision which is not only physical but mental. To understand why a thing is formed as it is, to look as with a giant magnifying glass at the structure of tree or shell or dune or bird, to see how it is made, and why, and to marvel at the astonishing repetition of forms in things both animate and inanimate is to understand ourselves and our universe more clearly than before. Form in nature represents order; and an orderly universe is a comforting thing to man who often manufactures chaos.

Man's creations themselves seem to be limited in their fineness. Under a microscope, our finest craftsmanship becomes gross, the more so with the higher magnification. But in nature nothing is coarse. The more it is magnified, the greater is its beauty.

In creating life, certain basic forms are used, as if nature had long since experimented and had finally settled upon nine patterns from which everything could be produced or compounded. Nature has kept some of these forms pure—the strength of the triangle and pyramid, the solidity of the cube and the growth potential of the cylinder, the universality of the sphere and the spheroid which form that basic cell. There are the spiral, the frond, and the wave, all pure designs.

The wave breaks over on the shore, disperses, draws back, forms, crests, comes forward white-combed, and breaks again as waves have been breaking on shores ever since there were waters and winds and shores, almost as long as the earth itself has existed. As the water draws back—sea-shore, lake-shore, pond-shore, mud-puddle in the path—the waves leave their mark in an undulating pattern. It is like an unwound spiral laid there. The same unwound spiral carves the dunes and rocks. The same wave pattern is plainly designed on many sea shells and in their contours, as if they were ornamented to fit their environment. The trees on the horizon present an undulating line against the sky. So do clouds, the wind over wheat, the course of a stream or river, the leap of a grasshopper, the grace of antelopes, the flight of bats—that same basic wave-form which archaic waters imprinted on beaches long since turned to stone. It is the same pattern which the flicker, the goldfinch, or the blue jay form in flight; as the snake makes in the dust; as the fish in the water; the worm in the mud, or the curve in the tail of the cat which prowls in the mystic summer dark. *(July 1962)*

LITTLE ESSAYS AND GENERALITIES

TO SEE THE YEAR

Let us resolve to see this year—to focus on the pattern of continuity in the timeless passing of seasons, in the plan of growth in bud and egg and crystal, in tree, flower and seed, in child, bird and caterpillar. It is all orderly. Each acts at the proper time and in the same tested manner which life has proved efficient and good.

To see the year is to adventure into deep truths laid freely open not only to philosopher and scientist but to any one of us on his way home from work, or out fishing, or gardening, or simply looking from a window, or laying a hand against a tree trunk, or examining with new vision the wonder in a snail, a stone, a star.

These are exciting personal discoveries. Look for the dynamic spiral of growth in pine cones, in fern fronds, in a Greek vase, in the curve of a lily petal. Look for repetition of form among all the myriads of diverse forms and designs of life. The oyster mushroom, as an example, has a close counterpart in a coral, the outward form translated from fungus to bryozoan dimensions in sea water. The many-forked dendritic pattern is found in river deltas, in erosion, in the nervous system, in the moss agate, in frost on window panes, in the fossil *Sigillaria*, in deciduous tree-branching, in the roots of grasses. Nature uses abundantly the efficient sphere, the spheroid, the circle, all smooth, rounded, cornerless, endless, varying from the great globe of earth and the circular form of the solar system, to the majority of the world's fruits, and the round perfection of the ball, the bird's nest, the egg, the eye, the dewdrop, the alga, the spore, the cell. Look for all round things. The year is full of them.

Look also for the mathematical law in plants—the remarkable integrity of the three-plan in trilliums, the four-plan in mustards, the five-plan in roses, the six-plan in lilies. Look for the universality of green and how it dominates, with reason, the living earth. Look for concealing coloration, the wizard's wand that transforms a butterfly, a tree frog, or a partridge into something patterned like tree bark or dead leaves. See how the law of geotropism, when a seed splits, sends the tiny stem and cotyledons up to light and the roots downward, though the seed is enveloped totally in the darkness of earth. Look for the growth of new leaves emerging in silent explosions on spring trees. Muse on the pattern of waves breaking on a shore, a pattern unchanged since there first was water on the cooling earth. See how grass, corn, oaks or nasturtiums react to wind; the way rain runs off each kind of leaf or flower; examine the symmetry of snow crystals, diatoms and pollen grains.

These multiple events, all ordered, all precise, all part of the span of the year, or the span of a hundred years, or of ten thousand, lie ahead to be discovered and savored as if they happened for the first time in the world. They provide a balance to the harassments of civilization. To learn of the world's natural orderliness is not to escape from the civilized world's challenge, but, with a calmer mind, to understand it better. To be able to see the small, timeless details of the year is to possess a special long-range insight into the greater span of centuries, an insight which may be balm to the nerves and the source of a broader tolerance of man and nature.

With the fresh new pages of the calendar before us, let us really see this year. (*Jan. 1961*)

A WALK INTO TOWN

To walk a mile in town may be something more than an exercise for the body or a means of getting from here to there. To walk with an awareness of one's surroundings is to discover new delights on every urban expedition.

February possesses an indefinable quality which is everywhere yet nowhere. It is visible in the higher-riding sun, in the brighter polish on the horse chestnut buds, in the quickening of the softened earth, in the apt mimickings uttered by starlings on rooftop and in tree. The starlings indicate a sure change in the season; they seem to imitate the voices of birds which will arrive next month—redwinged blackbird, grackle, meadowlark, bluebird, killdeer, as well as the bobwhite, cardinal, titmouse, and chickadee which stay all winter.

The cardinals have been whistling since sunrise. A tufted titmouse calls from a maple. A downy woodpecker attacks the loose bark of a dead elm across the street. English sparrows and juncos scratch about in dead grass on a lawn. Three blocks from home there are more starlings at their vocalizing. One sounds like a mockingbird, another like a crow. A fox squirrel, whipping its noble russet tail and chuckling and grinding its teeth in a frenzy signifying nothing, peers around a basswood trunk, then races in upward spirals in pursuit of another squirrel.

Ranged along the city streets, the trees themselves are a source of endless interest throughout the year. To learn all the trees along a twelve-block route is to become well versed in arboreal botany.

Although knowing them in leaf is excellent, recognizing trees in winter by bud, bark, and form is the way to fix them in the mind forever. Winter buds today are beginning to swell a trifle with the growth of coming spring while in the tips of maples and elms there are the earliest flowers, high-held and all but unnoticed. The bees, however, have not missed the event. A sunny day in February may be humming with bees long before the first crocus or forsythia has opened its flowers.

Five blocks from home there may be two old robin nests, an oriole's nest suspended like an old sock high above the street, and the shattered remains of the frail basket made last summer by a rose-breasted grosbeak. Old nests along the way fill a mile with interest.

Along the way, besides, cavities in old maple trees offer surprises. Fungi may grow on the rim; or a screech owl, the color of tree bark, may slumber all day in the cavity. On a cloudy day, the owl's head, little cat-ears erect, eyes closed, is visible from the street. Late in the afternoon the bird rises high in the hole and peers out to survey the five o'clock world of people homeward bound.

Nine blocks away . . . a large brown cocoon of the Cecropia moth. It hung in full view all winter in a privet hedge. It was close beside the side-walk, but no one saw the small treasure until today. In a garden up the street, a whitish cocoon the size of an English walnut, that of the Poly-phemus moth, hangs like a Christmas tree ornament from a birch twig.

Twelve blocks pass quickly when there is so much to look for. Above the twelfth block, over the busy part of town itself, there come the high, thin, tinkling songs of horned larks flying. On a February day this truly heralds the commencement of a new season. It is also visible in the green shoots of crocus and daffodil on the south side of a house, in the green tips of new grass, in the evergreen rosettes of dandelions, and in that glorious, new, golden, forward-looking dandelion flower just opening to the sun. The dande-lions bloom, the larks sing, the maples blossom, and the earth, during the time taken to walk a mile, has moved another small step of its own toward the actual coming of spring. *(Feb. 1966)*

BACKYARD ADVENTURE

We are the inheritors of all that great store of knowledge which has been the result of adventure, pain, hunger, death, and disappointment, and the ultimate triumph of truth, among the men who, from Columbus to the present, were the discoverers of American birds. Although the big adventures and discoveries may all be over, we of today have our own source of ad-venture, our own resource of delight, as long as there are birds. In spring we are most aware of our tremendous heritage.

Yet to only a comparative few of us does the strange mystery of the bird speak and call and offer unending excitement. The bird is always something of an unsolved mystery, even though its name and all its habits and physical characteristics are listed and known. The robin in my backyard, which has just come up from Kentucky to spend the summer here, is almost as much an unsolved mystery as was Henry Schoolcraft's newly discovered bird of sunset yellow and bone-white beak, as much a mystery as the forever-lost carbonated warbler of Audubon, or the voice of the limpkin before its maker was seen.

For a bird is not like other animals. It is unique. It has feathers, and the feathers are unique structures, too, their colors often glorious and often deceiving, their pattern a marvel of symmetry, planning, arrangement, and design for concealment or display. It is as hard to really understand a feather as it is to understand the bird—or its song, which may be pitched so high that we hear only part of it and stand wistfully, wondering what else we might hear if our ears were not so coarse or our senses so dull.

The song of the bird is a mystery, but *why* it sings is not half so puzzling as *how* it sings; and the flight of a bird is a mystery, too. Man himself has attained flight at last, though clumsily and not of his own body. The insects have perfected flight, but the handsomest moth or butterfly or beetle cannot compete with the hummingbird's incomparable flight; or gulls drifting translucent white, motionless, high in an ultramarine sky above a sea; or the route of a tern from the arctic to the antarctic; or even the strange nuptial flight of the woodcock on an April evening, a bird which, by all the laws of balance, should not even be able to get off the ground. Feathers, flight, song—these are the bird, yet there is something else which makes the whole bird, and that is the greatest mystery of all.

This is the quality which brings people, year after year, spring after spring, to look for them, study them, wonder about them. Yet the bird—the sparrow, the robin, the gull, the swift—is still a mystery as was the first bird which man ever looked at or wondered about.

Although the days of the real bird adventuring are past, and very likely all the new ones described, every person who first really sees a bird has his own life of adventure before him. He becomes a member of an old and honorable clan formed by all those men and women who, in the past and present, have found in birds a kind of fulfillment and an endless challenge.

There are as many ways of enjoying birds as there are people and birds, and the rewards though usually intangible are an enrichment of one's life. Thoreau was one who knew this well. He was the sort of man on whom the chickadees would alight and who could without being maudlin talk to owls and loons and robins, with no loss of dignity on either side. He said:

"I once had a sparrow alight on my shoulder while I was hoeing in a village garden, and I feel that I was more distinguished by that circumstance than I should have been by any epaulet I could have worn." *(Mar. 1962)*

A WORLD OF SMALL THINGS

When the old log was rolled back, a shiny brown millipede hastily curled itself into a flat spiral and lay as if dead. Half a dozen sleek black beetles pushed themselves hurriedly into greater depths of the decayed, soft old wood, while the colony of carpenter ants, inhabiting innumerable unseen apartments within the log, ran about in sudden distress when their world turned over. Thousands of microscopic creatures may have been aware that something had happened to their equilibrium. For the log was the world of many creatures—of ants, beetles, millipedes, snails, protozoa, of the newt, the white-footed mouse, and the chipmunk which, with the log as a roof, had set its deep burrow downward into the earth.

We, too, inhabit a world of small things. There are Rocky Mountains and Indian elephants and baleen whales, but the world is occupied mostly by little things. Man himself is not so very big, and the majority of the creatures are a good deal smaller. Yet the perfection of nature is nowhere more apparent than in those multitudes of little things.

When man himself turns to creating something, his finest works of art lack the minute and endless perfection as found in nature. Under magnification, the details of fabric, ceramic, paint, or carving become coarse, but the greater magnification of nature only reveals more astonishingly delicate and perfect details. The microscope is perhaps not yet made which will reduce to coarseness one of the particles produced by nature.

The spirals of the millipede and multitudes of other small wonders all lead toward an annual resolve to see more of them in the rich year that lies ahead. With that personal magnifying glass which stems first of all from curiosity, we may really see both the small things and the larger ones and at the same time grow more fully aware of other wonders. To focus on the arrangement of stamens and pistil in a flower, to look at a beetle's marvelous structure, to enjoy a frog's efficiency and the chimney swift's control of flight: they all add to the pleasure of a day in time.

Many of the small creatures, like the millipede itself, hiding in cool, dark places, must be sought carefully and handled gently. The millipede shuns the full light of the sun and prefers the haven, insulation, darkness, and dampness beneath an old log or dead leaves. The millipede is not a worm; it is an arthropod, akin to the insects, spiders, centipedes, and wood ticks. "Thousand-legger," it is often called, but probably none of them ever had so many appendages. A creature an inch or two in length would be no more efficient with a greater number; in fact, it would appear unnecessary to have the numbers of legs it does have, for with two pairs to every segment of its hard, cylindrical body wall, it seems to trundle along as with an effort. It usually avoids using its legs to carry it to safety. Instead of running, the millipede when alarmed often forms a spiral of itself and lies still as death. Its spiral has the appearance of that ancient one of the snail, the extinct cephalopod, the nautilus, the unrolling fern, the coiled cut-worm, and the sprouting seed, all part of a world of infinite wonder. *(Jan. 1966)*

THE SILENT WATCHER

A crowd would have spoiled it, midday would have lacked the magic, and night would have hidden it. It was a moment in time, a fragment of October, when man stepped for a moment inside the enchanted circle of the wild.

Night fog still blurred the woods and filled the lower parts of the meadow. So early in the morning before the sun woke their brilliance, the bright colors of the trees around the meadow were dim and hidden in the mists, and the moisture itself, almost like a gentle frost, had gathered in silver on every grass blade, on every leaf, on every twig. The maples dripped. The aspens shimmered. The meadow was all a soft blur of mist and dawn, and no bird sang.

There were two foxes in the meadow. In the place where the grass was short and thus not as wet as the long grass, one of the animals sat on its haunches, white-plumed tail resting on the ground but curled up at the end, quivering a little, ears pricked forward, watching something on the ground. When the thing moved, the fox pounced, picked it up lightly and tossed it gaily into the air, watched it come down, pounced again, tossed it up once more. It was a game. Down in the tall grasses the other fox was leaping on steel-spring, long black legs, bouncing high, looking down, plume waving—*bounce, bounce, bounce*—all intent on the motion of a mouse running for its life beneath the matted grass. The other fox continued to play with its catch. The pair were oblivious of being watched, oblivious of anything but the intentness of mousing. Mist on the lovely orange-russet fur made the foxes curiously dim, as if they were part of the foggy morning itself and would vanish in vapor with the coming of the sun.

Very high above the meadow, up against the clear sky and well above the ground mists, a flock of geese beat southward, their voices wafting down like voices of another time, another world. Their white bellies caught the gold of the rising sun long before it came to the foxes in the meadow. Up there it was morning, but down below it was still the edge of night. The jumping fox came down and stayed down, then trotted, mouse in mouth, to where its companion waited.

From the dogwood thickets at the edge of the woods, three deer in their gray and white winter fur emerged, and paused, their white-rimmed eyes wide, to survey the meadow before proceeding. The mists wreathed their legs as, with grace and sublime caution, the buck and two does stepped out to where a few alfalfa plants still were green and inviting. Nearby a black and white plume rose, waggling above the grass, as a skunk toddled about digging for grubs around the grass stalks. The feathery tail was draggled in the wet.

It was very quiet in the meadow. The blurring of the mists and the overwhelming stillness of autumn produced a charmed atmosphere in which the wild creatures moved about as if there never had been men to alarm them or any danger from creatures other than themselves. In a transient moment, the silent watcher could only watch through the mists which formed a screen that hid them from the dangerous light of day.

Then the rising sun, clearing the trees, pierced the mists and at the same time lit the creatures in the meadow. As if at a signal, the deer turned and stepped back into the dogwood thickets. The skunk waddled off to the woods. The foxes picked up their prey and trotted off into the thickets beyond the stone piles. Empty of animals, its mists burned off by the morning sunshine, the meadow lay waiting for the more forthright life of day. *(Oct. 1964)*

INHABITANTS OF A HILL

Take a hill, any hill, or any meadow or swamp or woods or shore, and you find that it and its inhabitants are governed by a complex, interlocking series of circumstances. It is not by chance that the woodchuck has its burrow here, facing the warm south sun; nor that a fox lives on the north slope, or that rabbits come here to feed, or that cactus plants grow here, or that hawks soar low over the wind-swept prairie grasses, and bumblebees grumble in the clover. It is not by haphazard chance that there is a brown thrasher nesting in a thicket of osage orange bushes, a Bell's vireo in a black-berry tangle at the foot of the slope, a shrike in a honey locust tree, a field sparrow peering up with quiet, watchful eyes from a grass nest set in the center of a clump of turkeyfoot grass, or orange-dog caterpillars feeding on the leaves of prickly ash. They are all here because they belong here. This is their proper haunt.

Long ago the barren hill was mantled by glacial dust (loess) blown by the prevailing west winds from the wide, dry flood plains of the river valleys. With the retreat of the glaciers, the rivers subsided, using only narrow channels in their gigantic valleys, the great flood plains becoming dry beds of alluvial soil from which dust was swept by every windstorm to cover the hills.

Because this harsh dust was open to sun and wind, only plants which could thrust a deep root down to moisture and food could withstand wind and brilliant light, and live. So tufts of sturdy turkeyfoot grasses came in and upholstered the hill with tall plants which stay a tawny fox-fur color all winter. And a brown thrasher one day ate the flesh of a prickly pear cactus fruit down on the sand banks near the river, flew back to the hill, dropped the seeds, and in a few years there were mats of spiny cactus plants with golden flowers in May and June. The brown thrasher nests in the osage orange bushes, which are there because a squirrel carried part of an osage orange fruit to this point on the hill, tore the fleshy fruit apart but did not eat all of the seeds.

The field sparrow, the brown thrasher, the shrike, the red-tailed hawk and the Bell's vireo live on or over the hill because the Mississippi Flyway guides their route up from the south. Instinct drops them off to occupy this par-ticular hill because it has what they require. The shrike nests in or near the locust trees and osage orange thicket. Here are thorns, good for impaling a captured mouse or sparrow to be eaten later by the shrike and its young. The meadow mice are here because the heavy grass forms shelter; beneath the tufts the mice cut passageways which are concealed from hawk or shrike hovering above.

The woodchuck is here because there is a good growth of bright green clover on the east slope, and clover and woodchucks go well together. The fox has its cool north burrow because it is handy to the young woodchucks and mice and rabbits. Clover seeds were dropped by a mouse; they grew and continued to multiply because there are bumblebees to pollinate the flowers; and the bumblebees come here *because* of the flowers, in an endless cycle of cause and effect. Just as there are the caterpillars of giant swallowtails feeding on prickly ash leaves, so are there bees and clover, foxes and woodchucks, shrikes and mice, grass and field sparrows, a wind and a hill, rocks and dust, and a broad river giving meaning to all. (*April 1959*)

THE TOUCH OF WILDERNESS

It was a deserted hill farm whose lands sloped to the river and whose surroundings, long since given back to the wild, had become a tangle of wild grape vines, a forest of poplar and maple saplings, and larger trees, living and dead, which were the property of woodpeckers, flying squirrels, raccoons, wood borers, tree fungi, and owls. Where the house had burned long ago there was only a cellar hole where a Carolina wren nested in a cranny of bricks, and a family of skunks foraged in the twilight, picking their way deliberately down the slope where bricks had fallen in, hunting grubs and beetles as they went. Beside the cellar hole stood the stark remains of a storm-shattered spruce, silhouetted against sunsets and picked out against stars as the likeliest stopping place for the night hunters as well as for the daytime hawks and flycatchers who used it for a vantage perch.

Across the twilight a shadow floated, and as it swerved upward to the crown of the dead spruce, it merged with tree and dusk and sky. There were only the quick movements of a head to show that the top of the spruce, black against the last glow, had life, and that that life was alert and wild, intent on what went on below. Golden eyes saw the last flirt of the wren's wings as it settled itself to sleep in the grape vine of the cellar hole, saw the plume of the skunk as it vanished into the hollow before there could be a sudden motion to follow. The shadow on the tree squalled a sudden, heart-stopping cat-yowl, an insistent "whocooo?" with a rising inflection at the end. The wren was still, the skunk ducked under the tumbled bricks, and all life in the dusky world below the tree froze at that voice of wilderness. The great horned owl was hunting.

In that voice, civilization vanished. Man might never have come to the hilltop above the river or built his fine house or planted his spruces or farmed his fields. The cry of the hunting owl was a sign that the touch of wilderness remained. It only draws back a little as civilization pushes in, only waits for the chance to return. The wild is prepared to move back in the instant that man lets go of an acre or a block or a clearing or a cellar hole—quickly, the grass sprouts between bricks, and tree seedlings enter cracks in concrete and split them wider. Jungles engulf temples, deserts reclaim ghost towns, and log cabins in the northern woods fall down under the onslaught of snow and carpenter ants and porcupines. Wild raspberries and bracken, given a year's time, quickly fill the neglected logging road and the clearing.

A chief concession which the wild makes to man's presence is to roam more at night than by day. Voices thus are our best proof that the touch of wilderness is still comfortingly with us. Its tonic is especially evident in the calls of the owls—in the melancholy wail of the screech owl on an autumn night, in the mellow tootling of the barred owl, and in that unutterably wild query of the tiger owl of the night as it detaches itself from the dead spruce and lightly swoops to the ground to snatch a rabbit palpitating, frozen, at that terrible cry. (*Oct. 1962*)

SQUARE YARD OF WILDERNESS

The nature of wilderness is a composite thing. It can only be produced by a great many forces working together in combination to produce an atmosphere as well as an environment, and a whole complex grouping of plants, animals, and earth. It is a situation only attained by age and the slowly changing patterns of growth. It is a matter of soil and of soil inhabitants; of vegetation and of inhabitants of that vegetation.

Forest wilderness is easily wiped out in its entirety, once a portion of it goes; but a square yard of prairie which has never known a plow may exhibit a cross section of that wilderness which once lay tremendously wild and wonderful from horizon to horizon.

Here and there in Illinois there still are a few of these untouched portions of the old prairie. Twenty years ago there were far more, for that space between the highway and the railroad right-of-way frequently was retained as a long narrow strip of original prairie land. More recently, however, flame throwers operated by the track crews, together with mowers and sprayers operated by the highway crews, have cut down and destroyed most of this priceless and irreplaceable heritage. But there are still a few persistent spots left. They are identified from a distance by the tall turkeyfoot grass or, even rarer, by the giant bluestem grass which once grew eight feet tall on the old prairie.

To measure off three feet of precious prairie remnant is to include some of the characteristic inhabitants of the past. The turkeyfoot grass itself, growing year after year from matted, perennial clumps of wide-spreading, fibrous roots, forms a cluster of dried old leaves at the base, leaves which are copper-pink in snow. By June, the tall, jointed new stalks are bright lavender-blue around the joints and pink, rosy amber, or green on the sections between. The flower raceme is usually in threes, like the toes of a turkey. Pale yellow stamens and purple pistils hang out of the waving racemes.

On the prairie, the tall grass is as the trees are to the forest, with accents of prairie clover, the spade-shaped, resinous leaves of prairie dock, a sunflower or two, an *Eryngium,* a *Liatris,* or a stout, pink-stemmed Sullivant's milkweed. Around, on, in, or beneath the forest of plants live the other inhabitants of the prairie, as they have lived for thousands of years.

The large yellow and black spider, *Argiope,* spins a web between grass stalks to catch grasshoppers leaping inadvertently squarely into the net. The jumping spider, *Phidippus,* leaps from grass to grass in odd little frog-like jumps. The singing of long-horned and cone-headed grasshoppers on a hot summer day is loud and sizzling and incessant.

Ants climb up the milkweed stalk, their sharp claws snagging the thin skin to bring out little spurts of milkweed milk. When the ants reach the clusters of fragrant flowers for nectar, they catch their feet in the blossom-traps and perish there, as ants have been perishing in the prairie milkweeds since they both began. The monarch butterfly, however, sips with impunity, then lays its eggs on the underside of a stout, thick milkweed leaf where the young green larvae will eat the leaf fiber and become jeweled, jade-green chrysalids by and by.

The matted tangles of dried grass and other plants on the ground hide the innumerable tunnels and escape routes of the meadow mice. They seldom dare to venture into the open, but in the security of the arched tunnels the mice can travel long distances and find grass seeds and other provender. The hovering sparrow hawk, from his vantage point on the nearby telephone poles, seldom catches sight of the mouse; but sometimes into the tunnel a killer shrew races in frantic search for meat . . . and one day there is the bleaching skull of a meadow mouse left in the tunnel to mark where the shrew had dined.

Quietly, well hidden in the clump of old turkyfoot grass leaves, that prairie bird, the dickcissel, sits on her nest with its five blue eggs. Her mate sings from a fencepost across the road. His monotonous chanting is as much a sound of the Illinois prairie as the sizzling of the grasshoppers.

The buffalo may be long gone from our prairie; the prairie itself may be all but vanished; but, as if in cross section or in a museum diorama, the smaller basic ingredients of life on the whole large prairie, as it used to be, are reduced to vividness in three square feet of prairie remnant. (*June 1961*)

THE FLOWER GARDEN

There was a wilderness, and there was the garden. It was separated from the wilderness only by a fence, and by the affection of the human beings who had planted seeds and roots and cherished them in the face of trials and adverse weather. Here were only simple flowers—a few marigolds and pinks, a tumbling Persian yellow rose, a tiger lily multiplying every year, some daffodils in spring, and some everlastings to put on the mantel when winter came—but garden flowers, as they do today, stood for civilization and human values and the art spirit.

Almost since the beginning of white habitation in America, there have been flower gardens. As soon as there were cabins at Plymouth and the food gardens and fruit trees had been planted, there were English blossoms thrusting their blooms into the remarkable American sunshine. They flowered and spread their seeds. Neighbors exchanged slips and seeds, one with another, so that everywhere soon there were flowers. They perhaps were the one expression of beauty and loveliness and impracticability in a harsh land, a land in which usefulness was a prime measure of value.

American gardens were as different as the people who planted them. There were the casual gardens that have come down to us as "old-fashioned gardens"; there were the elaborate, clipped, boxwood and knot gardens of Williamsburg, Boston, and Richmond. There were the azalea and camellia gardens of the South, the rose gardens of New York, the brilliant, impossible colors of statice and delphinium in the sea air of Cape Cod and Gloucester, the gardens of sun-loving flowers planted by monks and Spanish dons in California.

As folk moved west there were the unplanned gardens around the prairie cabins—a columbine or two, a clump of magenta phlox, a seven-sister rose— sheer luxuries as compared with the stark realities of cabin people. In river shack and squatter's cabin there appeared old tin cans full of opulent geraniums, or a Christmas cactus cherished from year to year.

Everywhere that people went, flowers went, too. Today this love for blossoms, even in the harshest lives, continues strongly. For flower gardening is a private, personal thing. It is the few moments snatched from other work, to dig in the soft moist earth and carefully plant a bulb. It is the deep satisfaction of seeing the shoot break through into the sunshine; it is the watering, the weeding, and the watching, and the fulfillment of a blossom. Gardening like this always has had its own private and personal reward.

Today's brilliant August garden with its phlox and bellflowers and morning glories is part of that love for flowers which has spread over America and lives in the hearts of Americans everywhere. (*Aug. 1946*)

SEED CATALOG

The turn from winter to springtime is noticed with the first seed and nursery catalogs which arrive almost as soon as the Christmas cards no longer flood the mails. The plant catalog is a magazine of promises and delights. No matter if asters seldom grow so gloriously or beans so large, the catalog is a bright tonic on a day when winter is the only obvious reality and spring is still a long way off.

But the catalog is more than pictures, more than promises. It is a compilation of the results of plant exploration around the earth. For almost a thousand years, seeds and plants, under some of the most difficult and impossible conditions, have been brought from far places to England and France and America to be coddled and cared for, to be propagated, improved, and then offered today at perhaps ten cents a packet or a mere three plants for a dollar, as if so much were not involved in the offering. The incalculable risks, the illnesses, the scurvy, the wounds, the savages, the deaths, the poor food, the weariness, the disappointments, and the persistence of the plant hunters are all represented in the catalog and, later in the year, in our gardens.

Even when growing naturally in the wild, plants through the ages have continually changed their habitats and their locations; but when men stepped in to help them along, the flora of the world became blended; it is continually merging and becoming one. If a plant growing in the mountains of Tibet can adapt itself to the latitude of Boston, experiments with it in the Arnold Arboretum soon have it on the market. If an Australian tree can grow in England, Kew Gardens and the Royal Society have seen to it that it grew there. But the botanical gardens and the botanical societies and plant nurseries and seed houses could not function without the intrepid men of the past who loved adventure as much as they loved plants.

Most of the early voyages around the Mediterranean, then into the East, and later around the world, all brought back seeds. The Crusaders brought seeds; so did caravans and caravels. Many early voyages were largely to bring to Europe valuable cargoes of those seeds, barks, or buds which were spices—pepper, cinnamon, cloves, nutmegs, cassia, and ginger. Herbs were carried to kitchen gardens. And roses were brought from Damascus, not for any usefulness but for their beauty. It was for the beauty of flowers that most of the later plant hunters sought their quarry.

Some of the most familiar species today were unknown in the United States when the Declaration of Independence made us a nation. Not until 1823 was the petunia discovered by a French explorer along the La Plata River in South America; and the seeds, by 1831, were growing in the Botanical Garden at Glasgow. The four-o'-clock was found in Peru; the nasturtium, prior to 1569, was brought by the Spanish from Peru to Spain, then to France, then to England, and it was cherished throughout Europe. Geraniums came from South Africa, cockscomb from Asia, portulaca from Brazil, salpiglossis from Chile, and zinnias, named for Professor J. G. Zinn, came from Mexico in 1750.

To bring seeds from afar was one thing, often filled with difficulties; but transporting plants was immensely more complicated and frequently resulted in failure at the end of a long voyage. Salt spray, heat, cold, and carelessness aboard ships could ruin the collections of months. But when Dr. Nathanael Ward discovered that plants in a sealed glass container could maintain themselves with their own moisture for years, the Wardian case came into being. After that, orchids, palms, and other plants of the tropics could be brought in miniature greenhouses to England.

We deal in generalities, but to know of the men themselves who are behind the flowers in the catalog is to meet a fascinating group of dedicated people. There is Ernest Wilson in 1910, struggling with a broken leg through mountain passes of China, with the first regal lily bulbs. We see Robert

Fortune smuggling the first chrysanthemum, the first bleeding heart, the first peony out of the forbidden territory of China, or David Douglas coming from Scotland to the western coastal wilderness of America, and finding the Douglas fir, the California poppy, the manzanita, and many more. There are William Bartram and the mystery of his lost *Franklinia,* and André Michaux finding, losing and finding again the rare *Shortia* in the Carolina mountains. There are Allan Cunningham finding Swan River daisies in Australia, Thomas Drummond finding *Phlox drummondi* in Texas, Joel Poinsett transporting the first poinsettias from Mexico. There are the *primulinus* gladiolus bathed in the spray of Victoria Falls and cyclamen on a mountain in Greece.

The catalog lies on the table. Face up on the cover are those *primulinus* gladioli and the lily of the Nile; there are hybrid amaryllis which originated in South America, tigridias from Yucatan, tuberoses from Mexico, Japanese anemones, and Chinese chrysanthemums. Inside there are Wilson's azaleas and rhododendrons, his pearlbush and tea crab and Chinese dogwood, Charles Wilford's Philippine lily, and gloriosa lilies from African jungles. In the catalog and in the garden, the world and men are one. *(Feb. 1964)*

THE STILL WATERS

The dark waters of the creek lie as quietly as a lake. There is no visible motion, even though its inner current is carrying it always to join the river. The waters are so still that the yellow leaves of cottonwoods, floating in becalmed fleets near shore, seem not to move, while the descent of a single leaf from twig to water is only a dreamwise part of the breathless hush of autumn.

For autumn, late autumn, is a time of such quiet that it rings in the ears. Our senses are so accustomed to accommodating themselves to many sounds at once, to the tumult of traffic, to the sounds of cities, that stillness comes with startling impact. Then, as we accept it, it becomes a gentle pleasure, a revelation of our awareness to what nature may be when sounds leave off and quietness takes over.

November is the time of the still waters and the silent woods. It is the time when the work of growth, reproduction, and the great hunt for food is past. Three-fourths of the birds, who are great sound makers, are gone to the south; the remainder are quiet, as if oppressed in the hush, or are respecting it by keeping their own voices low and small and far between.

Insects have been quelled by the frost, and only a hardy flight of wintering mosquitoes dances in the cool light coming down through the almost-bare willows and cottonwoods along the creek. A solitary cricket scrapes a painful ditty, a dolorous farewell to a world no longer filled with warmth, sunshine, other crickets, and the myriads of summer insects all a-sing. And even this one last cricket halts in mid-song, as if the effort were too great in the chill damp of the creek bank and the foreboding scent of winter which is in the air. A woodpecker's distant hammering stands out in staccato suddenness as the cricket stops. The hammering is almost as much a part of the silence as the silence itself, and then it is quiet again. Quiet.

And the still, dark, cool waters of the creek, slowly carrying its fleets of yellow leaves to the distant river, move on and on without any visible motion; yet, as surely as the year itself has come to November, these waters will reach the river and, one day, the still more distant sea.

Everywhere across the land the watercourses are quiet, filled with the final swarming of green diatoms and algae and protozoa, filled with the disintegrating jellies of the bryozoans whose reproductive cells are floating off to await next season's warmth and growth. Fish lie motionless in the depths. Frogs are already beginning to stay longer in the mud. Turtles have gone beneath for the winter. The crayfish shoves itself tail-first into soft mud and only emerges occasionally to get some food. Nymphs of dragonfly, mayfly, and damselfly lie half dormant on the creek bottom.

And in the waiting, cool, quiet of November's citron-colored sunset, one golden leaf detaches itself from a high twig and floats in sidewise dips and curvets, down, down, to land lightly on the dark and silent water. The leaves will all be down soon, and the waters of autumn will hold many of them. Some will freeze into the ice. They are a bridge between autumn and spring, for the trapped leaves, holding heat and energy in themselves, will permit sunlight to melt the ice faster when the break-up comes and spring returns to the still waters of the land. *(Nov. 1961)*

AMERICAN WATER

It is the same water, endlessly changing from liquid to vapor to liquid, since the beginning of the world. There is no more water in the world, and no less, than there was in the beginning but its distribution has been constantly varying since that moment long ago when a cooling planet held water in its hollows.

Water always tends to run into a hollow. The big hollows are oceans and the smaller ones are lakes or puddles; long hollows are rivers and lesser ones are streams or ditches. But they all contain water which is endlessly on the move, ever changing, restless, seemingly alive, as it dashes from a mountain top to become a water fall, or as it slowly and fetidly evaporates from a pool where dying fish gasp for breath. It is all water, American water.

Water determines man-desired boundaries. Oceans define continents; lake shores define states; rivers divide a continent; streams contribute to the load of soil materials carried elsewhere. American water has carved the continent, bisected the landscape, made known the secrets within the earth. It was the mad Colorado which gouged out the Grand Canyon, The San Juan which carved hundreds of gooseneck curves along its course, the Illinois which carried melting glacier water to the Mississippi and at the same time leveled a vast flood plain to mold the face of Illinois. The Mississippi's channel is never the same from month to month or from year to year; it is made up of waters from half a continent, from Montana to Pittsburgh and from Minnesota to Louisiana—all American water. The mountain stream dashing white with foam and sparkling over green boulders and past ferns dipping into its cool depths is as American as the almost motionless cattle pond where the redwings nest in the willows and catfish lurk in the mud. They are all part of the landscape, these waters of America.

Water puts interest in any landscape . . . the thousand lakes of the north, where there is either a lake or a marsh or a bog over every rise and around every bend in the road . . . the desert stream which is marked with water-loving cottonwoods and may be dry as dust in summer and deep with roaring flash-flood water in time of rain . . . dewdrops pearling the edge of a strawberry leaf . . . raindrops dripping through wild crabapple blossoms . . . a downpour which bends the trees and batters the daffodils . . . water which, in the form of snow, piles deeper and deeper on a silent winter night.

For proper distribution, water should go through its usual cycle of change, from evaporation from a body of water to the form of a cloud, to the form of falling rain, which drains down to tree roots and the surplus goes back to the streams and lakes. Sometimes the cycle is changed. In times of drouth all the water may be taken up and not let down in a certain area; there may be too much rain in another place and the run-off is too great for the soil to absorb, and there are floods. During the glacial era, it is believed that such a large part of the world's moisture was held inactive in the form of tremendous ice masses, that the water courses and oceans farther south of the ice sheets were noticeably lowered. Not until the melting, when the run-off was tremendous and soaked a continent with too much water, did the cycle get back to a better situation in providing a world with water.

American water. It is the flavor of a clear, cold spring running through beds of watercress. It is the taste of good pump water filtered through many feet of cold northern sand; it is the water flavored with iron or sulphur or other minerals which all tell mutely from whence that water came. It is the Finger Lakes, and Lake Mooselookmeguntic; it is Lake Michigan and Lake-of-the-Woods; it is Mud Lake and Catfish Lake and Lake Decatur; it is all the lakes which mark a map with blue. It is the yellow water of the Santee and the black waters of the Suwanee and the Styx; it is the grey-yellow of the Missouri and the clear amber waters of the Wisconsin; it is the muddy Sangamon and the tide-water smells of the Indian River in Florida, and the bright waters of the Kern splashing down from Sequoia heights.

American water—the blue springs of Wakulla, the red run-off from a Georgia cottonfield, green lakes set high up on Grand Mesa, white waves curling on the sands of Hatteras, and purple water hyacinths clogging the still waters of a Louisiana bayou.

It is water to drink, water to swim in, water to boat in, water to explore for sunken treasure, water to feel as mist on one's face and to hear pounding as rain on a cabin roof, water to keep motors cool and boilers hot, to keep factories running and to keep cities alive, to irrigate crops—water to sustain a world of plants and animals. Water. Part of the human body, part of the mechanism of the world, good, bad, admired, hated, changeless yet ever changing.

John Ruskin said of water: "Of all inorganic substances, acting in their own proper nature, and without assistance or combination, water is the most wonderful. If we think of it as the source of all changefulness and beauty which we have seen in the clouds; then as the instrument by which the earth we have contemplated was modeled into symmetry, and its crags chiseled into grace; then as, in the form of snow, it robes the mountains it has made, with the transcendent light which we could not have conceived if we had not seen; then as it exists in the foam of the torrent and in the iris which spans it, in the morning mist which rises from it, in the deep crystalline pools which mirror the hanging shore, in the broad lake and glancing river . . . what shall we compare to this mighty, this universal element for glory and for beauty? Or how shall we follow its eternal cheerfulness of feeling? It is like trying to paint a soul." (*Aug. 1950*)

THE RAINY DAY

The summer sun dried the earth until spring rains were forgotten. The back roads were powdered with dust. Roadside weeds were coated with it, and birds retreated to less uncomfortable areas with cleaner foliage. Day by day, as the sun beat upon cornfields, the shining ribbons of corn leaves began to roll into protective cylinders against too much evaporation. Grass was dry. The woods were dry. Everything needed the gentle restoration which rain would bring. And there had been no rain for many days.

And then in the night, from low clouds but without the disturbance of thunder and lightning and wind, rain began to fall. Even before the pattering of raindrops could be heard on roof or street, the wonderful aroma of newly dampened earth filled the air, and there was an excitement in the night as the rush of raindrops beat upon the thirsty earth.

By morning it was still raining and everywhere the land looked new and alive again. Corn leaves were unrolled and polished, a silvery gazing-globe of a drop hanging from the bending tip of each one, letting go to fall into the wet earth, only to be replaced by another. In the woods the rain came down hard on the tops of the trees, but the leaves diffused it, and many of the drops which fell on the upper leaves of maple and oak and elm would not reach the ground for half a day. The glossy leaves of the maples, as if oiled, held water in little puddles; it was channeled down the ribs, gathered in drops on each leaf lobe, let go and landed on another leaf; or ran smoothly down a twig, down bark furrows. Drops hung in a misting of moisture among the juniper needles and fell off in showers when a catbird flew in to reach its nest.

Ferns channeled drops down their midribs and off the curling pinnae of their fronds. Mosses and lichens, shrivelled and dry for days, had soaked the rain all night as if they were sponges and by morning were fresh and alive again. Even so quickly, with a return of moisture a few mushrooms were springing up in the wet moss beds, while old brackets on tree trunks looked polished and alive again.

On wet logs crawled snails. They left glistening trails behind as they hunted food. For days, as protection from dangerous drouth, the snails had drawn inside their shells and had sealed their openings with a film of mucus which had dried, insulating the creature from dryness and heat.

Chipmunks, for the most part, stayed in their burrows. Stored in them was food for emergencies. The chipmunk which ventured into the downpour was sure to come back with a tail that looked like an old wet bottlebrush, requiring a good deal of grooming in a dry place to restore its neatness. Rabbits stayed under bushes. Squirrels remained in their holes until, as the rain became only a gentle misting, a fox squirrel came out and raced across his tree-top route, shaking down a heavy shower of drops to mark his going.

A wood thrush, its cinnamon-brown feathers darkened by wetness, began to chime a splendid bell-song. Wood pewees darted out after gnats. Only a dripping from the trees and from the squirrel's cavorting sent down any rain. The sky grew lighter, and after a while the clouds broke and the sun came out, and the summer earth, revived in the life-giving moisture steamed a little in the warmth. (*July 1960*)

THE GIFT OF RAIN

What better boon to a sun-parched, heat-bedazzled land than this, the gift of rain? What greater benison can come to hard-baked earth and small creatures huddled in its unkindly, stone-like haunt; to the forest standing with roots in soil whose humus has lost its last moisture and now lies dry and friable, ready to burn at a spark? What better gift for pasture, cornfield and garden, for lawn and lily and hollyhock?

In Illinois in summer, the rains may be few and widely spaced, the sun an unremitting glare, the clouds too high, unrewarding and aloof, the country roads inch-deep in dust, and the weeds thickly laden with deposits laid there by warm-fingered winds. What kinder gift for summertime than summer rain? The all-night rain, the day-long rain, the voice of gutters running, the sliding drops on elm and fern, and that long, slow, sweet, living rain soaking into the parched and punished earth!

But for so long the earth had been denied this gift. There had been only that endless realm of drouth, of furnace winds, of heat-waves shimmering over grain, the desperate rolling of the leaves of corn. The robins, beaks agape, ran on rock-hard ground. Grass burned brown; daisies dimmed. The lessening brooks whose stones lay scabbed and dry, the ebbing pond shore marked with muskrat tracks, the green stagnation of the algae scum in what once was clear, clean, sparkling water of the lake, a dry land waiting—and still there came no rain, no rain.

And then at last—the darkening clouds, the sudden wind, the wash of chill, cool wind like surf across the heat, the declaration of the lightning flash, reply of thunder—and then the rain! The first drops raise perfume from newly dampened dust and stones. The ferns drip, the elm leaves sparkle, sweeping showers in the rain-wind, gusting and twisting, casting broken leaves adrift. Robins shout glorias, and swifts, oblivious to rain or wind, speed fast and gay, cutting the drops as with dark scimitars, chattering delight.

And so the earth drinks. The leaves are clean again, the streams are full, ponds brim, grass greens and robins rejoice, jabbing the worms brought up by rain. The catbirds sing. A lank-tailed squirrel comes out to see the day. Nighthawks swoop and squawk their wild gutturals into the retreating clouds.

Still dripping, still abrim with moisture slowly seeping into the depths of grass roots, down to meet the tree roots, into the cornfields and soybean rows, running like tears over the ripening cheeks of apples, the earth basks once again in moisture. It is nourished anew with supplies of nitrogen released by lightning from the atmosphere, and life, wherever the rain has fallen, is enriched with that vital food.

The great run-off, filled with life, works its way into the welcoming earth. The land lies at peace, relaxed and cool, breathing beatitudes for this, the gift of rain *(Aug. 1963)*

RAINY DAY

The car, that rainy April day, eased to a halt so quietly that even the turtles on the log only goggled a little in that direction and did not slide off into the pond. For wild creatures seldom fear a motor car. Man himself is to be feared, but not his conveyances. Therefore a car may come into a wild area without noticeably disturbing its inhabitants. And this was a wet spring day. Rain, except for heavy downpours, seldom disturbs the birds, and the presence of rain, besides, seems to give them a feeling of protection and security, as if they knew that hawks seldom fly in wet weather and that man prefers to stay indoors on puddly days.

And so the car stopped in the muddy little road, with the pond on one side and the sloping woods on the other. The pond itself was a place of quiet action. In the sedges near the shore a dozen fine shoveller ducks and eight blue-winged teal grubbed around in the shallows, nosed into the sedges, kept the water in motion. The rain had neither mussed nor dampened their spring-time beauty—the shovellers with their bright russet sides, their blue, black, and white backs, their green-black heads; the teal with their white crescent marks on face and sides, their soft brown feathers . . . but wait, here comes something. Cutting through the rain, dropping down suddenly with braked feet, sixteen cormorants hit the water and churned about in excitement. Their black feathers had green sparks; their wild eyes were green fire. Some of the big birds surface-dived; others sank, after the manner of submarines, their heads the last to disappear. Then up, with splashing, with silver fish in their hooked beaks . . . white shad slowly making lumps down those long necks. The cormorants stirred things up; the fish leaped from the water. A king-fisher, rattling, came and sat on the wire and dropped down for some fishing on his own account. Then, as suddenly as they came, the cormorants got up and went off in a long, straggling line.

A brown water snake slid quietly off the grassy bank and into the rainy pond. A song sparrow sang from a low willow where last year's nest still clung, an old fish head in it where a crow had left it. The ducks went about their business in the shallows, and a flight of bright blue and white tree swallows circled out of the rain and perched, preening and tweeting, on the wire just vacated by the kingfisher. The endless drama of the pond went on.

Just as things were growing quiet and nothing had happened for at least ten minutes, there was a splash and a scream that startled the teal and sent the swallows into the rain again. A big osprey, looking fully as large as an eagle at such close quarters and in such a little pond, had dropped down and with a shrill cry came up, splashing, with a big red carp flapping in the grasp of stout blue claws. Up went the osprey, the fish held pontoon-wise, up, up, and leveled off, heading for the swamp. And then it was discovered that the rain had stopped. A woodchuck, brown and heavy-furred, loped along its own private trail at the edge of the woods across the road, to the place on the slope where raw clay marked a new burrow. The ducks got up and headed for the lake, and then from the woods came a new song.

A wood thrush was singing. First of his kind to return this year to these woods, the brown and ivory bird perched high on an oak tip, against the sky that already was showing blue, and caroled long, low, fluting bell tones into the clean air of the April morning. (*April 1948*)

SAND BULLETINS

The dunes provide a haunt for creatures which must be well adapted to heat, wind, and dryness if they are to survive. Some not only survive but apparently choose this unkind area for their permanent homes. Although the temperature of the surface sand on a summer's day may reach 120 degrees or more, the air directly above is much cooler, as much as fifty degrees at about five feet above the dune itself, while six inches below the blazing surface of the summer sand the temperature remains, day and night, at about eighty degrees.

The ever-changing sand is an autograph album, a bulletin board, to present records of all that walked here. It takes the imprints of creatures and preserves them briefly until the wind or rain erases them to make way for the next day's records, for on this loose floor everything leaves a transient mark. When the wind swirls blades of marram grass and wild rye, they draw beautiful, compass-accurate circles on the sand. As a spider scrambles from one clump of grass to another, it leaves a lacy design of legs and body. A tiger beetle makes still another sort of trail; the hog-nosed snake marks a beautiful, sinuous track; and the mouse which may come out to collect grass seeds or the shrew which is foraging for prey leaves its own definitive mark. So does the killdeer with its three-parted tracks showing no hind toe, indicating that a plover has walked here, while the spotted sandpiper shows a hind toe to prove its sandpiper origin. The gulls on the shore leave their own special footprints and so do the foraging crows and herons.

Creatures live on and mark the surface of the sand. Some come out only at night, their movements revealed by the tracks and trails they leave on the sand to show where they have hunted. Most of the habitations of the sand are not easily seen, but the bullet-holes of the bank swallow nests under the crest of the inner dune are very much in evidence; and a peppering of small holes, no bigger than if they had been made by a lead pencil, were made by the sand wasps.

The wasp is one of the primary inhabitants of the dunes. Like a small and energetic dog, the female sand wasp digs a hole, kicking the sand back of her so fast that it flies in a fine showering. Soon she is out of sight in the burrow. An egg is laid in the bottom. The wasps may dig dozens of burrows, each one a nursery for their developing young. When the larvae hatch, they are fed by the females who catch and bring to them small flies which are found on the sand ridges. Other wasps are found in this habitat, some large, some small, some glistening, some dull, all a part of this world of the sand.

Still another creature of the dunes is the small, bristly, gray ant lion, larva of a delicate, winged insect, *Myrmeleon,* one of the Neuroptera. The larva lurks out of sight in the bottom of a conical pit in the sand. Into this open cone a traveling ant may stumble. Alerted at once by the sand grains tumbling under the ant's frantic scrambling, the concealed ant lion kicks out sand to further confuse the ant, then with large pincers grasps the victim and draws it down out of sight into the pit. After sucking the juices from the ant's body, the ant lion discards the empty skin like an old sandwich wrapper and then waits, ready for more prey. *(Nov. 1965)*

THE DRAMA OF DIAMONDS

Diamonds are the troublemakers of the world. Ever since man learned to covet them, these calm, clear chunks of pure carbon have caused ruin, bloodshed, and death; they have contributed violently to the making of human history.

During the hectic years of diamond-mining in India and later in Brazil and South Africa, only a few of all the gems found were outstandingly large and perfect, but it was these few, acquired by rulers of the world, which made history and caused a never-ending series of wars, hatreds, intrigues, and murders. Never in their history were they all gathered togther in a group; in the Illinois State Museum, however, there is an exhibit of realistic models of these huge diamonds. Their stories are vivid and dramatic.

Here we see the magnificent Kohinoor, and a thousand years roll back to the time when it was found in India's Godavery River and chiefs started an age-long battle for its possession. "Kohinoor, Mountain of Light!" exclaimed Nadir Shah many centuries later when first he saw it, and thereafter the great diamond was known as the Kohinoor. One by one we see its owners assassinated, tortured, exiled, imprisoned, because of a gem which, diamond-judges once said, was worth half the daily expense of the whole world.

Close by in the same case is the great round Orloff, which in spite of its Russian name originated, like the Kohinoor, in India. Once it was the eye of a Brahmin god, was stolen by a French soldier, and much later was sold at a fabulous price to Prince Orloff. He presented it to Empress Catherine of Russia in order to find favor in her sight, but although she accepted the diamond, the prince shortly afterward was executed. During the invasion of Moscow, Napoleon's soldiers tried to steal the Orloff and other jewels from a tomb where they were hidden, but a well-planned ghost rose up and frightened them away.

Death and disaster also followed the owners of the great square-cut diamond, the Regent. In its bright facets are the stories of the Hindu slave who was slain because he found a great diamond; of the sea-captain who stole it and who hanged himself when the money from its sale was gone; of poor, sensitive Sir Thomas Pitt who bought it honestly for $100,000 and then in disguise sneaked about with a furtive air, afraid for his life.

These diamonds still are to be found among crown jewels and national treasuries, all but the Grand Mogul, one of the world's finest jewels. The Grand Mogul has disappeared. Only one European, Jean Tavernier, the French gem merchant, is believed to have seen it, and he estimated its value at four million dollars; then the limpid treasure vanished. Some think that the Mogul was stolen and recut to become the Orloff, but others believe that perhaps one day a chest will be found moldering in some Kashmiri rose garden and inside, striking sparks in the sun, will be the Grand Mogul.

More stories are conjured up by the Nassak which once was the eye of Shiva in an Indian cave-temple; by the Shah of Persia which was the price of a man's life; by the Sancy which was owned by at least seven kings, three queens, and certain state dignitaries. More than for any other purpose, the Sancy was used by the thrones of Europe as security for loans. Many a time it saved a royal reputation or a national treasury. It was stolen in the famous Garde Meuble gem robbery in 1792 in Paris, and at the same time the glorious French blue diamond disappeared from the crown of Louis XVI. In 1812 a blue diamond that mysteriously appeared for sale in London was suspected as being the recut French blue, but no one could prove it. The blue diamond brought ill fortune to its European owners, but today the Hope, as it now is called, is the property of the McLeans of Washington and the bad luck for a time has subsided.

The climax of diamonds as to size, if not in drama, is the Cullinan, a chunk of pure carbon that looked like ice and weighed one and a half pounds, or 3,106 carats. It was cut into nine separate jewels, two of which, the Great Star of Africa and the South Star, are larger than those older diamonds in the exhibit. Before the war the originals of these two rested inside a double steel cage in the Tower of London and were guarded night and day, but their present hiding place is a British secret.

These are the troublemakers, the too-large, too-beautiful diamonds. Although no especial fury seems to brew around them at the moment, there is no reason to believe that their hectic careers are ended, until, like the Grand Mogul, they vanish from the sight of man. (*May 1945*)

"IN THE LONGEST TIME OF ALL . . ."

Stones on the shore bear the guise of permanence. They are rock, and it seems that rock must last forever. Yet change, even in rocks, is the one permanent thing in nature. The stone is no more permanent than the spring flower or the butterfly, yet the latter are geared to coming and going quickly while the former knows the long, slow change which, in the world of nature, has no need for hurry. The tempo of nature is different in each creature and in each thing, but not one will stay forever without changing. Men may not last long enough to see some of these changes; but they are there, moving inexorably on and on toward a future where change will still be the only stable thing.

The rocks on the shore . . . walk over them, sit upon them, contemplate them, study them; whatever one's interest or disinterest in them, the rocks remain. They have been broken from a long-gone mountain mass or from a sea-floor that solidified as limestone or sandstone four hundred million years ago. They are part of the beginnings of the world. They are part of today, will be a part of distant tomorrows. Yet the form they hold today is not exactly that of yesterday nor will it be that of tomorrow. The granite pebbles, their roughness smoothed, lie in a mosaic on the lake shore where waves placed them in an endless game of geologic chess. As each wave washes over them, some shift their places, or a fragment may wear away. Even their location on the shore is always changing, either by action of water or by the boy who comes along and, obeying that irresistible impulse to assist the forces of geology or simply to exercise the right arm, throws stones into the water. One day they will return as the movement of ice and waves brings them up again and pushes or nudges or throws them on shore, again part of the game of chess, yet not quite the same as they are today.

They have been moving and changing ever since they were part of the archaic mountain ranges far northward, in the early history of the earth. The action of cold and heat, of water entering cracks and inserting that potent force which breaks solid granite into fragments, of gravity rolling them down slopes, caused the whole mountain range to finally wear away. Fragments caught in moving rivers were smoothed and carried far away. No one can say where these rocks may have been before they lay with a deceiving quietude, lapped with water and bathed in sunshine on a Lake Michigan beach.

There was no Lake Michigan when they were on their way here. There first had to be the power of continental glaciers which gouged and scoured and built and tore away. Where the Great Lakes lie today there were once the valleys of old rivers. Filled with the mile-high ice masses, not once but four times, the valleys were gouged deeper, and, when the last ice had finally melted, water which filled the valleys became the five Great Lakes. The ice had, meanwhile, gathered up in its underparts the fragments of rocks torn from the archaic mountains long before, had further polished and shaped them, and littered the ancient lake bottoms and lake shores with them. Wave action continually brings more to the shore and takes others back. Quiescent they lie today, but the endlessness of change may one day have worn each one down to the ultimate unit of a grain of sand. The poet, Kathleen Raine, said:

> In the longest time of all come the rock's changes,
> Slowest of all rhythms, the pulsations
> That raise from the planet's core the mountain ranges,
> And weather them down to sand on the sea-floor.

(*June 1962*)

THE TOWNS THAT MINERALS BUILT

For ages man has mined minerals, set up his cities adjacent to the mines, and as the mines grew, so did his towns. But sometimes a mineral resource was unexpectedly exhausted, and the town which relied solely upon that resource for a livelihood was often left stranded, a village among the slag heaps. The traveller through Illinois finds the map dotted here and there with these lost hopes, and here and there, also, with others flushed with rising hope of a new boom. So cities since the beginning of history have risen and fallen.

In the early days of Illinois, when the prairie towns were mushrooming out of the sticky loam and Saturdays saw the village square crowded with horses and wagons, men were just beginning to find out something of what lay under that damp prairie sod, were discovering that here might be wealth.

As early as 1699 lead was discovered and mined along the Fever River in the northwest corner of Illinois. Much later a village grew up, and in 1828, when news of large lead strikes had reached the east, there began a lead rush almost equal in frenzy to the '49 gold rush which was yet to come. And, ironically enough, the new town, named Galena in honor of the mineral that made it, was ruined by that '49 gold rush westward, when a large portion of its population hurried to the new bonanza in California. Today it is a pleasant old town in the hills, a town that lives in the flavor of a romantic past, and remembers the mineral that built it up and let it gently down again.

In a similar way the cities of Braidwood, Coal City, Diamond, and Godley in northern Illinois rose with the discovery of coal to a promised greatness. In 1875 these towns sprang up quickly and grew to such size that, combined, they were at one time larger than Chicago. But the coal field at that point was thin, and the mines, that had burrowed down so enthusiastically for the black diamonds, soon stood deserted. With the breakdown of the mines, the towns decreased in size until they threatened to become a mere handful of people who were turning to farming. The dream of metropolis faded away. Today in this region, strip mining with huge mechanical shovels skims off the cream of thin coal lying not far below the surface.

Oil boomed the small prairie farming communities of south-central Illinois. LaSalle grew out of the zinc business, Wood River from its oil refineries,

Rosiclare from its fluorite, Granite City from its steel mills, Alton from its sand deposits and glass factories, and the little town of Depue, on a lake of the Illinois River, has also known many ups and downs. Once it was a thriving river port, but with the final departure of the river boats, Depue sank into a decline, until zinc mines were opened and smelters were operated. But the zinc smelters, which employed so many people, backfired by killing all the vegetation within reach of the fumes, and Depue began to sink again, until reforestation saved its greenery and its gardens.

Tales like these, too numerous to recount here, are told in Illinois towns and villages—tales of rising fortunes in lead, zinc, salt, or oil, in coal, fluorite or the occasional eddy of a false gold strike, and of that sudden drop from favor when fortune goes away. *(Sept. 1940)*

SACRED SMOKE

Perhaps it began as incense burned on an alter. Perhaps it grew out of inhaling the sacred smoke as it rose from offerings to the gods. But no one, actually, knows when or how pipe-smoking began, and although it is generally agreed that it originated in America, no one knows when a pipe was first made for the purpose of smoking. Not until Sir Walter Raleigh, proud of his new accomplishment, brought the pagan habit to England, did the rest of the world know the pleasure of tobacco. Yet something was lost when pipe-smoking went abroad. There it became a recreation, a social pleasure, a thing calculated to calm the nerves and soften the buffetings of fate. It lost the religious and cultural significance that had surrounded it since time unknown in the wilds of America. There it had always been a serious, reverent undertaking, performed with great and solemn ceremony; always it had been sacred smoke.

The earliest pipes were tubes made of stone or clay, perhaps smoked in the manner of the Aztecs who reclined in order to hold big stone tube pipes to the lips. Tubular pipes were often used by medicine men in exorcising illness. The hot end was placed on the afflicted part—and by the time the rite was over, the patient agreed that the medicine man's magic was indeed powerful, and there would be no need for any more of it.

The invention of the pipe bowl brought great changes in type and workmanship, and now the pipe became perhaps the most highly prized of Indian possessions. It could be used as a passport through hostile territory, and, according to Moorehead, "it ratified treaties and alliances; its acceptance sacredly sealed the terms of peace, and its refusal was regarded as a rejection of them."

During the tribal councils, in which braves and elders sat in a dignified circle in the bark house, the pipe was passed slowly from one man to the next, or was carried from one to another by a young brave. Early explorers in America soon learned that it was not only sensible to do so, but also it might save their lives if they accepted the peace pipe, took a puff of the burning, biting tobacco, and then reverently handed the pipe to the next man. To drop the pipe or dishonor it in any way meant sudden and drastic punishment.

Pipes for all these purposes were made of ground and polished stone, or of clay. Catlinite from certain quarries in Minnesota was the favorite. It was soft enough to shape well, and had a glowing, soft cherry color which to the Indian's sense of beauty must have been delightful. Tribesmen from hundreds of miles away came to chop out some of the splendid red stone from the pipestone quarries, where even enemies laid aside their weapons in strict observance of the sacred "Truce of Manitou" placed there by the Great Spirit himself. *(Aug. 1940)*

THE INDIANS IN ILLINOIS

The Illinois Country—for centuries it was the meeting place of Indians who travelled down the four great primitive waterways, the Mississippi, the Illinois, the Missouri, and the Ohio.

It was the home of early mound-building Indians who lived in the fertile river country. They were of two cultures. The Woodland people, the older of the two, were hunters who set up their villages of bark houses wherever they chose to camp for a while, and buried their dead in small round mounds.

The Mississippian people, younger of the two cultures, were southerners, it is believed, who came up the rivers and lived for a long time in Illinois. Their mounds were large and imposing, especially in the bottomlands opposite St. Louis. Their great pyramid at Cahokia was 710 feet wide, 100 feet high, and 1080 feet long.

When the French came here in the 17th century, Illinois from the Apple River to the Cache supported a large Indian population, partly dominated by many tribes of Illinois, the Cahokias, Kaskaskias, Michigameas, Moingwenas, Peorias, and Tamaroas. The largest Illini villages lay in broad meadows below Starved Rock. Northwestern Illinois was occupied by fierce Sacs and Foxes, the Chicago region by the Potawatomies, and the Kickapoos, a troublesome tribe, lived in the Sangamon country. The Shawnees held southeastern Illinois, the Piankashaws the lower Wabash.

The Illini, strong as they were, knew reverses. The Iroquois in 1680 raided and wiped out many of the villages. In 1796, when a Peoria Indian murdered Chief Pontiac, there was bloody war as the Chippewas, Ottawas, and Potawatomies descended upon the Illini. Twelve hundred, so the story goes, retreated to the top of Starved Rock, while the enemy waited below to thwart every attempt to get food and water or to escape. Now Illinois knew murders of unprotected women and children, of the Chicago massacre in 1812, of the battle of Stillman's Run in Ogle County, of the Black Hawk War, with atrocities on both sides. Finally in 1833 the remaining tribes ceded their ancestral lands to the white man, and the Indians left Illinois.

But everywhere there are reminders of their presence. Indian mounds along the rivers . . . arrowheads, spears . . . fragments of pottery where the villages were . . . an ancient tree with a branch bent down to mark an Indian route . . . roads that follow Indian trails . . . corn in fields where the Indians grew it . . . towns christened with Indian names . . . Algonquin, Itaska,

Maroa . . . they are as musical as an Indian flute, reminders of the past. For always there are the silent moccasined footsteps that still are sensed as they pass. *(June 1943)*

CAMPFIRE

Flames lick through the curls of bark, and the dry sticks burn red and blue. Thin smoke, almost invisible, spirals upward, and soft, white ashes drop silently in a growing heap. Around the campfire and its people stands the quiet, dark forest where the trees go up to the stars, but eyes are fixed on the magic of the fire. Here is a focal point of light in darkness, and the whole forest, with its wild eyes, watches the fire. A fox over on the ridge sees it. The owl, flying past, catches the glint of light in its shining eyes. Moths with softly luminous, bronzy eyes move in toward the flames. And a flying squirrel, off on a distant tree, comes in a series of flying glides, closer and closer, to watch.

This is the campfire. It is a heap of burning sticks and bark and a larger log or two. Campfires have been like this since the ancient day when a prehistoric man in Europe or Asia discovered what fire was and that he could tame it, build it, keep it, use it . . . a pile of sticks, burning. And ever since that day it has been a focal point, a point of attention, a lure, and an attraction which is not at once explainable in this day of neon, electric lights, and the cold and cheerless blue-white of fluorescent illumination.

They are harsh, and bold, and ugly when they are compared with the soft flames of a campfire. Neon is civilization; flames are timeless. They belong to all men. Flames are primitive, yet as new as each new fire. The flames require attention; must be fed with more wood; must be poked a bit to let in air so that the fire burns clearer and without smoke. The camp must be arranged so that any smoke does not pour into the eating place, nor the sleeping place. The fire must be guarded so that it does not go out, and, when the time comes to leave it, it must be completely extinguished.

Man's responsibility toward a campfire is far greater than his responsibility toward an electric light. The fire is still a wild thing. It may be tamed briefly, but it is still a wild thing, and when it gets out of bounds it devastates everything it touches.

In spite of the efficiency of cities and modern homes, the lure of the open fire remains with man. It is there, in the back of his mind. He may not know it is there, or understand why he wants to have a fireplace in his house or a barbecue pit in his backyard; but it is there, and it guides him in many ways. He builds his fireplace. He buys logs, he makes his fire on a winter evening. His house is sufficiently well heated by means of a furnace; he has no real physical need for a fire. But his inner need is still there, related to that ancient, distant need of his ancestor who knew that where the fire was, there was his home, and there danger could not approach. Fire was his protector and his counselor, his guardian and his comforter, his cook and his illumination. He was lost without fire. And so his descendant in his furnace-heated house has a fireplace, and when he goes camping he builds a fire. He rejoices in the flavor of meat cooked over open flames, of potatoes roasted in hot coals, in coffee brewed in a blackened coffee pot, in biscuits browned in a reflector oven before the fire. And when the night comes down all around him—even though his car and his city are not very far away—he feels that deep inner comfort of sitting beside his fire. The trees are tall and black above him, and the yapping of a distant fox out on the ridge is sweet music in the night. *(June 1951)*

THE SPIRIT OF THE FOG

The river world was very still. Fog moved pallidly along the shores, brushing the willows and leaving on them a condensing dampness of thin, cool silver, touching the banks with cotton-soft fingers . . . moving, voiceless, damp, chill, the fog. In the distance there was the faint sound of a receding boat engine, but the fog itself blurred the noise so that it might have been nothing more than the distant hammering of a woodpecker. Small wavelets lapped suddenly against the stony shore as the backwash from the boat came in, and then subsided, and the gray river grew smooth again in the November stillness. The rich smell of fallen willow leaves, the unique odors of riverbank mud, where raccoon and muskrat tracks lay imprinted, and the scent of water were all part of the day.

Autumn fog filled the river valley as with a thick white smoke. It was a breathing of the river itself, given off like human breath in cold weather, and it changed the whole aspect of the day. Boats, if they proceeded at all, did so at great risk, or else they traveled by means of their endlessly turning radar scanners; or they prudently tied up along the shore, seeking a good strong maple or sycamore that would not yank out by the roots at the first hard tug. A head line and a stern line made fast, the engines stilled, the boat became part of the November shore, part of the fog.

It was long past the end of summer, was really the end of autumn, was next door to winter, and the fog was like a theater curtain lowered between acts while the final changes were being made. When the curtain rose, it would be winter. The fog would vanish, the sky would clear to a cold brilliance, and the wind would be sharp, out of the north now, and day by day, through the rest of November and into December, on the shortening days and in the lengthening nights, in the lessening of the sun's warmth as it retreated into the south, winter would move upon the land. Along the river, winter would wait a little longer to take hold. The very presence of the fog indicated the effect of this great body of water in moderating the temperatures along its length. Along the Mississippi's banks, color had come later to the trees than it had on the hills inland. Even in the dimness of the fog there were pale yellow feathers on some of the willows, still a few amber leaves on the maples, though inland all the trees were bare. Even though the wind was chill, the water itself held the summer's warmth a little longer; but, when the river at last began to freeze, no clemency of temperature would stay it. Winter would have its way, and from Minnesota, mile by mile, the silent waters of the river would freeze.

But it would take a while. In November, the open pathway of water under its shroud of fog was still the guide which led the late migrants south. Out there, dim and half seen, now lost from view in the moving mists, swam a flock of scaup ducks. Trim mergansers got up and flew, streamlined, low over the water, through the drifting wraiths, and there were distant sounds of quacking and whistling where mallards fed.

And then, far off, there came the geese. They came—the compelling *ark-ark-ark* of their trumpeting passing overhead in a tempest of wings, going away, invisible in the murk, coming again, passing, still hidden in whiteness. When they had all gone at last, there came in the fog-filled dusk one laggard goose, groping as if lost, crying, circling, calling. It was the spirit of the fog, voice of the river, voice of the North, the atmosphere of November made vocal in the enfolding mists. *(Nov. 1963)*

THIS IS THE WIND

There is a wind that has the freshness of the sky and the never-ending excitement of the earth. It blows from the sea and from the mountains; it is a breathing of the plains and the whisper of the snow; it is the dancing of oatfields and the talking of the corn. It is flavored with whatever it blows across—good, bad, fragrant, malodorous—with its own meaning to whoever sniffs it. This is the wind, the American wind.

As it blows in from the ocean it brings the scent of waves that are familiar with far places. In it is the scent of tide beaches and sea-life—sponges and barnacles, starfish and clams. There are smells of the fish-wharves of Gloucester and the canneries at San Diego, of Georgia salt-marshes and tideflats of the Indian River beside a Florida orange grove; the rich scent of fried crabs at Nantasket Beach; the aroma of dead sharks on Hatteras. In that sea-wind are the commingled odors of the ocean, the sky, the land, and all the life therein and thereon. It is the storm wind that piles up mountainous waves and batters shipping. It is the hurricane that sweeps with ever increasing fury from the Caribbean and smashes Miami and Tybee City and Orient Point. It is the blizzard full of stinging snow, and the nor'easter that whips the weathered houses of Cape Cod and brings cold rain to New England.

The American wind is the rainy wind, the sunny wind, the dusty wind, the blossom wind. It is air set in motion by changes in temperature and the rotation of the earth. Here is the sundown wind that blows cold in the valleys of the Smokies and down the slopes of Lizard Head, wind that tears fog-wraiths into tatters and flings them across a morning sky, brings clouds low on the mountains, sweeps snow in July from Pike's Peak. It is the black wind that roars over the crest of the Blue Ridge and pours storm down in the Valley of Virginia . . . it is the gracious wind off Lake Michigan that cools a sweltering Chicago; it is the 230-mile an hour gale atop Mount Washington in the dead of winter. It is the dust-devil wind that dances along a road, wind that blows dry leaves in whirls and curvets in the street. It carries pollen at blossom-time and helps set the year's crop of seeds; it brings down apples and pears and nuts in autumn.

The American wind is relentless power that picks up fields and deposits them miles away; grain by grain it moves the dunes. The tornado splinters trees and farm buildings, yet leaves a wren-house unharmed; the glittering wind of the plains blows grasshoppers from their moorings, bends the wheat, and ruffles the ears of the jackrabbits loping to cover.

There is the desert wind, too, that blows broken sage and sand horizontally across the desert, shears off poles and posts, or, like a furnace blast, roars across the alkali flats of Nevada. It is the chinook of the Northwest and the williwaw of the Aleutians; it is kind to aircraft and sailing craft or mercilessly destroys them. It is the merry, obliging breeze that twirls windmills to water the Great Plains, gives nobility to every flag in the land, dries the Monday wash, flies springtime kites, and whisks smoke away from chimneys as fast as it emerges.

There is the pleasant evening breeze that comes at last after a hot summer day, wind that starts the conversation of the trees. There is the gentle talk of willows, the chatter of aspens, the murmuring of the maples, the churning of the oaks, the slashing round about and back again of the anxious *Ailanthus,* the sibilance of pines and the breathing of the spruces. This is the American wind that has its freedom from coast to coast and from mountain top to desert. In it is the fragrance of freedom, the greatness of American faith. Listen: that wind blows strong and clear. (*June 1944*)

PICNIC ON THE GRASS

Whether a picnic means sandwiches and lemonade or fried chicken and potato salad, or whether it means kabobs on a stick or steak broiler over hot coals, it nevertheless is an ancient custom which mankind has made part of his life. When summer comes, picnics come: even in ancient Greece it was so, when it was customary to put fruit and roast chicken and bread in a willow basket and go out to the nearest grove to dine. It was so in Rome, where even emperors, to satisfy their whims, ordered up elaborate banquets which were carried out to the mountainside or into the palace park, to be eaten on the grass. To carry food into the open countryside—to the shady spot beside the lake, to the pine woods, to the grassy space beside the temple—was one of the manifestations of summertime the world over. Perhaps even the miracle of the loaves and fishes, which fed a multitude assembed out of doors, could have been called a picnic.

They did not always call it a picnic. The word itself comes from the French—pique-nique—which originally meant an indoor social gathering to which everyone brought food to be served from one table—something like a pot-luck supper in an Illinois country church. Then picnics went out of doors, where they had been going on for years under different names, and there they have stayed. Madame DuBarry and her successor, Marie Antoinette, playing at being milkmaids, had their picnics under the trees at Petit Trianon, and the children of Victoria, with their devoted mama, often picnicked at Balmoral Castle.

In America, picnics are like nothing else anywhere in the world. Each one differs from the next in what is eaten and how it is prepared, just as every cook is different in her use of the same ingredients. Picnics always have been of two persuasions—the elaborate and the simple. In the past century, especially, picnics were feasts, or else they were simple bread and cheese and an apple, which the followers of Thoreau believed was enough to sustain a jaunt in the woods.

But most picnics to most people meant preparing for the feast a day ahead—layer cakes and cherry pies to make, a ham to be boiled or baked, chickens to dress and cool, to be fried next morning while the horses were being groomed and the carriage packed. The trip to the picnic spot was neither far nor long, though it might take several hours on a summer's day when the horses clip-clopped along without hurrying, so that the warm soft dust picked up by each hoof went down again in a gentle puff. Meadowlarks sang their summer songs; the bobwhites took their time crossing the road; spiders left curious tracks in the dust. The sky was clear and the sun was hot—you had to have a day like that for a proper picnic.

And to be correct, the picnic most often was laid on a table that was carefully spread with newspapers, and then the second-best damask cloth, the ten-footer, put over that, and the food set upon it in a tremendous parade. There were flies—picnics always had flies—unless there was enough wind to keep them off, and then you had trouble keeping the tablecloth and napkins down. There were mosquitoes and chiggers, and ants usually found the cake before dinner was over, and usually the children ate too much and one or two had a stomach ache. A picnic like this was infinitely more work than dinner at home, but it was as much a requisite of summertime as fly-screens at the windows or leaf-lettuce in the garden.

Today's picnics still belong to two schools of thought—the more elaborate, prepared-ahead-of-time kind, and the made-on-the-spot kind that may include a broiled steak, freshly made coffee, and a salad full of the sparkle of crisp vegetables. But though a picnic may be for two or for two hundred, it is still as much a part of today's summertime as it was in the leisurely eighties, as it was in the shadow of Mount Hymetus, or as it was in France, when mama and papa and the children took a daintily prepared pique-nique to eat beneath Marie Antoinette's trees in the gardens at Versailles. (*Aug. 1947*)

THE LONE TRAIL AND THE HIGH HILL

With summer comes the call to far places. Now comes the urge to visit mountains and shores—it is the time to travel the lone trail and the high hill. It is vacation time and, in the space of time allotted to each vacationer, there is encompassed the completion of a year's longings and plannings.

A vacation trip means first of all a journey into a different landscape, a landscape in which the living things and the geological background create those differences. The wild things are an inescapable and permanent part of any landscape, of any vacation. Green trees and roadside flowers cannot be avoided; neither can the arrogant chipmunks and the songs of larks and robins. They are not only part of the landscape—they are the landscape, and they are entwined in every vacation.

He who has watched the little cony gathering its hay piles among the rocks of the high country will always know the mountains better for that experience. The bleary-eyed marmot whistling on the top of the world, the bear that comes at dusk to eat doughnuts on a stump, the chipmunks racing around the doorstep or confidently taking food from one's fingers, the sudden deer beside the road, the porcupine climbing an aspen tree—they belong to vacation country. The Steller's jays and the Clark's nutcrackers which come boldly to eat crumbs at picnic spots in the Rockies, the hermit thrushes that chime among cool northern firs, the cry of a loon and the white wings of gulls drifting over blue water, the magnificent flight of pelicans, the yapping of skimmers over the Gulf —these, too, are part of it. Flowers, ferns, mosses, and trees all play a most important part in changing the landscape into something exciting and new. Tall spruces that climb high peaks, cypresses wading in southern swamps, purple jacaranda trees in California, the tiny white bells of the wintergreen, the flavor of blueberries with dew on them, the perfume of wild red rasberries, the scent of desert sage, the whip-lash spikes of ocotillo in moonlight, the pattern of seaweed washed on to a shore—to know them is to gain a deeper insight into any region. It is to know our country better and more intimately; it is to be aware of surroundings which may have had neither identity nor meaning before; it is to live more richly.

All this may be part of the annual vacation. It begins the moment the door is locked and the car is on its way to the tune of robins caroling in the summer dawn. The new landscape begins with the opening of blue chicory flowers along the road and continues ever more deeply to the lone trail and the high hill where riches wait for anyone to find. *(July 1952)*

CLIMB A WESTERN MOUNTAIN

Above the desert of western Colorado stands the great level bulk of Grand Mesa, a lava-topped, ancient peneplain left over from geologic upheavals in the Rockies. The lava topping the great mesa was too hard to be easily eroded, and so there it stands today, blue and distant across the irrigated orchards along the Colorado River. The mesa seems remote and a trifle mysterious, for this is the place the Indians called the Home of the Bahaa-Nieche, Dwelling Place of Departed Spirits. Yet as one makes the ascent of Grand Mesa, he sees the little intimate things along the way, the plants, the birds, the mammals, the reptiles, the earth and rocks themselves, all of which give meaning to the mountain and tell the story of how life changes as altitude rises.

The base of Grand Mesa rises steeply from the desert. Here, away from the irrigated lands, the desert is harsh and hot, with ancient cinder cones of the forgotten volcano, sage brush so dry in midsummer that it crumbles fragrantly at a touch. Yet in this stern and uncompromising environment there is life. The little desert horned lark, pale as the desert itself, runs across the ash and leaves long-clawed footprints to show where a bit of life raced past. On a rock a lizard, its throat palpitating in the growing heat of the morning, suns itself.

For the sun is high and the desert shortly will grow as hot as only cinder cones and volcanic ash in summer can become. But the mesa trail leads upward—upward to snowbanks which still remain on the sheltered northern slope.

To climb a mountain is to see a steady change in vegetation and in the wild things which live in that vegetation. For every one thousand feet in altitude, one reaches life zones which are found a thousand miles farther north. To climb from the desert zone and ascend to the summit of Grand Mesa at 10,000 feet is to travel from the desert to Canada.

To drive up—or better still, walk up—the tortuous little back road to the top of Grand Mesa and descend by way of the smoother, but less interesting, road leading to Grand Junction, is to see the life zones drop below, one after the other. On the ascent the sage grows greener and fresher and taller. Sage hens live here, and among the pinyon pines the magpies and Steller's jays squawk and argue in the morning sunlight. A western meadowlark carols on a post, and then quite suddenly the sage and pinyons are left behind and the road swings in among tall cool aspen trees. Here the blue columbines bloom in July and the harebells in August, and the mountain bluebird, blue all over —azure blue, not the deeper color of Illinois bluebirds—warbles among the pallid trunks. Above the aspens come the spruces, and with them the songs of white-throated sparrows, birds of Canada. Higher, and there are firs, where kinglets flit. Then ahead are the old, dirty snowbanks, and a snowshoe hare flops its great furry feet over the drift and vanishes among the firs.

There is the level summit at last, forested, cool, and sparkling, with open meadows and bright lakes. The western tanager, bright as a Kachina dancer, sings in the pines, and a troop of pygmy nuthatches explores the trunks of the spruces. The level top of the great mesa leads to the jumping off place at Land's End, below which lies the hot, remote, unreal desert a mile downstairs. *(Aug. 1952)*

WAR AND THE MUSEUM

Now when America is confronted with the forces of militarism which are striking at modern civilization, our first thought is to support our armed forces; our second thought must be to preserve our priceless culture. We must keep our artists and musicians, our writers and scientists, our inventors and bright-eyed youth, who have always been free to pursue their talents and enrich the world with their productions. Universities must be maintained; art galleries must be kept open; schools must function normally; museums must not be closed. If our culture is to survive, education must go on. And museums are essential in educating, in preserving, in showing the best in earlier cultures as well as in perpetuating our own.

News comes that great museums in England have been struck by bombs which destroyed whole wings, or let in water and wreckage to damage works of art and fragile collections—yet up to the time of bombing, these museums had been open to the public, and, in most instances, were cleaned up and reopened immediately afterward. People, in numbers often greater than in peace times, still pour in to visit them.

And the reason is this: Here in the museum is something of that good stability and sturdiness of life before there was war. Here are the long-lasting, unchanging things of the world. Here is no distortion of facts, no propaganda. Always there is the search for honesty and truth in explanation and in presentation of material, so that people walking into a museum feel the power of truth coming to meet them. In a troubled and oftentimes dishonest world, where lies and distortions are all about, where the solid foundations of human existence are besieged, the museum extends a calm and soothing hand and shows us that our culture lives on.

In a time of war, the museum must make even greater efforts to serve the people when they need it most. It must show the calm side of things as they have always been, as well as the trend of current history, and must always maintain the truth and sincerity which has long been the credo of museums.

Visitors in the Illinois State Museum step for a minute or two into some of the events of history that built mankind up to this day. In the dioramas one sees how man raised himself to his present level, from the ape man to Edison, and how, every step of the way, culture had to fight the barbaric forces of destruction. And from these very facts there comes once more a sense of certainty and calmness. Man has come a long way, has struggled to reach his present high state of culture, and this he cannot lose in a hurry. In the long, upward fight to Parnassus, he has had to combat wild animals and the Ice Age itself, has risen through the onslaughts of wild men and those first awful, uphill centuries when here and there a man's mind struggled independently for expression in ways other than those of beasts. Somehow, culture survived the hordes of the Huns and the Vandals, of the Visigoths and the legions of Xerxes and Caesar; though its libraries at Alexandria were burned, and Athens fell, books were not lost forever, nor was art permanently destroyed. Time after time, people have cried out in despair that the world was lost, that the age of goodness was gone forever. Yet culture somehow rises even higher, comes through and will not be downed.

And that is why the museum stays open. That is why the halls are filled with people who come in for a quiet hour, to look back at the pleasant days of peace and come forth renewed for the emergencies of the present. The benefit of a museum in a community cannot now be underestimated. For it is not just a series of exhibits to amuse. It is the tangible evidence that education and culture are not to be lost even if some men will it to be so, unless we shut out of our lives all the good, true, and worthwhile things that separate the human mind from the levels of brutism. (*Jan. 1942*)

KWAN-YIN, THE CHINESE GODDESS

She is a lovely, gentle figure, poised with that immobile grace of the Oriental woman. She is carved from rose quartz—Kwan-Yin, the Merciful.

Long ago Kwan-Yin sprang into being in an ancient Buddhist religion in India, but originally was represented as a man who symbolized mercy and justice. Kwan-Yin was not figured as a woman until about the 12th century A.D. when Buddhism came by devious routes to China—over the terrible Gobi Desert, through the dangerous passes in the Pamirs, or in frail junks over the menace of the China Sea. When Kwan-Yin became a woman, she became the most beloved figure in the new religion dedicated to soul-peace.

Perhaps it was the longing of the human heart for something motherly and kind in all that devine category of gods which created her. She was a gentle, lovely figure among Chinese demon-gods which inspired fear, never affection, and which illustrated with such terrible vigor the Ten Courts of Purgatory. Among these grimacing beings in the temples stood a calm woman, the mother goddess, Kwan-Yin, Hearer of the Cries of Anguish. To her came more prayers than to any of the others except to the Buddha himself. She watched over those in danger, listened to prayers of all who suffered or were frightened. She gave children to the childless, comfort to those who needed comfort. It was no wonder that Kwan-Yin has been depicted in more ways, in more mediums, and in more temples, shrines, chapels, and homes in the Orient than any of the more terrible gods and goddesses.

There are many stories about this goddess. The Chinese say she once lived in China, where she was known as Miao-Chen. According to the story, her father wanted her to marry, but she refused and escaped to the White Sparrow convent, where the nuns hid her. The king in anger sent troops to burn the convent, but when Miao-Chen prayed, a rain storm came to extinguish the flames.

The girl, however, was captured, tortured, and her body carried down to the underworld by a local demon in the form of a tiger. The underworld, as soon as she came, immediately blossomed with lilies and lotuses and became a paradise, which, of course, ruined Hell for its original purpose in the judicial system of the earth. Yen-Lo, the King of the Underworld, anxiously begged Miao-Chen to depart.

And so she was sent by Buddha to the island of P'uto, where today pilgrims travel by junks to worship her as Kwan-Yin, Madonna of China.

In the Oriental Room of the Museum you may see an exquisitely carved rose-crystal figure of the goddess, part of the Thomas C. Condell Chinese collection. There is the utmost grace in the lines of her garments, in the way in which she holds her hands, her head, her body. And in her sweet face is that inscrutable Oriental calmness, an assurance of invincibility, the certainty of goodness, kindness, and the salvation of mankind. (*Oct. 1940*)

THE RED EGGS OF SPRINGTIME

Long ago in the land of Galilee, as well as throughout all the hills and plains of Palestine, the early Christians held a yearly festival to mark the return of the growing season. When spring came with its new lambs and its blossoming almond trees, the Easter festival was celebrated by the symbol of resurrection and of life—by eggs. They were dyed red to represent the blood of Christ and to stand not only for this but for the tomb from which sprang life.

But it was even longer ago than this that there were Easter eggs in the springtime of the year. Three thousand years ago in Persia and certain other Oriental countries, spring was a time for feasting because winter was gone. It was a time to walk in flower-fragrant gardens, a time to dye hens' eggs with the colors of springtime and give them as gifts to one's dearest friends. So it may have been that the early Christians borrowed not only this custom from pagan peoples, but adopted the name of Easter itself from that of the goddess Eostre, who reigned in the springtime and spread new life upon the earth.

Ever since those far-off times, the custom of coloring eggs at Easter has had a varied and fascinating history. There were the scarlet eggs of Mesopotamia where the children each Easter held exciting egg-cracking contests. There were the wooden eggs of Italy, and the platters of boiled eggs which were carried to the church to be blessed on Easter morning, and eaten as the first meat after Lent. There were the old English egg-rolling customs which traveled over the ocean to find expression in the egg-rolling contests on the White House lawn.

And there were the sugar eggs of Germany which had wonderful pictures inside them; the thin glass and china eggs of Czechoslovakia; the chocolate eggs, the candy eggs, the cardboard eggs filled with candy, which are products of American confectioners; and the amazing and elaborate eggs which the Russian imperial family collected each year. These were magnificent creations of expert jewelers—eggs of gold and enamel, decorated with flowers and scrollwork and jewels, eggs that opened to reveal miniature scenes or pictures inside them.

And there were those eggs that "the rabbit brought." It is said that during a famine in Holland, a poor woman wanted to give her under-nourished children a surprise at the Easter season, so she dyed some eggs and made a nest for them in the garden. And the coincidence that made all March and April rabbits immortal took place on that Easter morning. A big brown rabbit bounded away from the nest just as the excited children discovered it. And as simply as that, a new Easter custom began.

No matter what their background, Easter eggs are part of springtime. Perhaps they are the eggs which grandmother decorated by wrapping them in calico and boiling them until the cloth pattern came off on the eggs; or perhaps she boiled them in strong coffee and polished them with lard to make them a lovely glossly brown. Perhaps they are eggs dyed by means of today's inexpensive vegetable dyes, or decorated with designs drawn in wax before the eggs are dipped. Or perhaps the tradition is that all Easter eggs, to be proper, must be red. For with every scarlet Easter egg one is carried swiftly back—back—back—to the villages of Galilee and the gardens of Persia, to the red eggs that stood for the rebirth of springtime and for the risen Christ. (Mar. 1948)

PINKLETINKS AND PUCKERBRUSH

Without the solid assurance of Latin names in identifying plants and animals of the world, we might become bogged down among the fascinating but confusing colloquial names by which the majority of us know our local wildlings. Usually the plants or animals which are most familiar over a wide range, known from the standpoint of the medicinal plant, the harmful plant, the common bird or animal, are the ones most often burdened by a multiplicity of names. This could have long since resulted in a complete breakdown in systematic knowledge of wildlife, without the steadying hand of the scientific cataloguer with his Latin names. Except when the scientists themselves disagree and then proceed to change even the old settled Latin titles, we can be fairly certain of what we know.

Hence, what might be familiarly and lovingly known as pinkletinks and puckerbrush in one place might be called peepers and candleberries somewhere else, until they are soberly identified as Hyla crucifer, the spring peeper, and Myrica pensylvanica, the bayberry, though admittedly pinkletinks and puckerbrush are a lot more fun. Among plants in particular a great many species are sometimes called by the same name in various parts of the country. Hence, an adder's tongue may be a fern or a dogtooth violet, though the latter is not a true violet but a lily. But calling the fern Ophioglossum and the violet-which-is-a-lily Erythronium clears the matter quickly.

Many plants were given their colloquial names through some real or fancied medicinal quality, such as boneset, convulsion root, or agueweed, or those with a fancied ability to scare off certain animals— dogbane, wolfbane, rattlesnake weed—or to cure their bite. Some were named from the difficulties they inflicted upon travelers or settlers. Knowing the nature of Smilax vines with their dreadful, wiry tangles and vicious thorns, we can easily understand why some of them were named tramp's trouble, blaspheme vine or hellfetter. We can see why the pitcher plant was called sidesaddle flower, huntershorn or trumpets. It is easy to see why the sticky sundew is sometimes called daily-dew; the early closing star-of-Bethlehem known as nap-at-noon; the plumy gray-white seeds of pasque flower called prairie smoke, or why that plant obtained its name of pasque flower—Pasque, for Easter, when the plant often blooms. It is easy to see why Indian pipe should be called corpse plant or wax plant, not so easy to know why Canada anemones should sometimes be called meetinghouses, but there is no doubt about why Hercules' club got its name or its alternate title of devil's walking stick; but who knows why it is also sometimes called life-of-man?

With some exceptions, such as the robin, which is a robin everywhere in America, though it is really a thrush, we find the least known birds with the fewest names, and the best known often over-burdened with colloquialisms which stretch out longer than the birds themselves. The little ruddy duck, for instance, has at least sixty-two aliases, varying from paddy whack, shot pouch, dinky and booby to butter-ball, to name a few. The old squaw duck is known variously as swallow-tailed duck, south-southerly, old wife, old Injin, old granny, John Connolly, Uncle Huldy, calloo, cockawee and hound, for no known reasons, while the pintail duck is burdened with sprig-tail, split-tail, spike-tail, picket-tail, sea pheasant, lady bird, harlan and smee. The puffin may be a sea parrot, pope, bottle-nose, Tammy Norie or tinker; a great black-backed gull a coffin-carrier; and the pied-billed grebe a hell-diver, devil-diver, water witch, dabchick, dipper, diedapper, or dive dapper, none of which are especially flattering to any bird. The big noisy pileated woodpecker is called logcock, cock of the woods, wood hen, Lord God Woodpecker and Wood Kate, while the flicker has innumerable names, among which are yawker, heigh-ho, yellow-hammer and yarrup, a list which could go on with unbelievable appellations to the end of the page.

But the cool, calm Latin names remain steadfast, a clearing in the jungle of confusion. The snow goose may have half a dozen common names from Hudson Bay to Louisiana, but its Latin name of *Chen hyperboreus,* telling more than any colloquialism, means Goose From Beyond the North Wind. Linnaeus and his later assistants, who first stabilized nomenclature to three names at the most and more frequently two, made it possible for naturalists and scientists around the world to understand each other. There might be a hundred or more different names for the same thing, but the Latin is the same the world over. Today in a book of Swedish wild flowers or Polynesian birds written in French, the only words which are understandable to American, French, German, Swedish or Japanese readers alike are the Latin names. To one who knows only his own language, these reassuring names stand out as examples of the universality of knowledge and the oneness of man's understanding of his natural world. *(June 1959)*

LIGHT IN THE FOREST

On a sunny June day, when the summer fields are sweet with the perfume of clover and the warm scent of growing corn and the dark green of well-developed plants everywhere absorbs the sun's heat and energy during the long days of June, the light in the forest is a strangly different and constantly changing thing. Light is vital. Sunlight continually renews energy to supply the forest—energy which, used each year by the animals and plants living in an acre of hardwood forest, has been estimated to equal the electricity used by an average home as power for nearly fifty years. The bombarding by radioactive material from the sun is utilized by every part of the forest, each in its own way.

Only the tops of the trees, however, receive the full impact of sunlight and energy. The leaf-canopy, spreading broadly in a green roof, reflects up to forty percent of the light, but most of the rest is absorbed and used in the manufacture of sugars and starches in the leaves while the remainder filters down to the lower levels of the woods. Here are plants with thin leaves—broad, thin leaves which require less light for maintenance of the plant than the thicker, darker green leaves of the tree canopy.

Only about six percent of the sunlight on a sunny day reaches the lower parts of the woods, and even less reaches the forest floor itself. This also produces great variation in temperature from top level to ground, often a difference of many degrees. In the dark, leafy, loose-textured forest floor live the forest's greatest populations, most of them microscopic—bacteria and protozoans whose billions in a square foot may be greater than the entire human population on the earth. In the glare of light and heat in the leaf-canopy, most of these would perish.

Tremendous changes in the quality of light take place in the forest. On a sunny day, it is direct and strong, but much of it is bounced off into the atmosphere as reflection from the upper leaves. On a cloudy day, however, there is a gentle diffusion of light which makes the forest floor more fully illuminated than on a sunny day. This is called *skylight,* a suffusion of light in dust particles, molecules of gases, and droplets of water in the air. Skylight, therefore, comes from all directions, and on a cloudy day the floor of the forest may receive up to twenty per cent of the light.

The results of changing intensity of light in the forest are plainly seen when mid-May comes—when spring merges with high summer. April and early May knew woods filled with spring flowers which were exposed to full, brilliant sunlight because there were no leaves on the trees. As soon as these began to grow, flowers waned. The early blossoms were quickly seeding, and their leaves were making food. As they yellowed in the lessening power of light in the woods, the food was sent to the roots for storage—sun-energy put away until next spring's growth. By June most of the spring flowers are not even visible. In their place are a few species which can live in decreased light.

In that dark, often windless, forest floor, the quiet life of millions of small creatures and the plants of lichen, moss, and fern continues busily. The scavengers devour animal and plant remains, reduce them to their mineral and chemical parts, and leave them in the loose leaf mold. Dissolved in rain-water, this food is carried by the tree to the leaf-canopy, which is using the summer sunlight to make other food. The energy stored from this endless font of supply becomes the subsequent energy for future dwellers in the woods. The light in the forest is its assurance of continuity and life. (*June 1962*)

THE WORLD OF DARKNESS

As the sun slides behind the farthest rim of trees beyond the cornfield and is gone until morning, the creatures of daylight retire. For an hour or two they have been preparing for darkness. Birds feed for the last time that day, the hawk cruises low for a final living morsel snatched from the meadow, chimney swifts swoop and twitter, the butterfly probes an ironweed flower for nectar.

Then as twilight grows and light diminishes, changes come to the activities of the wild. The locust leaflets fold down and hang closed for the night. Clover leaves in the lawn have done the same. The waterlily on the pond shuts its flower, the petals of the wild rose drop off. But the bud of the evening primrose has been growing larger all day. If you watch now at twilight, you may see the bud quiver. Then it is still. You wonder if it really did move after all; then it quivers again. A thin sheath splits and is pushed off. The tight furling of pale yellow petals opens a trifle at the tip, and suddenly the four-parted blossom falls open. A four-pronged pistil thrusts forth and there are eight polleny stamens. A gush of perfume floods out.

Almost at once there is a soft whirring of delicate wings as the hawk moth, creature of the dusk, comes with a hummingbird-like movement, unrolls a long tongue and thrusts it far down into the primrose's trumpet. This brings the moth's forehead against the stamens and some pollen adheres when the moth whirs away to another primrose flower. Brushing past its pistil, the moth leaves pollen there. And in the fragrant summer twilight, the flower's mission is accomplished. By dawn it will furl again and hang down, finished, while another bud or two will grow during the day and open in the dusk.

With the opening of the primroses there is an ending of daytime bird calls. The final chiming of the wood thrush, the calling of the cardinal, the last utterance of a wood pewee somewhere high in the trees, and it is night. Meanwhile ever since sunset the nighthawk has been swooping and uttering explosive squawks over meadow and marsh, over woods and the artificial canyons of town, and will continue all night long. The whip-poor-will calls endlessly; the yellow-breasted chat wakens and utters spasmodic calls and somewhat sleepy clacks.

The darkness is full of sounds, the small sounds that may be lost in the bustle of daylight, while a sudden silence may reveal more than the sounds themselves. As a wind moves through the leaves, the voices of their leaves tell what they are; for each tree has a different expression in the wind, from the rattle of the cottonwood and the tinkling of the aspen to the sibilance of pines and the dry rustle of the sycamore.

Deer walk about and feed in the twilight. During the full moon they may feed at intervals all night, but in the dark of the moon they eat at dusk, rest most of the night and feed just before dawn, and are frequently seen about in daylight. The deer walk quietly, or suddenly break a dry branch with unconcerned noise. There may be the soft thuds of a rabbit on bare ground, the rattle of a pebble where the fox leaped across a draw, the strange vibration of sound waves which the bat's wings make, the snarl of a raccoon challenging another. There may be the splash of a fish, the choking sounds of a bullfrog, the stony clicking of cricket frogs, the August concerto of insects soothed by the melodic songs of snowy tree crickets somewhere in the cool leaves of the trees. The summer night is full of sounds.

The night may seem to be an abyss of impenetrable blackness when viewed from a lighted place, but once outside in the dark, it slowly grows lighter with a strange, pervading, mysterious glow which comes from starshine —light scattered from the stars by gas molecules in the air. In little more than half an hour, the human eye can adapt to darkness and soon see well enough to detect trail and tree, meadow and bush. Then the human eye can see almost as well as the owl or the cat or the lynx, apparently sees better than either the rabbit or the cruising nighthawk.

The mysteries of night become friendly things, their identities discovered or forever mysteries. Night is a special world of blossoming, of hunting, of singing, of living, of dying, a world whose door closes gently with the coming of the sun and the awakening creatures of the day. (*Aug. 1959*)

THE SUCCESSFUL TREE

To each creature which uses it, a tree has a different evaluation. To the Polyphemus caterpillar, the birch must be a success because it provides in ample quantity the leaf-food required by the caterpillar to complete the metamorphosis into a moth, supplies the wherewithal for a cocoon's support, and a place to cling when the moth struggles forth. The wood pewee finds the tree's best use in providing a horizontal branch on which a neatly constructed, lichen-ornamented nest may be built with the assurance of ample support. The vireo looks for the forking twigs which are just right to hold a basket-nest swung beneath them.

To the woodpecker, a tree is a place to find food, a medium into which it may sink its powerful beak with rapid-fire hammer blows that send chips flying and the bird head-and-shoulders into the cavity. To the carpenter ants mining tunnels inside, the tree up to that moment has been a success as a place of habitation; that success is lost as the woodpecker tears open the massive wood fiber structure which was the trunk.

To the chickadee hunting a nest hole, the tree is now desirable because the woodpecker has left an unoccupied hole which is just right for chickadees. Into the pileated woodpecker's much larger excavation the wood duck may thrust her head and then slip inside to make a nest; or an owl may use a hole; or a raccoon may bed down in some rotted hollow which began years before as a woodpecker digging. For the uses of each creature, the tree is a success—to molds, mosses, fungi, ferns, birds, insects, mammals—a wood structure providing what they themselves require for life, or rest, or home, or reproduction.

In just such a manner does man evaluate a tree. To him it spells a myriad of uses for his own benefit. Trees from which he can find no benefit he labels useless. From others he obtains lumber or maple syrup or fibers or paper or shade or fruit or many other products into which human ingenuity has transformed the living trunk and branches.

But the tree in itself, unaided by other creatures or things, in its own perfection of growth—in simply being a tree—is a success. It has sprung from one small seed, in whose carefully arranged cells the processes of growth and the pattern of leaves, flowers, fruit, wood cells, twigs and buds were all preplanned and ready to proceed as soon as the first root went into the ground and the first leaves headed toward light—success in itself, this intuitive direction-finding. This is the tree's perfection. To expand its wood year by year; to draw up water and minerals from the soil by means of roots and root hairs, and conduct fluids up the pipe-line system of xylem tubes to the twigs and into the leaves which are manufacturing plant food by means of chlorophyll, sunlight and carbon dioxide; to transpire water into the air; to change starches into soluble sugars so that they may be transported down the food pipe-line, the phloem tubes, to be stored or used by the tree . . . this is magnificent fulfillment.

Thoreau felt this perfection of the tree, when he said of pines:

"Strange that so few ever come into the woods to see how the pine lives and grows and spires, lifting its evergreen arms to the light—to see its perfect success; but most are content to behold it in the shape of many broad boards brought to market, and deem *that* its true success. But the pine is no more lumber than man is, and to be made into boards and houses is no more its true and highest use than the truest use of man is to be cut down and made into manure. There is a higher law affecting our relation to pines as well as to men. A pine cut down, a dead pine, is no more a pine than a dead human carcass is a man. Can he who has discovered only some of the values of whale-bone and whale oil be said to have discovered the true use of the whale? Can he who slays the elephant for his ivory be said to have 'seen the elephant'? These are petty and accidental uses; just as if a stronger race were to kill us in order to make buttons and flageolets of our bones; for everything may serve a lower as well as a higher use. Every creature is better alive than dead, man and moose and pine trees, and he who understands it aright will rather preserve its life than destroy it." (*Aug. 1960*)

THE GREAT HUMBLER

"Hunger," said Homer, "is the great humbler of man." In his day, as it is now and always will be, hunger robs man of dignity, honor, morality, stamina, and civilization; it is a desperate thing, terrible in its power, at its worse reducing man to the level of beasts, at its best urging him to desperate action.

Probably there never has been a time in the troubled history of the world when there were not periods of great and gnawing hunger, with always the problem of satisfying that daily recurring urge for food. In the dim past when men hunted with clubs and pitfalls, hunger was a thing which came often and was not easily satisfied. Almost anything would do for food—tender-barked twigs, calamus roots, young birds in a nest, a red-eyed rat cornered in the cave, a long-dead mammoth from whose jutting ribs the squawking vultures had to be chased away again and again—anything would do. But always there was hunger, waiting like the vulture to find its prey.

One filled himself, yes, but in another day there was hunger again, insistent and gnawing, urging, irritating. In every living creature the demanding life processes needed food to exist. It was this demand which, perhaps more than anything else affecting ancient man's life, urged him to do something about making changes in his unsatisfactory food habits. One couldn't always depend upon a deer or wild cow coming along when the family was hungry; one could not always find wild grains or acorns handy; sometimes the fish wouldn't come to the spear, nor the bird to the snare. If a man was to live, he needed food. If he wasn't to be always chasing about the country in search of it, he would have to keep a reserve. So it came about that wild sheep, cattle, pigs, goats, and fowl were tethered, and little patches of grain were planted and harvested. Tending the food supply kept the families and tribes in one place; here was the nucleus of future cities. Yet hunger remained.

The years of change and growth came and went as slowly as time itself seemed to move in those deliberate days. Yet man seemed never able to prevent famines. Crops failed. The animals died of plagues. Rats and mice got into the grain and destroyed the seed for next year. There were wars that took men away from the fields and flocks. Still man battled hunger. His children wailed from blue lips and his women were gaunt. He had learned how to terrace slopes to conserve water; to irrigate; to battle predators and vermin; to lay away for the seven lean years that were almost certain to follow the seven fat ones. But when the battle once again was lost, when defeat came grinning at him through a death's skull of hunger, then he packed his belongings and his family and migrated. Some went peaceably, only seeking a place where there was more food. Others were desperate and ugly. Hunger roused hate and violence against those who were more fortunate. Famine sent the Barbarians down upon Rome when the grain crop failed; famine destroyed the defeated French army on the retreat from Moscow; famine sent the people of France in mad fury to overthrow the monarchy. There were bread riots and massacres; there was actual cannibalism in Europe during the centuries of famine in the Middle Ages.

Yet always the urge went on as men tried to combat this enemy who always—and still does—lay in wait for him. New crops were discovered, improvements made upon the old, new fertilizers and insecticides and fungicides discovered, the ills of animals studied, irrigation, crop rotation, milling, harvesting, sanitation, and many other angles learned. And if there had been no wars, no incombatable drouths, no floods, no hurricanes, no locust plagues—perhaps by this time men would have succeeded in saving themselves from hunger.

Most deadly of the hunger-inducers, perhaps, is war. It causes critical food shortages, dreadful famines. For many of the men who once produced food lie buried; the fields are ruined by battle, the cattle gone, the farms burned. Nature, once battered down, cannot rise again to full production at once, and so men starve.

It happens over and over again, yet in the individual who is desperately undernourished and perpetually hungry, whose rightful dignity is degraded to foraging as a vulture to keep his bony children alive, it does not matter that it is an old story. It only matters that he, like man in all his centuries of progress, has not found the way to guard himself from that most ancient and most persistent of killers—the slow death—hunger. (*Nov. 1947*)

COLORS FROM TREES

Out of the insatiable curiosity of mankind there have emerged the innumerable discoveries of secrets locked within the treasury of the wild. The wonder of it is how early man could have made his discoveries for uses of plants without any precedent or education to lead him to unlocking the secrets. Knowledge is a cumulative asset which grows in all directions from the initial opening of the door; the key which opens that door is perhaps the most important. Therefore, we must wonder about the person and the time, as well as his motivation and need, which brought about the discovery that colors contained in certain plants could be extracted and used. He needed, somehow, to be led into experimenting with mixtures and ingredients in order to discover the fixing agents or mordants which make a dye permanent or which might change one color into another. Ancient civilizations, which were dominated by the colors of nature, developed into a large commerce the search for dyes to change the dull grays, off-whites, and pale browns of natural wool, linen, and leather and to bring beauty to the raiment of mankind.

To pioneers in America there was some of this same urgency and need. Dyes from Europe either were expensive or they were not to be had, yet still the need for color was there. Therefore, as it was to fill many other needs, the people turned to the American herbs and trees which, like the European species, must hold dye secrets within leaves or bark or fruit.

Although in Europe the business of dye plants was a source of widespread trade, in pioneer America it played a more intimate role; for here the native dyes were not so much items for trading as for individual use in bringing the pleasure of color to homespun fabrics.

In pioneer America, the over-abundance of trees was put to many uses. Trees might provide items of food and fuel, material for building houses, furniture, and vehicles, might offer sugar and syrup and honey. These were fairly obvious uses, but hidden in certain trees lay secrets of dyes which had to be discovered one at a time. The sumac, *Rhus glabra,* was one of the most useful of the dye trees. It produced colors from almost every part of itself. The young shoots, bark, roots, leaves, and the fuzzy red fruits all had their uses. It was akin to the European sumac which in early colonial days was brought to America for use in dyeing before it was known that America possessed its own species.

Sumac was noted for making a fine yellow-tan color. The fruits were crushed, soaked, boiled for half an hour, then strained. Into this bath the wool or cotton, previously soaked in alum water, was placed and simmered, then rinsed and dried. The same liquid, however, might produce a good gray if no alum was used and if ferrous sulphate (copperas) was added to the dye bath. Tannin in the leaves and shoots of sumac, when they were chopped and boiled, produced an attractive tan or a rich brown, and required no additional ingredients.

An extract from the orange bark of osage orange or hedge apple gave an excellent gold color or a yellow-brown. The latter produced the color known as khaki and was used to dye army uniforms during World War I.

Some uniforms in other wars owed their hues to dyes obtained from trees. Colonial troops, often lacking any true army issue clothing, wore homespun pantaloons and shirts which had been dyed with butternut hulls to make a tan whose protective hue concealed its wearer in woods and fields, while the gaudily costumed British soldiers in all their glory were easy targets. Confederate boys in the latter days of the Civil War wore garments which their mothers had dyed gray from butternut extract, the gray achieved instead of brown by the addition of alum, tannic acid, and copperas to the dye bath.

Black walnut hulls, one of the oldest and best known of the pioneer dyes, were gathered when green and removed from the nuts by pounding. Anyone who has removed the hulls from walnuts remembers that indelible brown stain which clings to the fingers. The hulls were treated as butternut hulls to produce a rich black or a warm brown.

Black oak bark gave buff, gold, or orange, depending upon the treatment used. The bark of alder made a brownish-yellow while the leaves produced greenish-yellow. Apple bark gave yellowish-tan, sassafras flowers dyed yellow, but the roots were the source of a good brown. White oak bark gave dove gray, and the willow a rosy tan. There were no reds or blues or bright greens in the dyes to be found in the trees. These soul-satisfying hues had to be found elsewhere, from the coveted indigo for the best blue and from bloodroot or madder for a glowing red. Coreopsis flowers gave a fine orange; goldenrod produced one of the best yellows, almost as pure as that obtained from the European saffron, with peach leaves producing a lighter yellow. Cochineal, however, derived from an insect native to Mexico, was unequaled in the clear, glorious red it produced. The most coveted of the dyes in early times and the most costly was Tyrian purple, a coloring produced by certain varieties of shellfish found in the Mediterranean. This purple dye was used for the robes of kings and nobility, hence the long-time use of purple as a sign of wealth. There was nothing like it in pioneer America. No tree ever gave a purple dye. Pioneer garments were of quiet hues that were part of the woods from which they were obtained. *(May 1965)*

THE OLD SILK ROAD

In a piece of embroidered silk in the Museum's Oriental Room there lies the whole long tale of silk, of China, and the story of what is perhaps the oldest, longest, and most significant road in the world. This is the old Silk Trade Route which connected China and its culture with the major cities of the known world, in the days when there were great gaps of wilderness and barbarians between the dwelling places of civilized men.

The Old Silk Trade Route connected Shanghai and the Pacific Coast with Rome and pre-Christian Europe. It was an artery 6000 miles long, over which for five hundred years flowed trade and commerce, camels and Mongol ponies, Tibetans, Turks, Persians, Chinese, Mongols, and Russians, moving back and forth with silk between the cities of Europe and the old Chinese Empire.

About a hundred years before the Christian Era, so the story goes, old Emperor Wu-Ti of the Han Dynasty sent an expedition of 60,000 soldiers against Russian Turkestan to capture the blood-sweating horses of that land. By the simple means, the Emperor got his horses and the world had a new road, for his thousands of soldiers passing over a stretch of semi-desert country were bound to make a dent, a path, a highway.

When peace at last was made with Russian Turkestan, trade sprang up. Roads went farther and farther, were extended caravan by caravan, into Bactria and Media, to Antioch and Tyre and the coast of North Africa. A fork of the road went through India to Persia, to the Persian Gulf, and to southern Arabia, where trade was carried on with Egypt and Rome. The silk merchants of Shanghai or Sian-fu had only the haziest idea where their silk bales finally ended their journeys. Silk simply was sold to the caravan owners, who in turn sent it on, by camel and Mongol pony, on, on, from buyer to buyer, to the coast. From here most of the precious bales went to Rome, where the man of wealth who bought silk for his demanding wife paid its weight in gold.

The Roman silk-buyer did not know the story of the ancient road that brought silk to him—how, in the morning mists, a caravan issued from a door in the yellow-grey serpent known as the Great Wall of China and started out into the Gobi Desert. The caravan went through old Lou-Lan, home of the wild camel, and into the deserts of Central Asia, where the sandstorms howled and now and again a watch tower, beaten by the moving sands, protected the silk caravans from marauding bandits.

Then the silent-footed camels came into the populous bazaars and market places of old Samarkand and Kashgar, where the silk bales usually changed hands and went on in other caravans. The caravans cut a cross section across the Old World, taking silk to the peoples who wanted the precious, gleaming fabric, and who would pay huge prices for it.

From Arabian ports along the Mediterranean, Phoenician sailing ships loaded the silk bales from the wharves and set out on the last portion of the Old Silk Route. At the ports of Italy the silk was sold in the marketplaces and at last the Roman women had the fabric they coveted. But far away in the remote land of China, women who knew nothing of Rome and its fine ladies, patiently unwound the cocoons of silk from the fat white worms, dyed and wove the silk, and embroidered it in intricate designs. *(July 1946)*

THE BELLS OF TIME

When the bells at midnight rang to welcome the new year—when intangibly yet certainly there moved across the black winter sky the presence of a new cycle of days—the bells rang to announce one more year in the endless procession of the years. The bells clanged and rang and echoed, and time moved on a moment, and looked back across the eons of years and ahead to the eons beyond. Among people it was a time of celebration and merriment, but it also was a time of solemn looking forward and of looking back.

The bells rang . . . . and it was suddenly a time when there were no men or other creatures on the earth, and only the sun and the earth recorded upon themselves the certain passage of years. For although the calendar as a means of recording and reckoning time is new, time itself is very old, and it has forever left imprints of itself upon any substance it touched. And so the oldest calendar upon the earth is the earth itself, and its rock layers are the pages of a vast calendar which will close only when the earth ends. In the calendar of the rocks are imprinted all the records of the past. Seas and swamps, animals and plants, floods and drouths: they left their stories on the old calendar.

Even before man came along, there may have been a sense of time among living creatures. Animals that spent part of their year in hibernation would go into a deep sleep at about the same time each year and would emerge from it similarly at the proper moment. If birds migrated, they migrated according to an accurate calendar of their own which was spaced with summers and winters, autumns and springs. If birds made nests and laid eggs, they were made and laid according to an invisible calendar. And the bells of the past rang out as more years passed, thousands of years, millions of years, and there were men on the earth.

After man learned to farm, it wasn't long before he felt the need of knowing where his time went. He knew how days began with the rising of the sun and ended with its setting. He knew that the moon wasn't always the same and it rose at a different time each evening, and sometimes there was no moon at all. He discovered, after a long time of earnest cogitating which took a good deal of effort in this unfamiliar field of thought, that this sequence was repeated over and over again. Perhaps he tried putting a mark on a rock wall for every evening he saw the moon and finally discovered that there had to be twenty-eight sunrises and sunsets between new moons. And so, just as the sun marked a space of time in man's life, so did the moon. On his old, old calendar he had days and he had months, and the passing of the seasons told him of the passing of both months and days. He saw how the sun was high in the sky in midsummer and shone long hours and was hot; and he saw how, in winter, the sun lay far over in the south and rose late and set early and seemed in imminent danger of disappearing into the south. Yet he saw, too, in the month that later became December, how the sun did not continue to go away, but started back toward the north and stayed longer in the sky because summer came again. And so he had a year.

To many peoples, the new year began with the day following the shortest day of the year; it was a logical moment to begin a new cycle, to ring bells and to rejoice. Among some agricultural peoples, the year began with the spring equinox, March 21st—the beginning of spring was the proper moment to begin a year.

But whenever it was that the new year moved across the midnight sky and lay upon a world influenced by time and its relentless passage across it, bells rang and celebrations were held. For bells in themselves were one of the media to record time. They rang the hours, announced important events, opened the day and ended the day. It was fitting that bells with their clear, loud tones should shout out the news of another year, another beginning, until the black sky itself echoed with the sound. *(Jan. 1952)*

"BROAD STRIPES AND BRIGHT STARS"

This is the American flag: Thirteen stripes, alternating red and white, with white stars on a blue field as Congress decreed. George Washington added, "We take the stars from Heaven, the red from our mother country, separating it by white stripes, thus showing that we have separated from her, and the white stripes shall go down to posterity representing Liberty." And the thirteen defiant colonies, brought through a common rebellion to a hitherto unknown unity, were shown as a circlet of stars, "to form a new Constellation," said Congress.

As years passed and more states came into the union, Congress in 1818 decided that each new state-star would be added formally on the Fourth of July following a state's admission to the union. The delicate circlet of the "new Constellation" long since has been changed to orderly lines of Stars, with Illinois as number 21, and Arizona, which entered the union in 1912, as number 48.

Many flags have flown over this country, but when the new banner appeared in June, 1777, it superceded the flags of England, Scotland, Spain, France, and Holland, one or all of which, had the mere turn of fate been different, might be flying here instead of these broad stripes and bright stars. Only once after that was it seriously threatened, when a brave rebel flag called the Stars and Bars flew in the South, but came down forever in '65.

There they are—forty-eight stars, each one standing for a state which in turn stands for an integral portion of America. When the flag today flies grandly in the wind, it is telling about all the things that make up the nation . . . about Delaware and Peter Stuyvesant; about Pennsylvania and the

Susquehanna, Gettysburg, and witch signs on barn doors; of Ben Franklin, and the Blue Ridge. It tells of the birds of Barnegat, and the storms of Cape May, of the Marshes of Glynn and the Chattahoochee, of red dust and Georgia buzzards; of the Connecticut River and dinosaur tracks; of stone fences and blueberry pie, white pines and bayberry candles. The flag has tales of Kentucky rifles that could pick off a Redcoat as easily as a squirrel; it tells of Cape Cod, and the fishing boats coming in to Gloucester; of the Mohawk Trail, and the battles of Concord and Lexington; of Paul Revere riding Hell-for-leather through the night; of Plymouth and Myles Standish. It tells of American soldiers at Valley Forge and at Yorktown; of old Charleston and its earthquakes and wars, its great cypress swamps hung with moss and haunted with ghosts; of razor-back hogs whose ancestors were with DeSoto; of New Hampshire hills and the Great Stone Face.

There is the Valley of Virginia, and the Shenandoah bathed in fog, Jefferson and his Little Mountain, the Dismal Swamp, and Williamsburg, the tragedy of Roanoke, the fifty-one defiant ladies of Edenton, the battles of Manassas, Bull Run, and Appomattox.

The great city of New York lies behind another star; here the Hudson moves upstate, and Rip Van Winkle snores in the Catskills. There are the Great Smoky Mountains and the Cherokees, and from the dunes of Kitty Hawk the first successful airplane flies. The flag means Vermont maple sugar and Green Mountain Boys armed for trouble; it means Kentucky with Daniel Boone's Wilderness Road coming up through Cumberland Gap to the Blue Grass. It means the Ohio and the Wabash and the Mississippi, and George Rogers Clark taking Vincennes from the British, LaSalle building a fort on Starved Rock, Lewis and Clark setting out to the unknown west, and Audubon sketching birds in a Louisiana swamp. It tells of New Orleans and the Cajuns, of LaFitte, the pirate, of Vicksburg, and the Natchez Trace. It means corn in Illinois, Abraham Lincoln and the Black Hawk War, oil wells and apple orchards and coal mines, Chicago and New Salem; it means Mississippi roses in December, and the pelicans at Pass Christian, orange groves along the Indian River, Miami and palm trees and the Everglades.

There is so much, and the flag stands for it all—for the Great Lakes with their ore freighters going to Detroit, for Niagara thundering night and day, for little lakes with vacation cabins on them. It means Wisconsin Holsteins and the Longhorns of Texas, and Davy Crockett shooting it out in the Alamo. It is the Pueblo de Nuestra Senora la Reina de Los Angeles; the missions, the padres, and the gold hunters; it is the biggest trees in the world, and the Pacific on the rocks of Monterey. It is Death Valley and Mount Whitney, the Soda Lakes and Yosemite; it is Kansas wheat and jackrabbits pulling in their ears to get under a fence; it is the mad Colorado harnessed at Boulder Dam; it is rim rock and badlands and the great searing heat of the desert. It is a fighting chinook salmon in Puget Sound, a snow storm on Pike's Peak in July; Bryce and Zion and the Yellowstone brilliant as paint.

The flag tells of the Santa Fe Trail and the Donner Party, of Indians and Oklahoma and oil, of Spanish explorers hunting vainly for the Seven

Golden Cities of Cibola; of buffalo herds, and the Union Pacific. A great meteor crater and the Grand Canyon, the Painted Desert at dawn and the Navahoes with their sheep; it is the white heights of San Francisco peaks.

This is America. This is the flag. And you cannot have one without the other. It is this that brings a lift to the heart, suddenly, when the American flag snaps in the wind, this which gives one a deep sense of belonging, of being part of these shrines, this America, this flag. *(July 1943)*

LISTEN: THE BELLS!

High up in the church towers the bells are swinging, ringing, shaking the towers, shaking those who listen. So will they ring on the day peace comes.

Behind the bells is the story of man's adoration of a beautiful sound. Long before there were many musical instruments, the churches of Rome in the seventh century A. D. had their first bells. They were queer, four-sided, riveted things, but they were bells and soon were followed by shapes we know today. They first were made in monasteries and were intended solely for church use. Bells were tolled for deaths and funerals, tolled when a king or a bishop died, mournfully counting the years of his life with the strokes of the clapper. They rang joyfully for weddings, pealed for New Year's Day and church holidays and celebrations, and brought the faithful to divine services. And when there was fire, flood, invasion, or other disaster, the bells crashed and clanged and shouted in terror to warn the people.

In their place in the life of man, bells varied greatly in size from tinklers an eighth of an inch in diameter, to the Great Bell of Moscow which weighed 180 tons, stood 19 feet high and was 60 feet in circumference.

Much valuable metal went into bells both large and small, and many of them in times of war were melted down for guns and cannons. In making a bell, the proportion of metal was four parts copper to one of tin. A design was made on paper, then modeled in clay and baked, and a mold was made. Into this the molten metal was run; the bell, if large, often took several weeks to cool. When it was taken out, it was handled gently and usually needed no special tuning. A good bell gave out three tones, and the larger it was the lower were the tones.

Bells had their mighty influence on architecture; it was for these that towers and steeples were added to churches. Some bells in the towers were rung by hand by means of ropes, while others, some of them too large to swing, were played mechanically. In a carillon, a system of wires connected with small hammers, struck bells of many sizes, usually on their outer surfaces, and were arranged with the machinery of the clock to play tunes or chimes at intervals. The beauty of bell music came to rich and poor, to commoner and king, as the bells gave it freely into the air—poignant, soulful music that reached inside a person and touched chords of his inner being.

Bells played their part in America just as surely as they did in the Old World. There were those that warned of Indian attacks, bells that rang to announce news from England, ships' bells, the old Liberty Bell itself that never will have voice again because of its great crack suffered on the day of freedom, but whose sounds still are heard over the land. And there are so many other bells—bell-buoys clanging on a foaming reef; train bells ding-donging; dinner bells with their inviting persuasion; the hysterical fire-engine bells racing through the night; the old-time bell that tinkled when a visitor entered a dusty little shop. There is the bell around the cat's neck to warn the birds; turkey bells clinking, cowbells and sheepbells in the morning mists.

And always there are the Christmas bells, the happiest of them all. For life may change and times may change, but the ageless voices of the bells for many a year will ring Christmas into the hearts of men. *(Dec. 1943)*

THE CLOCK

Behind the striking clock stretches the long tale of time-telling—not long as time is long, but ancient in the brief story of mankind. In the early days when there were men on the earth, the rising and setting of the sun was the time-teller for all. Day began with the coming of the sun and ended when the sun vanished. There was no concept of hours, minutes, seconds: time was simple then.

Finally, perhaps, someone noticed how the shadow of an upstanding rock moved in a circular manner as the sun rose and crossed the sky. The moving shadow of the rock may have been the first marker of the day's divisions. Time in a timeless world gained meaning.

The moving shadow of the rock was the forerunner of the sundial, which, it is believed, was developed by the Greeks. Through the slow centuries, men struggled with the complexities presented by this simple mechanism, regulated the pointer or gnomon—called "the one who knows"—set the dial properly over and over again to fit the sun's position in that particular region.

But sundials recorded only sunlight time. On rainy days and at night, time had no measure. Yet man no longer went to bed with the sun; when he sat up late he wanted to know the hour. So about 2,700 years ago, there was developed a complicated mechanism called the Clepsydra, or water clock, which drop by drop lowered the water level in a jar and recorded upon a scale the passing hours.

Then the hour glass was invented. It was a simple thing composed of fine sand passing through a small hole between two glasses, a contrivance that was cheap, efficient, and wouldn't freeze, and which could be carried on journeys. But it only ran for a limited time, and at the end of that time it could not right itself and start running anew. Time stopped when the sands stopped.

Then the Dark Ages closed down upon Europe and time once again grew relatively unimportant. The church bells rang the hours for matins and angelus, rang to tell folk when to do things, told of fire, flood, victory, death, marriage, or the birth of a prince. In a village with a well-tolled bell there was little need for other time-telling devices.

But in the 11th century A.D. there came the clock. It didn't just happen. Involved in its complex mechanism was a long procession of invention, trial-and-error, and discovery, at a time when mankind's inventions still were relatively simple. A thing as complicated as a clock was a marvelous piece of achievement.

The early clock had only the hour hand, was large, clumsy, and often elaborate, with gears that were cut by hand. There were crude watches, too, but they were poor time-keepers; when they were carried about they were easily thrown off balance. Then the canny Swiss watchmakers studied and solved the problem of equalization in watch mechanism; they learned to use jewelled bearings to prevent friction.

Year after year the mechanism of watches and clocks advanced. Finally when man wanted his hours divided by seconds and minutes, the hour hand had company.

So humankind came to the present moment. Time obtained from the intricate passage of stars, for which great observatories are built; small watches that tick faithfully for years; electric clocks that go endlessly as long as the power is on; huge clocks, alarm clocks, sidereal clocks, dollar watches, tiny wristwatches—they all are proof that mankind, in advancing from his early timeless leisure, notes carefully but cannot halt the ceaseless passage of the hours. (*Jan. 1946*)

AUDUBON IN ILLINOIS

The heavy keelboat was loaded with trade goods, the hunters and crew were aboard; and John James Audubon and his business partner, Rozier, waved goodbye to their families at a little village near Henderson, Kentucky, and set off down the Ohio River during the latter part of December, 1810. The Audubon-Rozier store at Henderson had been far from successful, and in desperation the two decided to take their surplus stock and try to sell it in the prosperous towns of Sainte Genevieve and Cape Girardeau along the Mississippi.

When Audubon and his keelboat reached the Mississippi, an early freeze was filling the great brown river with masses of floating ice. Because of it, the keelboat could not shove across to the lee of the Missouri shore, as most keelboats did because the current was easier there; so the boat and cargo were taken by sheer manpower up the Illinois shore. The crew, including Rozier and Audubon, assisted in "cordelling" the keelboat up the river, breaking a path where there was none, stumbling over beached driftwood, dragging the boat along. Audubon, a great, strong, powerful woodsman, who was an asset to any keelboat crew simply because of his muscles, busily watched for birds as he helped pull the heavy craft up the Mississippi.

But the cold was deepening. The river was freezing solid. One morning the keelboat was caught fast in the ice opposite Cape Girardeau, Missouri, somewhere along the Illinois shore in Union or Alexander County.

The men shoved logs into the slush ice around the boat to protect it from the crushing floes and chopped a great supply of firewood. The crew rolled masses of soft, wet snow and built it into a high, circular wall, inside which they built a roaring fire and lived comfortably and warm. For six weeks the keelboat party camped in the snow. Audubon had a wonderful time. Living beside the Mississippi in winter was a new experience, and everything he saw, everything he did, was new and exciting. It was too cold to draw very much; his paint-water froze. But when some friendly Osage Indians came to the camp in the evening to visit, he often sketched their portraits, which amused them greatly. He made plans, however, for some of the bird pictures he would paint—the beautiful little green paroquets feeding on the hard, spiny seeds of clotbur in the river bottoms, the white-headed eagle eating a river catfish, a duck hawk with blood on its beak.

At last the break-up came and the ice floes ground their way down the river. On the journey across the Mississippi to the town of Cape Girardeau and up to Sainte Genevieve, the keelboat jogged among the remains of the great ice. It was there, in midriver, that Audubon discovered a big brown eagle soaring, as the bald eagles did, above the Mississippi. With delight he felt sure that he was seeing a new bird no one had ever described and decided that he would give it a name never before given to a bird—the Washington eagle.

Audubon did indeed paint a picture of the brown eagle, but it no longer retains the name he gave it that day among the ice floes of the Mississippi, for the the Washington eagle is simply the immature dark form of the bald eagle, a common bird along our rivers. We may remember it, however, as one of the highlights of this exciting keelboat trip, of Audubon's first experiences on the Mississippi, and his first and perhaps only camping trip in Illinois. (*March 1956*)

A HOBBY FOR STABILITY

Every day, said Mrs. Roosevelt, one should spend a little time out of doors. For one cannot worry too much over war and its effect on nations and families without soon feeling the strain in sleeplessness, nervousness, illness, and the loss of that precious possession, the sense of security. There must be a substitution for worry—something to replace it. Escape, some call it. It is not intended as an escape from responsibility and sacrifice, when such are called for, but rather to take the sting out of such trials and soften the blows before and after they fall.

Today's recreation tends toward simplicity, toward things which are of the spirit, things with the strength and charm which are found in nature. The out-door hobby is the solution to many war-weary minds. To be out under the sky, if only for an hour a day, to walk into a park or along streets and gardens, offers an invaluable balm to worry. Perhaps it is only in learning the friendly forms of trees on one's way home from work—in hearing a cardinal sing—yet this is something strong to take the place of uncertainty and fear.

Perhaps this is why the British have been able to come through sanely, with banners of courage flying. They still go out and collect butterflies, or flowers, some of them, or shells along the sea, when there isn't a raid on. There are Britons today, who, oddly enough, still find time to write books on the birds of Cornwall or Devon or the Channel Islands, and there are still a great many Britons who read such books and enjoy them. In these small, yet important things, they have found substitutes for worry.

That is why this year's annual Christmas bird census, taken by bird observers over the entire country, from Quebec to Key West, from Cape May to Alaska, was larger than ever before in its history.

Three weeks after Pearl Harbor, more than 2,400 people in America went out for birds, with 48 states represented for the first time in the entire 42-year history of the census. It is true that in many places the bird observers were thought by the jittery populace to be spies and saboteurs with their binoculars, notebooks, and generally suspicious actions, but the census went on, and was a great success.

These bird-watchers were finding a stabilizing satisfaction in birds which will be of good use during the days ahead. For morale is a curious thing: simple habits like watching birds and clouds and stars and hearing frogs in spring can strengthen it for our own deep good.

The Museum stands ready with sympathy for all interests and help in such pursuits. Because the Museum is a cross-section of life, whether it is that of nature or of men, life as it is today is the better understood and explained through the museum's assistance. It shows things from far away as well as things that are around us. It is an open door to developing a hobby, to a better understanding of the world—of life and the thrilling present—and it belongs to you. Use it! (*April 1942*)

BETTER THAN GAMES

"Make the boy interested in Natural History. It is better than games." These words were written by the lost explorer, Robert Falcon Scott, perishing in the Antarctic in 1909, as the final entries in a journal found by a rescuing party which came too late. Scott's young son was then three years old. His mother, following her husband's wishes, did indeed make the boy interested in natural history—he is Peter Scott, noted English naturalist and bird painter whose works contain a wildly glorious element of wilderness.

Interest in natural history—this indeed is important and it is a growing thing. The urgent trend is to go back toward our roots. We need to drink at the source, to know the wild places, to learn their truths. In the more than half a century after Robert Scott's death, Americans as well as Englishmen have more and more turned toward those truths. Yet now, ironically, when we reach out for nature, much of it has gone away from us.

This realization of our great inner need for nature is now a national concern. We must save what is left before there is nothing left to save; before America becomes a parking lot from coast to coast, with cities, cornfields, and trash dumps between. President Johnson has said: "For centuries Americans have drawn strength and inspiration from the beauty of our country. It would be a neglectful generation indeed . . . which failed to preserve and extend such a heritage for its descendants."

Although much is being done on the national level, it is even more important to people living in Illinois to know what is being done here to contain, preserve, and perpetuate some of our choicest wild areas before they are lost. *(July 1966)*

THE SEEING EYE, THE LISTENING EAR

There are as many ways to see and interpret the living world as there are people to use their senses out of doors. This awareness may be a sensitivity to the smells of the wild—to the odor of wet earth and pavement at the start of a rain, the fragrances of flowers, all different, the aromas of new leaves and autumn leaves, the different scents of night and day and what they convey, the awareness of the delightful fact that every kind of thing has a different odor, even though one's own sense of smell may not be keen enough to detect all of them.

The sense of hearing is something to be cultivated. It must first spring from a willingness to be aware, of not letting all the sounds out of doors become a blur which merges with the general, rushing undercurrent of the sounds of civilization. To listen—really to listen—is to hear the difference in the night songs of snowy tree crickets and black crickets, in orchard orioles and Baltimore orioles; it is to take note of small sounds of birds flying over on a spring or an autumn night; to hear the pulsations of a bat's wings swooping past; to distinguish trees by the rustle of their leaves. An acute sense of listening (which is not always the same as perfect hearing equipment) will bring alive the natural world in the multitudes of its small voices, its rustlings, its footsteps, and its wing-sounds.

The sense of touch sometimes comes to its best development in those who cannot see or who may not hear. Through the fingers comes another kind of awareness and appreciation of every thing which is within reach. The textures are different in every leaf and flower and tree-trunk and seed, in shell and fossil and bud and feather. Tasting is another sense to be used—but with a degree of discernment and caution.

Sometimes human beings feel too big and too clumsy in their blunted and unused senses to really comprehend some of the infinite details of nature. Unlike man's own creations, which do not improve under magnification, nature's creations only become more finely detailed and more exquisite under the greatest magnification devised by man. Microscopes show an astonishing world which is all about, yet is undiscovered without high enlargement in the laboratory. Still, because taking specimens into a laboratory and putting them under a microscope removes them from their world and makes them merely specimens, not ingredients of their surroundings, it is not a preferred means of discovery out of doors. But the small hand lens is the perfect auxiliary to the human eye and mind. The magnifier held to the eye, the flower or leaf or bud brought up to the lens (not the lens down to it) suddenly provides a greatly enlarged viewpoint and focus. It opens a door to a whole new world of discovery in one's backyard or along the woodland trail.

Ten-power magnification can do remarkable things to the appearance of a leaf-scar or a tree-bud. It can reveal golden hairs on a bitternut bud, splendid cinnamon-covered clubs of pollen in a lily, a "rabbit" in the figwort flower, an orderly garden of golden stars on a dandelion head, an orchid corsage in a red clover, and astonishing wonders in every seed, fern, fungus, pistil, flower, or moss.

Along with binoculars, bird book, or camera, a hand-lens should be part of one's outdoor equipment. The lens takes up where the senses leave off, thereby sharpening all of them. Life, say the enthralled initiates to the world of the hand-lens, is never quite the same after that first excursion into magnification, and the enlarging of human perspective, understanding, and appreciation of the world. (*June 1964*)

"NEVER . . . ENOUGH OF NATURE"

The somewhat belated concern of many communities to insure around themselves some safeguard of greenery against too many houses, too many highways, and too much civilization, is an innate alarm over the loss of an environment which, for too many generations, men took for granted. Early men in America fought against the wilderness as if against some living menace. They cut down trees, drained swamps, cleared woodlands; they rejoiced at the security which the resultant planted and cultivated open spaces seemed to insure. Yet it was not long before men were planting trees, laying out parks, enjoying an outing in the woods. No sooner had we lost the old wilderness than we began to long for manageable portions of it.

More than a hundred years ago, Henry Thoreau was an outspoken public conscience on the matter of keeping our wild places. For some of his radical views he was not especially popular with the more practical-minded citizenry, but this never affected his opinions or his utterances. He said:

"Our village life would stagnate if it were not for the unexplored forests and meadows which surround it. We need the tonic of wilderness—to wade sometimes in marshes where the bittern and meadow-hen lurk, and hear the booming of the snipe; to smell the whispering sedge where only some wilder and more solitary fowl builds her nest, and the mink crawls with its belly close to the ground. At the same time that we are earnest to explore and learn all things, we require that all things be mysterious and unexplorable, that land and sea be infinitely wild, unsurveyed and unfathomed by us because unfathomable. We can never have enough of nature. We must be refreshed by the sight of inexhaustible vigor, vast and titanic features, the sea-coast with its wrecks, the wilderness with its living and decaying trees, the thundercloud, and the rain which lasts three weeks and produces freshets. We need to witness our own limits transgressed, and some life pasturing freely where we never wander."

He was a stern man in his ideas, and few agreed with him then. Thoreau was several generations too early. But eventually the public opinion began to turn his way. Some of the great scenic areas were made into national parks; state parks were set aside even later; city parks, however, in some communities fortunate enough to have far-seeing planners, were often laid out early in the city's growth and never violated, no matter how large the city became. Wilderness areas, conservation areas, public lands, green belts —they all followed, decade by decade, in an attempt to halt the destruction which city progress and expanding populations necessarily demand.

The forward-looking plan to circle a town with unviolated green, to keep woods, lakes, and streams for the refreshment of the people, is following in the trend of Thoreau's words—"we can never have enough of nature." We may not visit them often, if at all; but it is an aesthetic satisfaction to realize their presence, to know that there are woods, and waters, and wild mountains and rivers, waiting and safe.

Thoreau said firmly:

"From the forest and wilderness come the tonics . . . which brace mankind. . . . I believe in the forest, and in the meadow, and in the night in which the corn grows." (*July 1961*)

"UGLIFICATION IS AGGRAVATION"

"I never heard of 'Uglification,' " Alice ventured so say. "What is it?"

The Gryphon lifted both its paws in surprise. "Never heard of uglifying!" it exclaimed. "You know what to beautify is, I suppose?"

"Yes," said Alice doubtfully: "it means—to—make—anything prettier."

"Well, then," the Gryphon went on, "if you don't know what to uglify is, you *are* a simpleton."

It would seem, from a glance about our big cities and along many American rivers, roads, and woods, that some of us have learned more about uglification than beautification. But uglification, as any Lewis Carroll character might have suggested, is aggravation, especially when we are the ones who have to look at it and live with it.

It is not the way of wild creatures to defile their own nests. There even are certain birds which bring shells, leaves, and other trinkets to adorn their abodes. The wild creatures have never had to live with ugliness, except that which man has wrought in a once pure and pristine landscape.

With an awareness now heightened all the more by the President's war on this defilement of our landscape and Congressional bills now doing something about it, we are even more aware of the state of some of our surroundings. Of course, there is still much beauty. There are still cool mountain brooks purling ice-water over stones, still fragrant forests and woodlands full of flowers; there are free-flowing rivers whose waters are clear and clean, and lake shores which are unlittered by beer cans and bottles. In contrast, then, the stark ugliness which has been perpetrated upon us inflicts shock and disgust. It is an affront to the senses, an insult to the innate love for the beautiful which seems to be part of all men until they somehow forget and let it be lost.

One day in April not so long ago, as a southbound train was leaving Chicago and passing through the usual shambles of slums and trash and unsavory dumps and mangled autos, an unforgettable vision suddenly presented itself. Over these miles of offensive landscape it was still spring, still April, and April would not be denied. In the midst of oil-soaked ground and piled-up oil drums, broken rubbish and no particle of greenery, a single, lovely, golden, unutterably magnificent forsythia bush was in full bloom. Who can say how it got there, how it managed to blossom so beautifully among its foul surroundings, or how many people its brief vision refreshed? A single candle of beauty, it stood in the midst of human ugliness, a proof that no landscape is devoid of hope.

It is not only places like this but the rivers and lakes which also have suffered blight. For a long time the majority of riverfronts became a repository for old motor cars, bedsprings, broken glass, reeking rubble, rats, and tin cans. It was easy to dump unwanted objects over the rim of the bank and let the river carry it all away—usually to deposit it on some other shore. Thus shores were defiled, rudders fouled, water polluted, fish poisoned, people endangered, and eye and nose offended. River clean-up campaigns are, however, creating miracles of rejuvenation; strict laws against pollution are having effect.

For America is noted for possessing a conscience. Although that conscience may take a while to stir, it usually awakens before it is everlastingly too late. In the past we could perhaps be excused for our tardy awakening because of that old notion of the endlessness of American land. With so gloriously much of everything, it was natural for man, coming from an often pinched and deprived Europe, to be prodigally wasteful. If the land was ruined by overgrazing or by poorly rotated crops, by erosion, by trash dumps and industrial desecration, it was easy to move on to new land rather than to handle properly the old. There was so much space. When forests were all cut off, men and saws were moved to the next tract of virgin timber westward, then "cut out and get out," on and on to the Mississippi River and beyond, until they ran out of forests. If a million wild pigeons were slaughtered in a season, it was confidently expected that there would be plenty more for the next year's shooting. The illusion of limitless natural wealth was easy to come by in a land as lovely and large as ours.

The sobering realization that forests do not in fact go on forever, that it is possible for a race of wild things to become extinct, that rich land may be ruined, that rivers may become sterile, ugly, gray, oozing messes contaminated by human carelessness, that mountains of mangled motor cars fill once-lovely meadows, all has come as a growing shock. We are not really like this, we protest, not really so bad; we did not mean to mistreat this land which we love . . . it just happened when we weren't noticing. It has been a humbling experience to realize that only we ourselves are to blame for defiling our own landscape, and that no one but we may effect the rejuvenation.

For nature is resilient. It is endlessly resurrected, is seldom totally ruined, except for the lost wild things which cannot ever be reborn. Now that the national conscience has been awakened, one day American uglification will have become a bad dream of the past.

In February, 1965, the President issued his "Message on Natural Beauty of our Country," excerpts of which are given here.

"For centuries Americans have drawn strength and inspiration from the beauty of our country. It would be a neglectful generation indeed, indifferent alike to the judgment of history and the command of principle, which failed to preserve and extend such a heritage for its descendants.

". . . our water, our soil, and wildlife are being blighted by the poisons and chemicals which are the byproducts of technology and industry. . . . We must not only protect the countryside and save it from destruction, we must restore what has been destroyed. Its concern is not with nature alone, but with the total relation between man and the world around him. Its object is not just man's welfare, but the dignity of man's spirit.

"Beauty is not an easy thing to measure. It does not show up in the gross national product, in a weekly paycheck, or in profit and loss statements. But these things are not ends in themselves. . . . Association with beauty can enlarge man's imagination and revive his spirit. Ugliness can demean the people who live among it. What a citizen sees every day is his America. If it is attractive it adds to the quality of his life. If it is ugly it can degrade his existence. . . . The beauty of our land is a natural resource. Its preservation is linked to the inner prosperity of the human spirit."

According to the Gryphon, anyone who doesn't know what uglifying is must be truly a simpleton. Because Americans are not simpletons, we are now spending billions of dollars in a great national movement to remedy our mistakes and turn ugliness into beauty. The lone forsythia bush in the oil dump may one day be surrounded by hundreds of its kind. (*March 1966*)

COUNTRY SUNDAY

It was a pleasant, warm, country Sunday. Out in the sand fields where the oak woods shaded the old cemetery, the white country church reared its steeple to a hot, clear sky. Beyond lay the low ridge of bluffs, green now from the rains, and wheat was a rich toast color in fields that only waited for Monday to be cut. Corn, planted late, grew lustily in lands that a month before were flooded.

The church bell rang, but almost everyone was there ahead of time. The sunburned men had come from baling hay all day Saturday. The women had come from country kitchens where they had canned peas and beans and raspberries all the week, had washed and ironed, and had fed their chickens. They had milked cows and driven cattle to the barn-lot to be vaccinated against black-leg that was attacking neighborhood herds, perhaps had helped in the hay fields because hired hands were scarce. Now in their Sunday clothes they were here with their children.

There was music. The organ sent chords out into the grove where the black-eyed susans gleamed in a mass of burnt gold, out across the sand fields where a sparrow hawk hovered for mice. A breeze blew the corn. The people sang. The young preacher spoke of the goodness of God and the sureness of faith; there was holy communion for everyone. And the organ softly played the closing hymn, "America," while the sunshine glinted on the black-eyed susans outside, and a wasp with long trailing legs sailed majestically into an open window and out another, and a robin carolled a lazy summer song from the steeple. Then church was over.

Outside, the people talked a while of the weather, of the crops, of the sick, of someone's son in the war, of the morning's sermon, of the cattle and hogs and how they did. Then they all went home. Most of them had company to dinner.

Dinner! It was still the typical country Sunday dinner which is part of the tradition of the middle west. The war seemed very far away as the platters of fried chicken and ham were passed, the green beans and beets from the garden, the great fluffy mound of potatoes mashed in cream and oozing butter, whipped cream salads and home-made bread with this year's strawberry preserves, new applesauce, coffee in enormous cups twice the size of city cups, and ice cream made of real cream turned in a freezer with ice and salt. And afterward while the women did the dishes and talked, and the small children napped, the men gathered on the cool porch and talked of the unstable weather, of how hard it was to get help; they argued about the government, the president, the war, the ration board, and taxes, and meant not more than half of what they said. It was good just to air one's views, and then go back to work again, harder than ever.

This is the Country Sunday. Here, whether anyone noticed or not, are the Four Basic Freedoms of Mankind, as they are desperately fought for now in nations throughout the world. Here they are taken as a matter of course, yet deep down they are none the less valued. Here is freedom from fear—that was the aim of the pastor's sermon, the security of the land itself. Freedom from want—a bountiful dinner, food at its source. Freedom of thought and speech—the after-dinner discussion, the right to criticize and complain and praise. Freedom of worship—that was the country church in its simple dignity, ministering to a scattered, faithful congregation in the sand hills. It is all very simple, very ordinary to those who live here. But it is a scene and way of life which, just now, cannot be visualized in battered Europe or, perhaps in any other place in the struggling world. (*Aug. 1943*)

THE COUNTRY ROAD

There still are small, winding country roads, and there still are people who like to walk them. For although there may be a good deal of talk about high-powered highways and the cars to match, many a person still finds no better substitute to inner peace than a pleasant, contemplative walk along a quiet country lane. The speed is not so great, but the personal rewards are undeniably greater, the benefits to mind, body, and blood-pressure inestimable.

The country road in November has reached one of its most comfortable points in the year. The summer's heat is gone, and winter's cold is not yet here. The dust is dampened, but there is seldom enough wetness to produce the sodden mud of early spring, nor is there the warm dust of summer. November is that almost-complete end of the year, and all along the road the fruits of the year's growth are in evidence.

Butterflies have left the weedy roadside, and now there are the cheeping of sparrows. They are usually not the sparrows of town, but the gentle-voiced finches of the countryside. Many of them have come down from Canada to spend the winter in these roadside weeds, while some will go on farther south. Tree sparrows pipe in the slanting sunshine; there may be big rusty fox sparrows, and slate-colored juncos flicking their white tail feathers, and song sparrows which, even so late in the year, still sing that bubbling carol which puts heart into the most downcast of men. A downy woodpecker energetically hammers a horseweed stalk with a gusto which resounds in the silent, cool, damp, brooding presence of November.

All of these sounds are separate. They are not a concerted medley as in spring and summer. They stand apart and are loud in their aloneness, emphasizing as they do the way in which the great numbers of birds and insects have vanished from the roadside and the woods, not to return until spring. In their quietness they are part of that great autumnal silence which seems to stretch almost unbroken from one country lane and woods to the next, to the silent forests of the North.

Walk along a little way, pause to watch the glint of sunlight on milk-weed silk, listen to the voice of a red-tailed hawk flying over, and see how the sunlight shines through its wings; listen to the rattling of locust pods in the November wind, and discover the tracks of a raccoon in the muddy place near the creek. There is a special fragrance, too, in the November air which is neither that of blossoms nor of growing things, but of things past, a mingling of the scents of dead leaves lying damp on the ground, of earth that has been productive all summer and now lies moistly fragrant in the cornfield, a scent of sun-and-rain-drenched dust and the cool, portentous perfume of shadowed hollows where the breath of winter already seems to lurk.

There will probably be no momentous events to discover on a walk on the November road. There are no mountains to climb, no cliffs to scale, no flowers in bloom (only the tiny white stars of chickweed, and a belated dandelion), no leaves on the trees (only the rattling dry leaves on the shingle oak, not yet fallen), few birds, fewer animals. Yet perhaps the secret of enjoyment is in that there are so few things to confuse and clutter the landscape. All the busy activity and greenery and growth and song and flight have been finished. It is a neat, Puritanical, inelaborate countryside with all the frills gone, stripped to the essentials, to the bones. And in this simplicity there can be a peculiar peace. (*Nov. 1955*)

LINCOLN AND OAK RIDGE

Every year thousands of people from every state and many countries visit the Lincoln Tomb in Oak Ridge Cemetery, Springfield. They feel the simple splendor of the tomb, the impressive silences within, the eloquent stillness of the sarcophagus, and something else, which is not so easily definable.

Oak Ridge Cemetery is a natural woodland at the northwest corner of Springfield. The area, once a genuine wilderness, is hilly and full of trees that grew there long ago, set with those which later were planted for variety and color, but the artificial planting has not changed the aspect of naturalness which is appropriate to the tomb of a prairie man.

Indians once roamed these woods and fished in the creek; arrowheads and flint spears have been found on the big hill. When the first settlers came to this region they, too, hunted small game in the forest and at last built their village not far away from the forest's edge. Here in 1855 a cemetery was laid out and named for the native oaks that grew there so abundantly. In Oak Ridge one by one were buried men who had fought in the Revolution and who came to Illinois with the westward trend. Here lay women who knew the hardships of the Wilderness Road and of flatboats on the Ohio, and men who had gone off to the wars. The people who built Springfield are buried here—poet and artist, banker and businessman, governor and president. American history is represented in Oak Ridge.

Yet unlike in so many cemeteries, the visitor is scarcely aware that this is a burying ground. The tombstones are there, of course, varying from the pioneer slabs with hand-carved legends all but obliterated by time to the granite shaft of the Lincoln burial spot itself. Trees predominate, bring a feeling of natural Illinois oak woods as they were when the Indians knew them. The trees eliminate the unpleasant characteristic of cemeteries whose living trees have bowed to the granite and marble of death.

Now in spring the oaks are leafing in the myriad pastel hues that only oaks produce, bringing a clear, illuminated look to the hills and ravines. Birds swarm in these peaceful acres, fill the trees and bushes and ravines with song and motion. Local bird students come here, especially early on a May morning, for their best look at tanagers, vireos, and migrating warblers.

There are barred owls in the spruces; wrens, thrashers, robins, thrushes, and a host of others already beginning to nest. Flying squirrels take up their abode in preempted bird holes, and the little striped chipmunk, tail erect, skitters around a stone and into a hole. Down in the floodplain woods there are 'coons and sometimes a fox.

Mentally subtract the monuments and there comes into focus a picture of the Illinois oak woods as Lincoln perhaps knew them as he travelled between Salem and Springfield. Here are the same sorts of flowers—violets and pussy toes and sweet william, dancing white dog-tooth violets, a few Turk's cap lilies in June, the perfume of wild plum and the unforgettable spice of prairie crab. It is this setting which visitors to Lincoln's burial place may feel yet cannot completely analyze. It is that fine sense of fitness, a sense of coming to a place to which Illinoisans and a Prairie President forever will belong. (*May 1941*)

THE QUIET NIGHT

Come out and watch the night, for night loses boundaries; it is all infinite space; nothing is distinct but the stars, and they are so far away that by their distance they convey peace. Since man first learned to sit by himself and meditate on the madness of the world, the quiet and peace of night under the stars has been as a healing balm.

Now in the west the sky is still a deep indigo-green, shading down to the horizon in a last clear lemon light against which jut the far-off silhouettes of trees. A night heron beats slowly across the last bit of glow, is gone, and out in the pasture a late field sparrow trills a song. In the woods the thrushes are still calling, sometimes uttering a last bell-note or two, and then they, too, are quiet. A wood pewee wails, and finally ceases. Yet night is not silent. The summer evening is full of quiet sounds that merge with silence until one can scarcely tell one from the other; when the thrushes stop, there is no noticeable hole in the night.

Now the tree crickets, hidden among the elm leaves, take up a refrain, a rhythmic, pulsating, jingling sound. The spasmodic sizzling of grasshoppers and other hidden insects breaks from the grass; the crackle of a beetle's footsteps is loud. The pleasant, slightly damp, warm aroma of evening rises from the clover fields, from the trees, from the damp woods, from wheat stubble, cornfield, and the river.

There is still enough light—owl's light, the Irish call it—to see the outlines of trees. Something on sharp wings flies across the crest of the hills, and then, full of pleasant eeriness, comes the crying of a whip-poor-will. Another answers. They call; they pause; they make duets. The whip-poor-wills are awake and night has come down.

By this time the stars are out, warm with the heat of July. They are sparkling and clear—blue Vega in the east, the Northern Cross high, the delicate circlet of Corona already past the zenith. Over in the west sink the white stars of Leo, with Spica, the water-lily star of Virgo, the writhing length of the serpent, the flapping crow, and the giant Hercules nearby. In the south burns the red flame of Antares, and on the other side of the sky sinks orange Arcturus. How bright the night, how far from dark and oppressive, with stars!

Where have the whip-poor-wills gone? They call no more, and the night echoes with silence. Then a field sparrow utters a single sleepy trill out in the wet pasture; in the woods a cuckoo clucks in its sleep; cricket frogs set up an incessant clicking somewhere near the river. And out of the darkness along the woods rolls the mellow hooting of an owl—a wildly resonant tone down there in the blackness.

The summer night is very far away from a busy world. On the quiet hill-top—or in the garden, by the lake, anywhere that stars and trees and night may be—the guns of warring nations are too far away for reality, too insignificant at the moment to be distrubing. The calm night does its work. It builds up an armor of serenity, so that, newly fortified, a man may face the harassing day; he has the placid sounds of whip-poor-wills and night-wind in his ears, the mystery of trees before him, and the stars above his head. (*July 1941*)

"INFINITE EXPECTATION OF THE DAWN"

Night passes through many changes between the time when dusk merges with darkness and when the darkness, in turn, gives way to the wonder of dawn.

Night moves up from the earth as the sun goes below the horizon. The sky itself is the last to darken. It loses its light so gradually that one cannot say when the final dark appears. Stars are visible long before the sky is black. The last birds of day have given their final calls. The great buzzing and jingling of night insects builds up as the insect chorus of day ends. In tree leaves cling hundreds of slender little green and white singers, the snowy tree crickets with their rhythmic calling. Katydids clack. It is time for the whip-poor-wills to sing, the time when young screech owls lined up on a bough or wire try out their voices.

The chorus slows near midnight. The whip-poor-wills are quiet, the owls say nothing; the tree crickets have a slower tempo as the night cools and midnight passes. Stars that were climbing up the east at nine o'clock now reach the top of the sky. Constellations that lay in the west when darkness came have now disappeared. Stars of autumn move up the east. The Big Dipper which was swinging around the west side of the North Star at sunset is now below it, lying low on the northern horizon. And as the hours move toward dawn, the Dipper begins to swing around to the east in its endless circumpolar route.

About three o'clock in the morning, in the dew-dampness and dark, a small wind springs up and moves with audible sounds through the trees. It has been very still before. Now there is a sudden sound of life, the moving leaves whispering and rustling as the wind moves off again, like the sound of distant surf. "It is the voice of the night wind, going to call the sun," a poet said.

As if the sounds of leaves were a signal, there is a swoop of pale wings to the darkness of the river shore. The night heron is fishing. A whip-poor-will tunes up again. Purple martins begin to gurgle and twitter somewhere in the dark sky.

And the world is wet with dew. It is the product of the summer night, the condensation of moisture given off by leaves during the cooler hours of night. And each leaf is different in the way it oozes dew. Some are covered with wetness; some are studded on their notches with separate drops. Willow leaves channel dew down their gutters and let drops run off as if in a fine rain. The lotus leaf holds a large, mercurial drop in its cupped center where it rolls about with any motion of the leaf.

In the darkness robins begin to sing, and a wave of song washes across the town and the river woods as a herald to dawn itself. The night heron gets up from its shore and flies in a slow, pearl-gray flight to the wet willows for a nap, and its place on the shore is taken by a green heron which has just wakened for the morning's fishing. The muskrats and raccoons which may have hunted on the shore are gone with the coming glow on the eastern horizon. The glow slowly increases for more than an hour before there is any real light, any true dawn.

As the sun climbs over the horizon at last, the night insects are quiet. The owls have sought their day-time roosts. The willows drip. And the creatures which slept all night are awake to a new day.

Thoreau said: "To be awake is to be alive. . . . We must learn to reawaken . . . by an infinite expectation of the dawn." (*Aug. 1961*)

THE OPPORTUNITY TO BE IGNORANT

When Henry David Thoreau in 1857 went on a camping and canoeing trip into the Allagash wilderness of northern Maine, in company with a botanizing friend and a Penobscot Indian guide, he kept a journal of the expedition. His account of those experiences is as vivid now as the experiences were more than a century ago and brings him closer to us than some of his more philosophical writings. He was in a delightful mood for discovery. Camping in a dark forest along the lake one night, he had wakened very late. It had been as if something had called to him—owl, loon, nighthawk, he did not know what it was. He simply woke to that summons and lay there in his blanket, listening, feeling deeply attuned to his wilderness surroundings. When he got up to fix the fire, which had fallen apart, he found a strange, glowing ring of white light at the end of a piece of firewood, and he knew that it had been this which had called to him. He touched it gingerly with his finger, and found that it was a cool fire with no heat. He picked up the piece of wood with its glowing end and pared back some of the bark, finding it all alight inside. It was his first look at phosphorescent wood in the damp forests of the north, and he was downright delighted. He said:

"It could hardly have thrilled me more if it had taken the form of letters, or of the human face . . . I little thought that there was such a light shining in the darkness of the wilderness for me . . . I did not regret my not having seen this before, since I now saw it under circumstances so favorable. I was in just the frame of mind to see something wonderful, and this was a phenomenon adequate to my circumstances and expectation . . . .I let science slide, and rejoiced in that light as if it had been a fellow-creature. I saw that it was excellent and was very glad to know it was so cheap. A scientific *explanation*, as it is called, would have been altogether out of place there. That is for pale daylight. Science and its retorts would have put me to sleep; it was the opportunity to be ignorant that I improved. It suggested that there was something to be seen if one had eyes. It made a believer out of me more than before."

The opportunity to be ignorant was the thing—if he had been all-wise and all-knowing, he might not have noticed the phosphorescent light shining out for him that night. It is this happy state of ignorance with which most of us are blessed. We are constantly alert and ready to discover whatever wonder chances to lie in our path—that opportunity to be astonished comes every day of our lives. It makes no difference if thousands of scientists may have seen this particular flower, commented upon that particular spider web, discoursed intensively upon a certain bird. Discovery is the heritage and personal enrichment of every person who sees for the first time a thing which he has never seen before. No night sky arching the city, no autumn morning in the backyard, no sundown across a cornfield, no thunderstorm over a lake is without the unending facility to reveal something new to wonder about. The libraries are full of books to answer the questions and improve the ignorance, but the seeing eye, the inquiring mind, and the excitement of finding something new must be there first before the books may attain their true meaning or are put to their best use.

It was Thoreau's experience in the northwoods country which perhaps brings him closer to our own happy sense of ignorance and personal discovery than does his more philosophical *Walden*. He was bitten by mosquitoes, soaked in bogs; he listened to loons; he was in a frame of mind to be delighted with everything he found. Like him, we can be thankful that no lifetime is long enough to know everything and that wonder is part of the experiences of each day. (*Oct. 1964*)

"SILENCE LISTENING TO SILENCE"

Quietly, with no comment, a leaf detaches itself from an oak twig and twirls to the ground. Around the leaf, around the tree, around the whole woods lies the insuperable silence of autumn, late autumn trending into winter. This is a stillness so filled with unheard sounds that a kind of echoing comes to the listening eardrums, a throbbing as of sounds not heard and of motion not seen. On uplands, in swamps and along the woodland trail there is to be found this trance-like spell of November.

Here is a silence stretching north to the Arctic Circle and but little altered by cities along the way. It is a stillness hovering over the grays and browns and purples of a landscape but lately green and gay, full of music and motion and sunshine, full of explosive life and activity.

But November, though so different from summer, is very far from dead. Although this trail between the trees would seem to be a pathway leading to the Great Silence which has closed down over the northern countries, it is far from lifeless or motionless. Sounds are still here. It is just that they are more widely spaced, are smaller . . . a lone hammering as a woodpecker works on a bed-hole for the winter . . . the thin, scraping rattle as a big brown pupa inside a Cecropia cocoon stirs in its cradle . . . the castanets of twigs clattering against twigs as a wind moves through bony branches held against a possum-colored sky . . . the blithe little chittering of a chickadee hunting katydid eggs.

Life is still here, but it is so much more quiet, its representatives so much fewer in numbers. Frost has already cut down the flowers; leaves have fallen from the trees; many birds have gone south. And the woodchuck has crawled into its deep burrow and rapidly sunk into a hibernating state skirting the fine borderline of death. But one fox squirrel doing death-defying leaps through the tree tops, or scurrying with a mad clatter through dry oak leaves, is enough to replace any number of clover-chewing woodchucks and long-departed birds. Yet the moment the racing stops, the instant the sounds end, that great stillness comes forth again, brooding like a tangible presence among the trees.

It is, as Thomas Hood once remarked, "Autumn . . . standing shadowless, like silence listening to silence." It is nature stripped to its skeletal essentials and beautiful in that basic structure. It is wild life so constructed, so attuned to trial, that few creatures now remaining in these woods, given their health, will fail in their ability to meet winter and its stringent needs.

And the silence deepens as a cool, damp, fragrant dusk closes early upon the November woods. Then in the dark vault of sky there may come an eerie flaring, a dim, green-white light wavering across the north, drifting in tenuous veils, dissolving into nothingness, taking form again in long shafts of upward-reaching light. A flaming color suffuses the stars as the tremendous spectacle of the Aurora Borealis develops on a frosty autumn night.

And there is no sound. The moving lights are unutterably still. There are only the faint, far calls of unseen migrants passing in the night and the tremulous crying of a screech owl somewhere in the lonely autumn woods, sounds which only point up a lack of utterance, voices which accent the Great Silence of autumn. (*Nov. 1957*)

RIVER WORLD

I stand on the shore and know that it was here yesterday, and will be here tomorrow, and that, therefore, since I am part of its pattern today, I also belong to all its yesterdays and will be part of all its tomorrows.

This is a kind of earthly immortality, a kinship with rivers and hills and rocks, with all things and all creatures that have ever lived or have their being on the earth.

It is my assurance of an orderly continuity in the great design of the universe.

V.S.E.